Images of
the Child

Images of the Child

edited by

Harry Eiss

Bowling Green State University Popular Press
Bowling Green, OH 43403

Contents

Preface

Our birth is but a sleep and a forgetting:
The Soul that rises with us, our life's Star,
    Hath had elsewhere its setting,
      And cometh from afar:
    Not in entire forgetfulness,
    And not in utter nakedness,
But trailing clouds of glory do we come
    From God, who is our home:
Heaven lies about us in our infancy!
Shades of the prison-house begin to close
    Upon the growing Boy
        But he
Beholds the light, and whence it flows,
    He sees it in his joy;
The Youth, who daily farther from the east
    Must travel, still is Nature's Priest,
    And by the vision splendid
    Is on his way attended;
At length the Man perceives it die away,
And fade into the light of common day.[1]
           —William Wordsworth

Here the child is seen as pure and angelic, embodying a natural spirituality lost by the adult. It is an important image, an intuitive and poetic grasp of the manner in which humans forsake their natural goodness and sense of wonder when they grow into the adult world of logic, reason, and explanation. However, as important as the image is, it is but one of several, many of them far less positive.

For hundreds of years, children were viewed as miniature adults, whose sole purpose was to become big adults as quickly as possible. Since childhood did not exist, or if it did, was viewed as a necessary nuisance to be gotten through as quickly as possible, there was no promotion of a child's perspective, no imaginative literature, either oral or written, expressing a child's view, and no distinguishing of a child from an adult in artistic depiction. When a child was included in a painting, it had the same face, body, and dress as an adult, only smaller.

There was education, more properly called training, specifically for preparing children to perform their assigned tasks as adults. Classical Sparta clearly had a highly regimented program in place meant to train boys for military duty and girls to bear strong babies. Classical Athens included some non-military subjects, such as politics, debate, and public speaking. Rome followed suit, mainly concentrating on the indoctrination of religious and patriotic feelings. In none of these cases was there any consideration of childhood as a special time of life. The child was simply the adult-in-the-making.

The Christian schooling that followed the collapse of the Roman Empire consisted in training priests and monks, and the main thrust was to deny the imagination and desires in preparation for the afterlife. The Crusades brought about a class of merchants and craftsmen, which, in turn, resulted in craft guilds, and the apprentice-ship of young boys in training for their future trades. Burgher schools, established under local governments, eventually absorbed many of these guild schools, and undertook to educate the children in similar practical skills, especially reading and reckoning. All of these forms of schooling concentrated on specific, narrow, practical matters, preparing children to fit assigned roles as adults. There was little written material, especially imaginative literature, for either adults or children; and there was no concern with childhood as a unique and special time in life.

However, there was a strong oral tradition, filled with myths and folktales, which, according to Robert Leeson[2] reached its climax in feudal Europe during the Middle Ages. These tales, sometimes called Castle Tales and Cottage Tales, were not meant for children. Rather, they comprised the great body of knowledge (tales of the origins of the universe or heroic deeds or ethical truths) that adults passed onto one another, helping create and preserve a cultural heritage. Castle tales, as the title suggests, were those tales told by or to the rich, ruling classes. They generally took the form of poetic epics about the great deeds of the lord of the manor (e.g., *Beowulf*). Cottage tales were the tales told by the poor around cottage fires, tales offering rewards for kindness or cleverness or the like (e.g., "Jack the Giant Killer").

Though these tales were being told by adults (often by traveling bards or minstrels) for the amusement of other adults, children undoubtedly were also in the audience, listening to, being molded by, and revising the tales when they grew old enough to retell them. However, once again, the tales were not told or modified for a child's perspective. There was no such thing as a child's perspective.

The Renaissance aroused a renewed interest in classical literature from Greece and encouraged personal development and self-realization. Nevertheless, this was still limited to a small audience of priests, nobles, and scholars. Few could afford the laboriously handwritten, parchment manuscripts that contained what there was of written literature; and children were still viewed as miniature adults with no special psychological needs.

With Gutenberg's discovery of moveable type, mass production of books became possible. In 1476, William Caxton established England's first printing press. Most of the material he printed relating to children was based on the idea that children should only read what would improve them. For example, *Caxton's Book of Curtesye*, 1477, contained instruction for combing hair, cleaning ears, and even cleaning one's nose (don't pick it!). This all fit the view of children as miniature adults simply needing certain kinds of training in practical matters to become big adults.

However, Caxton also published three books for adults that have since become classics in children's literature: *Reynart the Foxe* (The History of Reynard the Fox), 1481; *The Book of the Subtyle Histories and Fables of Esope* (The Fables of Aesop), 1484; and *Le Morte d'Arthur* (The Death of Arthur), 1485.[3]

Caxton's books were too expensive for the average person. However, cheaper reading was becoming available. The Reformation led by Martin Luther, arising out of the Renaissance, and promoting literacy for the purpose of reading the Bible, advocated schools for every community. These schools often used hornbooks, printed sheets of text mounted on wood, generally in the shape of a paddle, and covered with translucent animal horn. Unfortunately, their subject matter remained strictly within the practical and religious. They usually contained the alphabet, a syllabary, numerals, and the Lord's prayer—the practical knowledge needed for the Christian world children were being prepared to enter. Yet again, childhood did not exist as valuable in and of itself. It was simply a training ground for adulthood.

However, the image of children as nothing more than miniature adults, neither morally nor psychology unique, was about to change.

By the late 16th century, about the middle of the reign of Queen Elizabeth, England became enamored with a strict form of

Christianity based on the concept that we are all born in sin. In other words, children are evil and will die destined for hell, unless adults can literally scare the hell out of them. The people who believed this came to be known as the Puritans, and they both encompassed and embraced the victims of religious persecution. Crowds gathered daily at St. Paul's to hear the Bible read aloud, and the Bible became a standard book in homes. Foxe's *Book of Martyrs* (1563), filled with details of such things as death at the stake, was studied and given to the children.[4] James Janeway, a clergyman, wrote a long popular book for the Puritan nurseries with a long title to match: *A Token for Children: Being an Exact Account of the Conversion, Holy and Exemplary Lives, and Joyful Deaths of Several Young Children. To Which Is Now Added, Prayers and Graces, Fitted for the Use of Little Children* (1671).[5] In it, 13 good little children tried to reform, convert, and generally make better everyone they met, spending much of their time brooding about sin and eternal damnation. The point of it all was to literally scare the hell out of the children who were forced to read it.

Damnation, hellfire, sulfer and brimstone—the fiery, fear-filled sermons of the Puritans saw Satan everywhere, even in the innocent faces of young girls, who, after all, might well be concealing their true identities as witches, agents of the Devil, caught in a life of sin, children to be uncovered, to be exposed, to be cleansed or destroyed.

That's what John Bunyan thought. In fact, his preaching became so vehement that he was locked up for not conforming to the established Church of England. While confined with his copy of John Foxe's *Book of Martyrs* and his Bible, he wrote the one classic children's book from this time, *Pilgram's Progress* (1678), the story of a Christian soul on a pilgrimage through this world of sin to the heavenly paradise.[6] It is crammed with theological moralizing, but, in spite of this, it is a moving tale filled with the characters and adventure of high fantasy.

These same Puritans first landed in America in 1620, beginning a huge exodus that lasted for some 20 years, and transplanting the same harsh views of life and children. The first book published in America for children was written by John Cotton in 1646: *Milk for Babes, Drawn Out of the Breasts of Both Testaments, Chiefly for the Spiritual Nourishment of Boston Babes in Either England, but May Be of Like Use for Any Children.*[7] The famous *New England Primer*, published at least as early as 1691, began its also famous rhyming alphabet: "In Adam's fall/We sinned all."[8]

Harsh, frightening, and generally negative as it was, this view of children as vulnerable and in danger of going to hell if they died before they had been saved was the first to separate the child's world from that of the adult and take on the task of helping children get safely through it. Misdirected as it was, the intent was to comfort children and make them feel secure in the avoidance of hell and assurance of heaven.

In many ways, this Puritan image of the child remains with us today. Maintaining the view that children should be taught what to think, not how to think, powerful conservative religious groups, such as Educational Research Analysts (formed by Mel and Norma Gabler) and Citizens for Excellence in Education have led today's rapidly accelerating rate of censorship in the United States, especially in schools. But today's censorship (based on the same passive image of the child) is not as strictly religious as was the traditional Puritan image. It often extends into non-religious (and even anti-religious) concerns, such as male/female roles, multi-culturalism, and even environmental concerns.

Up to this point in time, children as miniature adults with no special needs and children as potential satanic victims who needed to have religion installed in them quickly (and the best method for doing this was through the fear of God) were the only two major images of the child to be formally embraced in western culture.

However, other images existed and were about to become important.

At the same time as the Puritans were preaching against traditional tales about witches, giants, fairies, and in general, anything that might be considered outside the strict Puritan code of ethics, the poorer, less educated people were buying this very same literature peddled by the "chapmen," peddlers of broadsides, newssheets, ballads, and chapbooks—popular and cheap books that often consisted merely of folded, unattached sheets of paper and badly written, poorly illustrated, severely condensed folktales. Though not specifically written or published for a child market, children, just as with the oral telling of these same stories, consumed the stories, and the market persisted, waiting for a future intellectual justification to move into more accepted circles.

In 1632, John Amos Comenius, a Czech educational reformer, wrote the *Didactica Magna*,[9] the first systematic treatise on education based on a psychological understanding of the learning process, and followed this with *Orbis Sensualium Pictus*,[10] the first illustrated textbook. It was embraced by educators, went through many editions, and was translated into 40 different languages. According to Comenius, children need interesting materials to entice them to learn.

In 1693, John Locke published *Some Thoughts Concerning Education*, where he stressed that children are rational, have individual needs, and should be taught through play, rather than force-fed through a fear of God.[11] According to Locke, children are born, not evil, but as blank sheets, tabula rasa, and they should be led gently in the right path. This view stressed a milder, more pleasant approach to teaching children, and called for books to provide pleasure.

Literature meant to offer pleasure means literature other than the strict non-fiction, rules-and-regulations literature previously given to children. In other words, it means imaginative literature. And the first true imaginative literature written specifically for children was about to appear.

First, Charles Perrault published *Contes De Ma Mere L'Oye* (Tales of Mother Goose), 1696, a collection of fairy tales, such as "Cinderella" and "Sleeping Beauty" that came out of a form of entertainment common in 17th-century salons of the Parisian aristocracy.[12] Then, two adventure stories, strong satires written for adults appeared and became classics of children's literature: Daniel Defoe's *Robinson Crusoe*, 1719,[13] and Jonathan Swift's *Gulliver's Travels*, 1726.[14]

But these were just sign-posts for the true beginning of children's literature. In 1744, a time when middle-class life began to center around the home and family, children were beginning to be thought of as something other than miniature adults or in desperate need of salvation, and people had more time and money for books and education, John Newbery, an advocate of John Locke, began publishing a line of books for children with *A Little Pretty Pocket Book*.[15] These books were not meant to teach or moralize, though there was something of a didactic tone to them, but to be entertaining. He was successful, the first to successfully publish the popular rhymes and tales for a specifically child public, and his success lead others to also begin publishing for a specifically child audience.

Though publishers had now begun to see a child ready to be entertained, the strong, religious-based school curriculum remained deliberately unpleasant, justifying its harsh, negative approach by claiming it strengthened children's characters. But this, too, was about to be seriously challenged.

Jean-Jacques Rousseau attacked the harsh, negative image of childhood and put in place the most important view of education yet developed. As he saw it, the apparent advances in civilization had, in fact, resulted in an evil, artificial, false existence, and the remedy rested in a return to the natural truths to be found outside of that corrupt culture. In a fictional biography, *Emile: Ou De L'Education*, 1762,[16] he put forth, through his imaginary pupil, Emile, that an educational program should allow unimpeded the unfolding and developing of a personality that was by nature good and would become bad only through the corrupting influence of civilization. Here, John Locke's image of the child as a blank sheet was replaced with the image of the child as inherently good. No longer should the adult lead the child in the right path. Instead, the child should merely be accompanied in his or her search for knowledge. Margaret C. Gillespie summarizes the importance of this:

His impact on the attitude of parents toward children was forceful and unmistakable. Now children were looked upon as "little angels" who could do no wrong. They were permitted to be children rather than "little adults." They became the center of the educational scene rather than satellites around the curriculum.[17]

Unfortunately, one important, immediate interpretation of Rousseau's views involved a strong didacticism:

The only thing these writers seemed to have carried over from Rousseau was the idea of following and developing the child's natural interests. In practice, they went at the business hammer and tongs. If the poor children picked strawberries, the experience was turned into an arithmetic lesson. If they rolled a snowball, they learned about levers and proceeded from those to wedges. If they took a walk, they had to observe every bird, beast, stone, and human occupation. Day and night these ardent authors stalked their children, allowing them never a moment for play of fancy but instructing and improving on every page. No longer did they threaten children with the fear of Hell, but the pressure of information hung almost as heavily over their hapless heads.[18]

However, though it was sometimes misinterpreted, Rousseau's philosophy had set in place a view of children that would shortly become extremely important.

The four most important images of the child in Western history were now in place. First, children were seen as little adults, only in need of gaining the strength and practical knowledge to become big adults. Second, children were seen as vulnerable, and the job of adults was to drive out the temptations of evil, to save their souls.

Third, children were seen as blank sheets, and the job of adults was to lead them gently on the right path. Fourth, children were seen as embodying a superior morality, as pure and uncorrupted, and the job of adults was to accompany them on the path to knowledge.

These views came together (perhaps, collided is a better term) in the late 18th and 19th centuries, and gave birth to modern child psychology and the many contemporary images of the child. In order to understand how this came about, it is necessary to dwell a moment on the larger, political, intellectual, and social developments of the time.

In the 18th century, the Western world was centered by the philosophical concepts of neoclassicism, which included the embracement of logic and reason as humans' highest ability, the belief in an ordered class system with the aristocracy at the top, and the promotion of form and order over content and the imagination.

Rousseau's views established a philosophical foundation for a revolt against this entire political, social, and intellectual world. All that was needed was a spark to set the European world aflame. That spark was the American Revolution. It burst into a roaring blaze with the French Revolution, and resulted in the great watershed in Western history. The neoclassic views embracing logic and reason were replaced by the romantic movement's views rejecting logic and reason in favor of the imagination and creativity. The neoclassic views embracing an aristocracy were replaced by the romantic movement's views embracing democracy. The neoclassic views embracing form were replaced by the romantic movement's views embracing content (form follows content).

More specifically related to the image of the child, the romantic movement embraced Rousseau's views that we are born inherently good, perhaps even more than that. The initial piece of poetry from Wordsworth for this essay finds the child, not just pure and good, but "trailing clouds of glory." In fact, the child is born out of the true world of nature, God, purity, and all of the positive qualities. Knowledge, or, rather, wisdom is to be found in the ability to recapture the child's sense of wonder. John Keats expressed it all the most directly and simply in the following line from his famous "Ode on a Grecian Urn":

Beauty is truth, truth beauty,—that is all Ye know on earth, and all ye need to know.[19]

This is not the kind of truth to be found in reason and logic. This is a truth beyond explanation. It is a truth to be known intuitively, a truth to be sensed, a truth to be related through expression (most specifically for these poets, through poetry) not reduced and made less than it is through explanation, reason, and logic.

This view, then, embraced the child's perspective, and still serves as the strongest supporting view for seeking out and attempting to see the world through a child's eyes, and it would lay the foundation for the Golden Age of Children's Literature.

Another important aspect of the romantic movement's views involved with this was their promotion of the culture's heritage and traditions over the artificial culture created by logic and reason. As they saw it, the intuitive understanding of life (wisdom) is more likely to be found in the stories and folklore of the common people, the peasants, than in the over-educated urban people or upper-class. This belief, in turn, would result in the serious collecting and study of folktales, which, in turn, would also lay a foundation for the Golden Age of Children's Literature.

This Golden Age began with the Brothers Grimm's collections of folktales, first published in 1812 and 1816, and grew, until it resulted in an explosion of great children's literature in the second half of the century, and finally ended with the publication of Kenneth Grahame's *The Wind in the Willows* in 1908.

The reason for the seemingly arbitrary choice of *The Wind in the Willows* as the final curtain for this Golden Age has to do precisely with its embracement of the views of the romantic movement, views long since succeeded by other views outside of the world of children, but remaining still important within it.

Though the entire book is laced with these views, the chapter titled "The Piper at the Gates of Dawn" combines them all in the best expression of this ethos in all of literature. The entire chapter needs to be read carefully to catch the interplay and nuisances, but here are a few central passages to suggest its import.[20]

Ratty and Mole have rowed up the river at night, searching for the lost baby otter. Ratty and, later, Mole begin to hear a beautiful music and feel a solemnness, a spiritual sense. They land on an island and moor their boat:

"This is the place of my song-dream, the place the music played to me," whispered Rat, as if in a trance. "Here, in this holy place, here if anywhere, surely we shall find Him!"

Then suddenly the Mole felt a great Awe fall upon him, an awe that turned his muscles to water, bowed his head, and rooted his feet to the ground. It was no panic terror—indeed he felt wonderfully at peace and happy—but it was an awe that smote and held him and, without seeing, he knew it could only mean that some august Presence was very, very near.

This continues with a description of Ratty and Mole coming upon Pan (god of nature), who holds Baby Otter in his lap. Ratty and Mole are overcome with "unutterable love" mixed with "fear." They bow their heads. At this moment the sun rises above the horizon and the "Vision" vanishes.

As they stared blankly, in dumb misery deepening as they slowly realized all they had seen and all they had lost, a capricious little breeze, dancing up from the surface of the water, tossed the aspens, shook the dewy roses, and blew lightly and caressingly in their faces, and with its soft touch came instant oblivion. For this is the last best gift that the kindly demigod is careful to bestow on those to whom he has revealed himself in their helping: the gift of forgetfulness.

As mentioned, this embracement of the child as the embodiment of natural goodness and spirituality was but one of the images of the child to come together in the 18th and 19th centuries. Another important force, economics, was seeing the child as a profitable source of labor.

Beginning in the 18th century and coming into full bloom in the 19th century, the Industrial Revolution swept through England, and the rest of Europe, and with it came a view of children that would separate them off from the family and the community, and that would necessitate a more careful consideration of the child as unique.

No longer could the average child develop naturally into social and economic maturity working hard but relatively healthy agrarian jobs or in small, family-owned shops, in either case receiving the strong, informal folk tradition for a life-centering force, in either case being a part of nature and the adult world, rather than separate from it.

Instead, the 18th and 19th centuries, operating under a laissez faire economy and without a system of popular education, transposed the working class acceptance of child labor in the domestic and agrarian world into the industrial world to counterbalance the high costs of equipment, and in so doing, etched an image of children as cheap labor, easily exploited. Now the long hours and hard work took place in mines and factories under dangerous and filthy conditions.

Coincidentally, in 1802, the same year Wordsworth was writing about the natural goodness of children as connected to nature, various labor leaders, philanthropists, and Tories (who were fighting against the rising power of the mercantile class) managed to get the first bill passed of what has come to be known as the Factory Acts (1802-46), sometimes called the first social legislation, which were aimed at easing the most serious of the abuses against children condemned to factories separated from nature. It should be emphasized that the first of these Acts were ineffective, because no provisions were made for enforcing them.

In the United States, because of the abundance of free land and the slower development of industry, the problem was not as widespread as in England. However, the cotton and textile mills of New England employed workers as young as seven for even longer hours than those of England. Many moralists saw such employment as an economic and social asset to the country, and even as a means of developing children's character (children factory workers were often required to attend church).

By mid-century, the separation and abuse of children had become so severe that several intellectuals took up the battle to redefine and protect them.

Karl Marx saw history as a class struggle, and highlighted the abuses of the proletariat and, specifically, of children in factories.[21]

Charles Dickens led a group of novelists who used the abuse of the angelic child of Wordsworth as an emotional tug to rouse the populace against the abuses of industrialization. Tiny Tim, the poor, crippled son of Bob Cratchet, who will die unless the hard-hearted Scrooge changes his tight-fisted ways, still represents one of the most powerful images of the child today—pure and idealized, not yet contaminated by a corrupt civilization.[22]

Johann Heinrich Pestalozzi (1746-1827) applied views similar to Rousseau's to the education of orphans in his Swiss countryside. He believed that education was the natural progressive and harmonious development of all powers and capacities of the human being, and he substituted pleasurable learning activities for the harsh discipline common at the time.[23] Horace Mann (1796-1859) and Edward A. Sheldon were instrumental in bringing his views to the United States.[24] Johann Friedrich Herbard (1776-1841) systematized the observational methods of Pestalozzian teaching, and Friedrich Froebel (1782-1852) applied Pestalozzian methods to pre-school training, in the process establishing kindergarten.[25]

However, the abuses of the Industrial Revolution remained. The bourgeoisie's view of children as cheap labor was not to be easily defeated.

Clearly, the time was ripe for a more sophisticated understanding of the child. It might be accurate to say that modern child psychology began with Charles Darwin's *Expression of the Emotions in Men and Animals*, 1872;[26] however, it really began, as did all of modern psychology, with the work of Sigmund Freud.[27] His theories, mainly dealing with the sexual instincts and how personality disturbances in later life are generally the result of early childhood experience, set in motion an ever growing concern with childhood experience; and though subsequent psychologists have disagreed with aspects of his theories, they have pushed and continue to promote his views on the importance of childhood experiences, until, today, children are seen as highly complex, very psychologically delicate creatures, easily damaged by the intentional or accidental actions of adults. Fragile, handle with care!

The study of child psychology has been further divided into several overlapping disciplines, including child development, child abuse, and child psychiatry.

Child development is generally divided into four aspects of human growth: physical maturation; mental or cognitive development; personality development; and socialization. In each category, the child is further broken down into stages of childhood (after all, a child of two is a far different human than a child of ten, and so on). Jean Piaget and Erik Erikson have developed elaborate charts of the stages that are often employed in education.[28]

Child psychiatry, of course, fits into the personality development portion of child development, but is also important enough to stand on its own. There are two important branches of it: the traditional psychoanalytic approach initiated by Freud, and a more recent neuro-chemical approach that relies heavily on bio-chemical research. In addition to Sigmund Freud, his daughter Anna Freud, Margaret Mahler, and Stella Chess have made important contributions to it.[29]

Child abuse, which may be defined as any intentional act of commission or omission that prevents or impedes a child's growth and normal development, drawing on the theories of child psychology, has become a major social issue. It is generally divided into physical abuse and/or neglect, mental and/or emotional abuse, and sexual abuse. Every state in the United States currently has laws against child abuse, and in 1974 the U.S. government established the National Center on Child Abuse and Neglect, which funds demonstrations and research projects to treat and prevent child maltreatments.

Related to this is child labor. As mentioned, the initial separation of children from the family and general society was closely related to the rise of industry, especially in the late 18th and through the 19th century. Today, as a result of the enactment of the Fair Labor Standards Act in 1938 and more recent state laws, children under 16 are prohibited from employment during school hours. Instead of the abusive employment of children, the current problem has reversed itself and become the unemployment of young people 16 and older who are no longer in school.

Obviously, the images of the child are complex and varied; and as has always been the case, children refuse to be caged.

For example, in the traditional nursery rhyme:

> Humpty Dumpty sat on a wall;
> Humpty Dumpty had a great fall;
> All the king's horses and all the king's men
> Couldn't put Humpty together again.

Father Gander, a popular rewriting of the traditional nursery rhymes meant to remove what some highly vocal adults see as negative sexual, classist, and violent images, changes it:

> Humpty Dumpty sat on a wall;
> Humpty Dumpty had a great fall;
> All of the horses, the women and men
> Helped put Humpty together again.[30]

In the meantime, a current playground version goes:

> Humpty Dumpty sat on a wall;
> Humpty Dumpty had a great fall;
> All the king's horses and all the king's men
> Stepped on him.[31]

Thus, the images of the child become ever more elusive, as Alice from *Alice in Wonderland* would say, "curiouser and curiouser."

What does the future hold? Which child in the famous poem "Monday's Child" is it to be?

> Monday's child is fair of face,
> Tuesday's child is full of grace,
> Wednesday's child is full of woe,
> Thursday's child has far to go,
> Friday's child is loving and giving,
> Saturday's child works hard for a living,
> But the child that is born on the Sabbath day
> Is blythe and bonny and good and gay.[32]

Whichever one or combination takes hold, I hope it will allow children the right to self-realization and self-responsibility, the right to dignity and respect, and the right to meaning, for without these qualities life has no value, and they cannot be obtained without being earned.[33]

This collection of articles on images of the child offers an excellent range of perspectives on an equally wide range of concerns, including advertising, girls' book series, rap music, realistic fiction, games, dolls, violence, and movies. I'm proud to be the editor of such a collection, and I thank all of the contributors. I also thank Ray and Pat Browne, and the entire staff of the Popular Press at Bowling Green for their help, encouragement, hard work, and willingness to publish a book on children's culture.

Notes

[1]William Wordsworth, "Ode: Intimations of Immortality from Recollections of Early Childhood," lines 59-78 (1802-4, 1807; rpt., *The Norton Anthology of Poetry*, ed. Arthur Eastman et al., New York: Norton, 1970). This poem begins with the following epigram, which also serves as the final three lines for "My Heart Leaps Up," another of his poems: "The Child is father of the Man/And I could but wish my days to be/Bound each to each by natural piety," also reprinted in the Norton anthology. *The English Romantic Poets: A Review of Research and Criticism*, 4th ed., Frank Jordan, ed. (New York: MLA, 1985) is an excellent source for further study of the Romantic Movement.

[2]Robert Leeson, *Children's Books and Class Society* (London: Writers and Readers, 1977).

[3]William Caxton, *Caxton's Book of Curtesye* (1477; rpt., ed. Frederick J. Furnivall, London: Oxford University, 1868). He is credited with 99 publications in all, mostly traditional literature, often translated by him into English. *Le Morte Darthur* (rpt., New York: Dutton-Everyman's, 1906).

[4]John Foxe, *Book of Martyrs* (1563). It began as a Latin account of the Christian martyrs, *Commentarii Rerum in Ecclesia Gestarum*, 1554, was enlarged in 1559, and then issued in English in 1563 as *The Acts and Monuments of the Church*.

[5]James Janeway, *A Token for Children: Being an Exact Account of the Conversion, Holy and Exemplary Lives, and Joyful Deaths of Several Young Children. To Which Is Now Added, Prayers and Graces, Fitted for the Use of Little Children* (1671).

[6]John Bunyan, *Pilgrim's Progress* (1678, a second part, 1684). The original title was *The Pilgrim's Progress from This World, to That Which Is to Come: Delivered under the Similitude of a Dream. Wherein Is Discovered, the Manner of His Setting Out, His Dangerous Journey, and Safe Arrival at the Desired Country*. Robert Lawson rewrote and illustrated a version for children, leaving out the moralizing (1939).

[7]John Cotton, *Milk for Babes, Drawn Out of the Breasts of Both Testaments, Chiefly for the Spiritual Nourishment of Boston Babes in Either England, but May Be of Like Use for Any Children* (1646). All of these writings are centered on the unity of the priesthood and the political body in the colonies. John Norton's biography about Cotton, *Abel Being Dead Yet Speaketh* (1657), was the first biography to be published in America.

[8]*The New England Primer*. Over 100 editions were printed in Boston from about 1691 to 1830. It was required reading for colonial children and was designed specifically to teach Puritan ideals.

[9]John Amos Comenius, *Didactica Magna* (1632).

[10]John Amos Comenius, *Orbis Sensualium Pictus* (1657; first English, 1659; rpt., *Orbis Pictus*, London: Oxford UP, 1967). This has an introduction by John E. Sadler giving historical and biographical background.

[11]John Locke, *Some Thoughts Concerning Education* (1693; rpt., *English Philosophers*, ed. Charles W. Eliot, Harvard Classics, Vol. 37, New York: Villier, 1910).

[12]Charles Perrault, *Contes De Ma Mere L'Oye* (1696; rpt., trans. Charles Welsh, *Classics of Children's Literature*, ed. John W. Griffith and Charles H. Frey, 2nd ed. New York: Macmillan, 1987).

[13]Daniel Defoe, *Robinson Crusoe* (1719). Important versions for children include Andrew Wyeth's (1920).

[14]Jonathan Swift, *Gulliver's Travels* (1726). Important versions for children include those of Charles E. Brock, Arthur Rackham, Fritz Eichenberg, and Louis Rhead.

[15]John Newbery, *A Little Pretty Pocket Book* (1744; rpt., New York: Harcourt, 1967). M.F. Thwaite comments on significance and in historical context.

[16]Jean-Jacques Rousseau, *Emile: Ou De L'Education* (1762). The gist of this can be found in *Jean-Jacques Rousseau, His Educational Theories Selected from "Emile," "Julie," and Other Writings*, ed. R.L. Archer (Woodbury, NY: Barron's Educational Series, 1964).

[17]Margaret C. Gillespie, *Literature for Children: History and Trends* (Dubuque, IA: Brown, 1970) 23.

[18]May Hill Arbuthnot and Zena Sutherland, *Children and Books*, 7th ed. (Glenville, IL: Scott, Foresman, 1986) 70.

[19]John Keats, "Ode on a Grecian Urn" (1819, 1820; rpt., *The Norton Anthology of Poetry*, ed. A. Eastman et al., 1970).

[20]Kenneth Grahame, *The Wind in the Willows* (1908; rpt., *Classics of Children's Literature*, ed. Griffith and Frey, 2nd ed. New York: Macmillan, 1987).

[21]Karl Marx. Along with Friedrich Engels, he drew up a statement of principles for the League of the Just, later renamed the Communist League, which was published as the *Communist Manifesto*, 1848. However, his writings did not gain notoriety until the publication of his *Critique of Political Economy* and *Das Kapital* in 1867. These writings set forth a powerful socialist theory that is still important today.

[22]Charles Dickens, *A Christmas Carol* (1843; rpt., *Classics of Children's Literature*, ed. Griffith and Frey, 2nd ed. New York: Macmillan, 1987).

[23]Pestalozzi's views on the natural development of children served as the basis for the later work of Maria Montessori, who encouraged the exploration and development of sensorimotor skills in teaching slum children. This embracement of the natural development was matched in the early 20th century by John B. Watson's more objective approach to studying children (what is called "behaviorism").

[24]Horace Mann was on the Massachusetts Board of Education, where he fought to incorporate European views on education, eventually reorganizing the entire Massachusetts school system, which became a model for other states. His writings on the subject include *Lectures on Education* (1840) and *Report of an Educational Tour in Germany, Great Britain, and Ireland* (1846).

[25]Friedrich Froebel worked under Pestalozzi and established a small school at Griesheim, shortly transferring it to Keilhau. Later, he was successful with a training school for teachers at Burgdorf. Nevertheless, he meet with opposition throughout his career. His views on early education were published in *Menschenerziehung*, Vol. 1, which was translated by S.S.F. Fletcher and J. Welton, *Chief Writing on Education* (1932).

[26]Charles Darwin, *Expression of the Emotions in Men and Animals* (1872). In 1877 Darwin also published his diary of his infant son, based on observations he had begun in 1840. His studies were used to attempt to draw support for the idea that humans are descended from animals, with the child seen as the link. This, in turn, led to the idea of recapitulation, which theorized that each child passes through the different stages of the evolution of animal life. *The Mind of the Child*, another famous study of this type, was published by William Thierry Preyer (1841-97) in 1882. G. Stanley Hall, often considered the father of child psychology, developed these approaches and did a great deal to promote child psychology in the United States. His quantitative studies were later improved by Alfred Binet, who developed the Binet-Simon intelligence tests, which were later revised by Lewis M. Terman and published as the Stanford-Binet test.

[27]Sigmund Freud, *The Standard Edition of the Complete Psychological Works of Sigmond Freud*. Trans. and ed. James Strachey, with Anna Freud (London: Hogarth, 1953).

[28]Jean Piaget and Erik Erikson. Drawing on the theories of Rousseau, they led the way in promoting the genetic/developmental approach to understanding children, which assumes that regularities in behavior exist and seeks to comprehend the biological programming and mechanisms that produce them. One of several good overviews of Piaget is *Piaget's Theory of Cognitive and Affective Development*, 3rd ed., by Barry J. Wadsworth (New York: Longman, 1984).

[29]Anna Freud (*The Ego and Mechanisms of Defense*, New York: Intl. Universities, 1946); Stella Chess (A. Thomas and Stella Chess, *Temperament and Development*, New York: Brunner/Mazel, 1970).

[30]Iona Opie and Peter Opie, *The Oxford Nursery Rhyme Book* (London: Oxford, 1955). One of several important collections by this husband and wife team.

[31]Douglas Larche, *Father Gander Nursery Rhymes: The Equal Rhymes Amendment* (Santa Barbara, CA: Advocacy Press, 1985).

[32]Michael Rosen and Susanna Steele, *Inky Pinky Ponky: Children's Playground Rhymes* (New York: Granada, 1982).

[33]Iona Opie and Peter Opie, *The Oxford Nursery Rhyme Book* (London: Oxford, 1955).

Brief Bibliography

Aries, Philippe. *Centuries of Childhood*. New York: Knopf, 1962. An excellent overview of childhood through the centuries.

Darton, Frederick Joseph Harvey. *Children's Books in England: Five Centuries of Social Life*. Ed. Brian Alderson. 3rd ed. New York: Cambridge UP, 1982. Scholarship on children's literature in England in the context of the social conditions and educational theories.

Green, Roger Lancelyn. *Tellers of Tales*. Rev. ed. New York: Watts, 1965. An overview of British authors of children's literature from 1839 to 1960s.

Lystad, Mary H. *From Dr. Mather to Dr. Seuss: Two Hundred Years of American Books for Children*. Boston: Hall/Schenkman, 1980. Deals with the social values and attitudes toward children expressed in a sampling of American books for children.

MacDonald, Ruth K. *Literature for Children in England and America from 1646 to 1774*. Troy, NY: Whitston, 1982. An overview of children's literature of the time based on social, historical, and cultural contexts.

Meigs, Cornelia, et al. *A Critical History of Children's Literature: A Survey of Children's Books* in English. Rev. ed. New York: Macmillan, 1969. An important study. The revised edition is still a bit dated, but a highly valuable survey.

Opie, Iona, and Peter Opie. *The Oxford Dictionary of Nursery Rhymes*. New York: Walck, 1955. The best scholarship on children's nursery rhymes, this is one of several of their books on the subject.

Pickering, Samuel F. *John Locke and Children's Books in Eighteenth-Century England*. Knoxville: U of Tennessee P, 1981. An excellent application of Locke and Rousseau to children's literature of the period.

Queen, S.A., and R.W. Habenstein. *The Family in Various Cultures*. 3rd ed. Philadelphia: Lippincott, 1967. A good comparison of views of children through history.

Townsend, John Rowe. *Written for Children: An Outline of English-Language Children's Literature*. 2nd rev. ed. New York: Lippincott, 1983. A direct account by a highly respected critic.

From *Seventeenth Summer* to *Miss Teen Sweet Valley*: Female and Male Sex Roles in Teen Romances, 1942-91

Joyce A. Litton

The innocent teen romance is a type of formulaic fiction which has appealed to preteen and young adolescent girls since the development of the junior novel. In the 1940s and 1950s, this genre was especially popular. By the late 1960s, authors and publishers perceived that the nature of American society had changed. Preteens and young adults had developed a more sophisticated view of society as a result of their own experience and their exposure to mass popular culture, especially television and movies. Authors began to write contemporary realism fiction for young adults; the problem novel displaced the innocent romance. Parents were no longer perfect; stable families were not the norm; and the wages of romance were often unwanted pregnancies.

At the beginning of the 1980s publishers reintroduced the innocent teen romance. Most of these books have formulas which are similar to those of the 1940s and 1950s, but significant contrasts exist in style, treatment of sex roles, and degree of realism. This study will compare and contrast male and female sex roles in teen romances during two distinct periods, 1942-60 and 1980-91. For the earlier era, it will use representative novels by five popular authors—Betty Cavanna, Beverly Cleary, Maureen Daly, Rosamond du Jardin, and Mary Stolz. For the later decade, it will consider representative books from five popular series: *Sweet Dreams, Sweet Valley High, Two Hearts, Wildfire,* and *Young Love.*

In the earlier novels, there are two major variations of the plot. First, the teenage girl becomes interested in boys and dating, but boys are not interested in her. Thus, at the beginning of the book, she is very dissatisfied with herself. As the story progresses, she makes changes in her image and is rewarded with one or more of the following: a date to an important school dance, selection as prom queen, a boy's class ring. In the second major variation, the girl must decide between two boys who are interested in her. One of the boys is exciting and dangerous; the second is stable, but usually dull. She always opts for the safe choice in the end.

There are a limited number of stock characters in addition to the female protagonist: the perfect mother who relives her youth through her daughter's developing social life; a loving, if bemused, father; a very close girlfriend or sister; and the chief female competition, who is either the former girlfriend of the ideal boy or a teenage flirt. In most cases, the setting for these novels is high school, but in the vacation version, the action may take place at a ranch, a resort, or even a foreign country. All the novels end with a chaste, if heartfelt, kiss.[1]

Some of the books of the 1980s and 1990s have the same formula. Often the same character types still appear. The most popular environment remains the high school, but there are also vacation locations. However, there are some cosmetic changes to adapt these novels, hybrids of the innocent novels of the 1940s and 1950s and the contemporary realism books of the late 1960s and 1970s, to the 1980s and early 1990s. Parents have imperfections. Many of the mothers work outside the home. There are some single parent families. Very occasionally, protagonists raise the question of whether to have intercourse; they invariably reject the idea. Infrequently, characters use mild profanity. Some authors recognize the existence of problems related to teenage drinking and drug use. Girls express an interest in having careers, and sometimes an author deals with feminist themes.

This study will evaluate the extent to which characters in the two sets of books are treated as stereotypes or as complex individuals. It will make use of the comprehensive list of sex role stereotypes developed in 1972 by Inge Broverman and adapted for use in analyzing adolescent literature by Melissa Mullis Kaufman. Almost all of the stereotypes apply today; in the 1940s and 1950s, all were valid. In addition, it will consider the following issues: 1) the extent to which girls are defined by the boys in their lives, 2) the extent to which mother-blaming is used, and 3) the ways in which fathers relate to their daughters.

Broverman presents two lists of male/female characteristics to denote sex role stereotypes. The first list consists of competency characteristics; in this grouping, the masculine characteristics are more desirable. For example, women are not at all aggressive; men are very aggressive. Women are not at all independent; men are very independent. Women are subjective; men are very objective. The second set of characteristics are warmth-expressiveness qualities; in that set, the feminine qualities are more desirable. For instance, women do not use harsh language, are very talkative, gentle and tactful. Men use harsh language, are not at all talkative, are very rough and blunt.[2]

Many of the more recent books are as full of stereotypes as the older ones, although there are refreshing exceptions. However, in some of the newer books women are sometimes shown in a more unfavorable light. In the earlier books women were placed on a pedestal, and parents of both sexes were almost perfect. Fortunately, the pedestal is gone in the newer books. However, in some of the more recent books, women simply cannot win no matter what they do. In some cases, women who stay at home to rear their children are neurotic and overprotective; in others, those who work outside the home do so to the detriment of their families. While some boys and men show sensitivity; many girls are devious. At times, there are positive females and negative males, but females are more often unlikable. The most important question one must ask is: In what ways will these new books affect the socialization process for preteen and young adolescent girls?

All of the authors who wrote teen romances in the 1940s and 1950s created characters who were clichés. If one were to arrange them along a continuum, the two with the most stereotyped characters would be Rosamond du Jardin and Betty Cavanna. Although the range of distinction is very slight, Mary Stolz and Maureen Daly would be at the other end.

Rosamond du Jardin's characters meet almost any stereotype model one might posit. The young girls define themselves by boyfriends. The most important things in their lives are clothes and dates. All of the young protagonists possess mothers who have retained their beauty, but have a few gray hairs to show for the rigors of child-rearing. Without exception, the mothers get misty-eyed and relive their youth through their daughters' dating experiences. Only two of the mothers work, and these are very special cases. Mrs. Howard is a widow who must work. An interior decorator, she has her shop in her home and has her mother live with her and her twin daughters to provide stability for the teenagers. In those romances featuring Tobey Heydon as the teen protagonist, Mrs. Heydon is a nurse. In the first book of the set, she provides unpaid services for the neighbors, and the family jokes about "mother's emergencies." In subsequent books, in which the youngest child is a teenager, she works because there is a shortage of qualified nurses.[3]

Almost all of the girls in the du Jardin novels are quite aware of what Melissa Mullis Kaufman has called the rules of "the game"—i.e. the means whereby one can catch an eligible boy or man. (In most of the books, the earlier authors refer to the 15- to 18-year-old protagonists as "girls," but the males whom they date are often referred to as "men.") The rules are quite numerous, but only the unsure protagonist must learn them. These guidelines are based on qualities which are very negative—indirection, manipulation, and deceit. At the top of the list is the rule that a girl should be interesting, but never acknowledge that she is brighter than the boy whom she wants to catch. (Competitive words such as "catch" are common when "the game" is discussed.) Pam Howard, a flirt, manages to "get lost" in the halls on the twins' first day in a new school so that she will have an opportunity to meet new boys. Tobey Heydon knows that it is important for a girl never to let a boy know she is very fond of him—even if she is wearing his class ring; such candor will go to his head.[4]

In Betty Cavanna's *Fancy Free*, set in Peru during an archaeology dig, Silence Crawford, a very bright archaeology student, learns from younger, flighty, but worldly-wise Fancy that the way to succeed with the less intelligent Jack McMahon is to concentrate on building his ego and to look like a girl—i.e. to abandon sensible clothes, have her hair done by a professional, and pay attention to her make-up.[5]

In the older books, the rites of passage from being a child to being an adult are usually different for girls than they are for boys. For a girl, dating or some other type of male/female bonding, such as an engagement constitutes a rite of passage. On the other hand, rites of passage for boys seem to require some sort of physical duress. In Cavanna's *The Boy Next Door*, Ken becomes a man when he has worked very hard to earn the money needed to repair his hot rod. In the older books selected, there is one exception to this rule. In *Fancy Free*, Fancy grows up when she must drive back from the hospital by going up a dark mountainous road accompanied only by an Indian boy who cannot drive. When she succeeds, she has done something which the Indians, including her companion, believe only a man can do.[6]

The men in these earlier stories are only aware of what goes on in their paying jobs. Du Jardin's fathers should receive prizes for being the most out-of-touch with their families. These husbands never seem to be aware of the source of their daughters' anguish— usually related to their latest male interest. They never lose sleep when domestic trouble is brewing, although their wives almost always do.

Boyfriends are clumsy and socially inept. Many of them will spend the better part of a novel pursuing girls who are wrong for them. Initially attracted to teens who are devious and shallow, they will often cruelly manipulate the girls whom they eventually love. They are usually insensitive. The main exception is Jack Duluth in Maureen Daly's *Seventeenth Summer*. When he takes Angie on a sailing date, he tells her about the beauty of the moon, nature, and his thoughts about God. This is rare indeed.[7]

All of the authors of the earlier novels use the idea that there are times when it is appropriate for men to think about, and sometimes resort to, physical violence. The most frequent excuse for an outbreak of fisticuffs is over a girl, and often the girl in question is truly flattered.

As the author who is the most prone to use stereotypes, it is not surprising that du Jardin is the one who resorts to presenting the idea that women like to feel anguish at the hands of their men. In *Wait for Marcy*, Ken tells Steve: "Women always go for the rugged, independent guys who make 'em suffer." In *Practically Seventeen*, Tobey tells her sister's fiancé that he should treat her sister roughly and make her like it.[8]

Of the five series from the 1980s and 1990s, it is possible to do a general ranking in terms of the degree to which a series is full of stereotypes. The early books of the *Sweet Valley High* series are the worst offenders. Although all of the books in the set are still in print, some of the more recent titles present a somewhat more enlightened view. Early volumes of the *Sweet Dreams* series are almost as bad as the early *Sweet Valleys*. Once again, newer issues are more moderate. The other three series are uneven; there are some cliché-laden books and one or two pathbreakers.

Sweet Valley High's *When Love Dies* is the ultimate soap opera and is full of stock characters who perform predictably. The main protagonists are Tricia Martin and her boyfriend, Steven Wakefield. The caption below the cover art asks: "What terrible secret is Tricia keeping from Steven?" Her secret is that she is dying of leukemia. She handles her problem like the ultimate martyr. She will not tell Steven that she is dying because she does not want to hurt him. She pretends that she has lost interest in him and manufactures a new boyfriend. Steven finds out through the luck and resultant intervention of his sister, Elizabeth. Tricia is completely blameless of revealing her awful news.

The subplot whereby Elizabeth learns Tricia's secret is also what one might expect. Jessica, Elizabeth's twin sister, decides that she and Elizabeth should become candystripers at the local hospital. Jess, a true flirt, does not have altruistic motives. She has learned that a local TV celebrity is in the hospital with a broken leg, and she wants a chance to meet him and possibly become a TV star. As usual, Elizabeth is kept in the dark about this ulterior motive. While Liz is working in the hospital, she has a conversation with Tricia in which the girl swears Elizabeth to secrecy about her illness. Liz talks with a trusted teacher and decides to break her promise. Liz also plots with the TV star to defuse Jess's infatuation with him. In the scenes between Jessica and the celebrity, the reader sees the conniving, dumb blonde at work.[9]

In almost all of the novels of the 1980s and 1990s, the young female protagonists have career aspirations; this differentiates them sharply from the girls in the novels from the 1940s and 1950s. In the earlier novels, the girls define themselves solely as appendages to young men. In the newer novels, their plans range from professional skater to psychologist, disc jockey, writer, and social worker.

What has not changed for the better in some of these newer books is the portrayal of older women. In the novels of the 1940s and 1950s, most women did not work outside the home, and they were perfect. In the more recent works, most women work outside the home, and all women have flaws. In some of the books the pendulum has swung too far in the direction of treating adult women unfavorably. By and large, there seems to be a great deal of friction between teenage girls and their mothers. Friction between parents of both sexes and their children at the time of adolescent separation is a normal psychological phenomenon. However, in many of the novels, the conflict is limited to mothers and their daughters, and fathers either intervene on behalf of the daughter or are silent. Thus, there is a lot of mother-blaming.[10]

There is a tendency for authors to show women who work outside the home as doing so to the detriment of their families. In Francine Pascal's *Double Love*, the twins and their father complain that the mother takes too much time away from the family for her outside work. In the *Two Hearts* novel *In the Middle of a Rainbow* by Barbara Girion, Corrie's mother is a sad, overworked woman who is insensitive to her daughter's needs. She drives Corrie too hard to make her succeed where she feels that she has failed. Her salvation is marriage to one of her late husband's former colleagues.[11]

Women who stay at home to rear their children do not fare much better than those who go out into the workforce. In Jill Ross Klevin's *That's My Girl*, a *Wildfire* novel, Becky's mother is a former competitive skater who seems to build her whole life around Becky's skating career. She makes all of her daughter's costumes, drives her to practice sessions, and at times pushes her too hard. It is the father who provides balance for Becky. There is at least one positive adult woman in the book, Becky's psychology teacher, Ms. Wing, who encourages her to further both her interest in psychology and her skating so that she will not become only an athletic has-been.[12]

Several of the novels of the 1980s and 1990s have things to commend them. This analysis will consider three: Terry Morris's *Just Sixteen*, a *Wildfire* book; Gloria D. Miklowitz's *The Day the Senior Class Got Married* from *Young Love*; and Francine Pascal's *Miss Teen Sweet Valley*. Adults do not play a major role in *Just Sixteen*, a story of what happens when Nancy Hughes and Roger Ames become lost when they go skiing and must survive until help comes the next morning. The adults who do appear—the parents of the couple—are balanced in terms of good and bad qualities, but the author does resort to some clichés. Nancy's parents are both likable and strong. Roger Ames does not get along with his parents, and both of them are portrayed negatively. Dr. Ames, a dentist, does not believe that Roger can do enough to please him.

He is a hard-driving man who left the early child-rearing of Roger to his wife because he accepted the traditional role definitions. When he realized that his wife was rearing their son to be a sissy who could not defend himself, he began to teach Roger to box and went overboard by setting up a rigid schedule for the boy. Roger's mother is overprotective of him. Since there are only two adult women of any significance, one wishes that the presentation did not resort to such a predictably negative treatment of Mrs. Ames. Presenting flawed characters is realistic, but these flaws should not perpetuate old stereotypes.

In spite of these weaknesses, the treatment of Nancy, Roger, and some of their friends is refreshing. Nancy has a nontraditional summer job; she is a lifeguard. She must, and does, deal effectively in handling disputes among the adolescents who frequent the pool. While Roger is away, she befriends Jerry, a brilliant science student who lacks social skills. While Jerry is interested romantically in Nancy, they maintain a platonic friendship. Above all, when Nancy and Roger must seek what shelter they can find when they become lost on a ski trail, both show their strengths and weaknesses. Roger berates himself for getting them into their predicament, rather than thinking constructively about what they must do to try to save themselves. It is Nancy who remembers that it is the person who keeps her head who survives in an emergency. Thus, she begins to devise a makeshift shelter for them and suggests that they ration their candy. Later, when Nancy is sleepy, Roger insists that they must both stay awake and do some exercises to keep from freezing to death. If either of the characters is stronger, it is Nancy, but both are human and multidimensional.[13]

There is little to criticize in *The Day the Senior Class Got Married*, a novel about Lori Banks's and Garrick Hamilton's decision to get married immediately upon their graduation from high school. The title of the book comes from the fact that Lori and Garrick are taking a course in consumer economics in which members of the class, all seniors, must participate in simulated marriages to learn about the economic, social, and emotional realities of marriage. This book has a pleasant twist; it is Lori who is brighter, more objective, and more level-headed than Garrick. Yet, as they work on projects for their simulated marriage and plans for their real wedding, Garrick tries to dominate her and override her sensible decisions. In the end, Lori rejects the idea of marriage in favor of a college education; Garrick will be an auto mechanic.

The treatment of the significant adults in the book—Lori's divorced parents and her father's woman companion—is balanced. Miklowitz shows how divorce and subsequent sexual involvement of parents with other potential partners affect children. She reveals how the estranged couple interact, and she insightfully demonstrates the ticklish position of potential stepparents. There is a strong bonding scene between Lori and her mother when they spend a Saturday morning alone. It is Lori's father who, in expressing his disapproval of her initial plan to marry at such a young age, makes a strong feminist statement.

It's stupid [getting married].... This is the twentieth century! Women go into professions, learn to stand on their own two feet before they settle down. What is it? Sex? You can't keep away from each other?...So there's the pill; there's other things. Don't get married just for that.[14]

Miss Teen Sweet Valley is one of the more recent *Sweet Valley High* titles which purport to deal sensitively with serious topics. *Miss Teen Sweet Valley* looks at the question of the sexism of beauty pageants, but Pascal has also come out with books on racism, anorexia, divorce, and Hispanic heritage. The stories are still soap operas with a fair amount of stereotyping, but there are more elements of the problem novel and some feminist teen characters in these later novels.[15]

In *Miss Teen Sweet Valley*, Jessica and Elizabeth are pitted against each other when Jessica decides to compete in the beauty pageant mentioned in the title in the hope of receiving prizes, fame, and the attention of her latest heart throb. Liz is opposed to the contest on solid feminist grounds—it demeans women by treating them as sex objects. Even though there are segments on talent and questions which are supposed to determine how the contestants can think on their feet, in the last analysis, beauty is all that is really important in determining the winner. Liz launches a vigorous campaign to get the pageant banned, and the twins are in violent disagreement once again. As Patricia P. Kelly points out, Jessica does show that she has a sense of the work ethic as she seriously prepares for her dance routine. Once again, Liz is willing to sacrifice her principles in order to stand by her sister. She pretends to be Jessica during the swimsuit portion of the contest. Jessica had fallen during her dance number and was so humiliated that she would not continue in the competition. In spite of doing badly in the talent portion, Jessica wins the title because she is the prettiest contestant. In the end Liz's views are vindicated, and Jessica concludes that her sister was right from the outset.[16]

There are differences between the novels of the 1940s and 1950s and those of the 1980s and 1990s, but the changes are not enough to eliminate the stereotypes. Having women work, giving teenage girls career aspirations, getting rid of the feminine pedestal, and presenting some feminist ideas are all improvements. However, there remain a number of problems which authors have not resolved: How do they make characters fallible without resorting to clichés? Why do they still have stock characters such as the dumb blonde flirt? Why are negative male characters counterbalanced with even more negative female characters? Moreover, preteens and young adolescents continue to have access to the older, more traditional teen romances. *Seventeenth Summer* and Beverly Cleary's romances of 1950s and early 1960s are currently in print.

Three significant questions about the reemergence of the innocent teen romance are more difficult to answer: 1) Why have they been reintroduced? 2) Although there are the noted exceptions in the newer titles, why do they seem to be so little influenced by feminism? 3) What effect will they have on the socialization patterns of preteens and young adolescents?

The romance genre has always been popular with young adult girls. Adolescents are fascinated with developing sexuality and love. One need look only at the continued popularity of classics such as *Jane Eyre* to see the validity of this generalization. Another reason for their proliferation is the current tendency in children's and young adult fiction for bad, cheaply produced literature to drive out more expensive books of above-average quality. The very best books will always find publishers. However, with the deep cuts in school and public library budgets, publishers have reduced the number of books for young people which they are willing to publish in hardback in favor of original paperbacks of much lesser literary quality. Series books prevail in this atmosphere. With some publishers issuing teen romances as often as one new title a month, they need cadres of authors. There are good writers within some series such as Miklowitz, but mediocrity is the norm.[17]

The reason for the lack of feminist influences on all but a few of the more recent books is complex and difficult to explain. One factor is related to the bad literature thesis. Many parents are conservative when it comes to picking out books for their children or, in the case of young adults, in letting the girls choose their own reading materials. Adults will buy slick, if badly produced, classics for their children because they regard these as safe purchases. Innocent romances do not bother parents' sensibilities. The books may be pap, but they seem innocuous.[18]

Christian-Smith attributes the reintroduction of teen romances and their lack of feminist values to conservative elements in the big publishing conglomerates; she almost, but not quite, relates these things to the rise of the Reagan right. This is an overreaction. Preteens and young adults are emulating older female role models in their reading habits, and there has been a backlash among parents against the very explicit problem novels of the heyday of contemporary realism in the late 1960s and 1970s. Furthermore, in a world where they are faced with enough real problems, girls want to escape. The very newest novels of this decade, like *Sweet Valley High*'s *The Perfect Girl*, which deals reasonably well with the problem of anorexia, may indicate that there is a moderate shift in interest from a relatively pure interest in romance to a greater emphasis on realism. This trend, if that is what it is, is probably a result of market research on the reading preferences of young adult girls.[19]

The far more interesting question which really deserves serious attention is the effect of teen romances on the socialization process. Will a more feminist approach in literature help to overcome current beliefs? Does sexist literature reinforce the prejudices which exist in reality? What really needs to be done is to analyze carefully what perceptions young readers have when reading these texts. Some very preliminary research which I have conducted suggests that the answers may not be simple.

In a relatively small sample of romance readers in the seventh and eighth grades, I found that regardless of class or even educational achievement, the girls knew that they were not reading about situations which accurately reflected real life. They were cognizant of the fact that the girls and boys were ideal types. They cared little about what the parents in the novels did or did not do.[20]

Even less scientific, but equally suggestive, was a conversation which I had with two of my women friends when we reminisced about reading the original versions of the Nancy Drew mystery series. All three of us, who range in age from 35 to 49, remembered Nancy as a strong, independent character. None of us recalled that the books are full of bigoted characterizations of immigrant Americans. So the question which scholars must address is what filters do girls use when reading texts? Do they pick up on the fact that girls have career aspirations or on the fact that some of the girls play "the game" with their boyfriends? If they do pick up on the sexism, do they necessarily buy it?[21]

An analysis and comparison of the innocent teen romances of the 1940s and 1950s with those of the 1980s and early 1990s leaves one with mixed emotions. One feels a sense of frustration, but also a sense of guarded hope. Most of the books are mindless and stereotyped regardless of the period in which they were written. In the books of the 1980s and 1990s, women have entered the world of outside work, but often, although not always, the authors do not present these women as complex human beings. Stock characters, like the flirt, and competition between the heroine and "the other girl" have not disappeared.

One might argue that, since formulaic fiction is based on formula and is escapist, change is not possible. This is not true. In the realm of teen romances, an excellent set of historical novels, the *Sunfire* series, belies this argument. These young women are strong, independent, and in love. Mothers often support their daughters' nontraditional behavior, and some fathers are over-protective.

If one wants to look at another genre of formulaic fiction for girls, the mystery, one can demonstrate again that change is possible. There is a marked contrast between an older series character, Nancy Drew, and Doris Fein, a modern day superspy. Nancy is perfect and has a steady boyfriend. Doris has a recurrent weight problem and does not have a permanent male companion. Neither set of novels will win any literary awards, and the later books are as escapist as the older ones. But, T. Ernesto Bethancourt (the pseudonym for Tom Paisley) has made Doris more human, even if she is still an ideal. The publication of books such as *Just Sixteen*, *The Day the Senior Class Got Married*, and *Miss Teen Sweet Valley* give one a sense of hope because amidst all the drivel which floods the market, it is possible for strong girls, nonsexist men, and independent women to have voices on the pages of some teen romances.[22]

Notes

The author is grateful to the staff of the Athens Public Library, especially Gloria Loomis, and to Karen Williams of Ohio University Libraries/OVAL for obtaining the novels for the period 1942-63 on interlibrary loan.

[1]Barbara Martinec, "Popular—But Not Just One of the Crowd: Implications of Formula Fiction for Teenagers," *English Journal* 60.3 (1971): 339-44; Rebecca Radner, "You're Being Paged Loudly in the Kitchen: Teenage Literature of the Forties and Fifties," *Journal of Popular Culture* 11.4 (Spring 1978): 789-99; Melissa Mullis Kaufman, "Male and Female Sex Roles in Literature for Adolescents, 1840-1972: A Historical Survey," diss., Duke U, 1982, 233.

[2]Kaufman 420-21. Kaufman cites Inge K. Broverman et al. "Sex Role Stereotypes: A Current Appraisal," *Journal of Social Issues* 28.2 (1972): 59-78. See my appendix for a reproduction of Kaufman's lists of the qualities which Broverman developed.

[3]Rosamond du Jardin, *Double Date* (Philadelphia: Lippincott, 1951); du Jardin, *Practically Seventeen* (Philadelphia: Lippincott, 1949); du Jardin, *Class Ring* (Philadelphia: Lippincott, 1951).

[4]Kaufman 13, 243-51; du Jardin, *Double Date* 32; du Jardin, *Class Ring* 23.

[5]Betty Cavanna, *Fancy Free* (New York: Morrow, 1961).

[6]Kaufman 156-58, 170-71; Cavanna, *The Boy Next Door* (New York: Morrow, 1950); Cavanna, *Fancy Free* 171-92.

[7]Kaufman 252-53; Maureen Daly, *Seventeenth Summer* (New York: Pocket, 1942) 14-15.

[8]Kaufman 248; du Jardin, *Wait for Marcy* (New York: Lippincott, 1950) 166.

[9]Francine Pascal, *When Love Dies* (New York: Bantam, 1984).

[10]Paula J. Caplan, Ph.D. and Ian Hall-McCorquodale, B.Sc., "Mother-Blaming in Major Clinical Journals," *American Journal of Orthopsychiatry* 55.3 (1985): 345-53; Catherine R. Cooper and Harold D. Grotevant, "Gender Issues in the Interface of Family Experience and Adolescents' Friendship and Dating Identity," *Journal of Youth and Adolescence* 16.3 (1987): 247-64; John P. Hill and Grayson N. Holmbeck, "Disagreement about Rules in Families with Seventh-Grade Girls and Boys," *Journal of Youth and Adolescence* 16.3 (1987): 221-46; James Youniss and Robert D. Ketterlinus, "Communication and Connectedness on Mother- and Father-Adolescent Relationships," *Journal of Youth and Adolescence* 16.3 (1987): 265-80.

[11]Pascal, *Double Love* (New York: Bantam, 1983); Barbara Girion, *In the Middle of a Rainbow* (New York: Pacer, 1983).

[12]Jill Ross Klevin, *That's My Girl* (New York: Scholastic, 1980).

[13]Terry Morris, *Just Sixteen* (New York: Scholastic, 1980).

[14]Gloria D. Miklowitz, *The Day the Senior Class Got Married* (New York: Dell, 1983): 54-55.

[15]Pascal, *Miss Teen Sweet Valley* (New York: Bantam, 1991). Pascal covers the topic of racism in *Friend against Friend* (New York: Bantam, 1990). She treats anorexia in *The Perfect Girl* (New York: Bantam, 1991). She takes three novels to deal with the potential for divorce in the Wakefield family: *Trouble at Home* (New York: Bantam, 1990), *Who's to Blame?* (New York: Bantam, 1990), and *The Parent Plot* (New York: Bantam, 1990). In *Rosa's Lie* (New York: Bantam, 1991) she deals with Hispanic heritage.

[16]Pascal, *Miss Teen*; Patricia P. Kelly, "Transitional Novels for Readers of Teen Romances," *The ALAN Review* 19.1 (1991): 19-21.

[17]Lois Kuznets and Eve Zarin, "Sweet Dreams for Sleeping Beauties: Pre-Teen Romances," *Children's Literature Association Quarterly* 7.1 (1982): 28-32; Maria Ricardi, "Young Love: How Teen Romance Novels Can Melt a Young Girl's Heart," *Cleveland Plain Dealer* 23 Jan. 1983: C1, C3; Betsy Hearne, "Children's Books: Bad Children's Books Drive Out Good," *New York Times Book Review* 3 Feb. 1985: 24.

[18]Hearne 24.

[19]Linda K. Christian-Smith, *Becoming a Woman through Romance* (New York: Routledge, 1990) 1-5; Pascal, *Perfect Girl*.

[20]Joyce A. Litton, "Sugar and Spice: Sex Role Stereotypes in Contemporary Teen Romances," unpublished paper presented at the

Annual Meeting of the Popular Culture Association, St. Louis, Apr. 1989.

[21]For early Nancy Drews, see, for example, Carolyn Keene, *The Whispering Statue* (New York: Grossett, 1937); Keene, *The Quest of the Missing Map* (New York: Grossett, 1942).

[22]Litton, "The Wild West, Floods, Wars and Boys: *Sunfire* Historical Romances for Young Adults," *The ALAN Review* 19.1 (1991): 22-23, 25; see, for example, Keene, *The Secret of the Old Clock* (New York: Grosset, 1959); Keene, *The Clue in the Diary* (New York: Grosset, 1962); T. Ernesto Bethancourt [Tom Paisley], *Doris Fein: Quartz Boyar* (New York: Scholastic, 1980); Bethancourt, *Doris Fein: Legacy of Terror* (New York: Holiday House, 1984).

Annotated Bibliography

Broverman, Inge K., et al. "Sex Role Stereotypes: A Current Appraisal." *Journal of Social Issues* 28.2 (1972): 59-78. A reevaluation of the validity of sex role stereotypes, questioning whether adherence to them by women and men is harmful to their development.

Caplan, Paula J., Ph.D. and Ian Hall-McCorquodale, B.Sc. "Mother-Blaming in Major Clinical Journals." *American Journal of Ortho-psychiatry* 55.3 (1985): 345-53. Investigation of the incidences of mother-blaming in major clinical journals to determine whether the women's movement has resulted in a reduction of this tendency.

Christian-Smith, Linda K. *Becoming a Woman through Romance.* New York: Routledge, 1990. Studies the view of femininity presented in teen romances and adolescent girls' interpretations of the novels.

Cooper, Catherine R., and Harold D. Grotevan. "Gender Issues in the Interface of Family Experience and Adolescents' Friendship and Dating Identity." *Journal of Youth and Adolescence* 16.3 (1987): 247-64. Finds that female high school seniors are more committed to dating than boys and that there is little difference between mothers' and fathers' approval of dating.

Hearne, Betsy. "Children's Books: Bad Children's Books Drive Out Good." *New York Times Book Review* 3 Feb. 1985: 24. Declining school and public library budgets have led publishers to reprint classics in slick editions and commission inferior series fiction.

Hill, John P., and Grayson N. Holmbeck. "Disagreement about Rules in Families with Seventh-Grade Girls and Boys." *Journal of Youth and Adolescence* 16.3 (1987): 221-46. Reports no significant gender differences between mothers' and fathers' disagreements with their adolescent children.

Kaufman, Melissa Mullis. "Male and Female Sex Roles in Literature for Adolescents, 1840-1972: A Historical Survey." Diss. Duke U, 1982. A comprehensive examination of sex role portrayals in adolescent literature.

Kelly, Patricia P. "Transitional Novels for Readers of Teen Romances." *The ALAN Review* 19.1 (1991): 19-21. Identifies transitional novels in teen romance series which might be used in classroom settings to encourage young adults to think analytically.

Kuznets, Lois, and Eve Zarin. "Sweet Dreams for Sleeping Beauties: Pre-Teen Romances." *Children's Literature Association Quarterly* 7.1 (1982): 28-32. Argues that preteen girls read *Sweet Dreams* romance series to prepare themselves for real romance which lies ahead of them.

Litton, Joyce A. "Sugar and Spice: Sex Role Stereotypes in Contemporary Teen Romances." Unpublished paper presented at the Annual Meeting of the Popular Culture Association, St. Louis, Apr. 1989. Preliminary analysis of what a small sample of seventh and eighth-grade girls perceive as they read popular teen romance series.

___. "The Wild West, Floods, Wars, and Boys: *Sunfire* Historical Romances for Young Adults." *The ALAN Review* 19.1 (1991): 22-23, 25. Points out the value of the *Sunfire* series, which fulfills girls' needs for romance reading with fewer sexual stereotypes and general historical accuracy.

Martinec, Barbara. "Popular—But Not Just One of the Crowd: Implications of Formulaic Fiction for Teenagers." *English Journal* 60.3 (1971): 339-44. An examination of the elements of the formula in adolescent fiction which finds similarities between books of the 1930s-50s and problem novels of a later generation.

Radner, Rebecca. "You're Being Paged Loudly in the Kitchen: Teenage Literature of the Forties and Fifties." *Journal of Popular Culture* 11.4 (1978): 789-99. An analysis of the messages of teen romances of the 1940s and 1950s.

Ricardi, Maria. "Young Love: How Teen Romance Novels Can Melt a Young Girl's Heart." *Cleveland Plain Dealer* 23 Jan. 1983: C1, C3. Argues that the phenomenal success of teen romance series is a result of young girls' desire for innocent romance in an era when most media products are sexually explicit.

Youniss, James, and Robert D. Ketterlinus. "Communication and Connectedness in Mother- and Father-Adolescent Relationships." *Journal of Youth and Adolescence* 16.3 (1987): 265-79. Concludes that sons and daughters agree that their mothers know them fairly well, but that their fathers do not know them as well. Daughters of blue-collar families felt that their fathers knew even less about them than did daughters of white-collar families.

Appendix

The following list of characteristics is from the study cited by Inge Broverman, and it is a good comprehensive listing of typical sex role stereotyping. The first grouping represents competency characteristics, in which the masculine characteristics are more desirable:

Feminine: Not at all aggressive; not at all independent; very emotional; does not hide emotions at all; very subjective; very easily influenced; very submissive; dislikes math and science very much; very excitable in a minor crisis; very passive; not at all competitive; very illogical; very home oriented; not at all skilled in business; very sneaky; does not know the way of the world; feelings easily hurt; not at all adventurous; has difficulty making decisions; cries very easily; almost never acts as a leader; not at all self-confident; very uncomfortable about being aggressive; not at all ambitious; unable to separate feelings from ideas; very dependent; very conceited about appearance; thinks women are always superior to men; does not talk freely about sex with men.

Masculine: very aggressive; very independent; not at all emotional; almost always hides emotions; very objective; not at all easily influenced; very dominant; likes math and science very much; not excitable in a minor crisis; very active; very competitive; very logical; very worldly; very skilled in business; very direct; knows the way of the world; feelings not easily hurt; very adventurous; can make decisions easily; never cries; almost always acts as a leader; very self-confident; not at all uncomfortable about being aggressive; very ambitious; easily separates feelings from ideas; not at all dependent; never conceited about appearance; thinks men are superior to women; talks freely about sex with men.

The second grouping represents warmth-expressiveness characteristics, in which the feminine characteristics are more desirable.

Feminine: Doesn't use harsh language at all; very talkative; very tactful; very gentle; very aware of feelings of others; very religious; very interested in own appearance; very neat in habits; very quiet; very strong need for security; enjoys art and literature; often expresses tender feelings.

Masculine: uses very harsh language; not at all talkative; very blunt; very rough; not at all aware of others' feelings; not at all religious; not interested in own appearance; very sloppy in habits; very loud; very little need for security; does not enjoy art and literature; does not often express tender feelings at all.

Exorcising the Devil Babies:
Images of Children and Adolescents
in the Best-Selling Horror Novel

Gary Hoppenstand

Prior to the 1960s, the American commercial publishing scene had rarely witnessed a horror novel enter the realm of best-seller status. Instead, horror fiction was generally delegated to the pulp magazine, or to the small press publisher which seldom released more than several thousand copies of a particular book. Even H.P. Lovecraft—who today is recognized as one of America's most important horror fiction authors from before the Second World War—during his own brief lifetime never experienced much commercial success with his writings.[1] In the 1970s, Lovecraft's work enjoyed a tremendous revival, a revival that coincided with the developing success of the best-selling horror novel as a popular literary genre. Lovecraft's weird fiction, relatively unknown outside of a small group of devoted fans and pulp magazine readers during his lifetime, was read and enjoyed several decades after his death by an audience the size of which he probably would never have dreamed existed. Obviously, something had transpired in the field of popular American fiction between the Great Depression and the 1970s that allowed for the widespread acceptance of a previously specialized, ghettoized genre.

During the late 1960s and early 1970s, the horror story was brought into the publishing mainstream. The design of the contemporary best-selling horror novel, in fact, was formulated by three American authors—Ira Levin (1929-), Thomas Tryon (1926-91), and William Peter Blatty (1928-). Three of these authors' novels, in particular, established the literary model subsequent mega-successful writers, from Stephen King to Dean R. Koontz, emulated. The literary critics may have hated the efforts of this new creature—the best-selling horror author—that has clawed its way into the company of the romance novelist, the thriller writer, and the pop, self-help psychologist, but the best-selling horror novelist's audience (that is, his or her *mass* audience) loved what they read, purchasing each successive King or Koontz book in greater and greater quantities. Reviewing the history of the genre during the late 1960s and early 1970s, Ira Levin's *Rosemary's Baby* (1967), Thomas Tryon's *The Other* (1971), and William Peter Blatty's *The Exorcist* (1971) established the three significant motifs of the contemporary American best-selling horror novel.

First, these three novels suggested to their readers that the appearance of normalcy may be deceiving, that what looks harmless and banal may, in fact, be nefarious and deadly. In *Rosemary's Baby*, an ancient apartment building in New York City called the Bramford is the home of a satanic coven, evil witches who otherwise seem on the surface to be doddering senior citizens. A handsome young boy in *The Other* harbors a dark secret, a secret that encourages him to murder in order to protect the revelation of truth. In *The Exorcist*, an upscale Georgetown brownstone is the site of a terrible demonic possession, where an innocent adolescent girl transforms into a demonic monster straight from our darkest nightmares.

Second, these three novels depicted grotesque violations of sacred American institutions and traditions. The sanctity of the relationship between husband, wife, and child is attacked in *Rosemary's Baby*, and the true horror of Levin's novel is not so much the evil magic practiced by the elderly witches as it is the evolving breakup of Guy and Rosemary's marriage. In *The Other*, the issue of the validity of the American rural myth is satirized by Tryon. The question of personal faith is Blatty's central concern in *The Exorcist*. He is most interested in the efficacy of the Church in the modern, pragmatic world. The possessed Regan's supernatural pyrotechnic displays are of lesser importance and serve in the novel as mere special effects.

Finally, and perhaps most important, collectively these three novels removed the horror story from the adult world and placed it securely within the realm of the child protagonist. *Rosemary's Baby*, *The Other*, and *The Exorcist* reinforced more than any other horror story published before them the notion that the tale of horror is intimately connected to contemporary social issues. Rather than interpreting traditional religious archetypes of good and evil (though, certainly, some of this exists in all three narratives), these novels primarily dealt with contemporary problems—and contemporary evils. For example, the identification of child abuse as a recognizable social problem is a recent development. Historically in America, sociologists began to document child abuse in the late 1960s and early 1970s, approximately the same period that Levin, Tryon, and Blatty enjoyed their initial literary successes on the national best-seller lists. The fact that these three highly successful horror novels paralleled a period in American history where the child became a more highly definable social entity is not entirely coincidental. Obviously, best-selling authors must tailor their work to a mass audience's taste. Best-selling novels, then, arguably must reflect at some level the society that buys them and reads them, since their very commercial success is dependent upon their intellectual accessibility. Horror fiction—which had previously been regarded as escapist, formulaic fiction—following the new patterns established by *Rosemary's Baby, The Other,* and *The Exorcist,* had rediscovered how to be escapist *and* highly entertaining to a much wider and more receptive audience. Yet the best-selling horror novel encouraged its reader to escape into the social issues confronting the modern world, not away from them. Levin, Tryon, and Blatty demonstrated, as had no other writers before them, the horror formula for commercial success: give the reader a story that reflects the reader's immediate world, a story that the reader can easily identify with, a story where evil possesses a recognizable face, a story where fictional horror is no less fantastic than today's front-page headlines.

Ira Levin, Thomas Tryon, and William Peter Blatty helped to establish in their respective best-selling horror novels three important images of the child that defined the social mores of the era. In Levin's *Rosemary's Baby,* the child reflected several strong and paradoxically conflicting feelings of parents. At one level, the child is identified as a love object, as something other than the mere propagation of the family line. At another level, the child is identified as a hindrance to personal or social success, as something that causes parents to ask the question: "How will a child affect my life?" In Tryon's *The Other,* the child is portrayed as victimizer. Adolescents presented American society during the late 1960s and early 1970s with a number of serious problems, including drug abuse, increased levels of sexual promiscuity, and antisocial behavior that rebelled against various authority institutions, most specifically against parental authority. Tryon's novel effectively incorporated these ambivalent feelings about children and presented a story where the child is a sociopathic monster preying upon society, thus reconstructing the readers' real-life apprehensions into a fictional narrative that resolves these apprehensions. Finally, Blatty's *The Exorcist* features the child as a victim. The young girl who becomes possessed in Blatty's novel not only becomes a test of faith for a priest who has none, but more important, she functions as a type of moral symbol warning of the dire consequences of an evolving family structure that places more emphasis on parental identity—such things as career success and personal fulfillment—than on the child's emotional stability. Blatty implies that one of the major reasons why the child becomes dysfunctional is because the family has become dysfunctional, stressed by the rising divorce rate and the drawbacks of single-parent households.

Since its initial publication in 1967, Ira Levin's novel *Rosemary's Baby* has sold more than four million copies, making it the top best-selling horror novel of the 1960s. The novel is not only significant in the history of popular fiction because of its impact upon subsequent best-selling horror fiction writers, such as Stephen King and Dean R. Koontz, but also because it updates the traditional Gothic narrative, creating in the process another strong link in the genre's evolution in American literature. In addition, Levin's use of several important thematic issues in his novel—including the function of personal and social paranoia, the detailing of a feminist argument against a male-dominated society, and the portrayal of the child as object of worship and object of vilification—established the modern prototype for the best-selling horror novel. Levin accomplished this by introducing traditional, supernatural evil of the Gothic novel's past into the commonplace lifestyle of the readers' present. Horror is thus generated in these narratives when those things that the reader normally takes for granted (social values, institutions, family) become morally corrupted, disfigured and inverted.

Ira Levin was born in New York City on August 27, 1929. He attended both Drake University and New York University, receiving his Bachelor of Arts Degree in 1950. Much of his early professional work was in the theater, where he wrote a number of plays, including *No Time for Sergeants* (1955; based upon the novel by Mac Hyman), *Interlock* (1958), *General Seeger* (1962), *Veronica's Room* (1973), and his most successful theatrical effort, *Deathtrap* (1978). Levin used his intimate knowledge of the theater in his development of Guy Woodhouse's character in *Rosemary's Baby*—the duplicitous actor husband who sells his wife to the Devil in exchange for a career break. Though Levin published his first novel in 1953, a suspense thriller entitled *A Kiss Before Dying*, it was not until 1967 that he returned to the novel with his immensely popular *Rosemary's Baby*. During a six-year period from 1970 to 1976, Levin published three more novels—*This Perfect Day* (1970; an antiutopian fantasy in the tradition of George Orwell's *1984*), *The Stepford Wives* (1972; a science fiction thriller detailing the nefarious efforts by the men of an upscale suburban community to replace their wives with android counterparts, thus achieving the male chauvinist's dream of the totally subservient "little woman"), and *The Boys from Brazil* (1976; another quasi-SF thriller that features a Nazi conspiracy to clone Adolph Hitler). Levin has also published another novel, *Sliver* (1991), in which he again returns to the genre of the suspense-thriller. In retrospect, Levin's small (yet immensely commercial and successful) literary output aptly demonstrates his effective use of science fiction and fantasy narrative motifs to construct contemporary fables about human nature that relate very effectively to modern-day social problems. These problems include the ongoing power struggle between men and women, the efficacy of religion in contemporary day-to-day life, the growing danger of the high-tech political state, and the moral issues raised by bio-medical breakthroughs like cloning. Indeed, Levin's influence upon contemporary horror fiction, both in sales and content, has been significant.

Yet among his many successes in the theater and with his novels, perhaps his single most important work is *Rosemary's Baby*. With *Rosemary's Baby*, Levin adopted the structure of a traditional literary form that was significant in American literature during the 19th and early 20th centuries: the Gothic narrative. Levin reshaped the Gothic, adapting it to a contemporary setting, and using it to house a contemporary social debate about the role and value of children in today's culture. Levin became a major influence in the development of the Gothic story in American literature. He joins the company of such notable figures as Charles Brockden Brown and Washington Irving (who brought the Gothic story from Europe to America during the early part of the 19th century), Fitz-James O'Brien, Ambrose Bierce, Robert W. Chambers (who first introduced modern-day settings to the Gothic), and H.P. Lovecraft (who, during the 1920s and 1930s showed how the Gothic story could be blended effectively with other literary genres, like the science fiction story).

Ira Levin structures his novel much the same way as Henry James structured "The Turn of the Screw." In both narratives, the respective authors create a powerful element of uncertainty, underpinning the supernatural events of their stories with equally rational explanations. This deliberate eradication of the boundaries between the world of fantasy and the world of reality creates a doubt in the reader's mind as to whether evil is psychologically or supernaturally induced, whether evil is created within or without the individual. Until the conclusion of the novel, when it is revealed that the Devil does indeed exist and that there indeed is a coven of witches living at the Bramford, the reader of *Rosemary's Baby* is, for the most part, unsure of the existence of supernatural evil. Rosemary Woodhouse's growing sense of paranoia about the fate of herself and her child (and most important, about the existence of satanic evil) is time and again diffused by seemingly rational explanations. As Rosemary's pregnancy comes to term and as she (in her role as detective) becomes more convinced of her impending peril, the reader is still offered rational, reasonable explanations for her otherwise hysterical, paranoid inferences. But we sense that Levin, from the beginning of *Rosemary's Baby*, has stacked the proverbial deck in favor of the Devil, and during the course of the story when it becomes more obvious that evil is external and supernatural, the fact that rationality could still be employed to mask the "truth" is perhaps the single most frightening element about the novel. Logic and reason are tools of alienation in *Rosemary's Baby*, and social alienation is what makes Levin's novel a truly contemporary horror story. Nothing is sacred—not religion, not love, not the institution of marriage, not even children. The accepted cultural stereotypes of what is "good" and what is "evil" are inverted by Levin, destroyed and reconstructed into something that becomes a modern-day fractured fairy tale of a mother's fear of, and eventual acceptance of, her newborn child.

In fact, there are two levels of paranoia evident in *Rosemary's Baby*. On one level, Levin's novel details the anxiety experienced by many pregnant women. *Rosemary's Baby* is divided into three sections. Part I recounts the events leading up to Rosemary becoming pregnant; Part II describes Rosemary during her pregnancy; and Part III depicts what happens after Rosemary gives birth. Much of Part II deals with Rosemary Woodhouse's apprehensions about reaching the end of her pregnancy. Many women feel some degree of nervousness about the physical changes happening to them as they progress through the term of their pregnancy, a discomfort about their changing appearance, for example, or an anxiety about the subtle or not-so-subtle variations in their health or appetite. In *Rosemary's Baby*, Levin accentuates these otherwise normal anxieties by having Rosemary undergo a literal hell with her pregnancy. Instead of gaining weight, she loses it, as though her baby were a vampire sucking the life force right out of her. Her "unusual" cravings for food include a taste for raw meat; at one point she devours a raw chicken heart. And she feels unrelenting, terrible pain all the time. Yet the worst aspect about her pregnancy is that those who should otherwise support her, such as her husband and her obstetrician, are instead forcing her to endure this physical and mental trauma so that they can get what they want. They are totally oblivious to her health and safety, and, in fact, function as her literal torturers. Thus, Levin has in his horror novel taken those otherwise normal fears experienced at some point by many expecting mothers and exaggerated those fears to the point where they become truly horrifying. Levin has written perceptively about the general paranoia surrounding the childbearing process in *Rosemary's Baby*.

The reasons why women subject themselves to the trauma of childbirth have changed as much over the years as has the perception of the child in society. Viviana A. Zelizer argues in *Pricing the Priceless Child: The Changing Social Value of Children* (1985) that prior to the 1870s children in an evolving industrial society provided a much-needed income for the financially impoverished family. Children had little worth, except as wage earners in the factories.[2] Women had children because the family needed them for economic survival, and they had as many as they could bear because the relatively high mortality rates during childbirth and the early adolescent years meant that a significant percentage of children would not even survive to the age where they could work in the factory. Yet Zelizer claims that a transformation occurred between the late 19th and early 20th centuries in which the perception of the child radically changed. Zelizer states,

The twentieth-century economically useless but emotionally priceless child displaced the nineteenth-century useful child. To be sure, the most dramatic changes took place among the working class; by the turn of the century middle-class children were already experienced "loafers." But the sentimentalization of childhood intensified regardless of social class. The new sacred child occupied a special and separate world, regulated by affection and education, not work or profit.[3]

Thus, according to Zelizer, children became fully identified in the 20th century as love objects, a social status they had historically never fully realized before.

In *Rosemary's Baby*, Levin essentially mirrors this transformation of the image of the child. The people involved in Rosemary's pregnancy (mainly the men) want Rosemary's child for some function. Guy Woodhouse sacrifices his wife for selfish career advancement; Roman and Minnie Castevet, Dr. Abe Sapirstein (her duplicitous obstetrician), and the other witches want the child for political reasons, to serve as the new anti-Christ. Theirs is a 19th-century perception that children must serve some sort of useful role. By contrast, Rosemary views her child in an entirely different (indeed, in a very contemporary) way. After she gives birth to the baby and discovers that the child is still alive, and although she is initially repulsed by her son's grotesque physical differences, she overcomes her revulsion and lovingly embraces her child. For Rosemary, the child's social role is irrelevant. She comes to love him unconditionally by novel's end, and this attitude is emblematic of the contemporary American parents' attachment to their children.

However, paradoxically conflicting with this feeling of unconditional love, many adults also possess certain reservations about having children, reservations concerning how children will change their lifestyles. Zelizer identifies this ambivalent attitude about the child in *Pricing the Priceless Child*,

Vance Packard...discerns a growing sentiment *against* children in the United States, expressed very concretely by those who refuse to have any children. Childlessness is emerging as an acceptable alternative to "child-creation." New instrumental considerations, claims Packard, may be depreciating the emotional benefits of the priceless child. Children are often feared as obstacles to "fulfillment," or a career, or as economic burdens, or even as impediments to marital happiness.[4]

Levin's *Rosemary's Baby* certainly expresses a number of these collective social apprehensions. Guy Woodhouse signs his literal Faustian pact with the Devil in order to enhance his career. His reasons for this terrible act are quite rational. He is insuring that his family will not become a financial burden to him or his wife. Ironically, however, by making a deal with the Bramford coven, he destroys his marriage. For Rosemary, her child will replace her husband as the focus of her affection. Rosemary's having her baby in Levin's novel, in essence, becomes a powerful reason why modern couples should not have children: because, according to Vance Packard, children will interfere with "marital happiness." This perception of the child as burden to parents serves as a common narrative motif in the best-selling horror novel (as readily evidenced in the fiction of Stephen King), and will soon reappear in William Peter Blatty's *The Exorcist*, to a quite similar resolution.

Author Thomas Tryon began writing novels as a mid-life career change. Before he published his first book, *The Other*, in 1971, he spent 19 years—from 1952 to 1971—as a moderately successful actor, appearing in television and in such films as *The Longest Day* (1962), *The Cardinal* (1963), and *In Harm's Way* (1965). Tryon was born in 1926 in Hartford, Connecticut. He married in 1955, and later divorced. He received an Ivy League college education, graduating with a B.A. from Yale University in 1949. Tryon's early artistic career included his working as a set painter, an assistant stage manager, a production assistant for CBS television, and a Broadway actor. After receiving his "big break" in Hollywood by landing the starring role in the Otto Preminger film *The Cardinal*, Tryon became disillusioned with the industry. He stated at one point, "If anyone ever picked the wrong profession, I did when I became an actor."

Tryon thus left a successful acting career to become a writer. He achieved best-selling and critical success with his effort, *The Other*. Following *The Other*, Tryon published a second horror novel, *Harvest Home* (1973), which is another countrified Gothic narrative about a transplanted urban couple who encounter the bizarre traditions of a rural community. With his third novel, *Lady* (1974), a story about a young man's long-term infatuation with a woman, Tryon departed the horror genre for fear of being typecast as a writer of mere genre fiction (much as Stephen King has later become). Tryon said, "I think the danger in writing or in being considered a 'bestselling author' is that you can as easily get typed in that as in acting. I waged a long battle in Hollywood for 15 years or something to avoid getting typed as an actor. By the same token, I don't want to be typed as a writer of thrillers." Tryon's other published novels include *Crowned Heads* (1976), *All That Glitters* (1986), *The Night of the Moonbow* (1988), the juvenile work *Opal and Cupid* (1990), and *The Wings of Morning* (1990). Some of Tryon's best work, such as *All That Glitters*, deals with the Hollywood film mythos, which was such an important component of his professional acting career for many years. Several of Tryon's best-selling stories, including *The Other, Harvest Home*, and the tale "Fedora" from *Crowned Heads*, were successfully adapted for film and television.

Tryon regrettably discovered that making the transition from successful actor to successful author was a difficult accomplishment, and not achieved without an emotional price. He stated, "I even changed my name to 'Thomas' to steer people away from that Hollywood image. But...no matter what I do, no matter how many books I write, it's always good old 'Tom' on TV shows and interviews ...It is very difficult for people to allow me to be a writer, because they have slotted me as an actor." Tryon died September 4, 1991.

In his first—and perhaps most famous—novel, *The Other*, Tryon co-opted a number of significant motifs from other authors of horror. From James Hogg and Robert Bloch, Tryon drew material about the pathological, split-personality protagonist. From Henry James, Tryon fashioned in *The Other* the ghost story that is not a ghost story. From Ray Bradbury, Tryon elicited thematic images of rural magic, carnivals, and demonic children. From Ira Levin, Tryon garnered the finished outline of his novel, recognizing that the tale of horror, if written for a wider, non-genre specific audience, still has the potential for commercial success. Tryon said about the writing of *The Other*, "I hadn't been long into it when I realized I had something. I knew if I finished the book that I had something, that it would be published, that it would make some kind of a mark. I did know that something had happened...the book was an act of faith." Tryon guessed correctly about the critical popularity of his first literary effort. In *The Saturday Review*, critic I.P. Heldmen called Tryon's book "one of the most compelling terror fictions written in this century."

Thomas Tryon creates this sense of horror in *The Other* by contrasting bucolic images with sadistic evil. Tryon manipulates his reader's stereotypical notions of American rural simplicity and emotional harmony by violating these notions with the intrusion of senseless violence and seething, irrational hate. For example, a location as innocuous as the apple cellar in the Perry barn is the site of a gruesome, senseless murder, as the boy Holland kills his father by slamming the trap door shut upon his head. The haystack beside the barn, where the doomed cousin Russell loves to play, conceals a hidden pitchfork, deliberately placed there by the Niles/Holland persona in order to remove swiftly a disliked member of the Perry household. The family parlor in the country farmhouse—the venerable site of weddings and other joyous family occasions—is also the setting for the novel's many funerals. A tea-party attended by matron aunts on the lawn becomes a scene of tragedy as an angered wasp is encouraged by Niles/Holland to sting one of the unsuspecting aunts who is mortally sensitive to the insect's poison. A simple country carnival provides the inspiration for a terrible act of infanticide, as Niles/Holland, impressed by the image of the dead baby preserved in a bottle of formaldehyde and displayed at the country carnival freak show, duplicates with his sister's newborn child, baby Eugenia, what he first observed at the freak show. The typical farm well is the site of Holland's intended cruelty to a helpless animal, and the place of his own accidental death.

Tryon attacks the surface appearance of our rural American mindset by undermining our preconceived notions of the mythic farm and farmer, which are, historically, from Thomas Jefferson to the present, two of the most powerful intellectual constructs in the secular pantheon of American belief systems. Tryon effectively counterpoises images of violence with images of pastoral serenity, in the process undermining the foundations of our belief systems, and our belief itself, in an important and sanctified segment of the American lifestyle. Tryon underscores this desecration of the American farm by employing a "bad seed" child as the facilitator of evil. Typically a symbol of innocence and renewal, the child in *The Other* is instead a harbinger of corruption and destruction. The innocence of Tryon's rural setting is violated by the duplicitous and inverted innocence of the child.

Indeed, *The Other*, as Gothic narrative of the pathological demon child, typifies the contemporary best-selling horror novel. The most frightening thing that happens in this story, Tryon suggests to his reader, is the characters' sense that they are not in control of their lives. The young Niles is unaware throughout most of the story that he is performing the evil acts that he attributes to Holland. Niles's immediate family, his overindulgent grandmother Ada, or his emotionally debilitated mother, Alexandra, have a difficult time arriving at the truth lurking behind the recent disasters in their family. These people are passive victims of events, and of the evil that perpetuates these events.

In the traditional horror story published prior to the advent of the best-selling horror novel, evil was perceived as being external. The individual was attacked by external forces—the lab-created monster, the blood-sucking vampire, the vengeful ghost. Evil was thus easily definable, understandable within a socio-religious context. But with the advent of the psychological horror narrative—such as seen in Robert Louis Stevenson's *The Strange Case of Dr. Jekyll and Mr. Hyde* (1886) or in Robert Bloch's *Psycho* (1959)—evil became internal, human made, and subsequently less comprehendible and more problematic. It might be argued that when the horror story became psychologically motivated, it also became more frightening because it argued that evil is relative in nature, that it lacks precise definition and, by lacking definition, it is terrifying by virtue of its incomprehensibility. What scares characters most in Tryon's novel is the state of not knowing things, not knowing the origin of evil, not knowing what lies beyond death, not knowing what motivates some people—like little children—to commit atrocities.

Perhaps a reason why contemporary best-selling horror fiction is so frightening is because it reflects the collapse of previously sacred and invulnerable belief systems that formerly could explain or account for the unknowable. Or perhaps today's horror fiction simply mirrors our modern understanding of human psychology.

The child as victimizer in Tryon's *The Other* reflects the paralleling sociologist's concern with defining and attempting to understand the social problem of juvenile delinquency. Certainly, juvenile delinquency appears as a narrative element in fiction, film, and television throughout the 20th century. But in the 1960s, the adolescent's individual antisocial activities began to become larger—a collective, political movement that was much more threatening because of its pervasiveness. Adolescents began violating what Thomas J. Cottle terms in his 1980 study, *Children's Secrets,* "The Myth of Traditional Values" and "The Myth of Normalcy." Cottle argues that "During periods of extreme pressure for people to recontextualize their values, one finds a retreat to or a reaffirmation of accustomed ways of living and familiar ideologies."[5] Certainly, the decade of the late 1960s and early 1970s embodied such a period of extreme social "pressure" for American adults, especially regarding the perplexing behavior of their children. Young men and women experimented freely with their sexuality (to an extent that had never been seen before in America). Parental anxieties about their children's sexuality readily manifested themselves in the mass media of the period, and were obviously apparent in the culture's popular fiction—the popular horror fiction—of the era. Adolescents were also experimenting with new forms of popular music like the "British Invasion" rock-and-roll of the Beatles and the Rolling Stones, which in itself articulated antitraditional philosophy. Accompanying the music was a pervasive drug culture which encouraged young adults to "tune in" and "drop out," a social violation of what Cottle identifies as "The Myth of Normalcy." Children, argues Cottle, require "their parents to be the 'straight,' traditional, almost conservative background against which they may experiment with their own 'twists' of behavior."[6] Thus, actions that may appear normal to children seem equally abnormal to their parents. The adolescent culture of the 1960s, the culture of free love and psychedelic drugs and political protest, by Cottle's definition, needed to "twist" or rebel against the dominant, older generation. The older generation, baffled by what it views as serious attacks against the dominant normalcy culture, sublimates its confusion and its anger in its entertainment, like the best-selling horror novel. Tryon's *The Other* discovered its great commercial success because it helped to examine and helped to resolve parental anxiety. Cottle's "Myth of Normalcy" is violated in Tryon's novel, and by having this fictional violation defined as formulaic entertainment, readers perhaps develop a type of psychological control over what they read as entertainment and, by inference, what they experience in real life.

In retrospect, reading horror fiction prior to the best-selling period (that is, prior to Ira Levin) is more of a comforting experience than a terrifying one. The reason for this is that traditional horror fiction does not challenge the reader's fundamental understanding of reality. It proclaims that there is a God in Heaven and a Devil in Hell, and that we should avoid the one in favor of the other. Contemporary horror fiction is much more problematic in its portrayal of evil. And, as Tryon fully understands, the effect of horror is best generated in popular fiction when it challenges both the characters' (and vicariously, the reader's) sense of security with life. What denies us this sense of security is not knowing the future, not knowing fate, and ultimately, not knowing where and within whom evil resides. Society tells us that children should not be evil. Instead, they should be innocent, loving, inquiring—emblematic of the best qualities of our society. Tryon's protagonists are the most frightened when they do not know what will happen to them (or when they begin to suspect who is causing the trouble). We are most frightened when reading Tryon's *The Other* for the same reason, and because these protagonists are an accurate reflection of our own emotions and our own phobias.

Things and people are not what they first appear to be in *The Other*. A young country boy's evil twin—the perpetrator of numerous crimes against family and friends—the reader comes to learn by the end of the novel does not exist. The evil twin is simply invented by a lonely, overimaginative, overindulged child. Yet the villainous accomplishments of the fictional boy are, in reality, performed by the real boy, and Tryon thus frames and enhances the horror of *The Other* (which, by the way, is an amazingly quiet horror novel; most of the violence occurs out of the reader's sight) by having a child as the instigator of the story's crimes. Niles accomplishes many of his vile deeds because, as an innocuous adolescent, no one initially suspects him. Co-opted from Ray Bradbury's short story, "The Small Assassin" (*Dime Mystery*, 1946), the image of the evil child is striking: sin is masked by youth; hideous violence is committed by the seemingly innocent.

Tryon's *The Other*, as well as Levin's *Rosemary's Baby* and Blatty's *The Exorcist*, as has been argued, exploited an American social preoccupation during the 1960s and 1970s with its young people. Nationwide (across most economic classes), adolescents were experimenting with drugs and increased sexual promiscuity. In an article entitled "The American Sexual Revolution," Pitirim A. Sorokin suggests of this period that "Increasing divorce and desertion and the growth of prenuptial and extramarital sex relations are signs of sex addiction somewhat similar to drug addiction."[7] Adolescents were collectively defying parental authority by defiantly engaging in what were previously closely sanctioned social activities. Young men were burning their draft cards in protest against the Vietnam War, and young women were burning their bras in protest against sexual discrimination. Teenagers emulated the appearance and lifestyles of international rock stars and began exhibiting, as had no other young people previously in America, a dislike of adults and the older generation. Naturally, the parents of these young people were gravely concerned about their children's apparent dysfunctional, anti-social behavior.

Levin, Tryon, and Blatty each capitalized upon this collective social paranoia, utilizing in their novels those things that the popular horror story should exploit: the conscious or subconscious apprehensions of their audience. These three best-selling authors contextualized their tales of horror by dealing with a subject that was then being defined for the first time as a social group—children—and that was also the topical concern at both the family level and the national level. In his study entitled *Social Psychology: A Sociological Perspective* (1983), sociologist Arthur G. Neal, working from Peter L. Berger's and Thomas Luckmann's theoretical model, terms this collective, cognitive process "constructing social reality." Neal states: "Symbolic communication [such as popular fiction] is the primary means by which those who are trying to make sense out of their environments or trying to understand what is happening to them share knowledge and information. In effect, through symbolic communication we create a social order and impose it on the physical world."[8] Thus, it seems to follow that victimized or victimizing children—as part of this social construction of reality in our highly pervasive vehicle of symbolic communication known as the entertainment mass media—should be a crucial motif in the evolving seminal best-selling horror novel as it developed during this period in American history.

In their book entitled *The Seduction of Our Children: Protecting Kids from Satanism, New Age and the Occult* (1991), Neil T. Anderson and Steve Russo argue the conservative far Right, charismatic Christian's view that deviant or antisocial behavior in adolescents is the literal attempt by Satan to possess young people. The method of this attack is revealed in the "seductive" power that sex, drugs, and rock-and-roll have on children. The authors claim: "The seduction of our children is no fairy tale or science fiction story. There is a real battle going on for our kids' minds. And the two major fronts of this battle center on two essential realities that, if not understood, will lead to the disintegration of the Christian family."[9] According to the charismatic Christian's paradigm, adolescent deviant behavior is religiously, rather than socially, motivated. Definitions of children's actions thus become polarized along a moral continuum, and hence are greatly simplified. Outside of a religious context, what is difficult to identify and deal with—rebellious youth—within the religious context, as articulated by Anderson and Russo, becomes something much simpler for adults to confront and resolve. Though more sophisticated in his treatment of the subject of children and demonic possession, William Peter Blatty in his novel *The Exorcist* pushes many of the same cognitive buttons in his readers as do Anderson and Russo. Blatty establishes a moral battle in *The Exorcist,* a battle for the possession of Regan MacNeil's soul. The child in Blatty's novel is a passive character in this epic moral conflict, a victim of powerful evil influences in the world. Regan MacNeil in *The Exorcist* is a symbolic victim of the modern age, and this is the third significant image of the child in best-selling horror fiction.

William Peter Blatty was born in New York City on January 7, 1928. He received his Bachelor of Arts degree from Georgetown University in 1950 (which also is the university setting in *The Exorcist*) and served in the U.S. Air Force from 1951 to 1954. He was an editor for the U.S. Information Service from 1955 to 1957, and Publicity Director of the University of Southern California from 1957 to 1958 and of Loyola University of Los Angeles from 1959 to 1960. In 1960, Blatty published his first novel, entitled *Which Way to Mecca, Jack?*, followed by *John Goldfarb, Please Come Home!* (1963), *I, Billy Shakespeare!* (1965), *Twinkle Twinkle, Killer Kane* (1967), *The Exorcist* (1971), *I'll Tell Them I Remember You* (1975), *The Ninth Configuration* (1978), and his sequel to *The Exorcist, Legion* (1983). Blatty also enjoyed a successful career as a Hollywood film screenwriter; he scripted the screenplays for *The Man from the Diner's Club* (1961), *Promise Her Anything* (1962), *John Goldfarb, Please Come Home!* (1963), *A Shot in the Dark* (1964), *What Did You Do in the War, Daddy?* (1965), *The Great Bank Robbery* (1967), *Gunn* (1967), *Darling Lili* (1968), *The Exorcist* (for which Blatty received the Academy Award for Best Screenplay in 1973), and *Twinkle, Twinkle, Killer Kane* (for which he won the Golden Globe Award for the Best Screenplay of 1981).

Blatty's most important literary work, however, remains his novel *The Exorcist*. Blatty claims that he first acquired the idea for *The Exorcist* in 1949 during his junior year at Georgetown University. He read an article in the August 20 edition of *The Washington Post* which documented a case of a 14-year-old Mount Rainier boy who was reputed to be possessed.[10] Blatty then began researching the causes and history of demonic possession, but when he tried to sell the idea of a book to his agent or his publisher, he was rebuffed.[11] William Peter Blatty, however, persisted in his efforts, finally completing his novel in the summer of 1970. Harper & Row published *The Exorcist* in 1971, and it became one of the year's best-selling novels.

Blatty establishes as the narrative frame of *The Exorcist* the archetypal battle between good and evil, or more specifically, the battle between the forces of God and the forces of the Devil. In the prologue of the novel, entitled "Northern Iraq," while working at an archeological dig in the area that was once ancient Assyria, a Catholic priest named Father Lankester Merrin (a name that invokes the famous magician of King Arthur's Court, Merlin) foresees an upcoming battle with his ancient nemesis, Pazuzu, a demon whose "dominion was sickness and disease." Father Merrin is described in the prologue as offering a profound sense of security to those Arabs who associate with him. Indeed, Father Merrin's goodness transcends religious differences. He is something nobler than his noble station in life. Yet despite his imposing moral strength, physically he is vulnerable, and it is this vulnerability that defeats the otherwise invincible priest. Blatty's message in *The Exorcist*, however, is not intended to be defeatist. Instead, he suggests to his reader that great adversity succors eventual moral triumph, that in the tragic death of a noble person or the equally tragic violation of an innocent child lies the catalyst for individual healing. After his fateful premonition (arrived at while observing the statue of Pazuzu in the ruins of ancient Nineveh), Father Merrin quickly leaves Iraq for America, there to await a new epic conflict, a conflict that will eventually result in his death.

The reader sees little of Father Merrin throughout most of Blatty's novel, except towards the end of the story when he is summoned by the Catholic Church to perform an exorcism for the possessed child, Regan MacNeil. Merrin is intended to function as a symbol, rather than as an individual—a symbol of traditional good. He provides the moral opposite to Regan's demon, and like the demon, Merrin is something much more than mere human. But Blatty's novel is meant to be more about human courage than about supernatural demons or white wizards. Blatty intends for his readers to examine the mortal, rather than the immortal, condition, and to witness the evolution of personal faith during the most trying and arduous of circumstances. Novelist and literary critic Anthony Burgess identifies something which he terms the "'nice irony'" in *The Exorcist*: the notion of "an atheist heroine who comes to believe that her daughter is possessed, in opposition to a Jesuit hero who does not."[12] Burgess' analysis of Blatty's novel is not totally accurate, however, because even the priest Damien Karras, without faith in himself or his Church, when confronted by the seemingly grotesque miracle of Regan MacNeil's possession, eventually becomes a true believer in both absolute evil and absolute good.

One of Blatty's significant thematic concerns in *The Exorcist* is the individual's search for personal faith. Blatty employs two characters in the novel to illustrate this search. The first character, Chris MacNeil, seemingly has the ideal life as the story opens. She is a famous actress who is starring in a film set in the Georgetown district of Washington, D.C. She is rich, and famous enough to receive adulation from an adoring public. Blatty writes, "They courted her [Chris's] company: cab drivers; poets; professors; kings. What was it they liked about her? Life?" Chris MacNeil is about to embark upon a new phase of an already successful film career. She is asked to direct a film segment that, if done correctly, will open new doors of career opportunity for her. Yet despite the vestiges of her material and social triumphs, her personal life, or more precisely, her inner life, is severely wounded and in need of spiritual soothing. She is the survivor of a recent separation and divorce, a divorce that resulted, for the most part, because of her husband's (Howard MacNeil's) inability to tolerate her rising success in show business. Chris's emotional sense of well-being is also hindered by memories of the death of her young son, Jamie, when she was but "an unknown chorus girl on Broadway." Because of these two crippling emotional wounds—divorce and death—Chris MacNeil is unwilling to embrace the unconditional love of her daughter, Regan.

Blatty also implies in the story that perhaps the reason why Regan became vulnerable to possession is because her mother, Chris, as a single, successful parent, was more interested in a career than in the social obligations to her daughter. Blatty's inference may seem antifeminist on the surface, but he otherwise portrays Chris MacNeil as a very strong woman. Instead, Blatty's message is allegorical. He desires to write in *The Exorcist* about the single parent's dilemma (especially the single mother's dilemma) of balancing the responsibilities of work with the responsibilities of nurturing children. Blatty, in addition, nicely articulates the paranoia that the single parent feels about the arduous process of successfully raising children.

In his book entitled *The Politics of Children's Survival* (1991), George Kent statistically identifies a strong link between high infant mortality rates and children raised in single-parent households.[13] Kent defines household wealth (or the lack of it) as an important element that determines the levels of child mortality.[14] The child in Kent's study is seen as being passive, as being a possible victim of imperiling social circumstances beyond the immediate control of the child. Interestingly, Kent's sociological definition of the child as potential victim corresponds with Anderson's and Russo's religious definition. Indeed, the child as victim is a powerful contemporary image that readily transcends defining boundaries.

Blatty utilizes this similar image of the child as victim in his novel. Regan is possessed, the author suggests to the reader, in part because her parents are divorced and because her mother is overly preoccupied with career advancement. Anderson and Russo would suggest that Regan became seduced by the occult (and by that New Age device of the occult, the Ouija board) because her mother, as a single parent, was not part of a strong, traditional "Christian" family. Kent might argue that Regan's psychological victimization occurs because of the physical lack of support she receives due to the limitations of the single-parent home. Blatty is aware of both of these concepts—the religious and the sociological—in his narrative, and he generates a sense of terror in his reader by playing upon this parental paranoia.

The other character in *The Exorcist* who exhibits a profound faith in the beginning of the story—but who later rediscovers a "misplaced" God through the ritual of self-sacrifice—is the Jesuit priest, Damien Karras. Blatty embodies in the person of Father Karras the paradox of the modern Catholic Church which is rooted more in the secular world than in the spiritual. Father Karras is both priest and psychiatrist. He is both holy man and man of science. His religious faith has been buried by his education, and also, in part, by the incapacitating guilt he feels about his mother's mental instability and subsequent death. When the reader first meets him at the beginning of Blatty's novel, Father Karras is emotionally numb to the suffering of others. Illness repulses him, as is demonstrated by his unwillingness to provide comfort for a destitute bum he encounters in a subway. He is equally numb regarding his belief in God. He demands some sort of proof as a foundation to base his faith upon. Blatty writes: "In the world there was evil. And much of the evil resulted from doubt; from an honest confusion among men of good will. Would a reasonable God refuse to end it? Not reveal Himself? Not speak? 'Lord, give us a sign...' The raising of Lazarus was dim in the distant past. No one now living had heard his laughter."

Along with children, one of the most victimized groups of people in America are the elderly, according to Richard V. Burkhauser and Greg J. Duncan in their article entitled "Life Events, Public Policy, and the Economic Vulnerability of Children and the Elderly."[15] Blatty provides his reader, in the character of Father Karras, this sense of individual (and collective) guilt concerning the treatment of the elderly in America. Damien Karras himself becomes the vulnerable child because of the tremendous guilt he experiences when his elderly (and perhaps neglected) mother dies. He blames himself for not taking better care of her as she grew older and began to lose control of her mental faculties. Her mental deterioration became an embarrassment to him, and he blamed himself for wanting to avoid her. Such guilt is, no doubt, a common experience in a contemporary society that has lost touch with its elderly, that has focused its attention too much on the advantages of youth and the disadvantages of age. Adult children dispose of their parents in nursing homes so that caring for them does not become a burden, and children have ambivalent feelings about such a practice. In Father Karras's case, his guilt is nearly debilitating, and Blatty intends it as a criticism against those who would readily dispose of their parents. Regan's demon attempts to use Karras's guilt as a psychological weapon against the priest during the rite of exorcism.

As we witness Karras's subsequent involvement with the possessed Regan, Blatty wants the reader to realize that faith and science are perhaps not psychologically compatible. The rational mind, Blatty implies in his novel, when confronted by miracles, attempts to dismiss those miracles with explanations that have no validity. During his investigation of Regan's condition in order to judge if the ritual of exorcism is required, the demon-possessed child attempts to confuse Father Karras about the real nature of Regan's possession by attempting to plant in his mind a strong doubt concerning the possessed Regan's apparent supernatural abilities. These include her speaking in foreign languages that she otherwise would not know, her bizarre physical stigmata, her superhuman strength, and her telekinetic ability to move objects physically. Speaking through the hapless Regan, the demon tells Karras that it cherishes "'all reasonable men,'" by inference because they doubt the evidence of miracles, no matter how nefarious or ugly those miracles may be. In the presence of the supernatural, Damien Karras eventually learns, rationality must be sublimated by a blind faith in the unseen and the unknowable. In fact, medical science alone has been unable to protect Regan MacNeil in *The Exorcist*. The physical and mental hardship of the tests that she undergoes to identify her dysfunction early in the narrative are as terrible in their own fashion as are the effects of her demonic possession.

Father Karras does regain his belief in the miraculous during his battles with Regan's demon, and demonstrates an ultimate act of faith when he challenges the demon to exit Regan's body and enter his. While in the throes of fighting the demon now within him, he commits suicide by hurtling himself through Regan's bedroom window to his death on the streets below. But before his death, he is absolved by his Jesuit friend, Father Joseph Dyer, who, like Damien Karras, is affiliated with Georgetown University. Regan is totally healed by Karras's sacrifice. Immediately before his selfless death, Damien Karras could do something he never could do before; he could confront pain and suffering, embrace them, and attempt to cure them.

Damien Karras's sacrifice is intended as a metaphor in Blatty's *The Exorcist*. It is meant to dramatize the responsibility of the concerned parent to protect and nurture the vulnerable child. To use Richard De Lone's phrase, as stated in his book, *Small Futures: Children, Inequality, and the Limits of Liberal Reform* (1979), American children may be perceived as being the "Bearers of the Dream,"[16] symbolic of America's future, emblematic of the best and the worst of our society. Blatty's novel is not only Damien Karras's and Chris MacNeil's internal dialogue concerning the discovery of personal faith, it is also the author's call to arms against the neglect or abuse of children. Blatty portrays the child as a helpless victim of the larger social/religious world, and he shows his reader that adults are responsible for nurturing and protecting society's most vulnerable class of people. As evidenced by the healthy sales figures of *The Exorcist* through the years since its initial publication in 1971, Blatty's metaphor is obviously a compelling one.

The contemporary, multi-dimensional method in which evil is depicted in *The Exorcist* clearly reveals why William Peter Blatty's novel is one of three seminal works of the mass market best-selling horror genre. Along with Ira Levin's *Rosemary's Baby* and Thomas Tryon's *The Other*, Blatty's *The Exorcist* articulated an intimate social reflection of the period in which it appeared. Prior to Levin, Tryon, and Blatty, the horror story tended towards the remote, fantasy-like Gothic setting of a Horace Walpole, an Ann Radcliffe, or an Edgar Allan Poe. The basic formula of this type of narrative depicted horror almost exclusively in supernatural terms, as an evil existing outside of the human condition, like the archetypal vampire or walking dead which seek to prey upon the unwary. The Devil and his minions were beyond us, extraneous to us, and like some virulent disease, something antithetical, and alien, and threatening to us.

With the development of the psychological Gothic in American literature during the 19th century—from Charles Brockden Brown to Ambrose Bierce—the origin of evil began finding its way inward to the dark crevices of our psyches. The recognition that people may do evil without the external support of demons and devils, that evil was indeed a human construct, paralleled the evolution of psychology and sociology as fields of scientific study. What Levin, Tryon, and Blatty ultimately contributed to the horror story, thus making it both contemporary and widely popular, was the notion that the greatest evil done is that which abusive husbands do to their battered wives, or that which abusive parents do to their battered children. The contemporary best-selling horror novel finds its mass appeal in its ability to illustrate collective social ills. *Rosemary's Baby*, *The Other*, and *The Exorcist*, for example, chart the break-up of the traditionally perceived American family. In all three novels, the dysfunction of the family plays an important role in helping to establish the context of supernatural horror. These novels discovered their respective successes on the best-seller lists at approximately the same time sociologists discovered that the most violent institution in America is the family unit. *Rosemary's Baby*, *The Other*, and *The Exorcist* also reflected a collective national paranoia concerning children of the late 1960s and early 1970s America. Adolescents rebelling against social and political authority were reflected in microcosm in Blatty's best-selling *The Exorcist*. Devils were possessing our children, which, in

the best tradition of popular formula, provided simplified explanations to complex problems. If children were becoming godless with
their addiction to sex, drugs, and rock-and-roll, then the Devil made
them do it, which then invoked parental responsibility to intervene in
preventing these external factors from seducing their vulnerable
children. An evolving sociopolitical crisis was defined in mythic terms
that provided not only a ready and easily identifiable definition for
what was wrong with today's children but also a ready and easily
identifiable response. The defeat of Regan's demon by a concerned
mother and a concerned Church in *The Exorcist* articulated a fairly
clear solution for the seemingly deviant child: unconditional love and
closer parental supervision. The worst devils in the best-selling horror
novel were not those who fell with Lucifer in Milton's *Paradise Lost*,
but instead were the personal, psychological devils of the alienated
family. Part of this familial estrangement was viewed as paralleling the
disintegration of our national moral fiber, the destruction of
traditional religion and religion's place in the American way of life. As
currently practiced by Stephen King, Dean R. Koontz, and John
Saul, the best-selling horror novel continues to define us in our
respective social moments. Because of this ability—the ability to
effectively blend dark fantasy with a type of documentary, in-your-
face reality—the best-selling horror novel finds its great commercial
success with American readers today.

Notes

[1]Part of Lovecraft's lack of commercial prosperity during his own
lifetime may perhaps be attributable to his professed disdain of the
professional writer. In his book entitled *Lovecraft: A Biography* (1975), L.
Sprague de Camp cites Lovecraft as saying that no author could produce
anything of value from strictly "commercial motives" (285). Donald R.
Burleson, in *H.P. Lovecraft: A Critical Study* (1983), admires Lovecraft's
professed artistic objection to professional fiction writing. Burleson states,
"Had he [Lovecraft] acquiesced in the artistic treason expected of him at
times by editors, many of his stories would scarcely have been worth
preserving, but he remained faithful to his principles to the end" (16). Of
course, Burleson assumes an invalid relationship between artistic integrity and
artistic profit. Robert E. Howard—who was one of Lovecraft's equally
popular literary peers at *Weird Tales*, and who also, like Lovecraft, had a
difficult time finding a book market for his pulp fiction during his lifetime—
made no such pretensions about selling his writing for as much money as he

could make. And regarding style, Howard was a much better writer than Lovecraft.

[2]Viviana A. Zelizer, *Pricing the Priceless Child: The Changing Social Value of Children* (New York: Basic, 1985) 24-25. Zelizer's study analyzes the evolving transition of the social value of children during the end of the final decades of the 19th century and the early decades of the 20th century. Zelizer argues that as the useful child (i.e., the child earning an income for the family) disappeared during this 60-year period, the useless child (i.e., the child earning no income), became more sentimentally valuable.

[3]Zelizer 209.

[4]Zelizer 217.

[5]Thomas J. Cottle, *Children's Secrets* (Reading: Addison-Wesley, 1980) 156. Cottle's book is a social history involving interviews with children who are "keeping secret some significant story about their family." The topics of the interviews in Cottle's anthology range in subject from family violence to mental illness.

[6]Cottle 183-84.

[7]Pitirim A. Sorokin, "The American Sexual Revolution," *The Family and the Sexual Revolution*, ed. Edwin M. Schur (Bloomington: Indiana UP, 1964) 149. Sorokin discusses in his article the complex sociological relationships within a given social system. Definitions of the family and of sexual activity are closely related to other types of social values and to other social institutions.

[8]Arthur G. Neal, *Social Psychology: A Sociological Perspective* (Reading: Addison-Wesley, 1983) 37. Neal's textbook provides one of the more comprehensive examinations of social psychology. Berger's and Luckmann's "Social Construction of Reality" theory offers an effective social science explanation for the myth/symbol approach to the study of literary formulas and genres (see also my book entitled *In Search of the Paper Tiger: A Sociological Perspective of Myth, Formula and the Mystery Genre in the Entertainment Print Mass Media*, Bowling Green University Popular Press, 1987).

[9]Neil T. Anderson and Steve Russo, *The Seduction of Our Children: Protecting Kids from Satanism, New Age and the Occult* (Eugene: Harvest House, 1991) 17. What is ironic about Anderson's and Russo's argument is that they themselves employ a famous dark fantasy/horror novel by Ray Bradbury entitled *Something Wicked This Way Comes* as a metaphor that introduces their religious discussion of how today's children are seduced by Satanism. They draw specific parallels between passages in Bradbury's novel and the Bible.

[10]William Peter Blatty, *William Peter Blatty on The Exorcist: From Novel to Film* (New York, Bantam, 1974) 4. This collection includes not

only Blatty's intriguing history of how the novel and film versions of *The Exorcist* were created but a first draft of *The Exorcist* screenplay as well. Regrettably long out-of-print, this is one of the finest examinations of how a popular story undergoes narrative translations from one medium to another.

[11]Blatty 7.

[12]Blatty 25.

[13]George Kent, *The Politics of Children's Survival* (New York: Praeger, 1991) 32. Kent examines the significant factors leading to worldwide infant mortality, including such things as "Individual Factors" (i.e., disease and malnutrition), "Household Factors" (i.e., education, ethnicity and religion, parental occupations and incomes, and parental marital status), "Poverty" (i.e., the sources of poverty), "War" (i.e., how war benefits and harms children), "Repression" (i.e., racism, gender discrimination, ageism), and "Population" (i.e., demographic interpretations), among others.

[14]Kent 77.

[15]Richard V. Burkhauser and Greg J. Duncan, "Life Events, Public Policy, and the Economic Vulnerability of Children and the Elderly," *The Vulnerable*, ed. John L. Palmer and Isabel V. Sawhill (Washington: Urban Institute, 1988) 55-88. Burkhauser and Duncan argue in this article that "economic hardship" is determined by the "magnitude" of the hardship, and also by the ability of the individual to cope with the hardship. They go on to claim that the two social groupings of people most vulnerable to economic hardship are children and the elderly. Children, the authors state, are "dependent" upon others for their support, while the elderly are less flexible than younger adults in locating jobs.

[16]Richard H. De Lone, *Small Futures: Children, Inequality, and the Limits of Liberal Reform* (New York: Harcourt, 1979) 20-34. De Lone's book looks at how certain social groupings of children have been denied social and economic opportunity in America, and how American social policy has failed to solve the problem of equal opportunity for these children.

Bring the Noise (Gently?):
The Role of Rap Music in an Adolescent Audience

Larry Juchartz

> I say a prayer for you every night
> I say a prayer that you will be alright
> Soldier baby of mine, while we're apart
> I hold your picture close to my heart
> —The Ronettes

> Listen for the lessons I'm saying inside music
> That the critics are blasting me for
> They'll never care
> For the brothers and sisters
> Now across the country have us up for the war
> —Public Enemy

When the "devil music" known as rock and roll came to life in the late 1950s, it quickly found an audience with teenagers around the world and a lasting place of importance in the canon of popular culture. We recall the national hysteria surrounding the Beatles' first U.S. concert tour in 1964, the national iconization of Woodstock, the national lyrical analysis and debate over Don McLean's "American Pie," in which rock and roll was alleged to have died with Buddy Holly—a pronouncement countered by The Who's Peter Townsend singing, "Rock is dead, they say? Long live rock!" During the 1970s, however, it seemed that McLean, and not Townsend, had been right: with the advent of "art rock" and disco, the strange and wonderful psychedelic backdrop which rock had provided for the previous decade's cultural unrest and introspection gave way to unwarranted self-importance or just general silliness in the form of such acts as Yes, Emerson, Lake, and Palmer, and the Village People.[1] Teen listeners hailed Freddie Mercury and Queen as visionaries when the band introduced itself to the record-buying world in 1973, but by the end of the decade Mercury's showmanship had replaced his musicianship, and young music consumers responded by staying away from Queen's new albums in droves. (The fact that the group enjoyed a mild renaissance in 1992 speaks more to Mercury's AIDS-related martyrdom than to Queen's musical importance; the concurrent inclusion of "Bohemian Rhapsody" in the score of that year's teen film *Wayne's World* helped quite a bit, too.)

The 1980s brought new music to teen listeners from two directions: in the U.K., Johnny Rotten and Sid Vicious fronted the Sex Pistols, while in the U.S., we got the Ramones. Both bands were masters of the three-chord, two-minute *blitzkrieg* song form, which remains with us today, in somewhat longer form, as a fairly new genre called "speed metal" performed by the likes of Metallica and Mötörhead. But this same musical metamorphosis drove a wedge into the cross-racial appeal that popular music had held in the 1960s, when young audiences of both African and European descent had enjoyed Motown acts like the Temptations, the Jackson Five, and Stevie Wonder. (During the same period, as Jimi Hendrix showed how a black guitarist could fit the blues into a white audience's definition of "acid rock," a blond-haired Englishman named Eric Clapton demonstrated how a white rock and roller could also play some pretty mean blues.)

With the advent of "punk" music, itself a backlash against the musical death called disco, such racial harmony in the form of shared musical appreciation gave way to a gradual division. And while A&R people from the record companies scoured the thrash clubs for new acts, another discovery took place in the inner city: a musical form known as "hip-hop" was transforming itself into what would become the single biggest musical genre of the 1990s. Today, that genre, now known as rap, is appreciated and admired by today's children and adolescents as the cutting edge of rock and roll, just as young listeners in the 1960s once viewed the work of Hendrix, the Doors, and the Beatles.

Rock critic and scholar Simon Frith has noted that "[e]ach moment in rock history fused moral and aesthetic judgments: rock 'n roll, rhythm and blues, and punk were all, in their turn, experienced as more truthful than the pop forms they disrupted" (266), and this continues to be the case with rap. Rap, to borrow the words of Theodore Roosevelt, is the "bully pulpit" from which this century's last sermons are likely to be preached, and toward which more and more young listeners are turning in search of social truth. "We will sing of great crowds excited by work, by pleasure, and by riot," Dada artist Bruno Marinetti wrote in 1909 (qtd. in Berman 25). "We will sing of...revolution in the modern capitals; we will sing of the nightly fervor of arsenals and shipyards blazing with violent electric moons."

While Marinetti's prediction regarding the *songs* of Dada was never quite realized (unless, perhaps, we count free-form jazz or the more avant-garde musical "Happenings" of John Cage), it did foretell the themes-as-images that the art form (or non-form) would present visually.[2] Today, the same types of images are captured in rap. Both Dada and rap share an artistic bravado: when Marcel Duchamp hung a snow shovel on the wall and called it "ready-made sculpture," he presented the same idea that rap uses today in "sampling" (recording) the music of other artists and re-mixing it to form a backbeat—thus finding fame through the use of "ready-made music."[3] Moreover, while Dada is described by two art scholars as "nihilistic, [with] its declared purpose being to make clear to the public that all established values, moral or aesthetic, had been rendered meaningless by the catastrophe of World War I" (Janson and Janson 381), so too are more militant rappers like Ice-T, Public Enemy, and Ice Cube nihilistic in their didactic rhymes against the empire. And although the catastrophe, in angry rap, is that of the inner city and the stasis of life there, the musical form has, like the Motown songs of the 1960s, once again crossed racial lines of appeal and brought white and black young listeners together. As Judith Lynne Hanna writes:

Rap is surely not at odds with the experience of many people, particularly in the inner cities. Others, including youth of the upper classes, often admire its attack on the establishment and identify with its rebellious qualities opposing mainstream life.... [Y]outh identify with performers as outrageous and provocative, as they fantasize themselves to be. (190)

Indeed, rap's appeal extends to white musicians as well as listeners. Hard-rock groups such as Red Hot Chili Peppers, Faith No More, and Anthrax have taken a shine to the form for its "outrageous and provocative" braggadocio, and the results are songs like the latter group's "I'm the Man," in which the band proudly tells listeners that

> Like Ernest and Julio, before its time
> Seven years later [this song's] holding up fine...
> We stretched our boundaries, we opened the door
> That no one [had] attempted before[.]

It's fitting that rap and metal have formed a bond, since both forms take music to an extreme. In rap's case, lyrics take precedence over individual notes, although there is always a strong beat, or riff, in the background; in the case of metal, lyrics are often obscured by the riffs and notes at the foreground. To merge the forms, both lyric and riff must come together and share a common foreground in a loud, proud, postmodern fugue. The best examples of successful early mergers may be Aerosmith and Run-DMC on "Walk This Way" and Anthrax and Public Enemy on "Bring the Noise"—each collaboration having been an important genre-crossover milestone for all four of the groups involved.

But metal rap, at best, is a hybrid: the pure origins of hip-hop are centered around the same kind of youthful rebellion against standard musicianship that the punk movement once championed around the same time. Punk pushed the envelope of the three-chord Chuck Berry riff to its variational limit, while hip-hop simply listened for a great note (or series of notes), sampled the sound electronically, and mixed it with others to form a usable backbeat. This backbeat, in turn, could be sped up, slowed down, or staccatoed by the deejay's "scratching" the record on the turntable. The whole process, again, mirrored Dada in its non-musicality, but for the children and adolescents looking for a new musical form, it was perfect. What better form of rebellion against bloated dinosaur bands like Yes and Queen than music that required no band at all to play it? "Rap embodies and reproduces perfect postmodern themes," writes James Lull in *Popular Music and Communication*, since it presents "songs that don't begin or end, [and] stories[4] that are never told" (11). The list of attractions for listeners goes on:

Lyrics are sounds. Segues match grooves and beats, not words.... Melodies disappear. Deejays *make* music [as opposed to simply playing it]. Popular music today may be the perfect soundtrack for life at the end of the twentieth century—a choreography of musical and cultural impermanence that matches the quickening pace and uncertainty of the times. (11)

To illustrate these ideas of impermanence and uncertainty, we can consider what's happened to an old song of the Woodstock era, "Everyday People," by Sly and the Family Stone. As John Leland describes in an article titled "Too Much of a Good Thing," the song was admired, borrowed from, and ultimately butchered to fit by the 1992 rap-crossover group Arrested Development, who included it on their first album as "People Everyday" with only its chorus remaining intact. The song had potential as a single, but the record company worried that the backbeat, deep bass, and sharp drums, might be too hard to appeal to young white listeners. No problem, the group responded, going into the studio to erase the original music and exiting with a new, softer, reggae-flavored version. Same words, same group, but a completely different genre, thanks to digital recording technology (57). Sylvester Stone, the original composer, had seen his musical score fade and disappear, and listeners who remembered his rendition of the song gradually lost the memory under the power and appeal of the new one.

Modern technology, Leland writes, has gotten us to a place where, "[w]ith the connective tissue gone, musicians are free to play mix and match" with every aspect of their art. Witness, for example, the group 2 Live Crew coming out a few years ago with two versions of the same album, titled respectively "As Nasty As They Wanna Be" and "As Clean As They Wanna Be." Certainly there's value in changing the message to fit the audience, but ultimately, young listeners are forced to wonder which message is true. Is it the clean group or the dirty one they're wearing on their T-shirts? The in-your-face symbol of rebellion, or the dinner-at-Mom's-house symbol of conformity? In the rhetoric of teen music, *pathos* may be the most important form of appeal. Lawrence Grossberg reminds us that "the relationship between musicians, music, fans, and history is constructed around an increasingly common celebration and production of energy in the midst of a global 'blackout'" (175), and this "blackout" idea can be explained by one college sophomore named Erica, who writes in an examination of literature courses:

Students born after 1972 have not had any social events of huge importance to identify with—no racial integration struggles, no Vietnam war (the quick and easily-forgotten Desert Storm barely counts as a "war"), no presidential assassinations…. [Finding out] about another generation's conflicts and conquests may give us something to think about, but not to identify with and savor. Contemporary works, more relevant to our lives, our world, and our conflicts, provide us with the opportunity to identify ourselves and our places in the narratives. (Juchartz and Hunter 3)

As with literature, so too with music: songs like the Ronettes' "Soldier Baby of Mine" may still be enjoyed by contemporary teens for their value as amusing antiquities, but the songs won't be "identified with and savored," simply because so many young listeners see the war fought by the modern "soldier baby" as the "quick and easily forgotten" enterprise which Erica mentions. Try as they might, it's difficult for adolescents to empathize with the emotion of the Ronettes' song when they apply it to military operations like

Grenada, Panama, or Desert Storm. But postmodern music, especially rap, finds application, for just as the written text forms a narrative, the rhymed and spoken word can also narrate some truth about the society and culture around it. As James Lull notes, the U.S. "has had a rich history of music as an agent of organized resistance to many forms of oppression" (5-6), including slavery ("Swing Low, Sweet Chariot"), labor abuse ("Joe Hill"), war (any of a hundred Vietnam-era protest songs) and poverty ("Coat of Many Colors"; "Livin' for the City"). Although some of these issues may appear to have been replaced to some extent by the unfocused "blackout" Grossberg mentions, it's only because they've been around for so long: the blackout consists of a Faulknerian series of "not-changes" in which, for example, children see that starving people are still not fed, education for inner-city youths is still not improving, wages for teen workers are still at minimum scale, and politicians are still not concerned with the welfare of their young constituents. And one thing more has not changed: children still become adolescents, and adolescents still rebel against the status quo. When the status quo does nothing, then, it stands to reason that youth will do *something* in protest—like reject the rock and roll genres their parents enjoyed and instead embrace a newer, louder, more radical form. As Grossberg asks (175), doesn't such a rebellion fit right into "the heart of rock and roll, and the soul of youth?"

Rapper KRS-One of Boogie Down Productions explains that, as a result of exposure to rap, "kids are becoming more socially and politically aware, I think…. Of course, music is not supposed to play that role" (qtd. in Denski 39). But this latter statement is made sarcastically. The role of music in an adolescent audience should be clearly visible to most of us when we simply recall our own youths and replay the musical soundtracks that played as those youths progressed. Chances are, we have a "first kiss" song, a "first love" song, a number of "driver's training" songs—along with the songs we turned to, during adolescence, for guidance and wisdom. For many young listeners in the 1960s, the spirit of the decade was captured not by the Ronettes, whose music had more of a 1950s feel, but by songs like the "I Feel Like I'm Fixin' to Die Rag" by Country Joe and the Fish, which could have offered the first seeds of doubt regarding the Vietnam War with lyrics like these:

> And it's one, two, three, what are we fightin' for?
> Don't ask me, I don't give a damn; the next stop is Viet Nam
> And it's five, six, seven, open up the pearly gates

There ain't no time to wonder why:
Whoopee! We're all gonna die.

According to Herbert Gans, all adolescents share a "taste culture" within the larger popular culture, from which they create social contexts for themselves (24-25). Many of them will form friendships based solely on shared taste in music, and these friendships are strengthened as they then share in the escape which the music can offer them. As a result, music forms a common background for the peer group—resulting in an *en masse* resistance to such things as military conscription in the 1960s, and to police brutality like the Rodney King and Malice Green incidents in 1992. James Lull writes that, for adolescents, audience participation takes place at five separate but interconnected levels (19), and these same levels can apply to the shared "taste culture" of a given peer group. Participation in the music begins at a physical level (e.g., slam-dancing in the mosh pit), then moves on to an emotional level in which anger, sadness, and joy are universally shared responses to the music. From there, young listeners progress to a cognitive level where they can, as Erica mentioned earlier, "identify themselves and their places in the narrative," which in turn leads to an internalization of the lyrics at a personal level: the song is no longer about a shared human condition, performed for a universal human audience, but rather about the listener's specific condition, and performed for that listener alone. From here, with time, participation moves beyond the personal level to a social one, and at last, the music offers some tangible insight for dealing with the world *outside* the peer group. Perhaps this is why, in high school, rappers tend to stick with rappers, metalheads stick with metalheads, and top-40 "party kids" tend to exclude each of the other two groups, while at the college level it's not uncommon to find, within a given group of friends, a wide variety of musical tastes that can be both shared with, and enjoyed by, all. Of all art forms, writes British psychiatrist Anthony Storr, music may offer the strongest form of rejuvenation for those who are "cut off from the life of the body and the capacity to feel" (qtd. in Gates 58), and as KRS-One says, kids are indeed experiencing, along with this energy infusion, an awareness revival not seen since the Vietnam era.

But rap—regardless of the musician's tongue-in-cheek claim to the contrary—is supposed to play a role in that revival, simply because it no longer has any choice. The "Charts" page in each two-week issue of *Rolling Stone* lists the 50 top-selling recordings in the

U.S., and listings from the May 27, 1993, issue can be categorized by musical artist and type as follows:

Rap	12
Country	10
Metal or hard rock	9
African-American ("Soul")	8
Pop/"light" music	7
Other genres	4

In brief, the chart says that rap and black music made up 40 percent of the record sales for that month, while the closest competitors, country and metal, made up 20 percent and 18 percent, respectively. Country music, as many Nashville analysts have proudly noted, is enjoying a huge revival in popularity, thanks largely to its serving as a safe haven for older listeners too alienated by the rage and hostility in the music young people have embraced, and as such it's been deemed deadly by many of today's adolescents. Metal, the next closest contender for rap's best-selling title, is the latter genre's close cousin, so if we overlook a few black artists (like Michael Jackson and Sade) in the "soul" category whose music relies on sung vocals and safely generic themes, we're left with over 50 percent of the market in mid-1993 being controlled by music with some form of social message.

How did rap get to be the leader of the record-selling pack? Many critics credit MTV and two specific programming decisions made by that network: first, to put the video for Run-DMC's rap version of Aerosmith's "Walk This Way" into heavy rotation back in the mid-1980s, and then to design a half-hour show—titled, with economy of creativity, "Yo! MTV Raps!"—to showcase the latest hip-hop "stylings" by the most recent challenger to Run-DMC's heavyweight crown. Every Saturday morning some new group climbed into the ring and was knocked out of it—and then came Public Enemy.

Although they'd been making records before Spike Lee included their song "Fight and Power" in the soundtrack to his film *Do The Right Thing*, rappers Chuck D and Flavor Flav assaulted the public consciousness for the first time during the movie's opening sequence. As the titles rolled and a young actor named Rosie Perez performed a street dance both provocative and threatening, Chuck D slapped a generation of Americans across the face with the lyrics:

> Elvis was a hero to most
> But he never meant shit to me, you see
> Straight-up racist that sucker was[,] simple and plain
> Motherfuck him and John Wayne

"With these lines," writes Elizabeth Wurtzel in *The New Yorker*, "Public Enemy dismisse[d] two white pop icons as if they were just a couple of flies that needed to be swatted" (113). And American youth loved it. To counter Mom's collection of Elvis LPs and Dad's John Wayne videos, they made Public Enemy's next two releases—*Fear of a Black Planet* and *The Empire Strikes Black*—gold records. Rap, said Chuck D in response, had become "black America's CNN," and white kids were free to watch it, too. The message was the music, and vice-versa. Public Enemy and its fellow rappers were bringing the noise to America's young, and none too gently. South-Central Los Angeles was just a CD player away from Mayberry, RFD, and membership in gangs like the Bloods and Crips was as easy as strapping on a set of headphones. Rap's image of the child was that of a street-smart and self-sustaining latchkey kid, against whom all the odds were stacked and for whom establishment symbols like police officers and educators held nothing but contempt. And its own self-image was all rough edges. Where black Motown musicians in the 1960s had been required by label head Berry Gordy to go to charm school in order to become "more palatable to white America" (Leland, "Rap and Race" 49), rappers showed up on MTV with gang attire and assault rifles, wearing dark glasses and scowling the most menacing "stay away" expressions they could muster. The establishment was frightened by the posturing—so it was only natural that teens of all races not only flocked to watch it but also adopted it for themselves, to experience, as Wurtzel writes, "the great high on rebellion which has been mostly sanitized out of music since the sixties" (112). Many of today's youth will echo the words of a young man named Apollo, who explained in the ABC news show *Day One* that, for him, "Rap ain't just a way of talking, it's a way of life." The producer of Public Enemy's song "Bring The Noise," Bill Stephney, takes it even further, claiming that the song began "an orthodoxy...of certain politics you can have, a certain look, a certain way that you refer to women, to whites, to homosexuals, a certain way that you comport yourself. There's definitely a *religion* that has developed out of rap" (qtd. in Leland, "Rap and Race" 49, emphasis added).

But if rap really has transcended its place as a musical genre to become a lifestyle and a religion, then who's attending the services? And why do they come? To find out what the music says to and about today's young listeners, *Newsweek* interviewed twelve New York teenagers, six white and six black, and while the sample is too small to be scientific, it is no less revealing. Asked what rap is "all about," Deonna McWilliams, 15, responds:

Rap is scaring people now. But if you remember back to the '60s and '70s, when everybody became hippies and had their own dress and music, people got scared [then, too.] It was just that kids wanted their own identity. They wanted to be noticed, they wanted to be understood. All of this [rap content] is just people crying out for help.

As for the particular appeal rap holds, Dan Morris, 16, explains:

I got into rap a couple of years ago because I have a lot of black friends who listened to it. I turn on the radio and [most other music] is mindless, it drives me insane. The words are so stupid. Every song sounds like, "I love you, hon." Rap has real stories and real things. It's interesting and I respect it as a form of music.

Finally, Jessica Jenkins, 16, shows how a musical form made up of so much racial content and context can also combat racism: "The white kids at my school listen to N.W.A. or whatever, and they'll have a black friend with them, bopping their head along with them and just chilling with them. It [forms] a bond with someone" (Leland, "The Lowdown on Hip-hop" 50-51).

Certainly, rap is too huge a part of adolescent popular culture to be dismissed. From it have come new forms of slang, dress, body language, dating etiquette, and even car customization, along with a complex, deconstructive inversion of Walter Ong's acclaimed theories of literacy and orality.[5] And the fact that many parents dislike what rap has brought with it only reinforces its popularity with adolescents—as was the case with punk rock in the 1980s, art rock in the 1970s, psychedelic rock in the 1960s, and the first amplified guitar in the 1950s. In each decade was rebellion by youth, *angst by* the establishment. But this time, the initials that 16-year-old Jessica Jenkins mentions—N.W.A.—stand for "Niggas With Attitude," and that group's first hit was titled "Fuck Tha Police." And this time, the cover art for censored rapper Ice-T's latest release, *Home Invasion,* shows a white teenager wearing headphones as he fantasizes about rape and murder. That white metal bands like Slayer have been singing about similar death and destruction for years is forgotten by society, or else forgiven in light of metal's high theatrics and ridiculous posing. Rappers don't wear capes or writhe in pentangles; they dress like thugs, talk like thugs, and, for much of white, established America, could very well *be* thugs. As a result, they are monitored and—in the case of Ice-T—silenced. Once upon a time, hip-hop music was a fun and joyful thing, consisting of two turntables and a bunch of people spinning on their backs on the dance floor. Today, it's metamorphosed into a serious threat to everyone's First Amendment rights.

"The 'danger' implicit in all the uproar [over rap] is of empty-headed, suggestible black kids, crouching by their boom boxes, waiting for the word," writes Barbara Ehrenreich regarding the controversy over Ice-T's song "Cop Killer" (89). "But what Ice-T's fans know and his detractors obviously don't is that

[this song] is just one more entry in pop music's long history of macho hyperbole and violent boast. Flip to the classic-rock station, and you might catch the Rolling Stones announcing "the time is right for violent revo-loo-shun!" from their 1968 hit "Street Fighting Man." And where were the defenders of our law-enforcement officers when a white British group, the Clash, taunted its fans with the lyrics: "When they kick open your front door/How you gonna come/with your hands on your head/Or on the trigger of your gun?"

This message scares adults because the messenger takes great pains to appear authentic. But just as Robert De Niro only acted the part of deranged taxi driver Travis Bickle, so too does Ice-T only take on the persona of a cop killer, Ice Cube the role of a loathesome misogynist, Dr. Dre the part of a bullet-spraying "gangsta." White rappers such as Vanilla Ice and 3rd Bass have even taken the personas of African-Americans, inventing "street" backgrounds and sometimes criminal records in order to be accepted by the rap community.[6] Just as metal can't succeed without allusions to Satan and death, rap can't make it without boasts, threats, and implied mayhem. Kids know that, so it's doubtful if any intelligent adolescent is going to take Chuck D seriously when he speculates that Muhammad Ali's brain damage, Richard Pryor's multiple sclerosis, Magic Johnson's HIV, and even Bo Jackson's hip injury are all part of a "big government conspiracy" ("Voices & Views" 9). And when no less a public figure than Oliver North threatens to have rappers tried for treason and sedition, rap's fans gladly find themselves guilty by their association with the music.

Danyel Smith, writing about female rapper Yo-Yo in *Spin* magazine, notes that the artist's persona plays a crucial role in rap's success, but that it also

benefits [listeners] by demonstrating that there is much more to us than our so-called blackness and our required "positive" responses to it; that being [black] is as much about personal impulses, and being vulnerable and confused and having a ball, as it is about displaying a don't-take-no-shit demeanor to disguise it all. (91)

That last sounds just like adolescence itself, doesn't it? Certainly, it's a fun time, but vulnerability and confusion come with it, and these are the most difficult things to express at a time when children are becoming adults. Rap sees the child as the child wants to see himself, brave and strong and fearsome. It tells the child she can wear a condom as an eyepatch if she wants to, just as the women in the group TLC do, as a sign to her parents that she's seen sex and is prepared to handle it. Rap brings the noise, and the child synthesizes it to make it fit his or her own personality, needs, desires. Parents hear the bottom-register bass, the monotonous spoken choruses, cover their ears and say, "That's not music," and forget that the child's grandparents said the same thing to the parents not too many years ago. Society hears the brutality in the lyrics, the rawness, the frustration, and yearns to make them more gentle for the kids, and rap says it will gladly do so when society itself becomes that way. Art and life, artist and audience, are inseparable, and are likely to stay that way for a long time.

Some day, though, rap will disappear from the musical horizon, just as every other musical genre has moved aside or been transformed into its successor. Already, some black artists are toning down their raps and mixing them with more traditional sung verses, and young listeners are encouraging the move by purchasing the records. Other musicians are keeping the hard beat but softening the lyrics; it has, after all, been 12 years since the shouting began, and many teens have been casting a wistful eye back toward the Woodstock and Motown days when things weren't quite so loud or angry.

But when rap dies, a little bit of history will die with it. There's some of Bob Dylan's speak-singing mixed in with Public Enemy, and some of Woody Guthrie's talk-songs mixed in with Ice-T, and some of the oral histories of the African *griots* intermixed with Ice Cube's narratives about a typical day in South Central.[7] In that sense, rap may not be so much a musical or cultural genre as it is the continuation of a tradition. As Alex Haley notes, "when a *griot* dies, it is as if a library has burned to the ground" (10)—and the same effect could with rap's demise. If the end comes through natural causes, because rap's content has ended, because there's no more cause for anger and alienation, then we can all dig out our old 45s and start dancing in the streets. But if rap dies of enforced suffocation, its young audience will surely take to the streets for a far less joyful reason, because its own voice will have been taken away with the music. Every musical decade, from swing to punk, has ultimately heard the words uttered, "Leave the kids alone; they know what they're doing." It would be a shame to take away that confidence and trust now, in an age when they need it most.

Notes

The author would like to thank his friends and colleagues Bill Bingham, Elizabeth Capwell, and Christy Minadeo for their valuable insights and suggestions during the drafting of this chapter. Thanks also to Harry Eiss, a most patient and considerate editor.

[1] I know that some readers might take mild offense to my digs at some of these bands—because I still like a lot of them myself. But one can serve as both fan and critic of a band and its music, and it is in the latter role that I point out Queen's often overblown music and melodramatic lyrics. Queen was certainly not alone in this, however, since other bands like ELP, Yes, Roxy Music, King Crimson—the "art rock" bunch—all seemed to suffer from an overdose of the "Gee Aren't We Terribly Clever and *Talented* Musicians" syndrome for a while in the 1970s resulting in too many songs by these groups going on for over ten minutes while impatient radio programmers responded by demanding no more than four minutes per track. In a way, then, these "dinosaur" bands killed not only themselves, but by association anyone else who tried to compose more than three verses, four chorus reps, and a guitar solo.

[2] Dada, by the fact that it is basically a non-art form, is a difficult thing to explain within the confines of this brief chapter. The concept of mocking the High Art elitists by forcing them to elevate commonplace things to artistic status played a part in the movement, which essentially established a presence based on absence, something made of nothing. A comprehensive art-history text will offer a much fuller view and explanation.

[3] An extremely obvious example of such "ready-made" music being used as the background for rap lyrics can be heard in the song "O.P.P." by the group Naughty by Nature. Anyone who grew up on the Jackson Five

will recognize whole strings of that group's song "ABC"—including a young Michael Jackson singing "Come on, baby, come on, let me show you what it's all about." Two other, more notorious examples are Vanilla Ice's "Ice, Ice, Baby" taking the main bass line from Queen's "Under Pressure" and MC Hammer's "U Can't Touch This" built around the bass line from Rick James's "Super Freak." Rap doesn't just sample single notes; it frequently takes whole chunks of older songs to create its new ones.

[4]Perhaps "subtexts" or even "countertexts" would be a better word here. My interpretation of Lull's line is that the *whole* story is often not told in rap. For example, if a song chastises a Korean shop owner for "dissing" a black customer, then the untold subtext/countertext would be the shop owner's point of view of the same event. Since first-person boasting is the main purpose of rapping, however, such a 360-degree viewpoint would likely be an odd inconsistency.

[5]Ong's theories, presented in his article "Literacy and Orality in Our Times," established a distinction between text-based cultures and those based on the spoken word. With rap, we have a largely orality-based culture expressing itself through text: the lyric sheets, and even the recorded music itself, fit the latter term. But rap also requires the ability to improvise, to add new lines for new contexts, so the text itself is in many ways non-textual. Moreover, an essential part of oral-based culture is continuity—passing the stories along unchanged—but since each rapper tries to outdo the other by amending the other's "truth," the orality is highly unstable. In effect, Ong's distinctions become blurred as they cross and re-cross their boundaries, and the concepts of "text" and "orality" become increasingly difficult to define.

[6]The recent arrests and legal problems encountered by rappers such as Flavor Flav, Tupak Shakur, and Snoop Doggy Dogg, overblown by the media as an omen of rap's inherent violence, are numerically equal to the number of well-known rock and roll or even country performers facing similar criminal proceedings at any given time (witness, for example, Axl Rose's ongoing string of court dates), and appear to be more problematic for the music genre—and those who would censor it—than they are indicative of an inability to separate role from reality.

As for the roles put on by rappers outside the African-American community, white rap loses much of its power because it lacks racial "authenticity." Acts like the Beastie Boys and (now-disbanded) 3rd Bass have had to address teen issues rather than racial ones, so in the listener's mind there's not as much substance behind the beat. White rappers, as a rule, sell fewer records as well, because (with the possible exception of suburban youth and preteens) many kids think of them as frauds. Black rappers and the audiences were angry about the incursion into their territory, at first—but now are less concerned that it could bring a repeat of the days when the African-

Americans who wrote so many of the early rock standards got a few hundred dollars while white singers such as Elvis Presley got millions. (This is probably the basis of Public Enemy's Elvis-as-racist line.) Many rappers now control their own record labels and oversee their own finances to ensure their financial and artistic well-being.

[7]As defined by Haley, a *griot* is a African storyteller, a tribal elder in charge of passing oral histories down from one generation to the next. The *griots* were the late author's primary help in discovering his now-famous ancestor Kunta Kinte.

Works Cited

Primary Sources

Anthrax. "I'm the Man." *Attack of the Killer B's.* Island #C125154, 1991. A rare "B-side" from the band's earlier recording sessions.

"Apollo's Story." *Day One.* Hosted by Forrest Sawyer. ABC 21 Mar. 1993. A segment of the news show documenting the life of "Apollo," a young African-American living in the New York projects and struggling to live a good life.

"Charts." *Rolling Stone* 27 May 1993: 63. A listing of the 50 top-selling albums for the second half of this month.

Country Joe McDonald. "I-Feel-Like-I'm-Fixin'-To-Die-Rag." *Woodstock.* Cotillion #SD3-500, 1970. An audience-participation song protesting the Vietnam War.

Haley, Alex. *Roots.* New York: Dell, 1977. The famous novel about this author's African heritage and his search to find it.

Juchartz, Larry, and Erica Hunter. "Ultraviolent Metaphors: A Reader Response to Bret Easton Ellis." Ms. Eastern Michigan U, 1993. An article manuscript discussing the violent fiction of Ellis and the reception of his work by freshman literature students.

Public Enemy. "Bring the Noise." *Apocalypse '91: The Empire Strikes Black.* Def American #CT47374, 1991. A rap song extolling the virtues of lyrical and musical integrity.

———. "Fight the Power." *Do The Right Thing Soundtrack.* Motown. #CK45406, 1989. A rap song appearing in Spike Lee's breakthrough film on race relations in the inner city.

The Ronettes. "Soldier Baby of Mine." *Phil Specter: Back to Mono.* Abkco 4-Disc Boxed, Sept. 1991. One of the biggest hits from Phil Spector's "Wall of Sound" production era.

"Voices & Views." *Detroit Free Press Magazine* 27 Dec. 1992: 6-17. A year-end listing of memorable quotes from several news stories in the past 12 months.

Secondary Sources

Berman, Marshall. *All That Is Solid Melts Into Air*. New York: Simon, 1982. An insightful and in-depth account of modernism in the 20th century.

Denski, Stan. "Music, Musicians, and Communication: The Personal Voice in a Common Language." *Popular Music and Communication*. Ed. James Lull. Newbury Park, CA: Sage, 1992. Quoting a number of contemporary musicians, Denski gives insight to the goals of musicians for their audiences and the responses they received from listeners.

Ehrenreich, Barbara. "...Or Is It Creative Freedom?" *Time* 20 July 1992: 89. The "pro" voice in a pro vs. con two-essay debate, Ehrenreich defends rapper Ice-T and his right to record and distribute the song "Cop Killer."

Frith, Simon. *Art Into Pop*. London: Methuen, 1987. Frith, a rock critic, offers a detailed and extremely informative history of modern popular music.

Gans, Herbert. "Popular Culture in America." *Social Problems: A Modern Approach*. Ed. H.S. Becker. New York: Wiley, 1967. In this article, Gans describes his theory of a "taste culture" and its applications to popular entertainment and modern life.

Gates, David. Rev. of *Music and the Mind* by Anthony Storr. *Newsweek* 28 Dec. 1992: 58. A review of a British psychiatrist's book detailing the history and role of music.

Grossberg, Lawrence. "Rock and Roll in Search of an Audience." *Popular Music and Communication*. Ed. James Lull. Newbury Park, CA: Sage, 1992. This article focuses on the purpose of rock music and its applications as a celebratory and social outlet for audiences.

Hanna, Judith Lynne. "Popular Music and Social Dance." *Popular Music and Communication*. Ed. James Lull. Newbury Park, CA: Sage, 1992. Dealing primarily with rap music and its role in the inner-city culture, this article offers both answers and questions to readers seeking information about the musical genre.

Janson, H.W., and Anthony Janson. *A Basic History of Art*. 3rd ed. Englewood Cliffs, NJ: Prentice, 1987. An overview of all art genres from cave paintings to modern architecture.

Leland, John. "The Lowdown on Hip-hop: Kids Talk About the Music." *Newsweek* 29 June 1992: 50-51. A listing of interview responses from teenagers discussing rap; a boxed sidebar piece to accompany "Rap and Race" below.

____. "Rap and Race." *Newsweek* 29 June 1992: 47-52. The subtitle of this article: "From hard-core rap to the boom in country (music,) the politics of color has (become) the driving force of pop music."

____. "Too Much of a Good Thing." *Newsweek* 25 Jan. 1993: 56-57. This article details modern recording technology and the trend toward excess in both musical production and contemporary singing.

Lull, James. "Popular Music and Communication: An Introduction." *Popular Music and Communication.* Ed. James Lull. Newbury Park, CA: Sage, 1992. The title of this chapter is self-explanatory: Lull offers a comprehensive introduction to the theme guiding the collection of essays that follow his own.

Rabhan, Jeffrey. Rev. of *CB4* Soundtrack. *Rolling Stone* 27 May 1993: 49. A record review of the rap soundtrack to the comedy film, *CB4.*

Smith, Danyel. "Dreaming America." *Spin* July 1993: 91. A black woman journalist's views of female rappers and the hip-hop audience.

Wurtzel, Elizabeth. "Popular Music: Fight the Power." *The New Yorker* 28 Sept. 1992: 110-13. The writer's opinion of the censorship furor over rapper Ice-T's song "Cop Killer" and the state of militant rap music in general.

Works Consulted

Jones, Steve. *Rock Formation: Music, Technology, and Mass Communication.* Newbury Park, CA: Sage, 1992. A step-by-step guide to the music industry, from the discovery of bands by talent scouts to the recording process and distribution of the product.

Kennedy, Michael. *The Oxford Dictionary of Music.* New York: Oxford UP, 1991. A valuable reference book for information about musicians and their work.

Light, Alan. "Ice-T: The Rolling Stone Interview." *Rolling Stone* 20 Aug. 1992: 28-32, 60. Censored rapper Ice-T offers his own explanations and insights regarding the controversy around his song "Cop Killer" and the music trade in general.

Morehead, Philip D., and Anne MacNeil. *The New American Dictionary of Music.* New York: Dutton, 1991. Another helpful reference for information on musicians and their work.

Ong, Walter J. "Literacy and Orality in Our Times." *The Writing Teacher's Sourcebook.* Ed. Gary Tate and Edward P.J. Corbett. New York: Oxford UP, 1988. 37-46. A well-known article in which the scholar presents his theory of a primary and secondary orality, one text-based, the other non-textual.

Stambler, Irwin. *The Encyclopedia of Pop, Rock, and Soul.* Rev. ed. New York: St. Martin's, 1989. A reference work with a light, journalistic tone that makes its information a pleasure to read.

The Shifting Imagery of Childhood Amidst Japan's Consumer Affluence: The Birth of the "5 Pocket Child"[1]

Millie R. Creighton

Ideology in Japan has long placed supreme value on children, with consistent assertions throughout Japan's cultural history that children are precious. For example, Japan's earliest poetry anthology, the _Manyōshū_, compiled in 753 A.D., proclaims, "as a treasure which excels everything else, could there be anything equal to children" (Kojima 123-24). Although the belief that children are treasures persists in present-day Japan, there have been significant shifts in the imagery propagated to capture the nature of this treasure. This shift is readily apparent in the transition from an earlier espoused cultural ideal of childhood, embodied in Ninomiya Kinjirō[2] to the genesis of a new image of childhood born from Japan's affluent consumer society of the 1980s, defined by the phrase the "5 pocket child."

From early in Japan's modern era, until the mid-20th century, the popularized hero of childhood, upheld as a role model for all Japanese children, was represented by the youthful image of Ninomiya Kinjiro, who came to be known as Japan's peasant sage. Although the life work of Ninomiya as an adult man has been the subject of much scholarly discourse both within and outside of Japan, it is the image of Ninomiya as a child that was, and still is, most familiar among the populace. Prewar schoolyards and public parks throughout Japan often contained a statue of this diligent child, some of which still remain, always with the same image—hardworking yet hungry for knowledge, Ninomiya Kinjirō was shown reading a book as he struggled along, stooped over, under the heavy weight of a large load of firewood carried on his back. This image of childhood was one which upheld the importance of education, but also presented children's labor as an important contribution to their households, and, perhaps above all, applauded the willingness to work hard and persevere despite a lack of material well-being (Plath 69-79).

In contrast, the persisting perception of children as treasures means that in present day Japan they are indulged with unprecedented consumer offerings. In addition to the expansion of children's goods, specialty lines and designer brand names for children, the decade of the 1990s opened with the rapid construction of shopping theme parks directed entirely at children. Significantly, 1990 also marked the 11th consecutive year in which Japan marked a new all-time record low birthrate (Shibauchi).

Japan's declining birthrate has helped transform the children's market into one of the most lucrative. Explaining this phenomenon, Takayama Hideo, director of the Children's Research Institute, says, "Fewer children are surrounded by more rich adults and that means that the money spent on each child increases" (qtd. in Blustein). Not only are adults spending a lot more money on children, but children themselves have more money at their own disposal. As its actual birthrate declined, Japan witnessed the birth of the "5 pocket child." This new phrase suggests that with so few children each child receives larger gifts of money during the New Year festivities, on birthdays, and on other special occasions, and hence metaphorically needs one pocket each for money received from parents, grandparents, aunts and uncles, neighboring households, and others. The modern image of the five pocket child reflects the shift to an affluent, indulged child who is no longer expected to contribute labor for the maintenance of the household. It is the image of a child still prompted toward educational achievement, but this time surrounded (and assisted) by a wealth of material goods and consumer services.

In this essay I will explore modern images of children disseminated via children's marketing in Japan, with a particular focus on the newly emerging shopping theme parks specifically designed for children. In doing so I, like Seiter, believe that not only consumer goods but the physical space defined by store layouts, and the images presented in promotional catalogues or displays constitute 'cultural objects' (Seiter 233). These cultural objects establish a physical reality heavily imbued with symbolic meaning which serve in Mukerji's terms, to "create a setting for behavior" which compels people toward certain forms of action (Mukerji 15).

Such an analysis of child shopping worlds is important for several reasons. Stores are embedded in a culture, both reflecting and shaping social trends within that culture (Creighton, "Maintaining" and "Depaato"). Although often ignored in childhood socialization studies, stores need to be considered as sites of socialization. Like other behaviors, consumerism involves learned, patterned actions. Despite Japan's burgeoning economy, and its frequent characterization as a 'consumer society' there is little research on how people are socialized as children into culturally appropriate forms of shopping behavior. As sites of socialization, stores not only compel people towards acceptable forms of consumer behavior, but prompt people more generally toward the values and behaviors society expects. The Japanese stores and shopping parks described here function, in Beauchamp's framework, as institutions of informal schooling. Education, according to Beauchamp, is conveyed through formal, nonformal, and informal elements "through which the values and behaviors of a society are preserved and passed on to new generations," with popular culture phenomena serving as arenas of informal education (Beauchamp 189).

The images of children proffered by Japan's large retailers reflect changing conceptions of childhood in Japan, and also have a role in the ongoing process of defining childhood. Three types of child images disseminated by Japan's marketing world emerge in this discussion. First, there are images of "real children" whether these are contained in advertising and promotional campaigns created by the stores, or the images of child visitors to the shopping parks—which in turn become part of the stores' image statement of Japanese childhood. A second type of image is found in the philosophical representations of the child often constructed by such stores. The third type of images to be discussed reflects Japan's consuming interest in 'internationalization'—a buzz word permeating all areas of Japanese life in the 1980s and 1990s. These are images of foreign (non-Japanese) children created for the consumption of Japanese children. I suggest these function less to enhance an understanding of foreigners among Japanese than to enhance concepts of Japanese identity and reinforce Japanese socialization for approved behavior, particularly in regards to expected gender roles.

Imaging the Modern Child in Contemporary Japanese Marketing
Distantly removed from the impoverished image of Ninomiya Kinjirō, modern children are depicted by the Japanese retailing world as the lords and princesses of modern Japan. They are still expected to work hard, but only at efforts directed toward their educational development. Balancing this image of the child is the suggested duty of parents and other relatives to pamper children as much as possible to make up for the grueling expectations of Japan's educational system, by providing expensive educational or developmental aids,

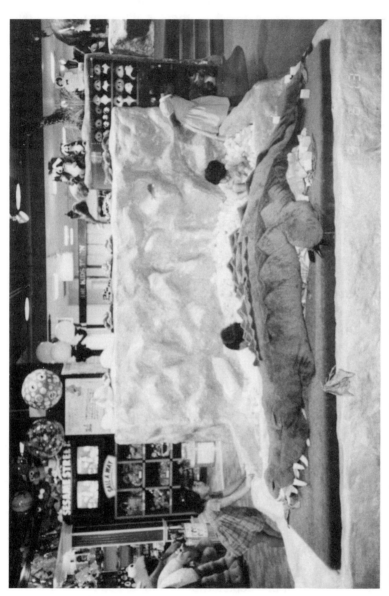

Children visiting the new specialty stores such as Dr. Kids Town can be seen playing throughout the complexes. In press reports the real children also become part of the stores' image-statement of modern childhood. (Photo by M. Creighton.)

along with extravagant toys and clothing in order to ensure adequate play opportunities and social acceptance.

Modern Japanese marketing images of Japanese children often also differ markedly from the images presented by the non-Japanese marketing world. An early 1990s ad campaign for American Airlines, offers a very traditional image of Japanese children, one which plays on American ideas of Japanese exotica. Five little girls are shown dressed in kimonos, with elaborate flower hairpieces, and faces painted white. This depiction of children brings to mind classical images of Geisha or young Maiko (young girls training to be Geisha) usually seen in kimonos and white face paint (Dalby). Japanese retailing images of Japan from the same period, are much less likely to play on traditional stereotypes. In the summer of 1990, in order to commemorate the opening of its new children's specialty floor designated, "kids farm,"[3] the main Seibu Department Store in the Ikebukuro district of Tokyo made images of children a focal theme statement of all its advertising posters. The children were dressed not in kimonos but in Western-style play clothes; their faces were covered not with white facial paint reminiscent of Geisha but with mud, suggesting the contemporary ideal of "nobi nobi" or free, unencumbered development (Katsube). The mud-splattered faces may suggest a free-for-all, but the children's body posturing was erect and controlled, showing that a long-standing respect for personal discipline has not been abandoned.

Although traditionalistic representations, as well as the parsimonious atmosphere that surrounded Ninomiya Kinjiro, have receded, images of modern childhood constructed by contemporary Japanese marketing still emphasize human embeddedness in networks of significant relationships. Individuality is recognized and even praised in Japan (Hendry, "Individualism"), but individualism and autonomous self-reliance have never been accorded the same value as in many Western traditions. Interdependency and inter-connectedness are instead upheld as the guiding canons for a human existence. Kondo describes this as the most prevalent idiom of Japanese life, writing,

In the factory, in the family, in the neighborhood, in language, in the use of space, in attitudes toward nature and toward material objects, the most insistent refrain, repeated over and over again and transposed into countless different keys of experience, [is] the fundamental connectedness of human beings to each other. (9)

With this emphasis on interconnectedness, child development is seen not as a process of separating and individuating, as much as a process of being drawn more and more closely into a nexus of human relationships. Material goods must not substitute for close personal ties; cuddly toys do not replace affectionate interaction with adults; games and pastimes are meant to develop skills not release mothers from time spent with young children. Store campaigns and promotional flyers do construct a relationship between young children and material goods, but it is one in which the material goods serve as a bridge introducing children to an interactive social world and furthering their ties to others. An example of this can be seen in a shopping catalogue aimed at Japan's youngest consumers—infants, which was designed by Seibu Department Store in the mid-1980s. Parents could enroll their infants (usually while still "fetusing") in Seibu's new infant shopping club, called "Baby Circle." Upon the announcement of baby's birth, Seibu would sent parents a congratulatory gift, and mail a birthday card accompanied by baby's first shopping catalogue directly to baby. The catalogue, appropriately called "Faasuto Guzzu" ("First Goods"), provided a brief poetic description explaining the importance of early consumer objects to baby's development as a social being.

> After mother's voice,
> After a smiling face,
> What are the things
>   that will become baby's favorites?
> The gentle strains of a music box,
> Or toys of many colors,
> Perfectly grasped by tiny hands.
> Perhaps the first meeting,
>   of baby and the world.[4]

The prototype for the close interdependent relationship esteemed in Japanese society is the mother-child bond (Doi 74). Since this bond is considered to form the basis of interdependency in later human relationships the cultural ideology of motherhood defines mothers as the best caretakers of their children, and calls for extensive maternal involvement, or 'togetherness' with children (see, for example, Fujita). Store layouts, services and special events reiterate the mother-child theme. In order to facilitate shopping outings for women with young children, large retailing complexes provide fully equipped baby and child care areas complete with cribs, kitchenettes and small rooms designated for breast-feeding. Many stores have specially built rooms divided into 'classroom' and jungle gym play areas that allow mothers to participate in free "seminars for housewives," while their children play near by. It is expected that mothers will attend and participate in special clubs or performances offered for children. Sometimes it is difficult to know whether events are directed at children or their mothers, as exemplified by the maternity concerts offered by many department stores twice annually so that mothers-to-be may help expose their unborn children to positive developmental influences.

Even toilet facilities reflect expectations of mother-child togetherness. Nearly all store women's restrooms contain small cribs, many are equipped with toddler-size potties. Because space is a premium concern in Japan's urban centers, a new type of 'parking place' for babies was designed to fit into a standard size stall for a Japanese-style floor toilet. This device straddles the corner of the stall about four feet from the floor. When a baby or toddler is placed on the protruding wall seat, bands automatically lock in place around the seated child. The device was named *bebii kiipu* ("baby keep"), a take-off on the more common phrase "bottle keep" (Smith 152-53). Bottle keeps, which are bottles of alcohol purchased by regular clientele of small drinking establishments and kept on the premises under the purchaser's name, symbolize the social world of adult men, consisting of late-night overtime work and socializing with business contacts. Conversely, baby keeps aptly reflect the social world of women in a society in which both child care and consumerism are constructed as 'women's work.'

Research on Japanese education has revealed resistance to breaking the mother-child bond. Instead, attempts are made to transfer this interdependency to childhood groups (Hendry, "Becoming"; Peak; Lewis). Store shopping clubs and activities reveal similar patterns; age appropriate shopping clubs exist for each stage of the life cycle such that group bonds are not severed but transferred to succeeding groups. Expectations for embedded relationships with others are also prominent in the newly emerging specialty shopping theme parks for children.

Strawberry Friends Playing in Strawberry Fields

Beginning with the pioneer project Strawberry House (*Ichigo no ouchi*) completed in 1984, then escalating rapidly from 1990, the boom in children's marketing resulted in the opening of numerous shopping theme parks for children which many observers claim rival

The author's daughter, Sayuri Kagami, models a "baby keep." (Photo by M. Creighton.)

the amusement offerings of Tokyo Disneyland (i.e., *Nikkei Sangyo Shimbun*). Many of these shopping theme parks were opened by toy companies or major department store chains, either as separate buildings dedicated entirely to children's goods and services, or as special floors within department stores themselves. These child-oriented stores, or store floors, no longer just sell merchandise for

Strawberry House, an early shopping theme building for children, consistently constructs a "sweet" image of children as strawberry friends. (Photo by M. Kagami.)

children, but instead emphasize 'lifestyle' approaches. Educational toys are endorsed by reputed centers of knowledge and Japan's leading scholars. Special in-store "learning corners" allow child visitors to participate in English conversation classes, or conduct science experiments under the guidance of specialist employees. Given the emphasis on 'high-class' and quality clothing for children, several of the stores have added sophisticated children's boutiques, with famous brand names such as Ralph Lauren, Christian Dior, and Tartine et Chocolat (a Paris-based designer line for children) all aimed at fashion conscious mothers, concerned from early on about which prestigious university their children will enter and hence referred to as "campus-minded mamas" (*kyanpasu maindo mama*) (Shibauchi 92).

As Japanese dwellings became increasingly satiated with consumer durables, retailers began to emphasize 'soft menu' or service offerings, under the retailing catch-phrase "*mono igai no mono*," or selling "things other than things" (Creighton, "Depaato" 53). This shift is also reflected in the children's shopping centers which typically offer child restaurants, coffee-shop-like shops, child beauty parlors, catering and travel services for children. In addition, complimentary offerings abound; clown, acrobat and theater groups regularly give in-store performances, there are clubs children may join and participate in, and opportunities to establish pen pal correspondence with children in other countries.

In 1984, the toy company Sanrio constructed one of Tokyo's first children's shopping theme centers, calling it *Ichigo no ouchi*, or Strawberry House. The physical structure of the complex, the specialty offerings, and the clubs operated by the store are all designed to create a particular image of children—the image of strawberry friends playing in strawberry fields. Strawberry House is a three-story strawberry shaped building, flanked on either side by brightly colored constructions, one shaped like a mushroom, the other like a smaller strawberry. The first and second floors of the strawberry building are devoted to the sale of Sanrio goods. Strawberry Parlor (*Ichigo Paaraa*), a child version of the coffee and treat shops ubiquitous to Japan's urban centers is located on the mezzanine level. The third floor contains a plaza known as *Ichigo no oheya*, The Strawberry Room. The Strawberry Room is furnished with strawberry stuff. There are strawberry-shaped tables, strawberry-shaped cupboards, strawberry-shaped light fixtures, and a strawberry-shaped mirror. Children can sit on the strawberry-shaped cushions found along the light, grass-green floor carpet.

The employees at Strawberry House are typically young women in their early 20s. Dressed in indigo blue uniforms with cardigan sweaters, they sing and tell stories to the visiting children, creating an atmosphere similar to a kindergarten or elementary school (Izumi 27- 51). These young women also serve as the emcees for special birthday parties for mothers and children, or thank-you parties held for teachers. Such events take place in the Strawberry Parlor.

The third-floor Strawberry Room is used as a special events plaza. Children, pre-teens and young teens can join a special club called Strawberry Mates (*Ichigo Meito*). Members receive the Strawberry Newspaper, a special periodical published by Sanrio. Once a month the Strawberry Mates attend a Strawberry Conference which is held in the Strawberry Room. Through the conferences, Mates (who are predominately girls) meet, socialize, establish friendships, and interact with their store *oneesan*, or "big sisters" (employees), discussing their lives and any problems they encounter.

On weekends and holidays, families come from distant parts of Japan on a 'pilgrimage' to Strawberry House. The shop chief finds nothing surprising in this, proclaiming that for children and Sanrio fans, Strawberry House is a "sacred place" (Izumi 27-51).

Everything about Strawberry House as a specialty retailing center, or theme park, directed at children, contributes to the fantasy and fairy-tale like image of children, mentioned above, as strawberry friends playing in strawberry fields. However, on a more realistic plane, it is also an image which again emphasizes human embeddedness and social connections to others. Unlike many shopping clubs in North America, for example, Strawberry Mates do not just receive newsletters, advertisements, and special discounts; they actually meet, interact, and establish relationships. The clubs and activities associated with Strawberry House reflect an emphasis found in Japanese society on strong bonds among same-age peer groups where these age-mates participate as equals, combined with expectations for vertical interactions between people defined in senior and junior (senpai/kōhai) relationships, such that seniors advise and serve as role models for juniors.

The image of human embeddedness suggested even for young children via the Strawberry House concept, can be related to Doi's work on the amae psychology of the Japanese (Doi). According to Doi, Japanese tend to repudiate extreme individualism, often considered desirable in the West, and instead value and cultivate dependency relationships, inherent in the word amae. The word amae, referring to indulgence and dependency, is related to the word amai meaning sweet. Dependency or interdependency relationships are conceptualized as "sweet" relationships (Creighton, "Sweet Love"; Arai and Kaplan). The image of children as Strawberry Friends radiates with pure sweetness and hence serves as a metaphor for amae, the validation of interdependency, and the recognition that human beings are not meant to be separate, but interconnected beings.

Imaging the Balanced Child at Dr. Kids Town[5]

Strawberry House was a pioneer project in a phenomenon that would skyrocket from 1990 when shopping theme parks designed as play floors for children began opening one after another. Seibu Department Store transformed the entire seventh floor of its main store, reopening it in September 1990 as kids farm. Tokyo Sesame Place, designed after Sesame Place built in the United States a decade earlier, opened in October 1990, along with Dr. Kids Town at the Kichijoji branch of Isetan Department Store. The supermarket chain Seiyu, opened Kids' Park in the Shibuya District of Tokyo in December of 1990, and Odakyū Department Store completed a mother and child shopping theme park in the neighboring Harajuku district in 1991. This new trend in child shopping parks could be seen not only in Japan's core urban centers but in outlying areas. A new shopping mall which opened in Okinawa in 1990, for example, is built around a huge central children's plaza containing a mountain and castle maze. This mountain and castle construction which children can climb, crawl through, and play on, rises through all three floors of the mall.

In order to present a better understanding of these shopping worlds for children, one of these, Dr. Kids Town, will be presented in more detail here. The highly innovative Dr. Kids Town, designed by Tsumura Pyxis International, shows that as in the world of adult Japanese consumerism, children's marketing is shifting from a focus on selling merchandise—clothes and toys—to an emphasis on 'lifestyle.'

Dr. Kids Town comprises the entire fifth floor of the annex building of Isetan Department Store in Kichijōji on the outskirts of Tokyo. A connection bridge, built in the shape of a train, provides a passageway to the main store building. As its name suggests, Dr. Kids Town has been designed as a miniature town for children, one that is said to be a representation of a small American rural town. Surrounding this town are forests with log homes (which are teddy bear shops). In town there is a zoo (with realistic and often life-size stuffed animals), police stations, a real fire engine (bought and remodeled at a cost of five million yen), the town's local businesses (such as an optical shop containing over 300 brand name frames for children) comprising stores within the store, a replica of the Statue of Liberty near a central fountain with a sponge pool, and, along the town's paved brick streets, the houses of five foreign character children. The employees at Dr. Kids Town are typically young women in their late teens and early 20s, who socialize and interact with the children. On the weekends they dress up as the town mayor, the fire chief, police officers, and nurses to further the playful interactions with young customers.

For the most part it is mothers who visit Dr. Kids Town with their children, although fathers are also seen, especially on Sundays. Parents and children are allowed to play freely throughout town. Children are frequently seen biking or skate boarding through town on store merchandise, climbing the fire engine, or playing in the

Accompanied by their mothers, children wait for a special performance. (Photo by M. Kagami.)

houses of the five fictive foreign playmates, while their parents rest on town benches. Mothers are commonly seen playing with young children on the streets outside of these houses, creating a scene reminiscent of real residential areas of Tokyo where, due to space limitations, mothers play with their children on the streets in front of their apartment complexes. The difference is that Dr. Kids Town presents a much more idyllic atmosphere than the real streets of Tokyo. While playing throughout Dr. Kids Town, the real children who are visitors to the store, themselves become images of children disseminated by the new project. Dr. Kids Town has become well-known to many Tokyo dwellers through extensive journalistic coverage of the new store concept. In most of the magazine and newspaper articles, views of customer children playing in the store, merge with constructed advertising portrayals of children, to enhance the image-positioning of the floor complex as something more than a store—a full developmental and play-stage arena for Japan's youngest consumers.

In addition to such images of "real children," the Dr. Kids project created a representational image of the child in order to project the store's educational philosophy of child development. This educational philosophy is presented on placards located throughout the store floor, and it is also found in the user's guide to Dr. Kids Town called *For Your Future Growth: Dr. Kids*, published by Tsumura Pyxis International as an aid for parents. The user's guide criticizes the emphasis on Japan's so-called academic-pedigree society, and the corresponding obsession with entrance examinations. It tackles social concerns of modern parents such as school bullying, school refusal syndrome, and what has been labeled "child-rearing neurosis," thought to be related to the extreme pressures on parents to make sure their children succeed academically. An example of such social commentary can be found in the following excerpt from the user's guide to Dr. Kids Town.

Parents tend to put heavy emphasis in their child care on making their children be smart and sending them to highly reputed schools and renowned companies. Given these phenomena, parents' goals have been distorted, so that they have lost confidence in growing their children up.[6]

A spokesperson for Dr. Kids explained the project's philosophy by asserting that all Japanese must really start thinking about developing children as Japan's resources for the 21st century. According to this woman, one problem is that all parents are most concerned with their own children, hoping they will get into good universities and thus onto the established track in life. But, she pointed out, not all children will be able to enter prestigious universities, and Japan as a society needs all kinds of people, with different abilities, doing different things.

Her ideas reiterate the Dr. Kids philosophy which emphasizes creating a balanced being by optimally developing all areas of human endeavor. In order to represent this approach emphasizing balance and holistic development, Dr. Kids developed an image of a stick-figure child. This drawn representation of a child stands with head high, arms and legs spread wide, creating the impression of a five-pointed star or revolving pinwheel. Various elements of human experience (such as motivation, imagination, appreciation, communicability, originality) flow toward the child from different directions. Each of the five body appendages is labeled to represent one important aspect of human life. Learning and playing were added to the common ideas of food, clothing, and shelter to make the theme concepts of eating, wearing, dwelling, learning, playing. These five theme concepts are represented on the child in the following way. "Learning" is written across the head, "eating" appears on the right arm, "playing" is located on the right leg, "dwelling" on the left leg, and "wearing" on the left arm. Across the torso of the child is written the word "balance." In creating Dr. Kids Town, the designers also constructed an entire philosophy of childhood development, which is projected in this image statement of the balanced child.

Images of Internationalization

To correspond with each of the five theme concepts found on the drawn image of the "balanced child," the Dr. Kids project created five foreign playmates. For each simulated foreign child a complete identity has been established, including physical appearance, personality, and abilities, and extending to details about other family members. Drawings of these children, along with information about their hobbies and habits, are found near their houses and in the user's guide. A brief profile of each foreign child image is presented below.

CATHY. Cathy represents "wearing," a category also referred to as "fashion life." Cathy is an eight-year-old second grader, who is 120 cm. tall with a slender build, and a sweet, feminine voice. Her father, Gerald, is a 38-year-old doctor, and her mother, Sophia, is a 35-

year-old flower arranger. Because she is an only child, Cathy misses having other siblings to play with, but does have an English sheep dog named Washington. Cathy plays the piano and takes ballet lessons; her favorite subjects are music and French. She belongs to the local drama club, and does community work signing for the deaf. Cathy has very good social skills, and is well attuned to the feelings of those around her. The user's guide also notes that Cathy has good "information gathering" skills, and she therefore serves as the secretary when the children travel over the world in the UFO they discovered. Cathy dresses in "French elegance" and her room design is "French floral." Her favorite foods are French pastries and croissants. Cathy is the only one of the five simulated foreign playmates who is not an American. Presumably she was created French, because of the Japanese association with French fashion, style, and cuisine.

JIM. Jim, who represents the theme "learning," is the child who excels academically. He is clearly headed for a prestigious university, and there is even a suggestion that he might become a future Nobel prize-winner. His shelves are full of books and educational aids developed by the Smithsonian Institution and other reputed centers of knowledge. Jim, who has a rocket ship in his bedroom, is going to be an astronaut when he grows up. For now, he is the pilot of the children's UFO.

DIANE. Diane is the representative child for "eating." Diane's illustrated image depicts a merry girl wearing a ruffled apron, the bodice of which is shaped like a big heart. She holds a box of cookie mix in one hand and a large measuring cup in the other. It is suggested that Diane has very creative cooking skills, and cooking is her job on the children's UFO. Someday Diane hopes to be a baker.

TOM. Like Jim, Tom, who is the representative child for "dwelling," is also brilliant. Although he does well academically, it is suggested that his abilities are not expressed best within an endeavor like pure science. He also has a great creative genius which the project philosophy suggests is too often sacrificed to Japan's examination-oriented education system. It is suggested that Tom will be an architect when he grows up.

GEORGE. Unlike the other two boys, George, the representative child for "playing," does not do very well academically. However,

This exterior view of Cathy's house reveals one of the "homey" rooms inside. Cathy's character image is a young girl who has good social skills, good "information gathering" skills, and who readily helps others. Cathy is the secretary on the children's UFO and does community work. (Photo by M. Creighton.)

This interior view of his house shows Jim's bedroom. Jim is a simulated foreign child, imaged as brilliant. He will be an astronaut when he grows up, and for now he pilots the UFO the children found. (Photo by M. Creighton.)

George is truly gifted athletically. George's house is full of camping equipment, sporting goods, and play gear of all kinds. It is suggested that someday George will be a professional athlete. The Dr. Kids philosophy hopes to encourage parents to realize that just because children like George might never be eligible for the academic track to prestigious universities, they nonetheless have abilities which should be developed.

Although the asserted purpose of the foreign fantasy playmates who reside in Dr. Kids Town is to provide Japanese children with glimpses of internationalization, and friendly images of foreigners, I suggest that these images of foreign children in actuality fulfill functions outlined by Barnouw and Kirkland, who contend that popular culture functions to provide the public with "a social repertoire of characters, relationships and outcomes that is used in the ongoing attempt to make sense of the world" (52). The five foreign-fantasy children most represent desired characteristics for Japanese children. In particular, the images of these five children are cast in gender stereotypes consistent with long-held expectations in Japanese society. The two children who excel in spatial, mathe-matical, and scientific abilities are both male. Both of these boys have very prestigious careers laid out for them, one as an astronaut and the other as an architect. Even though the child who does poorly in academic subjects is also male, his special athletic abilities are those more likely to be admired in boys. The two girl representations epitomize domestic and consumer roles expected of women. Their abilities and future occupations center around preparing food, creating fashionable outfits, arranging rooms attractively, assisting other people and making them feel good. Even the children's parents are cast in gender-typed relationships, with Cathy's father (who is three years older than Cathy's mother) as a doctor and her mother as a flower arranger.

The project designers listened carefully to my suggestions that the fantasy playmates evoked gender stereotypes, with some surprise. After all, the philosophical ideal of the store floor is that all areas of every child's development should be enhanced. However, it seems likely that given the strength and persistence of these gender concepts in Japan, they permeate retailing constructions even when this is not an overt objective. Images of foreign children, such as the image of a French girl who takes ballet lessons, studies French, lives in a French floral environment, and eats French pastries, presented at the shopping theme floor seem to perpetuate existing Japanese associations with foreign countries rather than introduce Japanese children to foreigners as more complex human beings. Like many of the other shopping theme parks, this specialty area helps socialize Japanese children into their future roles by introducing them to expected patterns of consumer behavior and by presenting "a social repertoire of characters, relationships, and outcomes" consistent with expected gender roles in Japanese society.

Conclusions

The imagery of childhood in Japan has shifted with changes in Japan's economic status and international role. When Japan was enveloped by conditions of poverty and material scarcity in the pre-World War II, and early post-war periods, the esteemed ideal child image was the hard-working Ninomiya Kinjirō, eager to study and support his household. Throughout the 1960s and 1970s, Japan experienced the rise of a consumer society, which flowered fully in the early to mid-1980s. In 1990, Japan marked a new all-time record low birth rate for the 11th consecutive year—a trend that has continued. With the declining birth rate, a new image of the child was born, the "5 pocket child." This new child image reveals the supreme place children are now given, partly because of their very scarcity, with adults willing to indulge them with extensive consumer goods and services, along with larger gifts of money to be used at their own discretion. This new image of an affluent, indulged, consumer-oriented "5 pocket child" has made the children's market a pre-eminent arena of Japanese retailing for the 1990s.

Marking this shift, large Japanese retailers began constructing specialty shopping theme parks directed at children. The rationale behind these shopping parks, the developmental philosophies they present, and their actual spatial layouts all contribute to particular image-statements about modern children. In many cases, the shopping parks also construct and present carefully crafted images of foreign children, which then become another consumer commodity for Japanese children. These glimpses of internationalization reflect the prevalent concern with, and dialogue about, internationalization reverberating throughout contemporary Japan. However, the images of foreign children, and frequently simulated foreign children, often serve as mirrors for Japaneseness. In the case of the five fantasy playmates residing in Dr. Kids Town, I have suggested that they function most to socialize expected behaviors for Japanese children, especially in regard to accepted gender roles.

Although the imagery of childhood has shifted with Japan's growing affluence, certain predispositions remain steadfastly reflected. Modern children are still depicted as hard-working, but at their own education, not to help support their families. An ideal of *nobi nobi* education, or allowing "free development" of child potentials, has gained great popularity, but is still balanced by expectations for discipline and the ability to function well within interactive groups. The images of Japanese children propagated by Japan's retailers, chosen for advertisements, depicted in catalogue commentary, and even suggested through the physical space of the new shopping theme parks, are above all images of embeddedness; images which suggest that the "natural" state of being for humans involves connections to others. Images of modern children still emphasize the strong mother-child bond, the importance of close ties with age-mate groups, and the need for interaction with senior role models.

The stores serve as sites of socialization, perpetuating themes common in Japanese society, and replicating gender expectations, by both providing casts of characters and constructing stages which compel children and parents towards accepted forms of behavior. Children are also socialized into culturally defined appropriate consumer activity. As the stores disseminate images of modern children, they are also imaging a particular social role for modern consumerism. Consumerism is presented less as a way of finding oneself, and more as a way of *linking selves* to others. Just as Japanese adults use gift-giving and other consumer purchases as a means of initiating or affirming networks of relationships, children are being drawn into a similar process of linking consumer activity to the all-important framework of human interactions. Images of humanness, images of children, and images of consumerism converge, such that consumerism becomes the operator connecting the young child to greater participation in the public social world.

Notes

[1] A grant from the Social Sciences and Humanities Research Council of Canada, awarded and administered by the University of British Columbia, allowed me to conduct the research on Japanese children's marketing presented here. This was enhanced by research conducted under an earlier U.S. Fulbright-Hays grant. An earlier version of this paper was presented at the national Popular Culture Association meetings held in New Orleans in April 1993. I would like to thank Merry White for research consultation, and

Tsumura Pyxis International for their assistance in this project and for permission to photograph.

[2]Ninomiya was also known by the name Ninomiya Sontoku, which tends to be the more common appellation when referring to his adult life.

[3]The name of this children's specialty floor, kids farm, is written in lower-case, roman letters with no apostrophe.

[4]From Seibu's *Faasuto Guzzu* catalogue, my translation.

[5]The name of this shopping area, Dr. Kids Town, is rendered in roman letters, without an apostrophe.

[6]From Tsumura Pyxis International's *For Your Future Growth: Dr. Kids*, company's English translation.

Annotated Bibliography

Arai Yoichi and Frederick I. Kaplan. "Growing Up and the Old Kentucky Home: An Examination in Japanese Popular Culture of Divorce and the Broken Family." *Journal of Popular Culture* 22.3 (1988): 131-41. This article traces the problems a young boy in a television drama faces when his parents divorce. It also provides an extensive discussion of *amae*, or "sweet" dependency relationships.

Barnouw, Erik, and Catherine E. Kirkland. "Entertainment." *Folklore, Cultural Performances and Popular Entertainments*. New York and Oxford: Oxford UP, 1992. 50-52. Barnouw and Kirkland argue that popular entertainments are not just providing us with amusement. Instead, people utilize the fictive characters and relationships encountered through entertainment to make sense of the real worlds and networks of relationships in which they interact.

Beauchamp, Edward R. "Education and Identity in Modern Japan, 1868-Present." *Asian Thought and Society* 16.48 (1991): 189-98. Choosing examples from literary works, Beauchamp explores the dialectic between education and Japanese identity crises during critical historic transition periods. He establishes a framework of three types of education, formal, nonformal and informal, which recognizes the significance of popular culture phenomena in socialization.

Blustein, Paul. "Catering to Children in Japan: Businesses Respond as Parents Lavish Money on Youngsters." *The Washington Post* 11 Feb. 1991: A15. Blustein looks at the expansion of the children's market in Japan, and the increasing tendency to lavish children with extensive consumer goods and services. The article also contains a section on the new shopping theme park, Dr. Kids Town.

Creighton, Millie R. "The Depaato: Merchandising the West while Selling Japaneseness." *Re-Made in Japan: Everyday Life and Consumer Taste in a Changing Society.* Ed. Joseph J. Tobin. New Haven: Yale UP, 1992. 42-57. This article gives historical background on Japanese department stores, then provides examples of the differential marketing of Japanese and Western goods. The concept of *mono igai no mono,* or selling 'things other than things' is introduced, revealing Japan's modern marketing emphasis on 'soft menu' consumer offerings.

____. "Maintaining Cultural Boundaries in Retailing: How Japanese Department Stores Domesticate 'Things Foreign.'" *Modern Asian Studies* 25.4 (1991): 675-709. This article provides a discussion of the cultural context of retailing, while discussing ways adopted holidays, foreign goods, and foreigners are juxtaposed with things considered 'traditionally' Japanese in order to reaffirm concepts of Japanese identity.

____. "'Sweet Love' and Women's Place: Valentine's Day, Japan Style." *Journal of Popular Culture* 27.3 (1993): 1-19. The symbolism surrounding Valentine's Day in Japan is situated within a discussion of persisting gender role expectations. The article contains a discussion of sweets as a metaphor for dependency relationships.

Dalby, Liza. *Geisha.* New York: Vintage Books, 1983. This book traces the historic development of Geisha in Japan, and explores their contemporary role. The sub-culture of the Geisha world is presented in reference to the cultural predispositions of the larger society.

Doi Takeo. *The Anatomy of Dependence.* Tokyo: Kodansha, 1973. A classic text in Japanese studies, this book outlines Doi's theory of the *amae* psychology of the Japanese, revealing a cultural predisposition to cultivate dependency, or interdependency, relationships while repudiating strong forms of individualism.

Fujita Mariko. "'It's All Mother's Fault': Childcare and the Socialization of Working Mothers in Japan." *Journal of Japanese Studies* 15.1 (1989): 67-91. Despite shifts in female work and career patterns, Fujita contends that the persisting cultural ideology of motherhood in Japan means that women are judged only by how well they mother, and given little credit for career accomplishments.

Hendry, Joy. *Becoming Japanese: The World of the Pre-School Child.* Manchester: Manchester UP, 1986. Hendry discusses the great importance Japanese social values place on small children, reflected in the Japanese proverb 'the soul of a three-year old lasts for 80 years.' She discusses the expected roles of various types of socialization agents including the family, the neighborhood, pre-schools, day cares and nurseries.

_____. "Individualism and Individuality: Entry Into a Social World." *Ideology and Practice in Modern Japan*. Ed. Roger Goodman and Kirsten Refsing. London and New York: Routledge, 1992. 55-71. Paying particular attention to the childhood period, Hendry argues that Japanese make strong distinctions between concepts of individualism (*kojinshuji*) and individuality (*kosei*). Whereas, individualism tends to have negative connotations, implying selfishness and immaturity, human individuality is recognized and appreciated.

Izumi Asato. *Okosama Gyōkai Monogatari* [Story of Children's Marketing Industries]. Tokyo: Shinchōbunko, 1989. Izumi explores the world of children's marketing in Japan, and provides an extensive description of Strawberry House, one of the first shopping theme parks for children.

Katsube Mitake. *Nobi Nobi kosodateron* [Discussion on 'free development' Child Rearing]. Tokyo: Tamagawa UP, 1984. The Japanese expression "*nobi nobi*" suggests a relaxed or free attitude toward child development. Katsube discusses the educational philosophy behind this approach and argues for a shift away from stricter practices of childhood socialization.

Kojima Hideo. "Becoming Nurturant in Japan: Past and Present." *Origins of Nurturance: Developmental, Biological and Cultural Perspectives on Caregiving*. Ed. Alan Fogel and Gail F. Melson. Hillsdale, NJ: Lawrence Erlbaum Associates, 1986. 123-39. Kojima discusses 'traditional' Japanese child-rearing attitudes emphasizing nurturance, and their reflection in modern society. He also explores modern impediments to nurturance created by extreme pressures for academic success that have resulted in such social problems as the so-called school-refusal syndrome and child-rearing neurosis.

Kondo, Dorinne K. *Crafting Selves: Power, Gender, and Discourses of Identity in a Japanese Workplace*. Chicago: U of Chicago P, 1990. Kondo provides an ethnographic account of a small family-run Japanese business, paying particular attention to the construction of gender through work and the context of power in which gender identities develop. The book contains an excellent discussion of the theme of interconnectedness in Japanese life.

Lewis, Catherine C. "Cooperation and Control in Japanese Nursery Schools." *Comparative Education Review* 28.1 (1984): 69-84. Describing activities and interactions in Japanese pre-schools, Lewis shows how children are socialized into a strong sense of identity with school peer groups.

Mukerji, Chandra. *From Graven Images: Patterns of Modern Materialism*. New York: Columbia UP, 1983. In exploring the nature of modern materialism, Mukerji looks at how desire is created and manipulated, in a system where human behavior is often compelled by commodity acquisition.

Nikkei Sangyō Shimbun. "Hyakkaten, TDL ni Manabu: Kodomo yōhin uriba teema paakugata ni" [Department Stores Learn from Tokyo Disneyland: Children's Goods Sales Areas Become Theme Parks]. 28 Nov. 1990. One of many journalistic articles appearing in the Japanese press about the new store specialty children's areas, this one suggests that the new stores have replicated the amusement park atmosphere of Tokyo Disneyland.

Peak, Lois. *Learning to Go to School in Japan: The Transition from Home to Preschool Life.* Berkeley: U of California P, 1991. This work on early childhood education focuses on the transition between a close family-centered life to participation in pre-schools. Peak shows how the emphasis on intense mother-child bonds is shifted to an expectation for intense involvement in peer group activities.

Plath, David. *The After Hours: Modern Japan and the Search for Enjoyment.* Berkeley: U of California P, 1964. This book describes the shift from early post-war poverty to the initial beginnings of Japan's consumer-oriented society, through the acquisition of new consumer goods and increasing leisure in the early 1960s.

Seibu Department Stores (Seibu Saisson Group). "Faasuto Guzzu" [First Goods]. Tokyo: store files. n.d. This is a shopping catalogue designed for new members of Seibu's "Baby Circle" and their parents. In addition to presenting consumer goods for sale, the catalogue reflects the cultural emphasis on drawing baby into closer networks of personal relationships.

Seiter, Ellen. "Toys Are Us: Marketing to Children and Parents." *Cultural Studies* 6.2 (1992): 232-47. Discussing the differentiated market of Toys "R" Us and upscale children's stores, Seiter suggests that educational professionals, by validating high-class "educational toys" while rejecting the more common mass marketed toys, tacitly reinforce a sense of inferiority among working class children who are more likely to play with the latter at home.

Shibauchi Ikuko. "'Hime-Tono Saabisu' ni hashiru kodomo yohin uriba" [Children's Sales Areas Running Toward 'Princess-Lord Service']. *Nikei Torendii* Apr. 1991: 92-93. This article in a Japanese economic trends magazine, discusses the children's marketing boom and provides descriptions of several of the new specialty shopping theme parks directed at children.

Smith, Stephen R. "Drinking Etiquette in a Changing Beverage Market." *Re-Made in Japan: Everyday Life and Consumer Taste in a Changing Society.* Ed. Joseph J. Tobin. New Haven: Yale UP, 1992. 143-58.

Smith shows that even for mundane, daily drinking occasions in Japan, certain forms of etiquette, reflecting expectations of social embeddedness, are expected. A discussion of "bottle keeps" and their prevalent role in male socializing and work interactions is provided.

Tsumura Pyxis International. *For Your Future Growth: Dr. Kids.* Tokyo: company files. n.d. This is the user's guide to Dr. Kids Town published by the company which designed it. The guide explains the educational philosophy behind the new theme park store floor, presents the Dr. Kids image of the balanced child, and gives extensive descriptions of the five foreign fantasy character children whose houses are found in Dr. Kids Town.

Boys-R-Us:
Board Games and the Socialization
of Young Adolescent Girls

Jennifer Scanlon

In a 1973 volume of *Ms.* magazine, Letty Cottin Pogrebin introduced a checklist for parents who wanted to buy non-sexist toys for their children. An acceptable toy would be "...respectful of the child's intellect and creativity, nonracist, moral in terms of the values it engenders, and nonsexist in the way it is packaged, conceived, and planned for play" (Pogrebin 48). One of the board games she recommended was Life, a Milton Bradley product, as it encouraged all players to pursue lives of their own, money of their own, careers of their own.

Now, readers, as the instructions on a game might tell you, advance 20 years. Enter the 1990s, a mall, anytown U.S.A. A parent looking for nonsexist toys for children might, at a Toys-R-Us store, find a few toys and games that Pogrebin would approve of. The game of Life remains popular, and consumers can find numerous trivia games, memory games, and games of skill on the shelves. Unfortunately, however, mall toy stores rely heavily on gender stereotypes for their displays, layout, advertising, and most importantly, products. This paper looks at four gender-specific board games directed at young adolescent girls, examines their messages in light of Pogrebin's now 20-year-old suggestions, and brings to light issues about a much-neglected time period in girls' lives, early adolescence, and a much-neglected area of popular culture or leisure studies, gender-specific games.

The least gender-specific toys and games in the stores are, arguably, those in the baby and toddler section. Primary colors predominate in these toys, and customers purchase chunky trains and boats for baby girls or boys. Sex-typing occurs quickly as you move either down the aisle or up in age, as trucks become masculinized, dolls feminized. Pastels replace primary colors in girls' toys, and the packaging, game boards and pieces, even the cover photographs become feminized. For boys' toys, camouflage greens and browns replace soft colors, and war toys and sports equipment fill the shelves. And now you arrive at these four games for young adolescent girls, where the players featured on the game boxes, girls only, dress in feminine clothing and wear heavy make-up and jewelry, even though the suggested starting age for the games is eight.

Heart-Throb: The Dream Date Game, and Sweet Valley High: Can You Find a Boyfriend in Time for the Big Date? are both produced by Milton Bradley, subsidiary of Hasbro, a company with $410 million in annual sales. Hasbro, with no women on its board of directors, produces board games for children and adults as well as a range of other products from teething rings to women's under-garments, baby pacifiers to girls' nightwear. The second two games, Girl Talk: A Game of Truth or Dare, and Girl Talk: Date Line, are produced by Western Publishing Company, which has annual sales of $495 million and produces, among other things, board games for children and adults, gift wrap and novelties, stationery, and books (Dun and Bradstreet, *America's Corporate Families* 813, 1831).

Not surprisingly, these four games invite girls to enter the consumer marketplace by encouraging players to use products such as clothing and make-up to enhance their looks. Another game for young adolescent girls, Meet Me at the Mall, more blatantly emphasizes the consumer side of things; players run around the mall, visiting stores like The Gap and Benetton, trying to outbuy the competition. For these four games, though, players must obtain boyfriends rather than consumer goods. Whether one steals one from a friend, wins one through her own matchmaking skills, or reads one into her future, a boyfriend rather than a career or a life remains the player's central goal.

A curious consumer might wonder whether the pursuit of a boyfriend is in fact a typical adolescent girl's primary goal. Unfortunately, researchers have not adequately studied the activities of young adolescent girls. Adolescence and pre-adolescence have most often been described as periods of conflict, with juvenile delinquency and violence the most frequently covered behaviors. Violence within this group, specifically male violence, receives the most attention from the media as well as from scholars. With this emphasis on delinquency and violence, both defined in male terms, issues in girls' lives are often overlooked (Coleman and Hendry 53-58). The recent debate over the proposed segregated schooling of African-American males, in order to meet their needs, largely ignores the needs of young African-American women and exemplifies this trend (Goodman A12).

Feminist scholars, however, recently began to take notice. As one puts it, we need to focus on the larger issue of adolescent culture rather than on delinquency and focus on what girls are doing, what their lives are like. Young adolescence may be redefined, in fact, not as violence vs. lack of violence but as peer identity vs. isolation. For girls, this often means close ties to the consumer culture rather than to so-called rituals of resistance (McRobbie 8; Coleman 53).

A quick review of the literature on adolescence reveals the problem. A recent handbook for parents about middle-school children encourages straight talk with children about the many issues that affect their lives. The book urges parents to examine questions of racial, ethnic, and cultural diversity, but it never discusses gender as a category of difference (Berla et al. 83). This is distressing when we know that during adolescence children become acutely aware of themselves as gendered beings, both biologically and socially. The exclusion of gender issues is typical, as is the tendency, when researchers do mention girls, to discuss them in relation to boys and in terms of dating or mixed-sex social encounters. Research virtually ignores girls' same-sex activities, an important aspect of pre-adolescent and adolescent growth.

Of course, gender is a crucial element in adolescent development for girls and boys. In no other period of life except infancy do so many biological changes occur so quickly, and many of those biological changes are sex-specific (Montemayor et al. 9). Those who study adolescence, however, argue that social expectations, even more than physical changes, shape gender roles (Huston and Alvarez 158). When young people respond to peers and television as socializing influences, they often become increasingly intolerant of deviations from traditional sex role norms; surprisingly enough, peers often promote more traditional roles than do parents. Stereotypical attitudes about girls and boys, while not born in adolescence, often solidify at this age into hard and fast rules rather than simple observations (Montemayor et al. 13; Coleman and Hendry 123; Chandler 150).

The implications of this rigid agenda for girls are dramatic. Studies show that girls' academic and career ambitions actually decline in early adolescence when they internalize the notion that females should achieve less than males. During this period females and males both come to view math, science, and computer skills as male domains (Huston and Alvarez 158, 169). Teachers and educational programs as well as the family encourage such messages. Girls also learn, by early adolescence, that in order to be defined as successful they must please others, putting the needs of others first. Girls have few illusions about how this translates into real life experiences. Sadly, while cognitive developments that take place in early adolescence can encourage children to look at roles, including gender roles, in a flexible way, social constraints encourage them to limit their thinking and conceptualize gender roles in highly conformist and predictable ways (Huston and Alvarez 173). For girls this translates to the rule that they must get a boyfriend, keep a boyfriend, and learn dependence on males to be successful in life (McRobbie xvii; Newman 150-51; Chandler x).

While children repeatedly get these messages at home and in school, they get them from popular culture as well. Widely documented studies of television's influence on gender role socialization reveal the connections between television watching and the likelihood that children and teenagers will have stereotypical beliefs about gender roles (Comstock 160-75). Adolescence heightens sensitivity about gender, and numerous studies demonstrate the extent of gender stereotyping on contemporary television. Males are overrepresented two or three to one in commercial television, and the voice-over in commercials remains male 90 percent of the time. This is significant, of course, as children in the United States watch an average of 40,000 commercials per year (Comstock 188). In addition to television, magazines and fiction addressed to preadolescent and adolescent girls stress traditional gender roles, the importance of girls' bodies, and the overwhelming and incessant need to find a boy. Magazines, for example, provide constant reminders that a girl must consciously and continuously cultivate sexual attractiveness, her greatest asset. Magazines, teen formula romance fiction, and other commercial enterprises replay the messages that come, in other forms, through the family and school.

However, unlike family or school, leisure pursuits like reading magazines or playing games do not appear to be coercive. Simply because of this, they demand attention. Associated with freedom, leisure activities for girls often carry heavy ideological messages wrapped in the context of an escape from limits (McRobbie 88). These activities define girlhood in class-, race-, and behavior-specific ways. Three out of four teen fashion magazines in the United States, with a combined circulation of almost four million, portray young American women as white, very feminine, carefree, boy-crazy virgins. A recent issue of *Teen* featured liposuction and plastic surgery as options for those readers dissatisfied with their bodies. *Sassy*, noted for its initial frank discussions of adolescent sexuality, bent to pressure and omitted much of what made it controversial and, not coincidentally, a favorite among many young women craving honest discussion of their needs. These forms of popular culture, rather than an escape from limitations, provide clear and limited definitions of what it means to be a girl.

Board games, another form of popular culture, are a significant aspect of same-sex play for girls. Girls do not play them with boys, nor do they play them to get boys' attention. As the back covers of the games illustrate, girls play in the company of other girls, often in the privacy of one of their bedrooms. The picture on the back of Heart-Throb is typical: four girls in a bedroom, one of them on the bed, the others lounging on the carpeted floor. The game board sits on the floor, and the background features a telephone, a radio/tape player, and a bowl of popcorn. In fact, three of these four covers show a telephone, a radio/tape player, and popcorn, which is, of course, a low-calorie snack. In this sacred space girls learn to define themselves. Real boys do not invade this very feminine scene, but the idea of boys takes up a good deal of space, as each game encourages girls to think about themselves in relation to boys. By playing these board games, girls learn a central rule: they need boys to complete their self-definition.

The four games featured here offer young adolescent girls a wide variety of messages, all of them gender specific. From the uniformly "pretty" boxes to the uniform goal of getting a guy, they promote traditional gender role behaviors, emphasize clear messages about race, class, and sexual orientation, and encourage play that is decidedly humdrum if not outright insulting to any young adolescent's intelligence. They clearly fail Letty Pogrebin's test for nonsexist toys, but the way in which they do so and fail young women in the process is worth examining further.

All of these board games promote the idea that the central object in a girl's life is to get a guy. In Sweet Valley High, girls literally race around the school trying to retrieve a boyfriend, a teacher chaperon, and all the accessories needed for a big date. In the process of trying to get it all done first, girls can steal other girls' boyfriends or fight over boyfriends; such behaviors receive rewards.

In Heart-Throb, each player chooses which boy she would like to have ask her out and guesses which boys her competitors will choose. The game pieces include 60 boyfriend cards, each picturing a different boy, and 162 personality cards, which reveal both good and bad qualities of boys. In Girl Talk: Date Line, players match up girl and boy cards they hold in their hands in order to create successful dates. While they travel around the board, trying to set up a date, the players date as well; if they do not secure a date for the imaginary characters they hold in their hands, they themselves must go stag or settle for a blind date.

In Girl Talk: A Game of Truth or Dare, the initial focus seems different. Girls spin a wheel and then must reveal a secret or do a stunt. Many of the stunts are unrelated to getting a boyfriend and include doing situps or sucking a lemon. Others, however, clearly promote the overall gender-enforcing plan and include pretending to put on make-up, calling a boy and telling him a joke, rating your looks from one to ten, or revealing what you would like to change about your looks. Anytime a girl does not complete the required stunt, she must peel off a red zit sticker and wear it on her face for the rest of the game. The game's instructions warn that the zit sticker must be visible: it cannot go under the chin or behind the ear.

The end goal of this game is to collect one of each of the fortune cards, which fit into four categories: Marriage, Children, Career, and Special Moments. However, dependency on boys or men dictates girls' experiences in each of the four categories except Children. Under Marriage, two possible fortunes are "You will marry _____'s boyfriend," or "You will meet your future husband while working together at _____ fast-food restaurant." Under Career, you could receive "After three weeks on your first job as a _____ (profession), you will meet the man that you will eventually marry," or "You will take a job as a carhop just to get a date with a certain boy who drives a _____." Finally, under Special Moments, fortunes include "A tall, dark, and handsome policeman will stop you for speeding and give you a ticket, but will make up for it by asking you for a date," or "While visiting a dude ranch, your horse will bolt and you will be rescued by a ranch hand who looks just like _____ (actor)." In the category of Special Moments, with 24 possible cards, 7 are specifically about boys but only one portrays a girl having a special moment with a girlfriend.

Each of these four games portrays girls in strictly feminine terms and boys in strictly masculine terms, with little overlap in traditional definitions. In the Sweet Valley High game, for example, students vote Jessica Most Popular Girl in the school; she is also, not coincidentally, co-captain of the cheerleaders. Elizabeth, Jessica's sister, receives an award for her newspaper column, a gossip column called "Eyes and Ears." The names used in the Sweet Valley game indicate which girls and boys are popular and which are not. The nerdy and nonmasculine boy is called Winston Egbert; Winston prefers feminine activities like talking and being gentle to masculine qualities like playing football and being aloof. The desirable boys in Sweet Valley, Todd Wilkins and Bruce Patman, do masculine things like skiing and driving expensive sports cars.

Names are used as indicators of appropriate levels of feminine or masculine qualities in Girl Talk: Date Line as well. When players land on a date space, they choose two of the character cards in their hand and set them up for a date. When they put the cards together in a microphone machine, girls discover whether or not the date they choreographed went well. The characters Gert and Homer stand out as nerds in appearance, name, and behavior. Both Gert and Homer wear glasses, but none of the many popular characters wear glasses, and the popular people have names like Nicole and Drew, Stephanie and Matt.

In Girl Talk: Date Line, Homer's personality profile reveals that he loves the computer club and collecting bugs but hates sports and school dances. Boys clearly should love sports, including the sport of pursuing girls at dances, whether or not they actually like to dance. Gert, the girl without make-up and hence without much personality, loves Latin and algebra, hates rock music and gym class. Obviously girls should not have academic aspirations. The attributes of the popular people in Girl Talk: Date Line confirm clear rules about what it means to be a girl or boy. Stacie loves talking on the phone and shopping but hates greasy hair and book reports. Tina loves pizza and make-up but hates computers and report cards. Eric, on the other hand, loves tennis and water skiing, hates shopping malls. Matt loves math and football, hates double-dating (wants to be in control?) and haircuts.

In Heart-Throb, girls and boys behave in gender-specific ways in dating. When the players choose which of the boys in the boyfriend cards they would like to date and which they think the other players will choose, it seems that at last girls are making choices. In actuality, though, the rules state that three boys from the boyfriend cards ask the girls first to dance, then to go on a date, then to go steady. The girls must choose from among the three boys. Players have some very limited choices: they can choose which boy they want, but they cannot choose not to accept a dance, a date, or a steady boyfriend. Refusing the advances of all three boys is not an option, regardless of how uninviting they appear in their personality cards.

These board games clearly promote male privilege, then; they also promote the privileges of race, wealth, and heterosexuality. In the four games, virtually all of the characters are white. In Sweet

Valley High, located in California, all of the students are fair-skinned, and the only ones with names that deviate from the most popular or trendy, which include Ken—who does in fact look like Barbie's counterpart—are the names of the nerdy characters, but Winston remains, nevertheless, a Waspy nerd. In Heart-Throb, a game with 60 boyfriend cards, not one of the boys even has an ethnic-sounding name. The only feature that distinguishes a few, and makes them appear perhaps somewhat "different," is the appearance of dark sunglasses. In Girl Talk: Date Line, the trendy names include, for the girls, Danielle, Tina, Allison, and Stephanie, and for the boys, Drew, Trent, Eric, and Brad. This game, interestingly enough, features one African American boy but no African American girls; one wonders who players match him up with for a date.

In addition to the privilege of race, the characters in these games have the privilege of social class. The Sweet Valley High game goes the furthest with this: one character gets rewarded for giving her housekeeper the day off and making her own bed, another for donating a large sum to charity, a third for taking everyone for a ride in her new sports car. In each of the other games, the girls playing the games or the character pieces in the games dress well, have access to income to buy clothing and make-up, and have private space all their own. No apartment living for these girls; they relax in their suburban bedrooms with plush carpet or scoot around town in their very own vehicles.

These board games promote the social control of girls' sexuality as well, with heterosexuality consistently privileged. In three of the four games, the only object is either to secure a boyfriend for oneself or secure one for others. The fourth clearly favors marriage and children as the end goal in life. Each game encourages competition among girls for boys, as girls steal others' boyfriend or find warnings in the instructions, as they do in the Sweet Valley game, that they need to keep an eye on their thieving girlfriends. Girls play these games together, but rather than promoting positive female culture or solidarity, the games teach girls that they cannot trust each other when it comes to their primary life definition: boys. The directions in the Sweet Valley game specify that girls can never have more than one boyfriend at a time; if they pick up a second, they must discard one. In Girl Talk: Date Line, the directions actually state in writing that players should not attempt to match up a girl with a girl or a boy with a boy for a date. According to these games, all girls, even the nerdy ones, can look forward to a shared future. What the games encourage players to share, however, is not the ability to laugh, intelligence, or even stereotypical nurturing qualities; instead, they share a future that must, apparently at any cost, include a man.

These four games rely on stereotypes about girls that stray far from the goal of promoting more egalitarian, difference-respecting play experiences. They suggest that the game characters represent the "ordinary" adolescent in the United States. Virtually all young adolescents, the games would have us believe, are white, long-haired, fair-haired, blemish-free, wealthy, heterosexual, and well dressed. The overall message does not necessarily suggest that all adolescent girls think the same way, because aside from their desire to secure a boyfriend we or the players learn little about what girls think about. What ties young adolescent girls together, through these games, is simply that they must acquire a boyfriend.

Interestingly enough, the stars of these games, the girls featured on the covers and on the boards and playing pieces, do not closely resemble the voluptuous and flashy young women of the teen magazines. In fact, they seem far closer to the "average" than that. It would be a mistake to think for a moment, though, that they represent anything but a carefully crafted version of the ideal, of the "average" ideal. Perhaps girls read fashion magazines and wish they could have the beautiful looks of the models. Perhaps when they play the board games they wish they could be the average girl, fit easily into developing peer norms, and blend into their settings as easily as the girls on the game boxes seem to blend into theirs. The games present a message just as damaging as that of the magazines, though, because if the game characters represent the norm, the average, they must represent the attainable. The truth remains, of course, that white, wealthy heterosexuality is not the norm, not the average, not what young adolescent girls have in common. Unfortunately, however, most adolescents share a strong desire to meet the established, if largely unattainable, norm.

The final way in which these games fail Letty Pogrebin's test and, in so doing, fail real girls' needs, is that they lack any challenge to girls' intellects or any inspiration of their creativity. Researchers have revealed that girls' games often provide fewer intellectual challenges than do boys' games. Girls, more restricted in their play than boys in terms of movement and noise, learn to appreciate indoor activities, in smaller groups, and at lower skill levels (Rivers et al. 105-07). These board games match those findings.

The most insulting of the four games is Girl Talk: Date Line. Girls match couples up and then hope that the date takes place. In fact, though, the individual qualities players match up do not determine whether or not the date takes place. Instead, a continuously running cassette tape determines everything. While the game instructs players that if the two individuals seem compatible the date will happen, sheer luck actually determines the course of action. If a player is fortunate enough to put her two characters in the microphone machine when the tape is about to play a successful date scenario, she wins. If not, she loses.

The next two games provide little more of a challenge. In Heart-Throb girls choose which boy they prefer, then they guess which boy their friends will prefer. A simple guessing game, Heart-Throb is packaged as though it contains something of consequence. Girls could easily play the same game, if they wished, using a magazine with pictures of boys in it; they hardly need the game board or pieces. Sweet Valley High is essentially a memory game. Girls have to remember in which classroom the corsage card sits, in which classroom their boyfriend sits. This game hardly differs from any matching game with cards played by young children, except for the ideological messages reinforcing gender and other stereotypes.

Girl Talk: A Game of Truth or Dare is the most sophisticated and potentially challenging of these board games. Girls actually do things in this game; they move around, they talk to each other, they share secrets. Were the end goals not so blatantly sexist, the packaging not so stereotypically feminine, and the zit stickers not so offensive, this might not be a bad game.

Games encourage players to develop particular skills. By encouraging large group play in a variety of settings, many boys' games urge them to achieve success in the world at large. Most girls' games, however, prepare girls for a life in one setting, the home, by emphasizing verbal skills in small groups rather than large, and by taking place indoors. Interestingly enough, although the object of many of the girls' games is to secure a boyfriend, the verbal skills emphasized do not apply to him. In other words, girls learn to talk to each other about boys, but they do not learn to communicate with those boys.

Further research may reveal that girls use these games in subversive as well as stereotypical ways or that, like the latest fashions, these trendy games spend more time in closets than they do in the center of girls' play areas. For the many girls who do play them as designated, however, these sex-stereotyped games promote damaging stereotypes, passive rather than active play, and skills that fall short of young adolescent girls' cognitive abilities. They assume that all girls share a common future of domestic work, subservience to men, and limited life experience. They also further the likelihood of such a future by failing to encourage intellectual growth. In an advice book for girls published in 1936, Mary Brockman wrote that "boys don't want girls to talk too much or try to appear too wise.... they want girls to know when to sit back and look interested" (Brockman 173). Apparently, the lesson lives on. These board games, as much a part of the toy-store world of the 1990s as they were of the 1970s, frame a world of limited possibilities for girls.

Works Cited

Berla, Nancy, Anne Henderson, and William Kerewsky. *The Middle School Years: A Parents' Handbook.* Columbia, MD: National Commission for Citizens in Education, 1989. Explores difficulties of adolescence, with attention to body image and self-esteem. Examines issues of cultural diversity but does not include gender in definition of diversity.

Brockman, Mary. *What Is She Like? A Personality Book for Girls.* New York: Scribner's, 1936. Traditional advice manual for girls, filled with gender stereotypes.

Chandler, E.M. *Educating Adolescent Girls.* London: Allen, 1980. Examines the ways in which adolescent girls are pushed into "covert delinquency," which is defined as allowing oneself to be pushed into a trivialized mode of life.

Coleman, John C., and Leo Hendry. *The Nature of Adolescence.* New York: Routledge, 1990. Examines dancing, club activities, sports, and community center activities to explore the nature of adolescence and, in particular, the importance of peer group identity.

Comstock, George. *Television and the American Child.* San Diego, CA: Academic, 1991. Traces portrayal of females and males on television over the past 15 years and finds little change in stereotypical gender portrayals.

Dun and Bradstreet. *America's Corporate Families.* Parsippany, NJ: Dun and Bradstreet, 1992. Provides financial information on corporations in the United States.

Huston, Aletha, and Mildred Alvarez. "The Socialization Context of Gender Role Development in Early Adolescence." *From Childhood to Adolescence: A Transitional Period?* Ed. Raymond Montemayor, Gerald Adams, and Thomas Gullotta. Newbury Park, CA: Sage, 1990. 156-79. Argues that gender roles become intensified in early adolescence, when girls and boys are themselves, even more than their parents, intolerant of deviations from traditional sex role norms.

Goodman, Ellen. "Girls Fail Too." *The Washington Post* 7 Sept. 1991: A21. Argues that schools fail not only young African-American males but young African-American females as well.

McRobbie, Angela. *Feminism and Youth Culture: From Jackie to Just Seventeen.* Boston: Unwin Hyman, 1991. Argues that adolescent girls receive less scholarly attention than do boys, partly because they are less likely to be violent. Examines the leisure activities of girls and argues that commercial leisure pursuits promote the separation of sex roles as actively as does any other social institution.

Montemayor, Raymond, Gerald Adams and Thomas Gullotta, eds. *From Childhood to Adolescence: A Transitional Period?* Introduction. Newbury Park, CA: Sage, 1990. Collection of essays on stages of growth—physical, psychological, and social—of children and adolescents.

Newman, Barbara and Philip Newman. *Adolescent Development.* Columbus, OH: Merrill, 1986. Traces physical and psychological development of adolescents from the onset of puberty to graduation from high school. Acknowledges challenges due to differences in looks, athletic ability, ethnic group membership, gender, etc.

Pogrebin, Letty Cottin. "Toys for Free Children." *Ms.* 11.6 (Dec. 1973): 48-53, 82-86. Advises parents to "resolve to take toy buying very seriously," and provides shopping lists of recommended dolls and age-specific toys.

Rivers, Caryl, Rosalind Barnett, and Grace Baruch. *Beyond Sugar and Spice: How Women Grow, Learn, and Thrive.* New York: Putnam, 1979. Explores the dynamics of indoor/passive play of girls and outdoor/active play of boys. Argues that this early conditioning has long-term ramifications in terms of intellectual development and social success.

Unfortunate Reality:
Fictional Portrayals of Children and Violence

Michael A. Grimm

We live in a violent world, one which increasingly involves children in violence. According to Carolyn Baggett, "In as many as two million American homes, family life is so violent it could not be shown on prime-time television" (371). Usually violence in the home takes the form of beatings or sexual abuse, and traditionally children have experienced this as victims of older family members, especially adults. *Time* claims that 88 percent of abuse cases are committed by family members and according to the National Center for Prevention of Child Abuse, approximately 2.7 million children were abused by their parents in 1991 (Toufexis 60). One need look no further than the local newspaper to find stories of parents abusing their children, or for those of us in education, to talk to the school counselor to find similar stories, some of which go unreported in the media. For instance, I know of one such incident in which a mother not only personally sexually abused her teenage son, but forced him to commit incest with his younger sister. Fortunately, the children were taken away from their mother, who spent time in jail for her crimes.

If children are victims of violence, they are also more than capable of committing it. Unfortunately, a new trend being seen in this country is the abuse of young children by other young children. A 1991 article in *Rolling Stone* gave insight into this growing trend with graphic, real-life examples, including a ten-year-old girl who stuck needles into her younger brother's penis; a ten-year-old boy, abused himself by an alcoholic father, who molested his four-year-old sister; and Frank, "who had been molested by three different people before he was five years old...[and who] at age six...sodomized his younger brother" (Terry 70). A recent case in the Lansing, Michigan area dealt with a 13-year-old boy "accused of raping a three-year-old and giving her gonorrhea" (Hoffman and Nichols A1). Most of these very young perpetrators, or "sexually reactive" children as they are sometimes called, are themselves victims of violence.

So it appears that Baggett is correct in her statement of family life and violence. But real violence, often sordid and disgusting, also involves children outside of the home and the immediate family. Take, for example, the case of the so-called wilding episode in New York several years ago, "when a 'wolf pack' of teenage boys set upon a nighttime jogger in Central Park, raped her, beat her senseless, and left her lying in a pool of her own blood" (Bauer 219). Or, looking at another example, social philosopher Myriam Miedzian asks "why do a bunch of boys in Glen Ridge, NJ, all of them on the high school football team, think it is fun to shove baseball bats and broom handles into the vagina of a retarded girl, a girl with an I.Q. of 64? This isn't sex. It is violence" (17). Miedzian says that "there has been an enormous increase in violent crime in this country in the past 30 years...There is such a culture of violence now that surrounds young people that I would suspect violent rates in all areas would be going up" (17).

Nor is violence involving children limited to abuse or sexual crimes. England was shocked in February 1993 when a two-year-old toddler was apparently kidnapped from a mall in Liverpool by two ten-year-old boys. The toddler was murdered and his mutilated body was found on a nearby railroad track. In a story about the crime on the *CBS Evening News*, correspondent Mark Phillips gave the following statistics: "In 1990 [in the U.S.] more than 2500 kids under the age of eighteen were arrested for murder, 283 under fifteen, five children under the age of ten arrested for murder in one year." *Newsweek* reports that according to the FBI, "while arrests for adult sex offenses rose by 3 percent between 1990 and 1991, the increase was three times as high for adolescents" (Ingrassia 17). And reports such as these don't even take into account places such as South Africa, Somalia, Bosnia-Herzegovina, and other numerous places around the world where children are taking up arms and killing people for political causes or for simple survival.

It is obvious, then, children are affected by violence of the worst sort, either as victims or offenders. Furthermore, many researchers and social scientists, including Miedzian, have postulated that exposure to gratuitous violence in all art forms, especially on television, not only makes children insensitive to the results of violence, but also causes them to act more aggressively and violently.[1] These hypotheses are hotly debated, and James B. Twitchell humorously tweaks researchers, saying that "the only firm conclusion that can be drawn is that television can indeed foster violence—among social scientists" (304). Again, these studies are mainly concerned with gratuitous violence, or what Twitchell calls preposterous violence, a type of violence that is "so exaggerated that most of the audience know full well that what they are watching [or reading] is make-believe" (3). Twitchell includes Stephen King novels, horror movies, comic books, and television (including *The A-Team*, professional wrestling, and MTV), among others, as examples of preposterous, or gratuitous, violence. These examples cover literature, music, television, cinema, and graphic arts to show that such violence can be found in virtually every art form.

Preposterous violence of the sort described by Twitchell, is, by its very definition, unrealistic violence. But some violent depictions in art act as mirrors, reflecting life, and if life is violent, such as has already been shown, then art will realistically reflect that violence. In fact, realistic art is, as Leland Ryken claims, "the explicit portrayal of human depravity in all its sordid forms" (239) which presumably includes violence. If this is true, then it gives us two possible boundaries to the violence portrayed in realistic works—little or no violence and too much violence. Either of these can cause art to shift to an unrealistic representation, just as mirrors in a funhouse distort reflections. No violence borders on a utopian view of life, one where violence is ignored and life is portrayed as idyllic, with no serious problems to be seen. This is not to say that all art which is free of violence is inherently suspect, for horrible violence doesn't affect every person every moment of his/her life, but most people don't live in a vacuum from the problems of the world. Other portrayals show either little violence or phrase descriptions of violence in such a way that they lose any emotional response that the reader could have possessed. For example, to say "the boys attacked the girl," or even "sexually attacked" invites a much more intellectual response than "they were holding her arms to the wall while Harry screwed her" (Cormier, *We* 10) which presents a much more emotional, even repugnant scene.

On the other hand, too much violence easily becomes preposterous. It steps past the purpose of realism, to accurately portray lifelike situations, and becomes violence for the sake of titillation or shock value. Realistic works of art must walk a line somewhere between these two unrealistic expressions of violence, and sometimes that line can be brutal, especially when it contains explicit, realistic depictions of violent behavior.

However, it is very important to emphasize that as realistic as art can be, it is still not real life. One of the purposes of art is to portray life as it can be, and to reveal some truth about life in the process. It can bring the reader or viewer some of the thoughts and emotions of characters in the work of art, but the reader/viewer cannot literally become those characters. Is it possible, though, that the use of realistic violence, as opposed to gratuitous violence, can show how violence often results in socially unacceptable acts, the opposite of those social science hypotheses mentioned above which claim that depictions of violence cause people to respond in kind? Can realistic images of violent actions involving children be shown as immoral, and can they, in turn, point towards a morality of some sort, or do such portrayals automatically warp the minds of children by encouraging them to commit similar acts? Works involving children and violence need not encourage copycat actions. As will be seen in the following examples from both children's literature and cinema, the artist's attitude toward his/her subject can have a profoundly positive influence on how the viewer accepts violent incidents, and such portrayals, while dealing with subject matter that may be considered immoral, are ultimately moral in their outlook on life.

"They entered the house at 9:02 p.m. on the evening of April Fools' Day. In the next forty-nine minutes, they shit on the floors and pissed on the walls and trashed their way through the seven-room Cape Cod cottage" (Cormier, *We* 1). So begins *We All Fall Down*, a recent novel by acclaimed writer Robert Cormier that examines violence and its aftermath. It is the story of the vandalism of a house by four teenagers and how various people involved deal with the event. Cormier starts the book in a strong, visceral fashion, describing the act of vandalism in graphic terms. He has said "Yes, I'm trying to shock them, but I'm trying to show them how it felt to find this on their walls...I wanted to put the reader in the place of these people" (Cormier, featured address). To use more polite terms such as feces and urine loses the emotional impact that those characters would have felt upon finding the violation of their home.

The violence doesn't stop with the vandalism, for Karen Jerome, a 14-year-old girl, arrives home to find the vandals still at work. The leader of the trashers attempts to rape her, but when she fights back and tries to escape, he pushes her down the basement stairs. The incident is graphically remembered later by one of the other boys:

Buddy closed his eyes against the sound of her falling. A long time ago, when he was a little kid, he had been in his father's car when it struck an old man crossing the street. He had never forgotten that sound. Like no other sound in the world. Not like a bat hitting a ball or a hammer hitting a nail or a firecracker exploding or a door slamming. The sound had a hollowness in it and in this hollow place was the smaller sound that had haunted his dreams for weeks. That small sound was the sound of something human being struck. And that was the sound Buddy heard as the girl tumbled down the stairs, a series of terrible bouncings, while Harry managed to pull up his trousers and zipped his fly as if he had just finished peeing in the bathroom. (Cormier, *We* 11-12)

Cormier's book is devastating in its graphic portrayal of violence, never backing off from a realism which is terrifying and yet never stooping to the level of literally describing blood spurting or bones breaking. His choice of words, *hitting, bouncing, exploding, slamming*, helps to reinforce the violence without blood and gore, and the violence is further dramatized and contrasted by the mundaneness of Harry zipping his pants.

One of the most disturbing aspects of the trashing and attempted rape is that the boys involved were normal kids, "not sleazies...or the rough guys and dropouts...they looked like high school baseball players or baggers at the supermarket or clerks at McDonald's" (Cormier, *We* 3). In some respects they were like the youths in the "wilding" incident, who have been described as "frighteningly normal" (Colson 170). *Washington Post* columnist Haynes Johnson has written that those teens "did not come from the classic 'pathology of poverty' background that is supposed to be a sociological breeding ground for violence and criminality" (Colson 170). They came from backgrounds that were more middle class than poor. This similarity to real life is a trademark of Cormier's novels for adolescents. Violent examples in Cormier's works include the brutal beating of Jerry Renault in *The Chocolate War*, the drugging of, and implied future murder of, Adam Farmer in *I Am the Cheese*, the deaths of two small children and Kate at the hands of terrorists in *After the First Death*, as well as several incidents of violence, including murder and attempted rape, in *Fade*. Realistic incidents such as these cause the reader to be uncomfortable because of "the power and consistency of his imagined world, which convinces readers that it bears a recognizable relationship to the 'real world'" (Patterson Iskander 7), and in Cormier's world, like ours, any child is capable of violence.

More physical violence takes place within a subplot of *We All Fall Down*, involving a character called the Avenger, who has witnessed the trashing and vows to take revenge. The Avenger was an 11-year-old boy with a penchant for ridding his world of wrongs.

His first act of violence was a cold-blooded stalking and assassination of a bullying classmate. After the murder, the Avenger took the time to carefully arrange the body and the gun to make it appear like an accident caused by the other boy playing with a gun. The Avenger's grandfather became suspicious of his grandson because his old police revolver was used in the murder, and so the Avenger shoved his grandfather off of a fifth-floor balcony. Finally he attempts to kill Jane Jerome, Karen's older sister, and ends up committing suicide instead. The first two scenes are particularly shocking because of the age of the Avenger and of the crimes he did. Even so, there are cases of children even younger than the Avenger using guns to deliberately shoot someone.

Cormier goes beyond showing graphic acts of violence as he explores the emotional effects on the Jerome family in the aftermath of the trashing. Of course, they are shocked, angered, and disturbed by the seemingly random vandalism, and they must also deal with Karen's being in a coma. But when Jane unwittingly falls in love with Buddy, one of the trashers, Cormier sets up a situation in which emotional violence plays a part, for eventually Jane must find out the truth about Buddy. She does so from the Avenger as he explains why he must kill her, and her initial response is "'No,' a harrowing scream of a word torn from her throat in a spasm of denial" (Cormier, *We* 167), which is itself a violent description of her reaction. Then her body reacts physically, vomiting violently as she thought of Buddy, "whom she'd loved with a love that was bigger than her own life. Buddy who had kissed her and caressed her, held her breasts so tenderly" (168), but at this point she is more concerned with survival. Later she has time for reflection, and feels empty and betrayed by "Buddy who had trashed her house and later trashed her, desecrated her" (182), for she had truly been in love with him. Five months later she runs into Buddy at the mall and is surprised to find she feels sorry for him, and "as pity moved into that hole inside her, she discovered how distant pity was from hate, how very far it was from love" (193).

In the final analysis, it is not so much the fact that Cormier writes about violent acts, but what he is able to do in examining the consequences of those acts. In writing about Cormier's other adolescent novels, Sylvia Patterson Iskander says that "he forces us to contemplate such subjects as the death of innocent hostages...the defeat of the nonconformist...all for the purpose of making the reader move beyond the close of the novels to a new sense of personal responsibility" (Patterson Iskander 17). With *We All Fall Down*

Cormier forces us to see beyond the physical acts of violence to understand the emotional and psychological effects of those acts on people involved in both sides of the story. Certainly the violence in this book is realistic, graphic, even degrading, but because it is portrayed in exactly those ways it causes revulsion rather than the desire to participate in such actions.

The random violence of *We All Fall Down* is nothing in comparison to the everyday violence that children must face in some segments of American society. Columnist George Will recently quoted a study from the *Journal of the American Medical Association*, which said in part that "the young child's attempts to master the age-appropriate fears of monsters under the bed are severely undermined when the child needs to sleep under the bed to dodge real bullets" (Will 78). Such is the world that was explored in 1991 by a 23-year-old writer/director named John Singleton in his movie *Boyz N the Hood*. It is a coming-of-age story of some black youths set in South Central Los Angeles, the scene of violent riots a year after the release of the movie. Violence is a part of the lives of the characters from the time they were young to the present when they are in their late teens, and yet Singleton makes it pointedly clear that the violence is a tragedy.

That violence is an omnipresent force from the very opening of the movie as the sounds of gunfire, sirens, and helicopters punctuate the opening titles. When visual images do appear, they are of four young kids discussing a shooting which occurred the previous night, perhaps the incident which was heard during the opening titles. The discussion includes not only the shooting incident, but how the children responded at the time, and the fact that two brothers of one of the girls had been shot in the past. One of the kids shows the others where the shooting took place, and they have a matter-of-fact discussion about the blood on the ground. Ironically, there is a bullet-riddled campaign poster for white-hatted Ronald Reagan, the 1984 law and order presidential candidate, hanging in the background.

Singleton uses a montage of pictures, presumably drawn by children, that portray images of violence to shift to the next scene, where one of the main characters, ten-year-old Tre Styles, is introduced in his classroom. After Tre makes some smart-aleck comments, his teacher invites him to teach the class, and he gladly complies by speaking about being from Africa. That provokes a teasing and then increasingly violent reaction from another student:

Tre: Like it or not, you from Africa.

Bobby: I ain't from Africa, you from Africa, you African booty scratcher.

   (laughter from class)

Tre: Punk, I'll kick your ass.

Teacher (quietly): Okay boys, that's enough, count to ten and be quiet.

Bobby (rising from seat): I'll get my brother shoot you in the face.

Tre: Get your punk ass brother, bitch. I get my daddy. Least I got one, motherfucker.

Bobby: Ain't your bitch. Ain't nobody's bitch, bitch. (*Boyz N the Hood*)

These verbal threats lead to Tre punching Bobby in the face as the teacher tries to stop them and the class cheers them on. As a result, Tre is suspended, and his mother takes him to live with his father, Furious Styles, who sets down rules and tries to teach Tre responsibility. The idea that these ten-year-old kids are not only used to violence, but resort to it so easily in the face of a minor disagreement is the first inkling of one of the messages Singleton is trying to convey, that violence is prevalent in South Central L.A., but that it need not be so.

That first night with Furious, violence strikes, as someone breaks into the house. Tre's father gets his handgun, shoots twice at the intruder, but the intruder escapes. When the police are called, Furious is subjected to verbal abuse by a black officer, but keeps his cool. The next day Tre goes to hang out with some of his neighbors, Ricky and his brother Doughboy, and their friend Chris. Chris takes them to see a dead body. Their attitude towards the body is so matter-of-fact that it almost seems as if it is routine to see corpses in the neighborhood, for not only do they discuss the smell, but they seem to be in no hurry to notify the police, and that attitude further reinforces the idea that violence is an everyday occurrence in their lives. Upon leaving, they are approached by a group of older youths who intimidate Ricky into giving up his football. Doughboy tries to get it back, gets into a scuffle with one of the bigger youths, and ends up being kicked viciously in the ribs. As they are leaving, Tre offers to give his own football to Ricky. Doughboy's response, which foreshadows his typically violent outlook on life, is "I wish I could kill that motherfucker" (*Boyz N the Hood*).

When the boys are seen next, it is 1991. Doughboy has just gotten out of jail and Chris is confined to a wheelchair, apparently as the result of a gunshot wound. Thanks to the strong, positive influence of Furious, Tre has stayed out of gangs and their associated mentality of violence, concentrating instead on his studies and job.

Tre and his friend, Ricky, serve as examples of how violence need not be the norm, even in the violent society in which they live. Several scenes continue that violence, and provide contrast to Tre and Ricky. In one instance, Tre sees a toddler playing in the street in front of traffic. He picks her up and takes her back to her negligent, crack addict mother. Walking across the street to his home, Tre steps in front of a customized car which slams to a stop. One of the back windows is partially lowered, and a double-barreled shotgun is pointed menacingly at Tre before the car is driven on.

Later, Doughboy and friends are hanging out on Crenshaw Boulevard, shooting the breeze and discussing things such as the existence of God. Doughboy asserts that "there ain't no god. Okay, if there was a god, why he be lettin' motherfuckers get smoked ever' night?" (*Boyz N the Hood*). As if to prove his point, Ricky is shoved by someone walking by, an argument ensues, and Doughboy pulls out his handgun. The other group backs off to their cars, where one of them pulls out a submachine pistol and begins firing into the air, causing the other youths in the area to scatter and leave.

Again, it is astonishing how quickly the youths resort to gunplay in the face of accidents or insults. Even more so is the apparent availability of automatic weapons. But while it may be tempting to condemn these portrayals, it is important to notice that until this point among the group of Tre and his friends, only Doughboy, a convicted criminal, has resorted to guns. Ricky and Tre have not, and so still provide a positive image. That positive, reasonable image is brought into focus by the contrast with negative images of violence, which are negative precisely because they are so senseless. And while much of America is shocked and dismayed by incidents like these, they come as no surprise to Singleton, who grew up in a neighborhood in South Central L.A. Like Tre and Doughboy, he had his own experiences with violence, including once in seventh grade "when a bully tried to take his money. He took a box cutter to school and threatened to cut the boy's throat if the harassment didn't stop" (Simpson 60). Fortunately Singleton never carried out his threat.

On their way home from Crenshaw, Tre tells Ricky that "I'm gettin' the fuck outta L.A. Fuck this shit. Fuck it. Can't go nowhere without it gettin' all shot up and shit" (*Boyz N the Hood*). As he finishes speaking, he and Ricky are pulled over by the police. Even though Tre is not threatening or rude, he is confronted by the same black officer who treated Furious badly years ago. The cop shoves his gun hard into Tre's neck and proceeds to lecture him:

You think you're tough. You think you're tough, huh? Scared now, huh. I like that. That's why I took this job. I hate little motherfuckers like you. Look nigger, lying shit, think you're tough, huh? Could blow your head off with this Smith & Wesson, and you couldn't do shit. How you feel now? (*Boyz N the Hood*)

The officer then backs down after hearing on his police radio that a car matching the description of Tre's has been sighted elsewhere, but the implication is clear that violence to the youths can come not only from the gangs, but also from those who are supposed to be the "good guys," those who are supposed to keep the peace and prevent violence. And what makes the scene even more powerful is the fact that it is a black officer, not a white one, who is threatening a black youth in this manner. In addition, it reinforces the opening titles which tell that one of every 21 black men will be murdered, most of them by other black men. Here is an incident where a black police officer, sworn to keep the peace, is threatening a black teen, almost to the point of perpetuating those statistics.

The movie comes to a climax when the "bad guys" from the Crenshaw incident see Ricky and Tre back in their neighborhood and give chase. Doughboy grabs his gun to try to protect his brother and friend, but arrives too late. Ricky is shot by a shotgun in a slow motion sequence that is graphic and bloodily realistic, yet not in any way gratuitous. The irony is that Ricky was not involved in ganglike activity but instead was a star football player being recruited by universities. He had just told Tre that he was going to join the army because he felt his SAT scores were not good enough for college admission. In another twist of fate, his scores arrived as he left for the store with Tre, and when they were opened after his death, they proved to be more than adequate for entrance requirements.

Understandably upset and angry over Ricky's murder, Tre goes home to get his father's gun in order to go with Doughboy, Chris, and the others to seek vengeance. Furious, trying to protect his son from commiting violence as well as potential danger from the murderers, confronts him in the house:

Oh, oh you bad now. You bad, you gotta shoot somebody now. Well, here I am. C'mon, shoot me. You bad, right? Look, I'm sorry 'bout your friend. My heart goes out to his mother and his family, but that's their problem, Tre. You my son, you my problem. I want you to give me the gun. Oh, I see, you wanna end up like little Chris in a wheelchair, huh, right. No, no, you wanna end up like Doughboy. Give me the motherfuckin' gun, Tre!

(Tre slowly gives him the gun.
Furious embraces him as Tre sobs.)
You're my only son, and I'm not going to lose you to no bullshit, you hear?
(*Boyz N the Hood*)

In spite of giving up the gun, Tre leaves to go with Doughboy, Dooky, and Monster. As Monster loads the magazine of an AK-47 assault rifle, Tre asks to be let out of the car and walks home. The others find the murderers of Ricky in a parking lot and Monster guns them down. Doughboy, not satisfied, gets out of the car and shoots two of them in the head, execution style. When Tre returns home he sees his father, who has a look of sadness, or loss of trust and respect for Tre in his eyes, for he believes that his son has fallen prey to baser instincts.

The contrast between the reactions of Doughboy and Tre to Ricky's murder is marked and it would be difficult to miss that fact. Tre, upon reflection, acts in a responsible, nonviolent manner which is the complete opposite of Doughboy, who is so consumed by the thought of revenge that he can't think straight. Doughboy ends up reacting not just violently, but with needless cruelty. Monster had already shot the murderers so many times they were sure to die, yet Doughboy had to get in those final taunts and shots. His reaction ultimately causes one not only to lose what sense of empathy that may have been felt for him, but also to feel revulsion for the violent acts that were committed.

In spite of that loss of empathy, the viewer learns something about Doughboy in the final scene of the movie when he sums up his feelings the next day to Tre as they sit on Tre's front porch:

Yo, cuz. I know why you got outta the car last night. Shouldn't been there in the first place. You don't want that shit to come back and haunt you. I ain't been up this early in a long time. Turnt on the TV this morning. Had this shit on 'bout, 'bout living in a violent, a violent world. Showed all these foreign places, foreigners live 'n' all. Started thinkin', man. Either they don't know, don't show, or don't care about what's goin' on in the 'hood. They had all this foreign shit, they didn't have shit on my brother, man...I don't even know how I feel 'bout it, neither, man. Shit just goes on and on, you know. Next thing you know, somebody might try to smoke me. Don't matter, though. We all gotta go sometime, huh? Seem like they punched the wrong clock on Rick, though. (*Boyz N the Hood*)

The viewer begins to understand some of the despair, anger, and frustration that motivate Doughboy after this speech. After all, when the media gives the impression that America cares more about the violence half way around the world than the violence at home in the inner cities, which is largely ignored or seen as a hopeless situation, it leaves a fatalistic and hopeless feeling in the inhabitants of those neighborhoods. Doughboy's words proved to be prophetic, for titles at the end of the film read, "The next day Doughboy saw his brother buried. Two weeks later he was murdered."

In spite of the abundance of violence involving children and its sometimes graphic portrayals, Singleton's movie strikes a strong chord of antiviolence. Cinema has often made use of images of violence in order to further a nonviolent message (Ansen 52), ranging from *The Ox-bow Incident* to more recent films such as Clint Eastwood's *Unforgiven*. In a review of the latter film, critic David Ansen proposed that "the darkness at the core of this film is in Eastwood's sorrowful view of human nature, Protestant in its sense of original sin" (52), a viewpoint suggesting the depravity of man and the immorality of violent acts that is echoed in Singleton's film and that also hearkens back to Ryken's conception of what realism portrays. But while the two aforementioned films are concerned with the actions of adults, it is *Boyz N the Hood*, along with other movies such as *The Outsiders* and *The Lord of the Flies*, that deal with the effects of violence and children. When Doughboy and the others "smoke" Ricky's killers, the attitude that comes across on screen is not one that celebrates their revenge and the ensuing violence, but rather one that shows how senseless such a retaliation really is. Nor does the film make any claims that the violence is only the result of the environment of the 'hood, for Singleton, through the words of his characters, especially Furious, makes it clear that each individual is responsible for her/his own actions. Doughboy is no more a victim of circumstances than is Harry in *We All Fall Down*, for they both make conscious choices to act as they do. And just in case the audience misses the point that the violence portrayed is not acceptable, the end title includes the message "Increase the Peace."

Situations where children find themselves in the midst of violent circumstances are certainly not limited to contemporary times, nor are they limited to the ghettos of Los Angeles or the suburbs of Massachusetts. Historical fiction can also reveal truths about our present reality, since human beings are essentially the same now as in the past. *The Machine Gunners*, by Robert Westall, shows this, as a group of children go about life in the midst of World War II in England. The novel is about Chas McGill, who finds a downed German bomber with the machine gun still attached. With the help of friends, he cuts off the machine gun and builds a secret bunker in order to shoot down attacking German bombers. The effects of violence from the war are apparent from the very beginning of the book, as Chas wakes up after spending the night in an air-raid shelter to hear his parents discussing the raid:

"You remember that lass in the greengrocer's?"
"The ginger-haired one?" said his mother, still bending over the stove.
"Aye. A direct hit. They found half of her in the front garden and the other half right across the house." (Westall 1-2)

While it is not entirely clear whether the "lass" was a child or a young woman, there is no doubt about what happened to her, and it sets a tone for the book that violence of the worst sort can happen to anyone. Shortly afterwards Chas discovers the bomber, along with the dead gunner, and Westall describes the scene of death: "The glass of the other goggle was gone. Its rim was thick with sticky red, and inside was a seething mass of flies..." (10). Admittedly both scenes are vivid and grotesque, but critic Pauline Kael says that "The dirty reality of death—not suggestions but blood and holes—is necessary...It is a kind of violence that says something to us" (Plagens 52). The scenes give the distinct impression that death exists and that it is not pleasant. While the scenes do not show violence done to children, they give the impression that children are vulnerable to its effects, that they, too, may be hurt by the war.

For the most part, the violence that occurs to children in the novel is done by other children, especially in fights between Chas McGill and his war souvenirs rival, Boddser Brown. Their first fight occurs when Chas and his allies try to escort Nicky, a favorite target of Boddser's, home after school. Boddser starts a fight with Chas, who retaliates with a handful of gravel in Boddser's eyes. "Calmly, full of murder, Chas picked up his gas-mask case and swung it. It hit the side of Boddser's head with a sound like a splitting pumpkin" (Westall 63). Chas's hate for Boddser causes him to go too far, and he has to be stopped by his own friends, Cem and Clogger. The reader gets the impression that Chas would have gone further had he not been stopped, and that this was somehow more than just the typical schoolyard fight, but a matter of life and death, just like the war.

Later, their relationship becomes just that, as Boddser tracks Chas, and confronts him alone. For over half an hour Boddser repeatedly dunks Chas underwater in an effort to gain the secret of the machine gun. When Chas escapes by feigning unconsciousness and putting Boddser off his guard, he calls for Clogger Duncan to help him, but is horrified by the violence that ensues after he tells Clogger to "do him proper." Clogger proceeds to beat Boddser in a manner that is even more alarming than the gas-mask incident:

He just kept on and on, white, silent, steady as a man chopping wood. He never touched Boddser's face; always hit his body where it wouldn't show...Clogger raised his boot and kicked Boddser in the ribs three times. It made a terrible noise, like a butcher chopping a leg of lamb. Then he kicked him three times more, and three times more. (Westall 143)

Finally he stops, after threatening to kill Boddser if he ever talks. The incident brings to a climax the rivalry between the two boys, but not before showing just how brutal and violent kids can be. The fights in one respect parallel the war, acting as a metaphor for the fighting between England (Chas's gang, the "good guys"), and Germany (the "bad guys," represented by Boddser's group). And the two fight scenes show two different types of violence. Chas's violence is more emotional, an act of passion like the majority of violent crimes, which is somehow understandable even if undesirable. On the other hand, Clogger's treatment of Boddser is cold, calculated, and methodical, brutality used to further the cause of the children, and, as a result, is less understandable and more frightening, although neither act is represented as desirable or appropriate.

The book ends with one more violent act. When the children see a group of foreign soldiers approaching the bunker, they panic and begin firing the machine gun. After the police show up with Mr. Liddell, the children's teacher, and their parents, the soldiers leave. Clogger fires a Luger pistol into the air to warn off the "advancing horde." Then Rudi, a downed German pilot who was befriended by the children appears, and Clogger shoots him, whether intentionally or accidentally. Remorseful for hurting their friend, they end up surrendering to their parents and to their respective fates. It was violence that brought them together as a group, and it was their violence in trying to act like their ideal of adults, rather than the adults they knew, whom the children perceived as helpless and impotent in the face of war, that split them apart.

With all the violence of war around them, the children in *The Machine Gunners* respond in kind. Partly their actions are just those of "normal" kids having petty squabbles and schoolyard fights, but more importantly, they are also responding to what they perceive as a situation in which the adults in their lives either refuse to act in the face of war or are just plain helpless. Because the kids feel threatened by the continual raids, and not protected by their parents or other authority figures, they take action to protect themselves and to fight back. It is this distinction that moves Chas and his colleagues from being victims in the violence of war to taking matters into their own hands by getting the machine gun and building the bunker.

As admirable as that sentiment may seem, and the reader does pull for them to succeed at least partially in their quest, ultimately the futility and wrongness of their actions comes out as the story progresses. One way takes place as they develop their friendship with Rudi and find out that the enemy, the dreaded Nazi, is much like the young men in their city. Then, when Rudi is shot, the children realize, along with the reader, that what they were doing was wrong, for an innocent man was hurt, and others, including their parents, were almost killed. Because the reader sees the humanity of the enemy and the destructive nature of the children, the book does not end up promoting violence, but instead shows that violence, no matter how good the intentions, is wrong.

Certainly the works examined here fall within the realm of realistic art, and the violence portrayed is also of a realistic nature. But some people might argue that images of realistic violence are needless and immoral, regardless of whatever message might be present in them. However, as Ryken asserts, "realism itself is not immoral, even though it may be distasteful" (240) supporting his claim by showing how the Bible, a moral book, uses "the technique of realism to tell us...the sinfulness of the human condition" (240). He goes on to ask and answer an important question:

How, then, does art (especially literature) embody an immoral perspective toward its subject matter? Essentially it does so by offering an immoral attitude for the audience's approval...[by] making immoral acts attractive;...generating sympathy for immoral characters and actions; belittling characters whose actions and attitudes are moral [etc.]. (248)

Conversely, Ryken argues that art embodies moral perspective by showing the opposite of these points, i.e., making immoral acts unattractive. It is this perspective of the artist and her/his work that becomes the moral determinant, for "the fact that something happens does not make it morally good either in life or art" (247). It is not so much the act itself which is depicted, but the manner in which it is presented that determines the moral perspective for the observer or reader. And it is here that the works examined embody the moral perspective spoken of by Ryken, because the writers have shown violent incidents in a negative light.

If art contains a moral or immoral perspective, then the question becomes, does art affect our actions? T.S. Eliot, in his famous essay "Religion and Literature," has said that it does, for

The fiction that we read affects our behaviour...When we read of human beings behaving in certain ways, with the approval of the author, who gives his benediction to this behaviour by his attitude toward the result of the behaviour arranged by himself, we can be influenced towards behaving in the same way...The author of a work of imagination is trying to affect us wholly, as human beings, whether he knows it or not; and we are affected by it, as human beings, whether we intend to be or not. (100, 102)

According to George Orwell, "every artist is a propagandist in the sense that he is trying, directly or indirectly, to impose a vision of life that seems to him desirable" (qtd. in Vanden Bosch 49). But is Cormier trying to say that vandalism, attempted rape, and murder are desirable? Does Singleton propose that gunning down people for insults, real or imagined, should become a way of life for America's youth? For that matter, does Westall suggest that vicious and brutal fights become a part of every child's growing up process? Certainly not. But as viewers we are affected, at least emotionally, by their art, and so the presentation of violent acts becomes ever more important to the perception of those acts by the reader, for it is the perception of the artist's intent that may affect our behaviour. Ryken says that

Sex, violence, and evil are not themselves immoral topics for artistic portrayal. It all depends on how the artist treats them — in other words, on the artist's perspective. The crucial moral determiner...is the degree of reticence and distance with which the artist portrays the experience. (248)

If the artist portrays a scene as sordid and disgusting, presumably the observer will not only recognize that fact, but will be changed or affected by his/her exposure to the scene.

Does this mean that portrayals which seem to approve of immoral acts can encourage observers to respond in kind? After all, we cannot assume that literature, in James Vanden Bosch's words, is "innocent of intentions" (58). It would seem that Eliot would answer yes, that it would encourage observers to do so. Susan Suleiman writes that "an integral part of the reader's response to novels has been an emotional reaction based on the explicit or implied judgments of the text regarding these characters or their actions" (163). Note that those reactions can come from implicit, as well as explicit, statements or attitudes. We have already seen the explicit portrayals of violence in the works examined here, but the writers have also implicitly shown the negative side of that violence. Cormier's entire book deals with the aftermath of a violent event, and *Boyz N the Hood* shows Tre turning his back on violence as well as the implicit disapproval of the revenge taken on Ricky's murderers. Chas's shock at Clogger is conveyed as disapproval of the extreme measures he used to subdue Boddser.

But is it the artist's responsibility to make sure we receive a moral message? Ryken lays the responsibility squarely on the shoulders of the reader to read those judgments and attitudes correctly, saying that "the ultimate responsiblity rests with the individual reader, viewer, or listener to be moral in his or her response" (249). If this viewpoint is correct, then art, no matter how moral or immoral its portrayal, is not responsible for the actions of an individual observer.

Why portray violent acts if some people might choose to copy them? Because "by presenting human depravity and misery for our contemplation, modern art, at its best and most responsible, aims to increase our understanding of the human predicament in the modern world" (Ryken 252). The works discussed here use violent incidents to do exactly that, to show how violence is a negative part of the lives of children. As a result, these works can be seen as inherently moral, because of the presentation of those incidents and the artists' attitudes toward those acts.

In looking at violent images involving children, one might ask the question, "Why show children being violated or being violent?" Speaking about *We All Fall Down* in an interview, Cormier has said that "when violence happens to adults, it is bad, but when it happens to young people they're even more vulnerable, and I find it more intriguing to write about from that point of view" (Cormier, "Kind" 31). That violence is used for the purpose of showing how violence adversely affects children, to shock the reader or viewer out of complacency, and it is not a new idea. Leland Ryken writes that

The presence of realism in the Bible refutes a common misconception that works of art automatically encourage approval of everything they portray. This is a totally untenable position. Art has two main themes—life as it should be and life as it fails to match that ideal. As with the Bible, much art portrays things that the artist wishes to reject and denounce. The only way to offer a negative perspective on something is to portray it in a negative light. (240)

The works examined here tend to portray life as it fails to match the artist's ideal, and so the violent acts are portrayed in a negative light. While *The Machine Gunners* is an exciting story, it does not imply that it is acceptable for children to steal machine guns in order to shoot down airplanes, nor that brutal fights are the acceptable norm for behavior. And in no manner can it be argued that Cormier condones the behaviors in his book. *Boyz N the Hood* not only portrays violence in a negative light, it also provides positive role models who try to counteract the violence. By showing these violent acts in this manner, the authors are following Bruno Bettelheim's suggestion that

we shall not be able to deal intelligently with violence unless we are first ready to see it as part of human nature, until we have gotten so well acquainted with it, by learning to live with it, that through a slow and tenuous process we may one day domesticate it successfully. In short, we cannot say that because violence should not exist, we might as well proceed as if it did not. (191)

That is what the artists have tried to show by using realistic violence in their works, for ignoring it does not mean that it doesn't exist. In a society that is perceived as being increasingly violent, it is important to continue the message that violence is not the answer to all of life's problems, and that violence toward children is never acceptable. Ironically, sometimes the message is clearer when violent portrayals are used, but in a society where violence is a part of life, it is likely that such images of children will continue to be a part of art in the future.

Note

[1]For other references regarding violence, including connections between violence and the media, see the following:

Myriam Miedzian, *Boys Will Be Boys: Breaking the Link Between Masculinity and Violence* (New York: Doubleday, 1992).

Deborah Prothrow-Stith, *Deadly Consequences* (New York: Harper Collins, 1993).

Brendan Gail Rule and Tamara J. Ferguson, "The Effects of Media Violence on Attitudes, Emotions, and Cognitions," *Journal of Social Issues* 42.3 (1986): 29-50.

Dorothy G. Singer and Jerome L. Singer, "TV Violence: What's All the Fuss About?" *Television & Children* 7.3 (1984): 30-41.

Jerome L. Singer and Dorothy G. Singer, "Family Experiences and Television Viewing as Predictors of Children's Imagination, Restlessness, and Aggression," *Journal of Social Issues* 42.3 (1986): 107-24.

Works Cited

Ansen, David. "Bloody Good and Bloody Awful." Rev. of *Unforgiven* and *Buffy the Vampire Slayer*. *Newsweek* 10 Aug. 1992: 52. Review of Clint Eastwood's latest western, *Unforgiven*, a violent film which ends up portraying an antiviolent message.

Baggett, Carolyn. "The Specter of Child Abuse In Realistic Fiction For Children." *Catholic Library World* Apr. 1985: 371-74. A basic overview of child abuse along with short summaries of some books for children that deal with the issue.

Bauer, Gary L. "The Battle Over Words." *Children at Risk: The Battle for the Hearts and Minds of Our Kids*. James Dobson and Gary L. Bauer. Dallas: Word, 1990. 217-26. A book written from a Christian perspective that tries to show how the authors perceive modern American culture is warping the children of today. Personally, I find that the authors have good intentions but take a shotgun approach, often repeating themselves from chapter to chapter. There are inaccuracies in the book and the tone is histrionic at times. They make some good points, but the material is not very scholarly in approach.

Bettelheim, Bruno. "Violence: A Neglected Mode of Behavior." *Surviving and Other Essays*. New York: Knopf, 1979. 185-200. Bettelheim recognizes the existence of violence as a natural tendency of mankind, but suggests that by attempting to suppress all expressions of violence, we increase the virulence of violent outbursts when they do occur. He writes that alternatives to violence need to be presented, as well as ways in which violence can be expressed in relatively harmless manners, and gives examples of children with violent tendencies who are allowed to express them in writing, so that they better understand their aggressive nature and can learn to deal with it.

Boyz N the Hood. Dir. John Singleton. With Cuba Gooding, Jr., Morris Chesnut, Ice Cube, and Larry Fishburne. Columbia Pictures, 1991.

CBS Evening News. Corr. Mark Phillips. CBS. WLNS, Lansing. 22 Feb. 1993. Report on a recent case in England where two ten-year-olds apparently kidnapped a two-year-old boy from a mall and murdered him.

Colson, Charles. *The God of Stones & Spiders: Letters to a Church in Exile.* Wheaton: Crossway, 1990. 170. A collection of essays by Christian writer Charles Colson on a variety of socio-political issues. Some of the ideas are repeated in several essays. Not as good as some of his other works, such as *Kingdoms In Conflict.*

Cormier, Robert. Featured address. Conference on Children's Literature and Drama. Ann Arbor, 19 Mar. 1993. In this address, Cormier spoke on his life as a writer, from boyhood when he was encouraged by nuns at school to the present, as well as why his books often deal with the darker side of life, and censorship attempts against his works.

____. "Kind of a Funny Dichotomy: A Conversation With Robert Cormier." By Roger Sutton. *School Library Journal* June 1991: 28-33. An interesting interview with Cormier before he was awarded the Margaret A. Edwards Award by the American Library Association. The interview covers his background in writing, and talks about some of his novels and characters.

____. *We All Fall Down.* New York: Delacorte, 1991. 1-3, 10-12, 167-93.

"Documenting Pain." *Time* 14 Sept. 1992: 25. A brief review of a television program, *Scared Silent*, narrated by Oprah Winfrey and aired in Sept. 1992, along with brief statistics about child abuse.

Eliot, T.S. "Religion and Literature." *Essays Ancient and Modern.* New York: Harcourt, 1936. 92-115. A classic discussion on the need for Christians not only to look at literature critically, but also to apply standards of their moral and theological beliefs to literature above and beyond the standards of the literary world.

Hoffman, Kathy Barks, and Sue Nichols. "Childhood Crimes Surge." *Lansing State Journal* 23 May 1993: A1. Story reporting the increase of crimes involving children in the mid-Michigan area as well as the nation at large.

Ingrassia, Michele. "'Life Means Nothing.'" *Newsweek* 19 July 1993: 16-17. Report on a June 1993 crime in Houston where six teens raped and killed two girls. Beyond the events of the crime itself is the shocking fact that the teens involved seem to have no remorse for the crimes they committed.

Miedzian, Myriam. "Why Johnny Might Grow Up Violent and Sexist." By Daniel S. Levy. *Time* 16 Sept. 1991: 16-19. An interview with the social philosopher who talks about the violence of boys in a society which encourages that violence even when it doesn't intend to do so. The major example she gives is sports, but she also addresses the media/arts.

Orwell, George. *My Country Right or Left—1940-1943.* Vol. 2 of *The Collected Essays, Journalism and Letters of George Orwell.* Ed. Sonia Orwell and Ian Angus. New York: Harcourt, 1968. 41. Qtd. in Vanden Bosch 49.

Patterson Iskander, Sylvia. "Readers, Realism, and Robert Cormier." *Children's Literature* 15 (1987): 7-18. This article addresses critics who feel that not only is Cormier too realistic but that he goes beyond realism because of the depressing nature of his books.

Plagens, Peter. "Violence In Our Culture." *Newsweek* 1 Apr. 1991: 48-52. This article primarily addresses the phenomenon of increasingly violent forms of art, especially in cinema and fiction, such as recent works like *Silence of the Lambs.*

Ryken, Leland. *Culture in Christian Perspective.* Portland, OR: Multnomah, 1986. 239-52. An interesting introduction to the arts from a scholarly Christian perspective. Ryken knows his material, although he seems to be a little quick to dismiss modern art in many forms, i.e., painting, poetry, etc., because of such movements as nihilism.

Simpson, Janice C. "Not Just One of the Boyz." *Time* 23 Mar. 1992: 60. A profile of John Singleton, writer and director of *Boyz N the Hood,* and also the first black as well as the youngest person ever nominated for the Academy Award for Best Director.

Suleiman, Susan. "Ideological Dissent from Works of Fiction: Toward a Rhetoric of the *Roman à Thèse.*" *Neophilologus* 60.2 (1976): 162-77. Suleiman asserts that all literature is rhetorical, and that all realistic novels are ideological to some extent. She tries to show that by studying how ideological manipulation works in the *roman à thèse,* one can better understand how more subtle manipulation occurs in other works, using *Gilles* by Drieu La Rochelle as her example.

Terry, Sara. "Sins of the Innocent." *Rolling Stone* 31 Oct. 1991: 67-72. Report on child sexual offenders, some as young as five-years-old, whose numbers are increasing. It includes comments from several experts in treatment who claim that many people deny the existence of the problem, that it's only children "playing doctor."

Toufexis, Anastasia. "When Kids Kill Abusive Parents." *Time* 23 Nov. 1992: 60-61. A discussion of children killing abusive parents, the article attempts to show that attitudes are slowly changing from the idea that parricide is one of the worst possible crimes to that of understanding for the children, who often feel like they have no choice if they wish to survive.

Twitchell, James B. *Preposterous Violence: Fables of Aggression in Modern Culture.* New York: Oxford UP, 1989. 3, 304. A scholarly treatment of exaggerated violence in several genres of art, primarily in the 20th century. Twitchell covers cinema, the comic books of the 1950s, Stephen King, and such televison fare as big time wrestling, MTV, and *The A-Team.*

Vanden Bosch, James. "Moral Criticism: Promises and Prospects." *Contemporary Literary Theory: A Christian Appraisal.* Ed. Clarence Walhout and Leland Ryken. Grand Rapids: Eerdmans, 1991. 24-71. The author provides definitions of moral criticism, the different varieties of it, along with criticisms by critics of differing perspectives. He encourages Christians (and others) to both read and teach literature critically, as well as to recognize the dangers of moral criticism gone wrong.

Westall, Robert. *The Machine Gunners.* 1975. New York: Knopf, 1990. 1-10, 63, 143.

Will, George F. "'Medicine' for '724 Children.'" *Newsweek* 22 Mar. 1993: 78. The conservative columnist writes about the efforts of Boston City Hospital to "treat" violence among inner-city children before it occurs, as well as after the fact, in the hope that preventative treatment may stop the flood of violence.

Realistic Works
Dealing With Children and Violence
1950 – Present

General – Books

Cormier, Robert. *The Chocolate War.* New York: Pantheon, 1974. The story of Jerry Renault, who refuses to be pressured into selling chocolates in the traditional chocolate sale at his parochial school by a group of students known as the Vigils. Jerry pays a heavy price for his refusal in the violent ending.

Golding, William. *Lord of the Flies.* New York: Putnam, 1954. A masterful story about a group of shipwrecked boys who slowly descend into ever-increasing violence and barbarism.

General – Film
Badlands. Dir. Terence Malick. With Martin Sheen, Sissy Spacek, and Warren Oates. Warner Brothers, 1973. Based loosely on the real life story of Charles Starkweather and his teenage girlfriend, Caril Fugate, this critically acclaimed film shows the spree of murder that the two go on across several states.

Abuse/Domestic Violence – Books
Byars, Betsy. *The Pinballs.* New York: Harper, 1977. The Pinballs are a group of foster children. One of the boys has been taken away from his father, who backed his car over the boy's legs. The book is spoiled by its sentimentality and its use of stock, one-dimensional characters.

Magorian, Michelle. *Good Night, Mr. Tom.* New York: Harper, 1981. Will, a young boy who is physically abused by his mother, is sent north from London along with other children to escape the bombing raids in World War II. He lives with an old man, Tom, who teaches him the meaning of love, until he is recalled to London by his mother, who beats him horribly and locks him in a closet with his new baby sister. The abuse scenes are vivid, realistic, and shocking.

Roberts, Willo Davis. *Don't Hurt Laurie!* New York: Atheneum, 1977. Eleven-year-old Laurie appears to be shy and withdrawn, even from her new stepfamily. Gradually, as she makes friends with Tim, her stepbrother, and George, the boy next door, she begins to confide that she is not clumsy, but that she is physically abused by her mother, Annabelle. When Annabelle beats Laurie unconscious with a broom and a poker, Tim takes the kids to their grandmother, who confronts both Annabelle, and her husband, Jack, with the truth. Most of the abuse that takes place involves beatings, but the story opens with Laurie in the hospital after her mother hit her with a butcher knife.

Smith, Doris Buchanon. *Tough Chauncey.* New York: Morrow, 1974. Chauncey is tough because he has to be. He is small for a 13-year-old boy, and he compensates by continually picking on people and getting into trouble. He also tries to be tough because of his family situation. He only sees his mother occasionally, although she lives only a few blocks away from his grandparents, where he stays. In addition, his grandfather beats him and locks him into the bedroom closet for hours at a time to "teach him a lesson." Yet for all of this, Chauncey is not as tough as he thinks, and he longs for a real family life, one where he will be loved and treated kindly. After falling from a train and almost losing a leg, Chauncey runs away from his grandparents and eventually goes to see about being placed in a foster home.

Abuse/Domestic Violence – Films

The *Color Purple*. Dir. Steven Spielberg. With Whoopi Goldberg, Oprah Winfrey, Danny Glover, and Adolph Caesar. Warner Brothers, 1988. The main character, Celie, is raped by her father, bears him children while she is still a child, and then marries a brutal man whom she addresses as "Mister."

The *Great Santini*. Dir. Lewis John Carlino. With Robert Duvall, Blythe Danner, and Michael O'Keefe. Orion, 1982. Robert Duvall stars as the Great Santini, a hard-nosed and hard-drinking Marine pilot. There are scenes of him beating a basketball against his son's head, as well as physically abusing his wife and children when he is drunk. In addition, there are graphic scenes of racial violence. Based on a novel by Pat Conroy.

The *Prince of Tides*. Dir. Barbra Streisand. With Barbra Streisand, Nick Nolte, and Blythe Danner. Columbia, 1991. Ostensibly the story of Tom Wingo, a man cooperating with his sister's psychologist in order to help the doctor determine how to help the sister, Savannah, after she tries to commit suicide. In acting as Savannah's memory, Tom and Savannah's abusive and violent childhood is remembered and played out on screen, from an abusive father, an older brother who shoots out the television in order to silence his father, to the time when three prisoners break into the Wingo household, rape Mrs. Wingo along with both Savannah and Tom and are killed by Luke the oldest brother, and Mrs. Wingo.

Gangs

Hinton, S.E. *The Outsiders*. New York: Viking, 1967. Ponyboy Curtis, along with his brothers Sodapop and Darry, are greasers, kids from the wrong side of the tracks who are continually battling the Socs, rich kids from the other side of town. One night Ponyboy and a friend, Johnny, are jumped by some Socs, and Johnny kills one who is trying to drown Ponyboy. That sets off a chain of events that leads to more violence, as well as some heroics by Ponyboy and Johnny. Besides the gang violence, the book contains many references to several of the greasers being beaten by parents, especially Johnny, whose father once beat him with a two-by-four.

Myers, Walter Dean. *Scorpions.* New York: Harper, 1988. Jamal Hicks, a 12-year-old growing up in Harlem, is asked by his jailed older brother to take over leadership of the Scorpions. When he is given a gun by Mack, one of the Scorpions, Jamal is unsure of what to do with it, although he feels the power it gives him. He uses it to scare a bigger boy at school who continually harasses him, but when he is called out by some Scorpions who don't want him as leader, he gives it to his best friend, Tito, who goes with him to the confrontation. Tito shoots the two other gang members, killing one, when they attempt to stab Jamal. The incident changes the relationship of the two friends, and Tito has to return to Puerto Rico to live with his father. Jamal is upset, yet still partly misses the power of the gun. A Newbery honor book.

Sexual Violence

Branscum, Robbie. *The Girl.* New York: Harper, 1986. The touching, yet matter-of-fact fictional story of an 11-year-old girl in Arkansas who is sexually harassed and abused by an older uncle. The scenes of sexual violence are not titillating in any sense, but are described in such a way that the reader may feel quite uncomfortable with the situations.

Peck, Richard. *Are You In the House Alone?* New York: Viking, 1976. When Gail Osburne finds a threatening, obscene note in her locker, she is frightened, but her friend Alison tells her to ignore it. Later, Gail starts receiving menacing phone calls whenever she is alone, and is eventually beaten and raped by a fellow classmate who has been stalking her. The novel also deals with the aftermath of the rape, especially the legal ramifications which cause Gail not to press charges against her assailant. While not as graphic its counterpart in *We All Fall Down*, the rape scene was considered to be quite frank at the time.

Political Violence/Terrorism

Cormier, Robert. *After the First Death.* New York: Pantheon, 1979. Cormier's story of a political hijacking of a school bus by terrorists. Two small children are killed, as well as the teenage bus driver and Ben, the son of a general who is used to try to resolve the situation.

_____. *I Am the Cheese.* New York: Pantheon, 1977. The convoluted story of a teenage boy trying to remember who he is and what happened to him. It includes not only the murder of one parent, and the potential murder of the other, but also the suggestion that the boy, Adam, would also be murdered. Most of the violence is implied, rather than described in detail, but it is a strong presence in the novel.

Racial Violence – Books

Gordon, Sheila. *Waiting For the Rain*. New York: Orchard, 1987. Frikkie, a
Boer, and Tengo, a black, are best of friends as children growing up,
but they go their separate ways as Tengo goes to a township in
Johannesburg in order to get an education. Eventually he gets caught
up in the struggle for black rights, and is in a confrontation with his old
friend Frikkie, who is serving his two years of mandatory military
service. There are some brief descriptions of violence and torture,
primarily done by the Afrikaners to black children.

Taylor, Mildred. *Roll of Thunder, Hear My Cry*. New York: Dial, 1976.
Powerful Newbery award winning story of the Logan family in
depression-era Mississippi. While the Logan children don't participate
in any violence except some minor fighting with schoolmates, one of
their friends, 14-year-old T.J., is badly beaten by some older white
youths and is almost lynched. Other racially motivated violence is
present, such as a tar and feathering incident.

Racial Violence – Films

A Dry White Season. Dir. Euzhan Palcy. With Donald Sutherland, Marlon
Brando, and Susan Sarandon. Metro-Goldwyn-Mayer, 1989. Set in
South Africa in 1976. Afrikaner Benjamin du Toit is asked by his
gardener, Gordon Ngubene, to help Gordon's son, Jonathan, who was
arrested by the police and beaten. When Jonathan is arrested again at
the scene of the Soweto riots at which children were tear-gassed,
beaten, and shot by police, Ben is asked to find out what he can about
Jonathan and his condition. Ben finds out that he is dead and buried,
and urges Gordon to drop the matter, which leads to Gordon's death
and Ben's subsequent investigation of the incident, at the risk of his
own career. Not all of the violent images involve children, but those
that do are disturbing. Based on a novel by André Brink.

War – Books

Cooper, Susan. *Dawn of Fear*. New York: Harcourt, 1970. Three young
boys in a small English village spend their time trying to build a small
fort or shelter in which to play during World War II. Their efforts are set
back when a rival group of boys destroy the fort, leading to a violent
confrontation between the two groups. The violence of the gangs is set
against the violence of the nightly bombing raids, which eventually take
the life of one of the main characters.

Maruki, Toshi. *Hiroshima No Pika*. New York: Lothrop, 1982. Mii is a small
girl who lives through the atomic bombing of Hiroshima. The very
nature of the book means that violence is included, and it affects

everyone. Mii is hurt by flying glass, which is still picked out of her head years later, and she never grows due to her exposure to radiation. The illustrations also serve to show the violence done to people. The story and illustrations are very strong in tone, and may not be appropriate for the very young.

Mazer, Harry. *The Last Mission*. New York: Delacorte, 1979. Jack Raap is a 15-year-old boy in New York who dreams about being in the Army and killing Hitler. To fulfill those dreams, he enlists using his older brother's name, and ends up being a waist gunner on a B-17 flying bombing runs into Germany. While Jack never personally commits a violent act against anyone, he is surrounded by violence, especially as he sees other planes shot down, his best friend killed as their own plane is shot down, and the effects of the Allied bombing runs after he is captured in Czechoslovakia, where he sees children missing limbs because of bombs. Upon returning home at the end of the war, Jack comes to the realization that war is not all it's cracked up to be, and that another way of dealing with problems must be found.

Battered Dolls

Allyson Booth

An exchange between two dolls on display at an exhibition in Rumer Godden's novel *The Dolls' House* exposes a few crucial features about the kind of hierarchies doll characters typically negotiate. Here, a haughty French walking doll makes small talk with a little wooden farthing doll named Tottie:

> The walking doll held her tiptilted parasol and her fan and glanced at Tottie. "What ees it you are made of?" she asked. "*Pardonnez-moi*, but la! I do not recognize ze substance."
>
> "I am made of wood," answered Tottie with dignity.
>
> "Wood? La! La! Tee-hee-hee." Her laughing sounded as if it were wound up. "Tee-hee. La! La! I thought doorknobs and broom 'andles and bedposts and clothes-pegs were made of wood, not dolls."
>
> "So they are," said Tottie, "and so are the masts of ships and flagpoles and violins—and trees," said Tottie.
>
> She and the walking doll looked at one another and, though the walking doll was quite ten inches taller than Tottie, Tottie did not flinch.
>
> "I am made of keed and porcelain," said the walking doll. "Inside I 'ave a leetle set of works. Wind me up and I walk." (Godden, *The Dolls' House* 61-62)

Like people, dolls who have it flaunt it: pricey materials, size, and gadgetry. But just as we have a mythology of rich and powerful people we love to hate, children's books invariably situate dolls who occupy the top tiers of such hierarchies in contexts that encourage readers to judge them rather harshly. Characters like the French doll quoted above become the Leona Helmsleys of doll literature.

Authors dethrone large dolls made of fancy materials first by emphasizing the relation between a doll's character and the material of which she's made and then by privileging strength over beauty: porcelain dolls are pretty but fragile while dolls made of good strong wood take pride in their wooden durability and advantage of the natural hardiness it gives them. During the conversation just mentioned, for example, "all the good wood in [Tottie] was standing firmly against the things...the haughty doll had said" (Godden, *The Dolls' House* 63). A wax doll, though beautiful, is often fearful of speaking her mind, for "wax is not very brave stuff" (66), while a china doll is liable to be dangerous because praise goes "to her head which, being china, [is] empty, which is a very dangerous kind of head to have" (34). The coincidence between a doll's mental disposition and her physical substance occurs in other books about wooden dolls (*Hitty*, published in 1946 by Rachel Field, for example); while in Johnny Gruelle's 1920s books starring Raggedy Ann and Andy, cloth dolls are lovable for their softness of temperament as well as for their sweetness of heart (Raggedy Ann has a candy one).

This attention to the link between anatomy and temperament speaks to our desire that a body be legible, as evidenced in a set of verbal connections which we habitually use to describe a person's character in terms of his or her physical characteristics. We refer to stout hearts, moral fiber, and rigid frames of mind in a way that conflates tangible and intangible constitutions. Even the assertion that we are what we eat—which, given the defensive attitudes adopted by people devoted to junk food, we apparently believe—suggests our fondness for the notion that bodies constitute the bottom line of selfhood. (That the character of the French doll I quoted to begin with plays on clichés of national character only confirms this suspicion.) Dolls' bodies, in other words, become the ground upon which we can transform the figurative into the literal—they figure our wish for physical legibility. Authors sometimes even endow dolls with a humorous ability to play on the expectation that bodies will body forth their meanings, as when Raggedy Ann and Andy "[pull] their foreheads down into wrinkles with their hands, so that they might think harder" (Gruelle, *Raggedy Andy* 81).

Doll heroines tend to be small, modestly priced, and simply constructed: they are, in addition, emphatically *un*mechanical. If likable dolls walk, it's only in private, and if they talk, it's only to other dolls. Dolls who talk to people in wind-up or motorized voices, in fact, fare astonishingly ill in the affections of authors and apparently draw on the tradition of the nagging shrew—such mechanized females are nightmarish characters of limited vocabulary, narrow mind and tremendously annoying powers of repetition. Mercifully, their voices often meet with abrupt ends when they wear holes in their tongues (Ross) or fall into bathtubs, water-logging their voiceboxes (Wells).

What authors most often seem to be privileging when they champion plain dolls with zero repertoires is not silent females but the imaginations of little girls. Dolls made of humble materials who, as far as children are concerned, just sit there are best in the end because they provide blanks for children to fill up with flourishes and curlicues of the imagination. Rumer Godden demonstrates this principle clearly in *The Fairy Doll*, whose heroine is the doll on top of a Christmas tree given to Elizabeth, the youngest child of a large family who is apparently incapable of getting anything right. Once Elizabeth has the fairy doll in her possession, however, she gradually begins to be able to master everything from multiplication tables to remembering to brush her teeth: all the right cues pop into her mind with a "ting[ing]" sound that Elizabeth attributes to the fairy doll.

The most interesting detail of this solution to Elizabeth's problems is the way that each new accomplishment is preceded by an act of the imagination in which she invents a fairy world for her fairy doll. In spring, she makes fairy bananas out of catkins, fairy lettuces out of hawthorn buds and French rolls out of beech-leaf buds. These inventions are followed by a report that for the first time (ting) Elizabeth remembered to brush her teeth, knew (ting) that seven times two is fourteen, and sounds out words (ting) in the story of Sleeping Beauty. In summer, the fairy doll has a Canterbury bell for a hat and eats daisy poached eggs, followed by Elizabeth's realization that she suddenly is able to remember a grocery list correctly and to keep hold of her bus money without losing it. This pattern linking the development of Elizabeth's imaginative prowess with other kinds of maturity allows Godden to position the imagination at the center not only of childhood and play but also of adulthood and responsibility.

Godden's story does not take up the fairy doll's point of view at all. She appears for a time to be responsible for the tings and the suggestions that accompany them: (ting) brush your teeth, L-I-L-A-C spells (ting) lilac. But when one day the fairy doll disappears, the tings continue, suggesting that Elizabeth herself has not only been creating the fairy doll's world but writing the fairy doll's script. As far as the fairy doll's character is concerned, her disappearance is only the final act of self-effacement in a whole sequence of self-effacements performed purely for Elizabeth's benefit. When Elizabeth feared responsibility, the doll took it on; when Elizabeth wished for responsibility, the doll disappeared, allowing the child to assume it.

Dolls do fashion themselves into models of altruism with frequent and rather appalling fervor. In a picture book by Rebecca Caudill (*The Best-Loved Doll*), a doll named Jennifer is taken to a party where prizes are given out for the oldest doll, the best-dressed doll, and the doll who can do the most things. Jennifer, however, is neither old nor talented, and her dress is "a fright." In addition, her "wig was loose and her hair was tangled. Her nose was cracked.... The toes on both her feet were worn away and her knees were scarred. But on her face she wore a smile that never went away." Jennifer's smile is clearly her definitive quality, and she administers it in large doses, grinning cheerfully and stickily (she has candy in her hair) as other dolls win all the prizes at the party. Finally, Jennifer herself wins acclaim when the mother of the child throwing the party pins a medal on her proclaiming Jennifer "The Best-Loved Doll." The book ends with Jennifer planning how she's going to give away all her party favors to other dolls and how they can all take turns wearing the medal. Such self-forgetfulness is clearly being held up to children as something to emulate; Jennifer is "The Best-Loved Doll" precisely because she is selfless, and the mark of that selflessness— her worn off toes and tattered dress—is what allows Mrs. Anderson to recognize her lovableness and to reward it with a medal.

That dolls should be blank slates onto which the imaginations of children can inscribe themselves makes good intuitive sense. The problem is that many fictional dolls overflow the position of blank slate by displaying idiosyncrasies and personalities of their own. Tottie and Hitty, the little wooden doll characters of Rumer Godden and Rachel Field, for example, are difficult to think of as blank in any sense of the word. Their status as toy objects stands in tense relation to their status as speakers, personalities, and even moral nerves in the novels that center around them.

For one thing, dolls like Hitty seem conscious of their bodies in a way that is not only closer to a human than an object, but closer to an adult than to a child. Near the end of the book, for example, when Hitty is quite old, she lives with a pair of elderly spinsters who are constantly made to confront the discrepancy between what they are now and what they were years ago, because a portrait of them as young women hangs in their drawing-room. Hitty is understandably struck by the difference and comments that

Sometimes I think they, too, were surprised at the change in their appearance. I have seen Miss Hortense stand a long time before the picture with a queer expression on her lips, and once I caught Miss Annette peering with just the same look into the long mirror between the French windows. But I never heard them mention such thoughts, not even to one another. It was only because I, too, knew what it was to change that I could understand all that must be passing in their minds. (Field 157)

Despite the fact that Hitty remains a toy and wishes most to belong to a little girl who will play with her, her concern with her own fading complexion is unmistakably the concern of an aging woman—for, after all, the beauty of childhood (at least as adults imagine it) is an ideal of physical unselfconsciousness inhabiting a perfectly pristine body. Hitty's self-consciousness regarding her skin allows her to empathize with the two old ladies who dress Hitty up for an exhibition in a bridal gown fashioned from a handkerchief each of them had hoped to carry on her wedding day.

Dolls like Hitty and Tottie participate in an alternative hierarchy that extends across a great deal of children's literature and over a number of generations. Instead of concern with size and material, this hierarchy reduces gradations of price and mechanism down to a pair of simple categories: real toys and not-real ones. Famous examples of this intense desire of toys to become "real" are Pinocchio, who is rewarded at the end of his adventures by becoming "a real boy" and Margery Williams Bianco's Velveteen Rabbit, who experiences two levels of reality—first an interim stage in which the Boy believes he's alive, and a later another one in which actual rabbits with real hind legs confirm that he's alive. Unlike Pinocchio and the Velveteen Rabbit, most dolls don't become real people but rather stick to the verbal and imaginative reality which consists of being loved and played with by a child. The Skin Horse explains it to the Velveteen Rabbit this way: "'when a child...REALLY loves you, then you become Real.'" When the Velveteen Rabbit asks worriedly whether becoming real hurts, the Skin Horse admits that it sometimes does. But he adds that "'When you are Real you don't mind being hurt'" (Williams 17).

Dolls, then, do best when they're made of durable materials because that way they can survive the often painful process of becoming Real. The ethos of use—for a toy to be loved and played with by a child—is articulated in and confirmed by the vocabulary of reality. And reality means accepting the fact that to be alive means to be vulnerable. Tottie makes this point beautifully when she intercedes in a conversation between a wax doll, who is insisting that it is children who give dolls life, and an evil china-headed doll, who notes that children also "'tumble one about and spoil one.'" "'Isn't that life?'" Tottie asks, pointedly (Godden, *The Dolls' House* 66). It's difficult, of course, not to agree with her.

The problem is that dolls, being unusually susceptible to harm on the one hand and unable to act or even to consent on the other, occupy a precarious territory somewhere between subject and object. They speak, but only to the reader. They wish, hope, and worry but often to no effect. Rumer Godden comments on this hazardous state of events in an aside to her readers, reminding us that "It is an anxious, sometimes a dangerous thing to be a doll. Dolls cannot choose; they can only be chosen; they cannot 'do'; they can only be done by; children who do not understand this often do the wrong things, and then the dolls are hurt and abused and lost; and when this happens dolls cannot speak, nor do anything except be hurt and abused and lost. If you have any dolls, you should remember that" (*The Dolls' House* 12-13).

This tension between subject and object emerges in the difficulty of articulating the damage suffered by a doll's body. On the one hand she's an object which would suggest that when she falls out of a tree or down a staircase she would be ripped, torn, or scratched but not hurt, fractured or bruised. On the other hand she's frequently a subject with a voice and a personality independent of the child to whom she belongs (in the Raggedy Ann and Andy stories, Gruelle makes a point of saying that Marcella's dolls are invariably thinking of other matters when Marcella pretends, in the course of her play, to speak for them). Given, then, the insistence with which we're made aware of dolls not as objects but as characters, mishaps *do* seem like injuries.

Authors frequently add the problem of gender to this verbal quandary, for dolls are not always, but almost always, female. What we're faced with is, therefore, a convention of female characters who are supposedly subjects but are actually objects and who inhabit, furthermore, a context that teaches the best of them to accept battering as the price not only of love but of life. Battered women wear sunglasses over their black eyes until the trace of their abuse heals, but battered dolls like Jennifer, "The Best-Loved Doll," wear the signs of their having been played with proudly, delighted to have been broken and mended over and over. There's no middle ground for a doll, only the extreme alternatives of offering herself up to the play that at once erases and confirms her, or resigning herself to the neglect that keeps her body intact but her disposition either depressed (if she's a nice doll) or sour (if she's a nasty one).

The most acid charge one doll can level at another is that "'You are not a doll.... You are a *thing*'" (Godden, *The Dolls' House* 103). Since most dolls wish fervently to be "real dolls" rather than things, subjects rather than objects, they develop strategies for negotiating the damage suffered by their bodies. Probably the most startling of these tactics is the one Johnny Gruelle relies on in his Raggedy Ann and Andy stories, where dolls simply declare that what looks to us like hurt doesn't actually hurt. Raggedy Ann and Andy lose arms in pillow fights without even noticing it, laugh at the memory of being dismembered by spinning wheels and emerge from accidental launderings that involve being boiled and then cranked through clothes wringers sporting cheerful smiles on pancake bodies. After having been dropped into a can of paint, Raggedy Ann tells her friends the story of the "'kind lady'" who "'took off my yarn hair and cut the stitches out of my head and took out all the painty cotton...'" adding that "'It was a great relief, although it felt queer at first and my thoughts seemed scattered.'" Next, Raggedy Ann gets hung, apparently brainless, upon the clothes-line: an illustration shows her in this condition, gleeful as ever. Here, in her words,

"...a dear little Jenny Wren came and picked enough cotton out of me to make a cute cuddly nest in the grape arbor!"
   "Wasn't that sweet!" cried all the dolls.
   "Yes indeed it was!" replied Raggedy Ann. "It made me very happy."
(Gruelle, *Raggedy Ann Stories* 46)

Dolls like Godden's Impunity Jane and Johanna Johnston's Sugarplum take a cost-benefit approach to the issue of bodily damage: the adventures to which they have access are worth the price of being tattered or lost, having your clothes taken off or your body nicked and scraped. Sugarplum, who at first suffers because the big dolls tell her that she's too small to be a real doll ("'You're only a trinket, a knicknack, or a bangle, not a *real* doll'") later is frustrated by receiving a set of clothes she had wished for for ages, but which turn out to make her too good to play with ("'Sort of like an ornament, a showpiece, or a statue. And I wouldn't care for that. No *real* doll would, I'm sure,'" the big dolls sniff). Impunity Jane chooses the adjectival prefix to the name Jane given her by her original owner because she hears a shopkeeper remark that "'This little doll is very strongly made.... Why you could drop her with impunity'" and then explain that "'Impunity means escaping without hurt'" (10). Impunity Jane and Sugarplum both prefer being banged up a little to the alternative of boring safety.

Hitty, the Rachel Field character who writes the story of "Her First Hundred Years," takes the approach that the physical discomfort she endures is nothing compared to the emotional trauma that accompanies it. Hitty describes her life at its most miserable when her current mistress, a child called Thankful, responds to criticism of both herself and Hitty by thrusting the doll into the crevice between two sofa cushions and abandoning her. "I was really too big to go in," Hitty confesses, "but [Thankful] was determined, and her fingers forced and pushed me out of sight. The sofa was done in horsehair, which scratched me cruelly as I went in" (Field 104). There she is, upside down in a crack of upholstery, and to make matters worse, the sofa is soon afterwards relegated to the attic, so that Hitty spends a significant amount of time there—perhaps years, she has no way of knowing. "It is a bitter thing indeed, to realize that those one holds dear are ashamed of one," Hitty says. "I think I have never suffered more in my life" (Field 104). But despite the discomfort of her physical position, "that discomfort," she asserts, "was less hard to bear than the humiliation I suffered" (107).

Hitty's claim is one that we would like to believe but which unfortunately is not at all borne out by the human experience of physical pain. Elaine Scarry, in her analysis of torture, has described how "Physical pain is able to obliterate psychological pain because it obliterates *all* psychological content, painful, pleasurable, and neutral" (34; emphasis mine). Much as we may be invested, then, in the idea that betrayal hurts more than being stuck upside-down in a horsehair sofa for an extended period of time, surely the suggestion that matters of the brain will always win out over matters of the body—that battering doesn't hurt, that battering is worth it, or that loyalty takes precedence over physical harm—surely all these suggestions are disturbing ones.

Picture books, with their reliance on illustrations to help speak their stories, present some of the most arresting images of battered dolls. Here, depictions of damage are not explained away but rather exposed in all their distressing detail by dolls who don't speak at all. *Amanda Remembers*, by Robert Kraus, consists almost entirely of a catalog of ways in which Amanda's doll and her toy dog have been damaged over the course of time. The story begins when Amanda's mother puts the toys in the garbage, which loss becomes the occasion for Amanda's remembering. What she remembers about her toys, though, is in every case an accident in which one of the toys gets hurt. The incidents are fairly innocuous in the beginning—the toy dog is startled and upsets the pot of tea onto the doll's dress; the doll falls into the toy dog's bath. They become more and more frightening, though, as the book goes on: they are attacked by a cat, the toy dog slips on an icy street, the doll is lost in the woods, the pair of them suffer a terrible fall down the stairs. This litany of damage increases in severity throughout the book and constitutes the entire plot.

The pictures showing us Amanda's nameless doll certainly suggest that the doll is suffering; there is no indication that she is able or inclined to rationalize away her lifetime of traumatic experiences. Like fairy tales which when we look back on them as adults suddenly seem terrifically harsh, the picture books revolving around battered dolls are surprisingly disturbing. By combining the excruciating honesty of children themselves with a child's acceptance of almost any situation as the unassailable norm, the battered dolls in picture books seem—by their eloquent silences, their refusals to reassure—to express some of our very real concerns about mute passivity.

Works Cited

Caudill, Rebecca. *The Best-Loved Doll*. New York: Holt, 1962. At a party for dolls where prizes are to be awarded to the oldest doll, the best-dressed doll, and the doll who can do the most things, Betsy's doll Jennifer prompts the establishment of a new category: the best-loved doll.

Field, Rachel. *Hitty: Her First Hundred Years*. New York: Doubleday, 1946. Hitty, created by a peddler from good mountain ash wood, experiences several generations' worth of adventures and writes her memoirs from an antique shop.

Godden, Rumer. *The Dolls' House*. New York: Viking, 1958. Two little girls learn (much later than the doll family that belongs to them) that certain dolls belong only in museums, not in dolls' houses.

——. *The Fairy Doll*. rep. in *Four Dolls*. 1955. New York: Dell-Yearling, 1983. Elizabeth grows up with the help of the fairy doll that sits on top of the Christmas tree.

——. *Impunity Jane*. 1954. New York: Viking, 1966. Impunity Jane finally is allowed to participate in a life of adventure after she is adopted by a little boy.

Gruelle, Johnny. *Raggedy Andy Stories: Introducing the Little Rag, Brother of Raggedy Ann*. 1920. New York: Dell-Yearling, 1948. Raggedy Ann and Andy, originally made by the mothers of little girls who lived next door to each other, are reunited in the next generation and have good times with their playmates in Marcella's nursery.

——. *Raggedy Ann Stories*. 1918. New York: The Johnny Gruelle Company, 1947. Raggedy Ann survives the mishaps of being a doll with astonishingly good humor.

Johnston, Johanna. *Sugarplum and Snowball.* New York: Knopf, 1968. A kitten rescues Sugarplum from the curse of new clothes which made her too good to play with.

Kraus, Robert. *Amanda Remembers.* New York: Harper, 1965. After her mother puts the toy dog and the doll in the trash, Amanda remembers all the things they have been through together.

Ross, Geraldine. *Benjamin Brownie and the Talking Doll.* Racine, WI: Whitman, 1962. One of Santa's elves learns the hard way that dolls should be seen and not heard (or only minimally heard).

Scarry, Elaine. *The Body in Pain: The Making and Unmaking of the World.* New York: Oxford UP, 1985. Scarry analyzes the structures of war and torture (unmaking) as well as the Old Testament's preoccupation with making in a compelling analysis of physical, verbal and political representation.

Wells, Rosemary. *Peabody.* New York: Dutton-Dial, 1983. Peabody the bear regains his place in Annie's affections after the talking doll falls into the bathtub.

Williams, Margery. *The Velveteen Rabbit, or How Toys Become Real.* New York: Doubleday, 1958. The Velveteen Rabbit finally becomes a real rabbit as a reward for having been loved dearly by the Boy.

Towards Empowerment:
Reflections on Children's Literature

Monica Hughes

In *The Story of an African Farm*, Olive Schreiner speaks of

> ...the loneliness, the agonised pain!...There are some of us who in after years say to Fate: "Now deal us your hardest blow, give us what you will; but let us never again suffer as we suffered when we were children." The barb in the arrow of childhood's suffering is its intense loneliness, its intense ignorance.[1]

This is the cry of the 19th-century child, articulated in the novels of Dickens: the Oliver Twists, the Nicholas Nicklebys, who are seen through the eyes of authority as "limbs of Satan" to be tamed and civilized, in order that they might become useful members of the new industrial society. These were children seen as unfinished human beings, their minds a page from which all erroneous material must first be expunged, so that an education and correct social behaviour might be imprinted upon it. From the child's viewpoint, as with Waldo in *The Story of an African Farm*, it is a world of loneliness in which adults are frequently to be feared rather than trusted.

Simultaneously, there appeared the contradictory idea of the Romantics that children were "angels of God." In Wordsworth's view, childhood was a time of bliss and our progress into adulthood a journey away from our Paradisical beginnings...

> Trailing clouds of glory do we come
> From God, who is our home;
> Heaven lies about us in our infancy!
> Shades of the prison-house begin to close
> Upon the growing boy.[2]

Depending on one's own biases, these dichotomous views could be rationalized by thinking of girls as angels and boys as devils, or the children of the middle class as angels and those of the lower orders as

153

devils; this view, expressed in literature as well as society, persisted for many decades, forcing the children into an artificial mould, offering them little in the way of empowerment.

Frances Hodgson Burnett embraced the Victorian ethic in her earlier works but began to move away in her last writings. So we find in *The Little Princess*, written in 1905, that Frances Hodgson Burnett draws an improving picture of a good child, Sarah, untouched by adversity, for the edification of her young reader. The protagonist is still powerless. The events that change Sarah's life from better to worse and back again lie outside her control; all she is expected to do is to endure gracefully.[3] But her last book, *The Secret Garden*, written in 1911, has been read by generation after generation. Once more, the protagonists, Mary and Colin, are not children living in normal circumstances, while Dickon, the throw-back to the nature child of Wordsworth and Rousseau, is perhaps the most unlikely character of all. But the strong-willed Mary is actually able to manipulate events to her desired end; it is through her persistence that Colin walks again. It is the beginning of "empowerment." Most importantly, this book acknowledges *the need for a secret and imaginative life for the growing child.*[4]

As with their Victorian predecessors, the Edwardian family had little intercourse between parents and children and this is reflected in the world of Edith Nesbit's Bastables, whose adventures reflect their lack of understanding about the way in which the adult world functions. The scrapes they get into would never have happened to today's street-wise kids, while their perception of their parents, as remote as the Gods on Mount Olympus, is far removed from that of today's children.[5]

But in her fantasy novels, Edith Nesbit does more than enhance the imaginative life of her young readers. Here, the situations in which her protagonists find themselves are the result of the chanciness of magic and they are able to overcome their problems. In the background are the occasional parents, servants or governesses who have to be kept in the dark for their own sanity. These are decisive children, risk takers, freed from the daily constraints of Edwardian life by the magic ring of *The Enchanted Castle* or the reluctant wish-granting phoenix in *The Phoenix and the Carpet.*[6, 7]

A generation after Edith Nesbit, following the social and economic disruption of the First World War, a new breed of child protagonists appears. Arthur Ransome's children live in a world marvellously devoid of adult supervision and interference. At the beginning of *Swallows and Amazons* a symbolic handwashing sets the stage for the stories to follow. Their father gives the four children permission to spend their holidays unsupervised, sailing and camping in the Lake District, in a telegram that reads:

BETTER DROWNED THAN DUFFERS IF NOT DUFFERS WON'T DROWN

This unlikely permission gives the children a temporary power, but is it real? The mother appears in a traditional nurturing role, after a particularly stormy night, with a bucket of hot porridge for the adventurers, and they are no longer shipwrecked mariners. The holiday is over.[8]

In the era between the wars, the plots of many books for children reflect this somewhat unrealistic freedom in a fictitious world frequently devoid of adults, despite the fact that most children were growing up in close proximity to their parents in small suburban houses. But children grew up, for the most part, unaware of world tensions or of their parents as vulnerable human beings. The stories of this time reflect this in the shadowiness or total absence of adult characters. It is an unreal world, with no real empowerment.

In the 1950s, a series of very different books appeared, as pivotal as Edith Nesbit's *Story of the Treasure Seekers* and *The Enchanted Castle*. These were C.S. Lewis's Narnia chronicles.[9] Lewis's Narnia is a more complex fantasy world than that found in *The Enchanted Castle*. The Ugli-Wuglies of *The Enchanted Castle* are made out of brown paper bags and walking sticks and string and their life is ephemeral at best; though frightening at first glance, they are seen through for what they are. The land of Narnia is very different. It was there before the children find their way through the back of the wardrobe and it exists in their absence. The characters are strong and the mythic struggle between good and evil, evident in C.S. Lewis's adult writing, is powerfully developed here, as it is not in Nesbit's books. The juvenile protagonists suffer, are afraid and have real interior and external conflicts. C.S. Lewis never condescends to his young readers and his stories are without the overt preachiness of some earlier fantasy novels, such as George MacDonald's *At the Back of the North Wind*.[10]

After the Second World War, television's global village plunged children in the adult world. They can no longer help being aware of the emotional, financial and social worries of their parents, as well as of the world around them. Three generations after Edith Nesbit the adults are back, but they are no longer Olympian; they are frequently emotionally frail and have to be coped with, like the vagrant mother in Peter Dickinson's *The Gift*.

"I don't know about Mum. I wonder what she'll come back with this time." Davy laughed. Last time Mum had gone off on one of her "holidays" she'd got home with a black eye and two brand-new suitcases, scarlet, with gold plated clasps.[11]

The squabbling parents in the blended family of Robert Westall's *Wind Eye* project the children into the uncomfortable role of peacemakers.

A quick furtive marriage in the registry office and the trouble really started. Bertrand began talking about *my* wife, as he had always talked about *my* daughters and *my* house. The gay logical arguments turned into screaming matches, as Bertrand strove to tidy up Madeleine's life, and Madeleine resisted with increasing wildness.[12]

Coping with such adult problems, or at least learning to live with them, often constitutes an integral part of the structure of today's novels. The protagonist may have to act out the role of Lucy in the Peanuts cartoons, becoming psychiatrist to the whole family. The anxious elderly looking Ida in Maurice Sendak's *Outside Over There* seems to be a commentary on today's children, growing up too fast, too soon, without any buffer of innocence between them and the often violent adult world.[13]

Lately [Momma'd] go to the store for bread and come back with a can of tuna and just put her hands over her face, sitting at the table. Sometimes she'd be gone for a couple of hours and then wouldn't say where she'd been, with her face blank as if she couldn't say. As if she didn't know.[14]

So Dicey, in Cynthia Voigt's *Homecoming*, must assume the role of caregiver upon the abdication of the children's own mother, in a situation that reflects that of many parentless children in the aftermath of wars and natural disasters. Indeed, in many modern juvenile novels like *Homecoming*, there is a deep sense of loneliness, of ignorance of the "rules" that govern the world "out there," similar to that expressed above in Schreiner's description of Waldo; the thrust of the plot may be in the search for family, for roots, for a symbolic key to the meaning of life, but, like Dicey, the *modern* child protagonist realistically overcomes her problems.

Today's children do have a certain power. There is power inherent in the spending potential of the young person, reflected in the enormous clothing and entertainment industries. There is also political power. Nowadays it sometimes seems that children are running their parents—*and* the schools. Yet this power is accompanied by a sense of helplessness, not the helplessness of a child, but a more adult helplessness in the face of the seemingly insoluble problems of poverty, unemployment, pollution, nuclear destruction. It is a sad paradox that in their time of greatest freedom, children *should* feel so powerless. Much of the negative behaviour of young people in our society today is due to anger at their inability to see a way out of this apparently impending doom.

How to handle and transform this frustration into good? In the foreword to his new book, *The Cry for Myth*, Rollo May states:

As a practising psychoanalyst I find that contemporary therapy is almost entirely concerned, when all is surveyed, with the problem of the individual's search for myths. The fact that Western society has all but lost its myths was the main reason for the birth and development of psychoanalysis in the first place...I believe there is an urgency in the need for myth in our day. Many of the problems in our society, including cults and drug addiction, can be traced to the lack of myths which will give us as individuals the inner security we need in order to live adequately in our day. The sharp increase in suicide among young people and the surprising increase in depression among people of all ages is due...to the confusion and the unavailability of adequate myths in modern society.

Later in the book he affirms that

The myth is formed by the child's endeavour to make sense of strange experience. The myth organizes experience, putting this and that together and brooding about the result.[15]

Mythology was always part of the human experience, from the first stories spun by preliterate peoples to make bearable the inexplicable around them: thunder, volcanoes, earthquakes, death itself. Then, as tribes became communities, new myths evolved: stories such as Prometheus stealing fire from the gods, Icarus flying towards the sun, Pandora opening the forbidden box; stories about sassy and curious humans stepping out of line, asking too many questions and coming to no good. These stories, though acting as warnings, also celebrated the humans who *stepped out of line*, who asked the forbidden questions. They might be horribly punished, but they became elevated to the stature of HERO, replacing the tribal hunter hero of the early stories.

Later, as property was accumulated and the rights and duties of the individual members of society needed to be defined, a new kind of story began to be told, folktales with human protagonists: the stories of Cinderella, Red Riding Hood, Briar Rose, teaching social ethics and warning of the consequences of disregarding them.

With the Industrial Revolution, it seemed we no longer had any need of myth and folktale; we had the sciences and a legal and police system to protect our property. The stories, no longer passed on through word of mouth by nursemaids and live-in grandmothers, finally vanished from childhood culture, to be replaced by...what?

Jane Yolen, in her fascinating book *Touch Magic*, mourns the loss of the great myths. She compares today's youngsters to feral children who, even when reclaimed from their animal foster parents and returned to civilization, are never able to acquire language: they have lost touch with their humanity. It is in recognising and understanding the mythology that is our human inheritance, that we may learn to understand the complexity of our humanity.[16] *Those who do not learn from their past are condemned to repeat it.*

Children, in particular, are hungry for myth and will find it in whatever form their environment provides. Whether it is true myth or false, whether it will provide a serviceable guide for their journey through life or leaves them rudderless and lost, will depend on that environment. In *Touch Magic*, Jane Yolen mourns the loss of meaningful symbols. To the American child, the winged horse is no longer Pegasus but a symbol of a gas company. Children's myth culture has not improved since she wrote that book. Today's youngsters grow up associating Michelangelo not with a towering figure in Western art but with a turtle that lives in a sewer. There is a frightening symbolism in this: that the new heroes come not from Olympus or Valhalla but from the sewers.

Children need myth. Where there is a need, something will fill it, whether it is Ninja Mutant Turtles or a good mainstream or science fiction story. What makes a good modern mythic story? Often the protagonist is a solitary person, perhaps a youngest child, misunderstood and underrated, or a person out of sync with their society—somebody curious. Frequently a journey is an important constituent in the story and the force that drives the story is the need to right a wrong, symbolically slay a dragon, whether external or internal, to overcome evil with good. On the way to this objective the protagonist meets obstacles and, in overcoming them, grows in stature and even becomes "heroic." So the children in E. Nesbit's fantasies, the children in the Narnia chronicles, Dicey's family in *Homecoming*, Davy in *The Gift* and the family in *The Wind Eye*.

Science fiction and fantasy in particular are valid carriers of myth for the 20th century, and most especially for young people. The success of Tolkien's *Lord of the Rings* lies not only in the fascinating minutiae of Middle Earth but in the story of the Hobbit Frodo, who is drawn, against his will, into the search for the Ring, without which Evil will overcome. In so doing he gains strength and knowledge—as does the reader, because mythic fiction is *empowering*.[17]

In a sense, young people today are already living their myth: the dragons are here; the need to right the wrong, to make things whole again, are all here. What is lacking is the symbolic gift: the magic sword or shield given to the young man or woman before they set out on their quest. *Empowerment*. In the real world this begins with understanding. Good literature, whether it be mainstream or science fiction or fantasy, makes tomorrow's ogres real and present, within the unthreatening framework of an imaginative world. It is within this framework that the writer can challenge the readers, through the persona of the protagonist, to find answers to the questions that exemplify their own powerlessness. Hopefully, as they identify with the main character, they begin to understand the possibilities, the greatness of being fully human. They are *empowered*.

Notes

[1]Schreiner, Olive. *The Story of an African Farm*. New York: Caldwell, 1883. An evocative account of life on an Afrikaaner farm in the 19th century, this would probably be considered unreadable by most of today's teens.

[2]Wordsworth, William. "Ode on the Intimations of Immortality." *Oxford Book of English Verse*. New York: Oxford UP, 1939. This famous poem (1836) argues that learning in the adult mind is only a recollection of a child's intuitive memory of paradise.

[3]Burnett, Frances Hodgson. *The Little Princess*. 1905. New York: Warne, 1975. A wealthy orphan is relegated to the status of servant after her father's money is lost, but she regains all and is reinstated. The TV movie may interest avid readers in this story.

[4]Burnett, Frances Hodgson. *The Secret Garden*. 1911. Philadelphia: Lippincott, 1962. The unloved Mary's spunky attitude, as she overcomes

her problems, discovers the secret garden and bullies Colin back to health, makes this still a magically appealing story for the confirmed reader.

[5]Nesbit, Edith. *The Story of the Treasure Seekers*. 1899. London: Benn, 1932. The humorous day by day adventures of a large Victorian family may still appeal to the confirmed reader, but the lifestyle will seem very curious to the North American child.

[6]Nesbit, Edith. *The Enchanted Castle*. 1907. London: Benn, 1931. In this humorous fantasy, the children discover a castle with a "princess" who shows them some supposedly "magic" jewelry. The fact that one ring is magic leads to complications. This will appeal to the thoughtful +11 reader.

[7]Nesbit, Edith. *The Phoenix and the Carpet*. 1904. London: Benn, 1931. In this fantasy, the irascible phoenix guides an impoverished family on adventures, most of which end in disaster, via a magic carpet. Will appeal to the avid +11 reader who does not let the outdated language and customs get in the way.

[8]Ransome, Arthur. *Swallows and Amazons*. 1930. London: Cape, 1934. Four children camping and sailing in England's Lake District discover two local girls whose prior claim to the island leads to a pretend war. Particularly appealing to children who love boats. +10.

[9]Lewis, Clive Staples. *The Lion, the Witch & the Wardrobe*. 1950. London: Macmillan, 1983. In this first great fantasy for children, a family finds the world of Narnia and is precipitated into the ongoing war between good and evil. An eminently readable classic for the +10 child.

[10]MacDonald, George. *At the Back of the North Wind*. 1871. London: Macmillan, 1950. The dream fantasy adventures of a child from a Victorian London slum is heavy on the moralizing, but still appeals to some young readers in the +12 range.

[11]Dickinson, Peter. *The Gift*. New York: Little, 1973. The terrible "gift" of second sight gives a modern boy insight into a crime in which his own father is involved. Realistic and enthralling, set in industrial England and in Wales, this is appropriate for the +12 reader.

[12]Westall, Robert. *The Wind Eye*. London: Macmillan, 1976. In this time-travel fantasy, a blended family with problems journeys into the time of St. Cuthbert and the Viking invasion. An enthralling realistic story for the +12 reader.

[13]Sendak, Maurice. *Outside Over There*. New York: Harper, 1981. Only Ida seems aware that a changeling has replaced her small brother and she must rescue him. The dark overtones of this picture book make it more appropriate for the older child than the preschooler.

[14]Voigt, Cynthia. *The Homecoming*. New York: Atheneum, 1981. Abandoned by their distraught mother, Dicey and her siblings find their way to their grandmother's home. Dicey's obstinate determination to avoid adult

help is logical, the story is believable and engrossing, with fine values. For the +11.

[15]May, Rollo. *The Cry for Myth*. New York/London: Norton, 1991. The author uses examples of folktale, Greek tragedy and the stories of Peer Gynt and Faust to explain the need for myth in today's world and to suggest methods of healing. Adult.

[16]Yolen, Jane. *Touch Magic*. New York: Philomel Books, 1981. Yolen retells folktales with wit to develop her theme, that myth stories are necessary guideposts in life. A brilliant innovative work suitable for young adult to adult.

[17]Tolkien, J.R.R. *Lord of the Rings*. 1954. Boston: Houghton, 1982. In this trilogy, Tolkien introduces the reader to a mythic alternate world, with its own language, geography, history and mythology. Its strength lies in the believability and vulnerability of the characters struggling against the power of evil. 12 to adult.

Growing Up in the Phoenix Award Books

Alethea K. Helbig

Most stories for young readers involve children or teenagers who, through their experiences in the book, become informed about life and begin to see themselves as part of the larger unit. They mature, or become more mature, emotionally and intellectually, and often also physically, in the book. Terms sometimes used interchangeably with "growing up" for this kind of novel are "maturation," "apprenticeship," "developmental" and *Bildungs-roman*," and they all mean much the same thing. Another term occasionally employed is "rites of passage," and while the rites-of-passage and the growing-up stories come to the same in the end— the young persons see themselves as part of the larger community and are better able to take their places in it—the rites-of-passage novel differs significantly from the growing-up story.

The term "rites of passage" derives from the work of a French anthropologist and folklorist of the very early 20th century, Arnold van Gennep, who published his findings in *Les Rites de Passage*. After an extensive survey of old and contemporary societies, he concluded that such rites have been experienced everywhere. Richly symbolic ceremonies, they move people from one social stage in life to another. He declared that each of these sets of rites wherever practiced at whatever stage in life is characterized by three phases: separation, transformation and reincorporation.

The rites of passage into maturity (which is the one we are interested in) always involves a rebirth and represents a dramatic departure from the previous condition of youth. During the ceremonies, initiates are ritually "killed" from their former way of life and made to mature in their new states. The rites usually involve a task or ordeal of some sort, the acquiring of special knowledge and physical alteration of the body, perhaps tattooing or incisions. The process dramatically severs individuals from their previous states and launches them into a new stage in the life of their community.

The rites-of-passage story has an element of dramatic intensity, then, that the growing-up novel lacks. In the growing-up story, the maturing is a gradual process. It may involve many events in the

163

book, some, of course, more important for that outcome than others. But a rites-of-passage or initiation novel features one or a couple of very closely related incidents that are intense experiences in themselves and that move, maybe even catapult, the young person into maturity. The experience, like the initiation rituals in primitive societies, strips away old ideas and behaviors and forces the young people to see themselves and life differently from before.

The Laura Ingalls Wilder Little House books are growing-up novels. Laura quite literally goes from childhood to adulthood in the seven books. She also grows up psycho-socially from an independent, tomboyish child often at odds with authority to a responsible self-controlled young matron of whom her social environment approves. Although there are many tense scenes in the books, Laura's maturation is a gradual process. Hers is a growing-up story in the purest sense. Similarly, *Anne of Green Gables* by L.M. Montgomery takes its heroine, another bright, strong-willed girl, from childhood to adulthood physically, psychologically and intellectually, like Laura.

Among boy's growing-up stories a notable example is Esther Forbes's *Johnny Tremain*. One might argue that the maiming of Johnny's hand in itself makes the novel a rites-of-passage one, since that traumatic experience plunges him into a different world. But a careful consideration of the plot suggests otherwise. The book focuses on how Johnny will handle his physical handicap: whether he can overcome his anger, resentment, despair and his own self-destructive tendencies, and whether he will make a worthwhile life for himself again. No one single incident changes Johnny's outlook on life, but rather an extended series of happenings matures him.

On the other hand, *The Yearling* by Marjorie Kinnan Rawlings is a fine example of a rites-of-passage book. Flag, Jody's pet deer, becomes a threat to the family's existence, damaging and eating their small crops. When Jody procrastinates about shooting the animal, Jody's mother steps in, but succeeds only in severely wounding the deer. Confronted by the necessity of relieving his pet's suffering, Jody forces himself to kill Flag. He runs away in his grief but returns with the realization that the family's welfare must take precedence over his personal wishes. He understands that he must put away childish things and assume the responsibility of provider and protector, the man's estate. As in cultural initiations, the rites-of-passage novel may involve the doing of an actual deed that is a test of one's readiness, as in *The Yearling*, and may be painful physically, emotionally and spiritually. It may also include a sudden insight into self or circumstances, but it always involves trauma. Jody's initiation into manhood is all these.

The winners and honor books from the Phoenix Award[1] have been singled out for critical acclaim because of their high and lasting literary quality. The list, begun in 1985, shows how frequently these two types of novels occur and also clearly demonstrates the difference between them. Of the 14 books named to the list through 1992, 11 are either growing-up or rites-of-passage stories.

Of the three that do not qualify as either type, two are honor books, Milton Meltzer's *Brother, Can You Spare a Dime?* and *Ravensgill* by William Mayne. The former is a well-written and gripping account of the Great Depression, which was certainly a traumatic period in United States history, but since the book is nonfiction, it is out of the scope of this discussion. *Ravensgill* is a mystery-detective novel in which a long-standing feud between two Yorkshire families is laid to rest by the persistent sleuthing of a young man of one of the families. The teenaged protagonist does not change as a result of his experiences, beyond gaining knowledge about his family and the people of the region as he solves the mystery. For a book to be a growing-up book or rites-of-passage story, something more than that must happen to the person. The change in this book is too outer localized to fit either type.

Of the remaining honor books, *Sing Down the Moon* by Scott O'Dell is only marginally a growing-up story. Bright Morning, a Navaho girl, does gain new strength, which is particularly revealed in her ability to make decisions, and she shows great fortitude. But what one carries away from reading this book about the forced removal of the Navaho from their Arizona homeland by the United States soldiers in the mid-19th century is a keen sense of the Navaho tragedy, and thus Bright Morning becomes representative of what happened to these Native Americans in the face of the white advance. Bright Morning is less interesting than what happens to her people on the death march now known as the Long Walk. Her story is subordinate to that of the Navaho.

Three honor books do qualify as rites-of-passage stories: *Pistol* by Adrienne Richard, *A Game of Dark* by William Mayne and *The Tombs of Atuan* by Ursula LeGuin.

Pistol is a richly detailed and substantial story set in Montana ranch country at the very beginning of the Great Depression. In addition to the problems of survival that face Billy Catlett's family because of the economic crash, much of the story's conflict revolves around the father, who is the sort who chases rainbows. When the ranches shut down and businesses in Great Plain fold, Mr. Catlett simply takes off, leaving his two teenaged sons to provide for themselves and their mother however they can. Later he returns, having decided the family shall move to Deal, a wide-open town on the Missouri River where the federal government is erecting a huge dam. When Billy summons the courage to tell his father they must leave Deal because the unsavory environment is killing his mother, he learns Mr. Catlett has already decided to move back to Great Plain. Billy moves too, but he has grown apart and makes the big decision to leave home and find out what the outside world has to offer. He sees himself now as part of a much larger unit than his family and in breaking the ties with them he joins that larger unit. The book's end finds him punching cows on a cattle train heading for market in Chicago. Billy's decision is difficult and significant and of rites-of-passage calibre, but it by no means involves the pain Jody suffers in *The Yearling*.

Except looked at as a convincing psychoanalytic picture of a rapidly disintegrating personality, *A Game of Dark* is less compelling for its real-world story than for the fantasy one that is woven throughout the real-world narrative. Donald's father is an invalid who is often in great pain. Donald's mother's life revolves around that of her husband, a rigid, demanding and fault-finding man. Donald's self-esteem is so low that he is driven to find solace in a fantasy world of chivalry that exists only in his head and where he progresses from errand boy to squire to knight.

When, in the real world, a family friend tells Donald how his father came to be injured and something of how the man became so difficult to live with, Donald kills the dragon in his made-up world. In the real world he knows his father is dying, but, with this new knowledge, in his heart he becomes reconciled to his father, "whom he knew now how to love" (142). When his father's breathing ceases, "Donald lay and listened to the quiet, and went to sleep, consolate" (143). In the fantasy world, he has killed the dragon that symbolizes the resentment and guilt that have plagued him in the real world and thus he is at peace with his father and feels better about himself. This is clearly a rites-of-passage story.

The early part of *The Tombs of Atuan* is a growing-up story because it summarizes the physical maturation of the protagonist, Arha, the priestess of a temple complex in the world of Earthsea. A rites-of-passage incident, however, occurs about halfway through the novel, and in that way this book is different from both *Pistol* and *A Game of Dark*, where the initiation takes place near the end.

Having suffered tremendous guilt for allowing three prisoners to starve to death (a customary mode of capital punishment in her country) and faced with having to kill another, Arha rebels, turns on her mentor priestess, lays a curse on the woman and thus becomes a new person in her own right. She calls herself Tenar, a name symbolic of her new personhood. The characterization of Tenar presents a problem, however. Overall she is a passive, unself-reliant figure, and at the very end she is described as walking beside the man she has helped to escape "up the white streets of Havnor, holding his hand, like a child coming home" (163). This is the second novel in the Earthsea series and the remaining two books must be considered in completing the picture of Tenar. But the particular incident in which she curses the priestess marks a distinct turning point in her life, and the episode is certainly dramatic and traumatic.

Among the Phoenix Award winners, only *The Night Watchmen* by Helen Cresswell fits into neither category. In this charming story about a plucky little boy who becomes friends with two engaging, middle-aged tramps and helps them evade terrible night villains called Greeneyes, little happens to Henry as a person. He is the vehicle by which we follow the tramps who are more central and more interesting than Henry.

Four winners are growing-up novels. David of *The Rider and His Horse* by Erik Christian Haugaard changes gradually as he learns about circumstances in the dark and turbulent world of conflict between Jews and Romans in first century Palestine. He learns much about human nature, too. But themes dominate this book—the futility of war as a means of problem solving and the human tendency to engage in heroics or exhibitionist behavior and to make symbolic statements, which in the end may hurt more people than are helped.

Calling Sylvia Louise Engdahl's *The Enchantress from the Stars* a growing-up story may be laboring the term, since the emphasis in the book falls not upon what happens to Elana herself so much as on whether the Imperialists can be stopped from taking over the Younglings' world of Andrecia. As in *Ravensgill* and *Sing Down the Moon*, the main action is outer directed rather than inner localized. Elana, however, does learn something about people and about the objectives and procedures of the Federation, the secret service group of which she is an agent. She also learns the importance of self-control and of thinking before she acts. Like David in *The Rider and His Horse*, she becomes a soberer and more intellectually and emotionally mature young person by the end of this gripping science fantasy.

A Long Way from Verona by Jane Gardam is an amusing, sharply characterized story of a year early in World War II in which independent, outspoken English Jessica Vye experiences first love, narrowly escapes death in a bombing and wins a poetry contest. It might be argued that, at the point where Jessica goes to the house of her favorite teacher, Miss Philemon, finds the place bombed to rubble and realizes that the woman is really dead—no one could have survived such terrible destruction—one might claim that at that point Jessica grows up. But there are several other places that are also important in her development. This is just one of a number that contribute to her maturation. Jessica's is a growing-up novel.

The last of the growing-up stories among the Phoenix winners is Mollie Hunter's *A Sound of Chariots*, an autobiographical novel of a Scottish girl who copes with the death of her beloved father and pursues her dream of becoming a writer. Here again, a memorable scene might be taken as a rites-of-passage episode but really is only one of several that contribute to Bridie's development. The girl goes one night after dark to take her mother's coat to her where she works. Unable to find the servants' entrance, Bridie blunders into the front hallway, tracking dirt on the carpeting. The English lady of the house, Bridie's mother's employer, scolds Bridie's mother and the lady's son openly scorns the Scottish people. For the first time, Bridie sees the high price her widowed mother must pay not only physically but also emotionally to hold her family together. This scene clarifies the girl's image of her mother and helps alleviate tension that has arisen between them. But the mother-daughter conflict is only one of the book's problems. This novel fits better as a growing-up story where the maturing comes through a series of episodes over a period of time than a rites-of-passage where the maturation is more sudden.

The three remaining winners are clearly rites-of-passage stories, *Smith* by Leon Garfield, *Queenie Peavy* by Robert Burch and *The Mark of the Horse Lord* by Rosemary Sutcliff. In *Smith*, a scroungy, 18th-century London street urchin of that name picks an old gentleman's pocket of a document. The boy's efforts to learn to read and to evade assassins hot on his trail make for action-filled, extremely suspenseful reading. Two places in the book figure in Smith's initiation, the first best taken as a balance and foreshadowing of the second, bigger one. While fleeing from the assassins who murdered the old gentleman and will also kill him, in the dark city streets Smith quite literally bumps into a blind man, a magistrate or justice of the peace. This blind man arouses feeling of sympathy in Smith—a most unusual emotion for the boy. Smith helps the blind man get home and the magistrate becomes his mentor. Smith's rehabilitation, his entry into life, has begun.

Events tumble over one another to happen in the Dickensian convoluted plot and eventually to his horror Smith realizes that the villains have also marked the blind magistrate for murder. The culminating rites-of-passage episode occurs in a blinding snowstorm on Finchley Common, after Smith discovers that the magistrate's coach is to be waylaid. Smith intercepts the coach, yanks the magistrate out and hides him in the bushes. In his effort to save the man, Smith forgets that he, Smith, has ironically become a fugitive from justice and that the magistrate is, of course, a representative of the law. Saving the man's life has wiped from Smith's mind what he has always thought of first—himself. A little later, he again saves the blind man's life in the melodramatic showdown with the villains in a cemetery. In the ensuing fracas, most of the evil-doers are slain. Smith is rewarded financially, but beyond that and more importantly, he emerges with a new sense of self-respect and life-direction. He is a human being, or as he puts it, a "yoomanbeen," a person in spite of his gutter-rat background, and he sees possibilities in life he never before dreamed existed.

Georgia schoolgirl Queenie Peavy, in the novel of the same name, persists in causing trouble. She acts out her anger and resentment at being the object of scorn because her father is in jail. When she causes her arch-enemy and chief tormentor, classmate Cravey Mason, to break a leg, the principal threatens to expel her. Then she is wrongfully accused of throwing stones through the windows of the Baptist Church and fears she will be sent to the reformatory. She is sure, however, that when her father is released from prison, all will be well. Once home again, however, he shows no interest in her, even snubs her, soon gets into trouble with the law and is sent back to jail. Realizing he does not really care for his family, near to despair, Queenie experiences a flash of insight. Ready to pitch a stone through the one remaining church window, she has an inspiration:

She took aim again, but her own voice nagged: "Just you wait...Go wild if you want to, see if I care! But who are you hurting in the long run?" (155)

Suddenly she sees that she herself and she alone is responsible for the course of her life. She cannot blame her problems on what has happened to her father; she can no longer make him her excuse. She decides she does not want to live in the "shadow of the jail"

(104) anymore and starts to put her considerable energies to work becoming a productive member of society.

The most moving rites-of-passage episode of all the Phoenix books appears in the first winner, a book set in Roman Britain, *The Mark of the Horse Lord*. Here, as in *Smith*, we have an initially unlikeable protagonist. Phaedrus kills his best friend in the gladiators' arena and wins the wooden foil that ends his bondage. Never having had freedom before, Phaedrus does not know what to do with it. He goes out on the town, causes trouble and lands in jail. Asked under mysterious circumstances to impersonate a Scottish tribal king, he accepts. It seems an interesting diversion, and he has nothing better to do. After undergoing a period of training in the ways of the tribe, he is introduced at assembly as the rightful king, and the woman who has usurped the throne and declared herself queen flees.

Phaedrus grows into the kingship, ironically showing a surprising amount of leadership ability and an aptitude for handling himself well in tense situations. He finds, to his surprise, that he likes these people and sympathizes with them in their struggles to maintain their sovereignty. He even marries, as the king is expected to do. When war comes, he directs the enterprise, showing resource and ingenuity. The tribe succeeds in defeating the queen's forces, but she gets away and goes to the Romans for refuge. In the attempt to kill her—because as long as she lives she will be a threat to the tribe—Phaedrus is captured by the Romans. They agree to free him, but at a very high price: they will release him in return for 1000 fighting men from the tribe to serve in the legions. What this proposal amounts to is the life of the king at the cost of the life of the tribe, because surrendering so many males will result in eliminating the tribe as a people.

Phaedrus has grown fond of these tribespeople and now thinks of himself as one of them and sees himself as their leader. It is the custom of this tribe that the king must always be ready to die for his people; this is one of his responsibilities. At this point Phaedrus realizes that if he is going to be their king—and not just in title—he must die for them, and he does. He takes his own life rather than command his people to surrender their men.

He had been playing idly with the great enameled brooch at his shoulder...working it free. He had it in the hollow of his hand now. His fingers closed over it so that only the tip of the deadly pin that was almost as long as a small dagger projected between them. He had plenty of time to find the place, the two-inch place just to the left of the breastbone...

The freed folds of his cloak fell away from him as he got a knee across the rampart coping and next instant had sprung erect...He opened his fingers, freeing the whole deadly length of the great pin, and drove it home.

The taste of blood rushed into his mouth. He plunged forward into the sun dazzle and felt himself falling. He never felt the jagged stones in the ditch. (243)

Thus ends *The Mark of the Horse Lord*, with Phaedrus's death, his rite-of-passage into the tribe. Death is Phaedrus's initiation. In death he earns his kingship. In death he becomes the king he has thus far only pretended to be. His story is a rites-of-passage novel. The growing-up and rites-of-passage genres are similar, but this book and other Phoenix books demonstrate the essential difference between the two forms.[2]

Notes

[1]The Phoenix Award of The Children's Literature Association (ChLA) is given annually to the author, or the estate of the author, of a book for children published 20 years earlier that did not win a major award at the time of its publication but is deemed worthy of special recognition for its high literary quality. Recipients are determined by an elected committee of ChLA members. Honor books may also be named.

[2]A collection of essays about the Phoenix Award books was published in 1993 by Scarecrow Press, Inc., in conjunction with The Children's Literature Association.

The Phoenix Award Winners
(listed by year of award)

1985—*The Mark of the Horse Lord* by Rosemary Sutcliff. Oxford, 1965; Walck, 1965.

1986—*Queenie Peavy* by Robert Burch. Viking, 1966.

1987—*Smith* by Leon Garfield. Constable, 1967; Pantheon, 1967.

1988—*The Rider and His Horse* by Erik Christian Haugaard. Houghton, 1968.

1989—*The Night Watchmen* by Helen Cresswell. Faber, 1969; Macmillan, 1969.

1990—*Enchantress from the Stars* by Sylvia Louise Engdahl. Atheneum, 1970.

1991—*A Long Way from Verona* by Jane Gardam. Hamilton, 1971; Macmillan, 1971.

1992—*A Sound of Chariots* by Mollie Hunter. Hamilton, 1972; Harper, 1972.

The Phoenix Award Honor Books
(listed by year of award)

1989—*Brother, Can You Spare a Dime?* by Milton Meltzer. Knopf, 1969.
Pistol by Adrienne Richard. Little, 1969.

1990—*Ravensgill* by William Mayne. Hamilton, 1970; Dutton, 1970.
Sing Down the Moon by Scott O'Dell. Houghton, 1970.

1991—*A Game of Dark* by William Mayne. Hamilton, 1971; Dutton, 1971.
The Tombs of Atuan by Ursula LeGuin. Atheneum, 1971.

Works Cited

Burch, Robert. *Queenie Peavy.* New York: Viking, 1966.

Cresswell, Helen. *The Night Watchmen.* London: Faber & Faber, 1969; New York: Macmillan, 1969.

Engdahl, Sylvia Louise. *Enchantress from the Stars.* New York: Atheneum, 1970.

Gardam, Jane. *A Long Way from Verona.* London: Hamish Hamilton, 1971; New York: Macmillan, 1971.

Garfield, Leon. *Smith.* London: Constable Young, 1967; New York: Pantheon, 1967.

Haugaard, Erik Christian. *The Rider and His Horse.* Boston: Houghton, 1968.

Hunter, Mollie. *A Sound of Chariots.* London: Hamish Hamilton, 1972; New York: Harper, 1972.

LeGuin, Ursula. *The Tombs of Atuan.* New York: Atheneum, 1971.

Mayne, William. *A Game of Dark.* London: Hamish Hamilton, 1971; New York: Dutton, 1971.

———. *Ravensgill.* London: Hamish Hamilton, 1970; New York: Dutton, 1970.

Meltzer, Milton. *Brother, Can You Spare a Dime?* New York: Knopf, 1969.

O'Dell, Scott. *Sing Down the Moon.* Boston: Houghton, 1970.

Richard, Adrienne. *Pistol.* Boston: Little, 1969.

Sutcliff, Rosemary. *The Mark of the Horse Lord.* London: Oxford UP, 1965; New York: Walck, 1965.

Winslow Homer's Lost Boys

Joseph Stanton

Winslow Homer's depictions of children have at least two tales to tell. Two separate, but not incompatible, narratives can be discovered in certain of Homer's pictures of children: a popular narrative growing out of a largely conventionalized late-19th-century nostalgia for childhood and a private narrative that gives form to some unresolved personal dilemmas with which the artist was struggling at the time the pictures were made. In telling these two tales I will emphasize three important paintings: *Snap the Whip*, *Dad's Coming*, and *Breezing Up*.

Snap the Whip

Snap the Whip is Homer's most famous contribution to his era's romanticization of boyhood. The cult of the barefoot country (or small-town) boy in the arts of the late 19th century is a prominent feature of the mentality of the age. Literary cultivations of the fad included Charles Dudley Warner's now little-remembered volume of musings entitled *Being a Boy* as well as Mark Twain's timeless tales of Huck and Tom. John Greenleaf Whittier perhaps best captured the appeal of the idea in his poem "The Barefoot Boy." The condition of barefoot boyhood was celebrated in Whittier's poem both for what it seemed to be—an endless "laughing day" filled with "painless play"—and for what it seemed to provide escape from—entrapment in "the mills of toil" and "the prison cells of pride" symbolized by the shoes that irrevocably separate the adult from "the freedom of the sod."

Homer was heavily implicated in the popularity of images of children through his work as an illustrator for a broad range of materials. His pictures of boys and girls at play appeared in *Harper's Weekly*, *Our Young Folk*, and several other journals. He also illustrated a number of books that required him to depict children. By the 1870s when Homer was doing his best pictures of children, his reputation was such that his images were often printed for their own sake. Toward the end of his career as an illustrator there were several instances of the reversal of the normal pattern: Homer was some-

173

times asked to provide pictures, which then served as inspirations for the writing of poems to be published beside the pictures. For instance, poems by Lucy Larcom, John Trowbridge, and Richard Henry Stoddard were composed for *Our Young Folks* to accompany a suite of Homer pictures of childhood activities. These pictures—*Watching the Crows*, *Green Apples*, *The Strawberry Bed*, *Bird Catchers*, and *Swinging on a Birch Tree*—which were entirely of Homer's invention—are among the best of his pictures of childhood subjects to appear in popular journals (Tatham, *Winslow Homer and the Illustrated Book* 91-93).

Although Homer's labors in the depiction of kids certainly made business sense with regard to the wide audience that welcomed such images, there are a multitude of signs that his interest in the theme was more to him than a canny choice of products to peddle. An indication that Homer's depictions of children were motivated by more than the marketplace can be found in the earliest Homer pictures extant, drawings and even paintings of his brothers at play and doing chores. Homer was making remarkable pictures of children when he himself was yet a child. A drawing of his brothers Charles and Arthur playing "beetle and wedge" that Homer sketched at age 11 is cited by Homer's first biographer, William Howe Downes, as evidence of the young artist's precocity (25-26). An awkward oil painting of Arthur Homer feeding chickens is another interesting example of Homer's boyish attempt, as a participating observer, to chronicle barefoot boyhood.

All Homer biographers agree that Winslow loved his younger years growing up in a Cambridge that was at that time an "overgrown village," a country place that offered ample opportunities for "fishing, boating, and other rural sports dear to the heart of boyhood." For Homer the celebration of country childhood was not merely a fashionable exercise. He looked on his early years "with pleasure in after years as a period of joyous freedom" (Downes 24-25). Homer's affection for boyhood—unlike the contrived affections evident in many of the hackneyed stories and pictures that flourished in abundance in the magazines—was the direct result of his personal experiences. His renderings of childhood activities have an authenticity that comes from actual recollection as well as actual observation. Lloyd Goodrich sums up the achievement of Homer's pictures of boys: "Rarely has such sympathy with childhood been united with such utter unsentimentality" (29).

One sign of the truth to experience of Homer's renderings is the prevalence of schools in Homer's pictures of children. In the boyhood books of Warner and Twain schools seldom put in an appearance—a circumstance highly contrary to the actuality of childhood. In Warner's *Being a Boy*, school only appears when a little boy is seen walking a girl home from one. For Warner even winter is an endless summer of boyish country fun. But Homer renders the one-room country schoolhouse so often and so well that his depictions provide, in certain respects, the best historical record available to historians of the way those places looked from both the inside and the outside. Besides the several versions of *Snap the Whip*, other Homer pictures that show the schoolhouse exterior are *School Time* and *The Red Schoolhouse*. Among the best known Homer interiors of the schoolhouse are *The Country School, New England Country School, Kept After School*, and *Blackboard*. All of Homer's one-room-schoolhouse pictures from the 1870s appear to show the same basic building, which has given rise to the supposition that all or most of them grew out of one or more periods of observation of a particular building. As Cikovsky has pointed out, Homer captured the American school just shortly after women had begun to predominate as teachers, taking over the profession from the formidable and frequently pompous male schoolmasters who had become the objects of fun in a good many popular literary and pictorial works ("Winslow Homer's School Time" 53-57).

Homer's school scenes portray the duality between the outside world of play and the inside world of educational captivity that structures the experience of childhood. Although it is clear that outside is where fun and freedom are to be had, the interiors are not made to seem bad places to be. In *The Country School*, all the children, with two exceptions, appear to be contentedly attending to their assigned tasks. The little boy who has put his book down and is crying and the little girl who is watching him weep are minor exceptions that do not detract from the overall orderliness of the pretty young teacher's apparently well-managed and pleasant classroom. The teacher is by no means a villain here. In fact, in several of the pictures we can identify with the teacher as readily as we can with the students. In *Kept After School*, for instance, the boy who is being disciplined is contentedly reading an assignment, while the teacher stares out the window, daydreaming; the image suggests that the teacher is at least as anxious to escape to the outside as is her young scholar.

Snap the Whip is probably America's most famous image of energetic children joyously freed from schoolhouse confinement. In *Snap the Whip* we see the classic little red schoolhouse as a backdrop for a boyish rough-and-tumble game that was an inspired choice of subject matter for a picture. The advantages, and difficulties, of a horizontal line of figures for pictorial composition were well known to Homer through the lessons learned in his long apprenticeship as an illustrator. *Prisoners from the Front*, Homer's celebrated Civil War painting, was one of his first good solutions with its line of defeated Confederates exhibiting subtly contrasting expressions and postures. In *Snap the Whip* the solution is more than good. The poise of each boy is separate and energetic, yet the line exhibits a continuous ripple of motion that has an attractive unity. Each child is charged with the energy of the game as the effect of the pulled back "whip" passes down the line causing the last two to tumble to the ground. Perhaps Homer's later mastery of the seascape can be deduced from this breaking wave of boys.

Homer seems to have endeavored to keep alive in his mind the happy memory of his childhood. Tatham's recent examination of "Winslow Homer's Library" revealed that Homer kept in his limited collection of books a volume entitled *The Boy's Treasury of Sports, Pastimes, and Recreations* that was probably given to him when he was about 11 or 12 years of age; perhaps he received it from his father shortly before the elder Homer's ill-fated journey to California that I will be discussing later. Some of Homer's earliest surviving sketches were made on the flyleaf of that volume, including a lively sketch of a man fishing. Homer's preservation of this boyhood book about boyhood things is indicative of a lingering interest in the activities of youth. The book may have served him both as a sentimental momento of his own childhood and as a reminder of the recreational pursuits of children.

It could be argued that Homer never had to grow up. His work as an artist was for him a kind of play as well as a most serious vocation. Furthermore, the solitary and self-directed nature of his artistic career, as well as the fact that he never married, allowed Homer considerable freedom of movement. He was, thus, able to continue for his entire life the activities he loved as a child— particularly hiking, boating, and fishing. Homer can be regarded as an eccentric Peter Pan figure of relentless, stubborn boyishness, but there also appears to be a dark side to his choice of a manner of life.

Dad's Coming

The young boy depicted in *Dad's Coming* gazing out to sea from a perch in the prow of a small, beached boat bears some resemblance in his dress and general appearance to the boys depicted at play in *Snap the Whip* and other Homer works of the happy-nostalgia type, but this boy is not at play and the work as a whole has no happiness to its nostalgia. What we have here is, rather, a highly personal statement of the artist's concerns about his own life—past, present, and future. To say that this picture can be understood as expressive of Homer's personal life and concerns is not to say that he meant it to embody any such revelations. Homer was an intensely private man and had he known that anything could be inferred about his life from his pictures he might have given up picture making. The personal narrative inherent in this work can, in fact, only be gathered because, like most artists, Homer was obsessively repetitive about the themes that had for him the greatest personal resonance. Although it is easier to focus on one or two works for purposes of discussion, it is the careful study of all available works by an artist that allows for the discovery of the person in the art. A presence emerges from the whole that is elusive when the parts are considered in isolation.

Homer's few statements about the art of making art tend to emphasize his awareness that he was engaged in a business enterprise. He was proud of his success in the business, but avoided discussions of his artistic strategies whenever he could. His decision to do seaside scenes at Gloucester harbor in Massachusetts and his choice of particular seaside motifs could be entirely explained as business decisions. Homer knew that customers would like images of barefoot boys down by the shore. He painted what he thought would sell, but, as we witness Homer's developing mastery of his art at Gloucester—especially his ongoing discovery of some of the roles the ocean can play in his work—we are witnessing something more profound than a successful business venture. Beginning at Gloucester, Homer's pictures conceived on the edges of various seas seem those that most powerfully unlock "the stern poetry of feeling" (Van Rensselaer 19) that was to mark his greatest later works.

Although Homer loved being a boy, as *Snap the Whip* and many other pictures show, a cloud hung over the later years of his boyhood because of his father's misconceived pursuit of a pot of gold that remained out of reach. When Homer was about 12 years old, the elder Homer caught the "forty-niner" gold fever and sold his hardware business to finance his travel west in hopes of gaining riches. When he finally returned home to stay several years later, his family had been through an ordeal of waiting and worrying. The family finances remained precarious from the time of the elder Homer's expedition until the time when the business successes of

Winslow's older brother Charles put the Homer clan on solid footing again.

Dad's Coming[1] and related Gloucester images as well as the large number of watching-the-sea-for-the-return-of-the-husband pictures Homer did at Cullercoats in England are probably unconscious commentaries on the crisis that complicated Homer's world just at the time of his transition from childhood to adolescence. Homer's staring-out-to-sea pictures are picturesque seaside scenes. We could simply confine ourselves to appreciating the strength of these pictures as pictures without regarding the artist's life and personal anxieties, but Homer's preoccupation with the staring-out-to-sea motif suggests a powerful underlying narrative that must be addressed in any attempt at a full critical description of these works. The narrative can be stated with stark simplicity, as it relates to Homer's childhood anxiety. The boys are waiting for the return of their fathers just as Homer, when he was their age, had waited for the return of his. But simplistic biographical interpretations are always problematic. An image has multiple lives. I will say more about this later, but it is also important to note that Homer, who was to remain unmarried and childless, may have also felt some sense of identity with the nonarriving father.

Indeed, always implicit in such scenes is the dire possibility of nonarrival. The sea is a highly effective means for suggesting this grim possibility. The sea can quite literally be a killer of fishermen—this immediate and palpable danger will be more explicitly considered in Homer's Cullercoats pictures—but the equation of the sea with the possibility of death also has a broader appropriateness.[2] Whether in the poems of Tennyson or the paintings of Caspar David Friedrich we easily understand that facing the sea means the facing of an image of a vastness that seems to be infinite. Coupled with this sense of vastness is our instinctive understanding of the nature of water. To enter water is to lose human form, to be consumed; hence the importance of water in religious rituals involving concepts of death and rebirth. A submersion involves loss of form and a rising out of water, a rebirth (Eliade 139-31).

The sea-gazing-boys theme became prominent in Homer's work all at once in the Gloucester watercolors of the 1870s and the oil paintings that grew out of those more spontaneous works. The question of fatherhood was becoming important for Homer in a double way at that time. He was observing the aging and decline of his own parents at a time when he was considering marrying and raising a family of his own. Significant in this set of circumstances was

the outcome of his marriage prospects. Whether it was his decision or
the decision of the woman in whom he was interested, Homer did
not marry, and, after the masterworks of childhood depiction of the
1870s and the babes-on-the-backs-of-their-mothers images he did at
Cullercoats in 1881-82, children largely disappeared from his work.

Before looking closely at *Dad's Coming* it will be useful to
examine briefly a few other of Homer's images of boys pondering the
horizon. The many pictures Homer did of boys staring out to sea,
treat the boys yearning for the father's return in a gentle way. Despite
a vaguely meditative quality to these pictures, which has sometimes
been referred to as a tone of sadness, there seems little suggestion
that tragedies are in the offing—again this is in contrast to the
Cullercoats pictures where it is obvious that loss of life is a real and
present danger for the fishermen. It is not surprising in fact that not
much has been said about the likelihood that all of Homer's
Gloucester watchers were waiting for their dads. So quiet and
dreamy and free of apparent anxiety are these pictures that it is easy
for the sadness and yearning of these pictures to be overlooked. In
Three Boys on the Shore, Schooners in Gloucester Harbor, and
Marblehead we can enjoy the composition and feeling of leisure
implicit in these scenes of boys sprawled on harbor rocks to scan the
horizons without concerning ourselves about what the boys are
doing. Similarly, the boy in *Watching the Harbor* is set by Homer in a
patch of flowers that is so visually satisfying that we could easily be
distracted from considering why the watcher is watching. *Waiting for
the Boats* is an image that has often puzzled writers on Homer—
Cooper, for instance, calls it "oddly disturbing" (23)—but, when we
consider it in relation to *Dad's Coming* it loses its mystery. Why is the
one boy putting his hand of the shoulder of another boy, as if to
comfort him? It would seem likely that the boy who is in need of
reassurance is concerned about an unreturned father.

Dad's Coming makes the narrative implications clear. As John
Wilmerding has pointed out, it is "a painting at once about family and
about isolation" (209). A small boy is perched in the prow of a small
boat tied up on the shore. He stares out to sea from this position of
slight elevation. His stance and gaze suggest that he has not yet
spotted his father. The alternative title, *Waiting for Dad,* although not
used by most art historians, would be a more accurate description of
the situation than *Dad's Coming* with its implication of safely
accomplished resolution. The boy's yearning for the dad to come is
accentuated by the centrality of the boy's placement as well as by the
way he is silhouetted against the sky, sitting, it seems, on the

horizonline at the apex of a dramatically triangular substructure. The boy and his desire for dad has been placed on a kind of pedestal that is saved from sentimentality by the austereness of the painting's style and the contrasting nature of the mother's stance.[3]

We know that the boy came first in the conception of this design. In the first version the boy poised in the little boat was the only figure—the mother and baby were absent. Despite the importance that waiting wives would later have in the Cullercoats works, it is a waiting son that dominates this most substantial early depiction of seaside watching.

The figure of the woman is, however, also of considerable importance, in the narrative of the picture and, apparently, in the largely unrecorded narrative of Homer's life. Lloyd Goodrich, Helen Cooper, and others have discussed the possibility that the flower painter Helena de Kay, who became Mrs. Richard Watson Gilder in 1874, may have been the "mystery woman" in whom Homer had some degree of marital interest (Cooper 51). Homer's sympathy for and identification with the nonarriving father in this picture can be easily understood to be more than a trivial consideration when one notices that the waiting wife is, in fact, a depiction of Helena de Kay. This resemblance is born out by other depictions of de Kay by Homer—the definitive image being the *Portrait of Helena de Kay*, dedicated to her as a wedding gift in 1874. A strong case can be made that the female figures in a variety of other pictures—including the paintings *Shall I Tell Your Fortune?* and *Moonlight* and the book illustrations for Longfellow's "Excelsior"—are also images based on de Kay. Except in the case of the *Portrait*, however, these other "portrait" designations are merely speculations based on general resemblances of face, hair style, and wardrobe. It is important to note that de Kay was working in the Tenth Street Studio Building in New York at the same time as Homer. That de Kay posed for several Homer pictures proves nothing about their relationship; however, her starring role in *Dad's Coming* adds a further, possibly ironical, dimension to that important image.

In 1873, when he painted *Dad's Coming*, Homer did not realize the tremendous importance the wife-waiting-by-the-sea motif would have for him in the future. If all my speculations are correct, *Dad's Coming* is an enormously important biographical document. It is, in any case, a key image within the set of images he did of boys. He freezes for our contemplation the yearning of the son for the absent and at-risk father, a scene with implications for any time, any place, any life.

Breezing Up

In 1873, the same year he painted *Dad's Coming*, Homer began working on preliminary sketches for what eventually became *Breezing Up*. This image of a lively boyhood adventure on the sea clearly fits in with other Homer images celebrating boyhood. These boys are as thoroughly involved in the great fun of sailing as the boys of *Snap the Whip* are in their rollicking game. There is, however, a key difference that is seldom noted and never given much weight in the picture's narrative. One of the figures in this picture of a boyhood recreation is not a boy. This difficult and somewhat dangerous form of nautical play is taking place under the supervision of an adult. The man partially concealed by the vigorous boys is crucial to the picture's narrative. What we have here is not a Twain-like version of Huck and Tom and friends off on a lark. The dad, in this picture in control of the sailboat, seems to occupy the position of greatest importance. In view of the biographical speculations to which I have accorded some importance in this essay it is interesting to note that *Breezing Up* depicts what could well be a group very like Homer's own family. He shows a father taking out his three sons on an important excursion. The dad is quite literally showing his boys the ropes. It could be that what is depicted here is an excursion that should have happened in Homer's family but did not because of the father's absence during some critical years in the development of the Homer boys. They were all boys when he left, but, when he came back, Charles and Winslow were already young men. This is the first of Homer's many great pictures of seafaring on the open sea that are among his most famous images. Though we do not want to accuse Homer of allegorical intent, it is inevitably the case that this image of a father captaining his sons bears a relation to Homer's pictures of men struggling, not always successfully, to survive dangerous waters. This image shows boys at play, but it is a serious play. They must learn to stay afloat in all weathers, even when the father is not there to guide their navigations.

Once again we must remember that each picture may have many lives. Homer may have identified with the father as well as with the boys. The motif depicted in *Breezing Up*, which he started working on in 1873 but did not complete as an oil painting until 1876, may have, as one of its interests for him, enabled Homer to imagine himself as the father he was never to become.

Homer's images of barefoot boys were among the most famous images of childhood in post-Civil-War, 19th-century America. His genius for capturing the popular image of the country boy was largely due to his clear-eyed but affectionate remembrance of his own childhood and his ability to work from the observation of available scenes. Although Homer's pictures of boys may have had appeal for audiences caught up in the fashionably sentimental celebration of boyhood, the feelings that underlie his pictures are of a highly personal nature having little to do with the nostalgic narratives of Twain, Warner, Whittier, and company. Homer was creating his images of childhood at a crucial stage in his adulthood. These pictures tell us much about Homer's lingering need for boyhood and, paradoxically, hint of a troubled longing for fatherhood.

Notes

[1] *Dad's Coming* became the title of choice for this work largely because an engraved version of the picture was published with a poem, inspired by the picture, that chose the upbeat *Dad's Coming!* over the more appropriate *Waiting for Dad*. The choice between the two titles is an important one: the happy, enthusiastic declaration of the father's appearance within the boy's range of sight conveys implications that differ strikingly from those of the scene of obviously unresolved waiting that all three versions of the picture present. I will not go against the accepted practice of using *Waiting for Dad* only when referring to the watercolor image that shows the boy without the mother and baby, but it is my conviction that *Waiting for Dad* should be accepted as the title of the oil painting. *Dad's Coming* seems acceptable for the print since it is printed beside the poem, but it should be abandoned for the other images simply because it mis-describes the scene.

[2] The contrast between the degree of dangerousness of the ocean in the Gloucester and Cullercoats pictures, cannot be completely ascribed to the actual differences in the dangers of the two fishing spots. Fishing off the New England coast could be just as dangerous as fishing in the North Sea off Cullercoats, as Homer suggests in *The Fog Warning* and a number of other important New England pictures he did as a post-return-to-America continuation of his Cullercoats preoccupations.

[3] The sentimental side to this narrative is given full rein in the poem by an unknown author that appeared in the 1 Nov. 1873 issue of *Harper's Weekly* in the company of the engraved version of Homer's picture. Wilmerding seems to feel there is some doubt about whether the picture or the poem came first (220), but in view of the gradual evolution of the picture through its early version that did not include the woman and child it seems obvious that the painting came first. One of the points to my essay is to show that Homer's *Dad's Coming* grew out of impulses that Homer felt

compelled to express. The poem, quoted in full below, is awkwardly maudlin, but it does reflect the urgent concern for the father, crucial to Homer's compelling image but often overlooked in art historical discussions of it.

Dad's Coming!

Out where the waters are sparkling and dancing,
  Crested with sunlight all purple and gold,
Turn the true eyes that so long have been watching
  To welcome the wanderer back into the fold.
Lightly the billows are foaming and tossing;
  Freshens the breeze as the sun goeth down:
Softly the light, ere it dies in its glory,
  Lays on the heads of the watchers its crown.

Now in the distance a white sail is gleaming,
  Flutteringly spread like the wings of a dove;
Nearer and nearer the light breeze is wafting
  The wanderer back to the home of his love.
"See, he is coming! Dad's coming! I see him!"
  Shout, little Johnny! Should loud in your glee!
Only God heareth the prayer that is whispered
  For thanks that the sailor comes safely from sea.

Ah, happy mother! while clasping your treasures
  How little you think of Eternity's shore,
Where hearts true and loyal have parted in anguish,
  Where souls have gone out to return nevermore!
And eyes that were bright have grown dim with long watching
  While yours overflow with your joy and your pride!
But sing, little Johnny! "Dad's coming! Dad's coming!"
  The husband and father is safe at your side.

Works Cited

Cikovsky, Jr., Nicolai. "Winslow Homer's *School Time*: 'A Picture Thoroughly National.'" *Essays in Honor of Paul Mellon*. Ed. John Wilmerding. Washington, D.C.: National Gallery of Art, 1986. 47-69.

Cooper, Helen A. *Winslow Homer Watercolors*. New Haven: Yale UP, 1986.

"Dad's Coming!" *Harper's Weekly* 1 Nov. 1873: 970.

Downes, William Howe. *The Life and Works of Winslow Homer*. Boston: Houghton, 1911.

Eliade, Mircea. *The Sacred and the Profane: The Nature of Religion*. Trans. Willard Trask. New York: Harcourt, 1959.

Larcom, Lucy. *The Poetical Works*. Boston: Houghton, 1884.

Tatham, David. *Winslow Homer and the Illustrated Book*. Syracuse: Syracuse UP, 1992.

Twain, Mark. *The Adventures of Huckleberry Finn*. Many editions available.

____. *The Adventures of Tom Sawyer*. Many editions available.

Van Rensselaer, M.G. "An American Artist in England." *Century Magazine* Nov. 1883: 13-21.

Warner, Charles Dudley. *Being a Boy*. Boston: Houghton, 1877.

Whittier, John Greenleaf. "The Barefoot Boy." *One Hundred and One Famous Poems*. Ed. Roy Cook. Chicago: Contemporary, 1958.

Wilmerding, John. "Winslow Homer's *Dad's Coming*." *American Views: Essays on American Art*. Princeton: Princeton UP, 1991. 209-22.

Annotated Bibliography

Adams, Henry. "The Identity of Winslow Homer's 'Mystery Woman.'" *The Burlington Magazine* Apr. 1990: 244-52.

____. "Mortal Themes." *Art in America* 71.2 (1983): 112-26.

____. "Winslow Homer's Mystery Woman." *Art & Antiques* Nov. 1984: 38-45. Henry Adams is a provocative commentator on American art. Some of his biographical interpretations of Homer's work are more persuasive than others. His various attempts at resolving the mystery-woman controversy seem to miss the mark, but his accounts of Homer's "mortal themes" are largely convincing. Homer's concerns about the imminent deaths of his parents were, no doubt, important factors in his conception of many of his pictures.

Beam, Philip C. *Winslow Homer at Prout's Neck*. Boston: Little, 1966. Beam gives us a fascinating look at Homer in his later years. We learn much about his eccentric, old-bachelor style of life from the anecdotes that Beam relates. Beam is one of the many to mention Homer's lifelong affection for children. He would allow children to watch him paint but would chase away any adults who might attempt to approach him while he was working or preparing to work.

Cikovsky, Jr., Nicolai. *Winslow Homer*. New York: Abrams, 1990.

_____. "Winslow Homer's *School Time*: 'A Picture Thoroughly National.'" *Essays in Honor of Paul Mellon*. Ed. John Wilmerding. Washington, D.C.: National Gallery of Art. 47-69. Cikovsky's book offers high-quality reproductions of Homer's oil paintings and much intelligent commentary on Homer's work. The article on *School Time* does an excellent job of relating the nature of American education in the 1870s to Homer's schoolhouse and schoolyard pictures.

Cooper, Helen A. *Winslow Homer Watercolors*. Washington, D.C.: National Gallery of Art, 1986. The reproductions of the watercolors are beautifully done. Cooper has many useful things to say about Homer's watercolors of children.

Downes, William Howe. *The Life and Works of Winslow Homer*. Boston: Houghton, 1911. Written the year after Homer's death and recently brought back into print by Dover, this admiring account by a Boston art critic remains fresh in some ways and seems quaint in others. A reader seeking an introduction to Homer's work might find the small price and pleasantly antiquarian flavor of Downes's book to be attractive. He characterizes Homer's childhood briefly but vividly.

Flexner, James Thomas. *The World of Winslow Homer: 1836-1910*. New York: Time-Life, 1966. The popular Time-Life format works well here. Flexner, one of the most important historians of 19th-century American art, does a good job of placing Homer in the context of his time. Flexner's three-volume *History of American Painting* helped establish, or re-establish, the greatness of Cole, Homer, Eakins, and others. His work has served to remind America that there are great American artistic traditions that reward serious study.

Gardner, Albert Ten Eyck. *Winslow Homer, American Artist: His World and His Work*. New York: Potter, 1961. An important life-and-works study of Homer. One of its useful features is its careful examination of evidence of European influences.

Goodrich, Lloyd. *Winslow Homer*. New York: Macmillan, 1944. This book remains the fullest and most persuasive account of Homer's life.

Hendricks, Gordon. *The Life and Works of Winslow Homer*. New York: Abrams, 1979. A huge book containing a compendium of information about Homer and his art. Hendricks supplies numerous photographs, maps, and other materials—much of which is not available in other studies of Homer. Many documents relating to Homer's childhood and to his depictions of children can be found in this weighty tome.

Larcom, Lucy. *The Poetical Works*. Boston: Houghton, 1884. Larcom's work is typical of magazine verse in Homer's day. Her poems about children reflect the conventional romantizations.

Tatham, David. *Winslow Homer and the Illustrated Book*. Syracuse: Syracuse UP, 1992. This book is a valuable resource for students of 19th-century popular culture. It shows the range of work one of our best artists produced to earn a living as a popular illustrator.

Twain, Mark. *Huckleberry Finn*. Many editions available.

____. *Tom Sawyer*. Many editions available. These familiar classics have seldom been studied in their popular-culture context.

Warner, Charles Dudley. *Being a Boy*. Boston: Houghton, 1877. This odd and entertaining work contains extended descriptions of the legendary barefoot boy and his style of life. It is interesting to read in conjunction with Twain's Huck and Tom tales. Warner's essays strongly convey the yearning for a simpler boyish mode of life. He is the most explicit spokesman for a widespread shared nostalgia. Since this book was published in 1887, it was composed not long after Homer's preoccupation with the depiction of boys in the 1870s.

Whittier, John Greenleaf. *The Complete Poetical Works*. Boston: Houghton, 1894. Barefoot boys run through many of Whittier's most popular verses. His poems catalog the joys of boyhood. Many readers who had no personal knowledge of barefoot boyhood took pleasure in the romantic view of country childhood offered by Whittier and many other popular poets. Many poets of the day found audiences through the lyceum circuit of public readings as well as through their publications in journals and books.

Wilmerding, John. *Winslow Homer*. New York: Praeger, 1972.

____. "Winslow Homer's *Dad's Coming*." *American Views*. Princeton: Princeton UP, 1991. Wilmerding has written widely on Homer. His comments on the pictures are always careful and wise. His essay on *Dad's Coming* is of great usefulness. He recognizes this picture's crucial importance but avoids biographical speculation. It is an assumption of my essay, however, that biographical matters should be considered.

Wood, Peter, and Karen Dalton, eds. *Winslow Homer's Images of Blacks*. Austin: U of Texas P, 1986. My essay does not consider the important topic of Winslow Homer's pictures of black barefoot boys. Wood and Dalton's pioneering study makes clear that Homer, though a man of his times, rises above most of his fellow artists in his serious depiction of blacks in the south as well as in tropical Caribbean locales.

Targeting Baby-Boom Children as Consumers: Mattel Uses Television to Sell Talking Dolls

Kathy Merlock Jackson

From 1946 to 1964 America was immersed in the greatest baby boom it has ever known. All told, over 76 million babies were born, comprising approximately one third of the current population (Jones 2). At the same time that Americans in record numbers were having children, a new technology—television—was taking hold, quickly becoming the nation's dominant medium. Baby boom children embraced television and immediately became one of the medium's heavy viewing audiences. By the 1960s, children from the ages of 2 to 11 were watching approximately 25 hours of television per week (Comstock with Paik 61). This phenomenon did not go unnoticed by television advertisers, particularly those representing the toy industry. Thus, children were perceived in a way in which they had never been before: as a target audience for television advertising.

Prior to the age of television, advertising for toys was generally geared to the adult consumer, who would then make the purchasing decision for the child. However, along with television came the realization that advertisers could reach children directly, and children, in turn, could make their own consumer decisions. It also became apparent that children frequently preferred toys advertised on television. As toy historians Sidney Ladensohn Stern and Ted Schoenhaus observe of television-advertised toys, "They are the toys that children choose for themselves. Children want the products they see on television, and if their friends have them, they want them even more" (29).

One of the first companies to tap the potential of television to sell toys to baby-boom children was Mattel. Although best known for its Barbie dolls and Hot Wheels, Mattel unveiled in the early 1960s its popular series of Chatty dolls. Mattel, in its conception of this innovative product line and its use of television to promote it, provides a telling case study for identifying the image of the child as a consumer and understanding subsequent marketing strategies in the toy industry.

TALKING DOLLS

NEW! SINGIN' CHATTY™
#3055 Blonde #3056 Brunette
IT'S FANTASTIC! SHE CAN
ACTUALLY SING!

Huggable, lovable new doll! Just pull the
CHATTY-RING®, and SINGIN' CHATTY
will sing long, long phrases like "Row, row,
row your boat, life is but a dream" and
"Hi-ho, the merry-o, the farmer in the
dell." (No batteries required.) Girls can
finish the song that SINGIN' CHATTY
starts, or sing right along with her! SINGIN'
CHATTY sits, stands and has moving eyes.
She's 17" tall in her bright red dress. Her
rooted hair can be brushed, combed and
styled. Self-display packaged.

Std. Pack: 6/12 Doz.   Wt. 17¼ Lbs.

CHATTY CATHY®
#0745 Auburn #0746 Blonde
#0747 Brunette

The world's most famous talking doll . . .
CHATTY CATHY will say one of 18 different phrases at random. She has Mattel's
proven patented voice unit (no batteries
required). She's dressed in red velvet
bodice, white taffeta collar, white lace
skirt over taffeta underskirt, red satin sash,
white panties and socks, and red velvet
shoes. Her rooted saran hair can be
brushed, combed, and styled. She's 20" tall,
has movable head, arms and legs. Individually packaged; beautiful 4-color label.

Std. Pack: 6/12 Doz.   Wt. 19 Lbs.

NEW!
Baby CHERYL™
#3040

She's a soft, wonderful, cuddlesome new
baby doll, who actually says nursery
rhymes in baby talk! Pull her CHATTY-
RING, and Baby CHERYL says 10 different
things like "Jack and Jill, up the hill" and
"Three little kittens, meow." (No batteries
required.) Baby CHERYL, 16" tall, is dressed
in a cute lace trimmed daisy-print dress
with matching panties and booties. Her
eyes close, and she has rooted hair that can
be brushed and combed. Beautifully illustrated package.

Std. Pack: 6/12 Doz.   Wt. 14¼ Lbs.

48

Mattel, which a young couple named Elliot and Ruth Handler founded in their garage in 1945, introduced the first of its Chatty series dolls in 1960. It was a logical step for the small toy company that had begun as a manufacturer of doll furniture and musical toys and, just the previous year, had introduced a teenage fashion doll, Barbie, who—despite her phenomenal success in subsequent years—got off to a lackluster start. The year 1960 appeared as though it would be an unpromising one for the toy industry. On March 8 of that year, the New York *Times* reported the opening of the Annual Toy Fair at the Sheraton Atlantic Hotel in New York City. Describing this prestigious event, which showcases for toy buyers the top lines to be sold during the next Christmas season, the *Times* noted "that there did not seem to be as many items shown as in former years. Many toys were redesigned, repackaged, had changes in color or sizes but were variations of items on the market last year" (*Times*, 8 March 1960: 53). One item, though, took the buyers by storm: the talking Chatty Cathy doll by Mattel. Although Chatty Cathy was not the first doll to talk, she was the first with the capability of uttering 11 different phrases. And she did so easily—a child need only pull the ring attached to a string at the back of the doll's neck to hear, at random, one of Chatty Cathy's sayings. Inside Chatty Cathy was a small voice recording, the sound of which emanated from a hexagonal-shaped grill positioned over her chest and stomach.

Chatty Cathy was also different from other dolls being marketed at the time in two other important ways. First, she was the same age as the children for whom she was purchased. While most other popular dolls—among them Baby Chrissie and Betsy Wetsy—were models of infants or small babies, Chatty Cathy appeared to be five to eight years old, approximately the same age as the children who played with her. It is interesting to note, too, that with Chatty Cathy, her creators Elliot and Ruth Handler also made a conscious decision to break away from the teen fashion doll phenomenon. According to A. Glenn Mandeville, "the lukewarm reception which *Barbie* received in 1959, made the Handlers reevaluate whether Americans really wanted such a sophisticated doll as *Barbie* or whether 'traditional' dolls were...the answer" (165).

Chatty Cathy also broke the mold in another way: she had physical imperfections characteristic of real children. Unlike the beautifully formed baby dolls with sweet smiles and golden curls and the attractive and shapely Barbie, Chatty Cathy had unruly hair, freckles, buck teeth, and a bulging belly. She was, in essence, the typical baby boom child. As one doll collector observed,

Her slightly buck teeth told of future orthodontics work needed (that is, 'braces,' the status symbol of the boom children), and her hair was longish and straight. Her body typified the ice cream indulged child with the slightly protruding tummy, while her hands were posed creatively. All in all, *Chatty Cathy* represented...the ordinary adorable child of her day, the early 1960s. (Mandeville 165)

Even her name, Cathy, was one of the most popular of the time, reflective of the little girl next door.

Given Chatty Cathy's age, physical flaws, and ability to talk, the doll found her niche among children's playthings. Traditionally, dolls are vehicles with which children can model adult roles. As Sigmund Freud believed, through play, children rehearse the roles of adult life and also repeat life experiences in order to gain emotional mastery over them (Newson 108). What, then, does Chatty Cathy suggest? Children between the ages of five and eight, the age group which Chatty Cathy depicted and for whom she was designed, typically reach new levels of verbal competence and become more aware of speech patterns; thus, they would be intrigued with a talking doll. Chatty Cathy's character also gave them the opportunity to act out the same relationship that they had with their mothers. Chatty Cathy's imperfect appearance suggested vulnerability: she was so ugly she was cute. Thus, the child playing with her would take on a parental role. The concept of Chatty Cathy as a helpless child in need of care was further exemplified by her phraseology, which included the following:

> Please brush my hair.
> I'm so tired.
> Will you play with me?
> Let's play school.
> Give me a kiss.
> What do we do now?
> I love you.
> Do you love me?
> Please change my dress.
> May I have a cookie?
> Let's have a party. (Bagala 104)

In essence, Chatty Cathy typified the normal baby boom child: she was innocent, talkative, adorable but in an imperfect way, and needing love and attention. As Mandeville asserts,

Here is Chatty Cathy — the famous original Mattel Talking Doll—with a brand new sales-sparking, attractively colored display guaranteed to sell more than ever of her distinctively detailed costumes.

Four dolls, 2 blondes and 2 brunettes, come already dressed in various costumes for display purposes (and for extra sales help).

Each doll is individually packaged in her own carrying case and each open stock costume is individually wrapped in a clear plastic display package.

MATTEL'S CHATTY CATHY®
DRESSED DOLL ASSORTMENT

#390 Retail Value $103.50

DRESSED DOLLS

		Retail Value Each
1 ea.—#681	Blond Chatty Cathy in Basic Costume	16.00
1 ea.—#684	*Chatty Cathy in Sleepytime Pajama Set	$15.50
1 ea.—#685	*Chatty Cathy in Nursery School dress	$15.00
1 ea.—#687	*Chatty Cathy in Playtime Set	$15.00

* *Dressed Dolls #684, 685,687 Not Available Except in the #390 Deal.*

COSTUMES ONLY

2 ea.—#691	Blue Party Dress costume	$ 4.00 ea.
2 ea.—#693	Peppermint Stick dress costume	$ 4.00 ea.
2 ea.—#694	Sleepytime costume	$ 3.50 ea.
2 ea.—#696	Party Coat costume	$ 3.50 ea.
2 ea.—#695	Nursery School costume	$ 3.00 ea.
2 ea.—#697	Playtime costume	$ 3.00 ea.
1 ea.—Display		FREE
1 ea.—Window Banner		FREE
	Total Retail Value	$103.50

Std. Pack: 1 ea.—1 carton   Wt.: 21½ lbs.

"CHATTY CATHY" IS A REGISTERED TRADEMARK OWNED BY MATTEL, INC.

NATIONALLY TV ADVERTISED

MATTEL, INC.
5150 ROSECRANS AVE., HAWTHORNE, CALIF.

This fulfilled perfectly the stereotype [sic] image of the word 'doll' during the past several decades. A helpless little waif that needed a 'mommy' to take care of her, and at the same time, nurture that 'mother' instinct that some say is inborn to all females (though many today question such a statement). Through playing with dolls, a little girl would learn how to prepare for the future, perhaps the ONLY future she would ever be offered. (105)

Chatty Cathy may have conformed to the early 1960s image of childhood, but that alone does not explain how she became the first toy priced over ten dollars to sell a million units (Schneider 37). For that, one need look at another phenomenon of the early 1960s—television. As one advertising executive who worked on the Chatty Cathy campaign recalls,

In testing and ongoing observations of children with Chatty Cathy, it became apparent that the talking mechanism was relatively unimportant *after* the doll was purchased. Girls quickly tired of the talking novelty and went back to playing with Chatty as if she were any other baby doll. Ultimately the talking feature was important to make her more attractive on television. (Schneider 37-38)

A sampling of television advertisements for Chatty Cathy shows this to be true. In one television commercial, a boy enters a kitchen where a girl is playing with Chatty Cathy. He is unimpressed with the doll until she utters, "Please brush my hair." At this point, both the boy and girl look adoringly at Chatty Cathy, and the girl notes that part of the fun of playing with her is "you never know what Chatty Cathy will say next." As this and other Chatty Cathy advertisements suggest, Chatty Cathy could be a little girl's talking companion. In addition, the doll could help that same little girl to become the envy of her friends.

It is important to note that Mattel was not a novice in the strategy of television advertising. In 1955, when Mattel was still a fledgling company, Elliot and Ruth Handler invested $500,000—an amount equal to the entire net worth of the company—to assume the sponsorship of a new television show, "The Mickey Mouse Club," which debuted on October 3, 1955. They hired an advertising agency to produce three advertisements, including one for a new toy called the Burp Gun; the advertisements, which became the first toy commercials ever put on film, cost a staggering $2,500 each to produce (Schneider 21). However, they proved well worth the cost. "The Mickey Mouse Show" became a runaway hit, reaching an astounding 75 percent of the nation's televisions (Thomas 291). Although the Burp Gun ads did not seem to have an immediate impact on sales, approximately six weeks after they first appeared, the Mattel staff arrived at work on the Monday morning after Thanksgiving to find the telephones ringing off the hooks and the doorway blocked by bags of mail—all requests for reorders (Schneider 21). As one advertising executive affirms, "The lesson we learned, and it has not changed since, was that the long chain of distribution then dominant in the toy industry had simply taken its time to produce results that could be felt at the factory" (Schneider 22).

The Burp Gun, with its popping sound, was the perfect toy to be advertised on television. However, what made the Burp Gun advertisement especially effective was its emphasis on the product's brand name—Mattel. The final moments of the advertisement depicted the Mattel logo—a seal featuring a little boy named Matty Mattel wearing a crown and sitting atop a capital letter M with the words "Mattel Toymakers" encircling the image. The visual was accompanied by a male voice proclaiming, "You can tell it's Mattel. It's swell." Mattel advertising executives reasoned that young children who could not read would nevertheless recognize the seal with the character of Matty Mattel. Further, the slogan was intended as a mnemonic device to get children to remember both the logo and the Mattel name (Schneider 21).

Unquestionably, the strategy worked. The Mattel Burp Gun became the first televised toy to become a sensational hit, selling more than a million units, each priced at $4, by Christmas. In record time, Mattel had more than doubled its sales volume and become a household word. The company even received a personal letter from then President Dwight D. Eisenhower, who requested a Burp Gun for his grandson David (Schneider 22). Baby boom children had spoken: they wanted Mattel Toys. And their parents, many of whom had experienced deprived childhoods during the Depression, had spoken as well: they wanted the best for their children, and that meant brand name toys. In the status-conscious 1950s, a time when parents were buying more toys for their children than in any previous generation (Stern and Schoenhaus 37), brand name toys carried other ramifications as well.

Like the Burp Gun, Chatty Cathy reached a pinnacle of popularity due to savvy television advertising and an emphasis on the Mattel logo and name. All told, three different versions of Chatty Cathy dolls were manufactured between 1960 and 1965 and, despite their $16 price tag, sold briskly; additional outfits for Chatty Cathy were also available. Realizing the marketability of talking dolls, Mattel added more to the line. In 1962, Chatty Cathy's chubby little sister, Chatty Baby, appeared. She was followed in the next year by three new family members: the round-faced, wide-eyed twins, Tiny Chatty Baby and Tiny Chatty Brother, and their big sister, Charmin' Chatty. All operated by means of a pull string at the base of the doll's neck, which activated an internal voice box. Charmin' Chatty, however, possessed a much larger vocabulary than her siblings. Dubbed in her commercials as "the doll who plays with you," Charmin' Chatty said a total of 120 phrases. This ability was made possible due to five small interchangeable records that fit inside her. Despite this innovative sound mechanism, Charmin' Chatty, with her tall, gangly body, poker straight hair, glasses and impish grin, failed to meet Mattel's expectations. In the words of one disparaging advertising executive, the

smart alec pixie...could say *hundreds* of different things and say them in Spanish and in French. While the talking mechanism was obviously new and improved, the new smartie look that went with such an intelligent little creature left the kids absolutely cold. They hated her glasses and snobbish attitude. They didn't want...a smart friend. No amount of television advertising could move Charmin' Chatty off the shelves. Mattel experienced its first expensive flop. Television demonstration and heavy advertising simply could not move a product with a poor concept. (Schneider 38)

Despite the Charmin' Chatty debacle, Chatty series dolls continued to appear. In 1965, Singin' Chatty, who recited several nursery rhymes, joined the family, and she and other Chatty products—including plush toys of Beanie and Cecil, Matty Mattel, Sister Belle, and Casper the Friendly Ghost—were produced until 1967 (Lewis 42). In 1970, Chatty Cathy, Chatty Baby, and the twins Tiny Chatty Baby and Tiny Chatty Brother were reintroduced with new looks; however, the toy line sold poorly and was quickly discontinued (Lewis 42). Today, classic Chatty dolls—especially Chatty Cathy, who is edging toward her 35th birthday—remain popular among doll collectors, particularly those who remember such dolls from their or their children's youths (Mandeville 166).

Although Chatty Cathy remains Mattel's second most popular doll, she lags far behind the company's seemingly ageless doll wonder, Barbie, who turns 35 in 1994. Still, Chatty Cathy's legacy is significant in many ways. First, she helped to solidify Mattel's position as a toy manufacturing powerhouse. By catching on shortly before Barbie, she contributed to Mattel's financial growth. As *Time* magazine reported, Mattel earned $4 million in 1961, a whopping 73 percent increase in its sales over the previous year (22 October 1962: 90). Today Mattel, which in August 1993 bought Fisher-Price for $1.1 billion, is one of only two American toy manufacturers that have sales that hover in the $1 billion range (Stern and Schoenhaus 25).

Second, the success of Chatty Cathy's voice mechanism inspired Mattel, as well as other toymakers, to develop their research and development staffs. In 1962, Mattel employed a staff of 200 toy developers, among them chemists, sculptors, and engineers; the annual research budget was $1,500,000 (*Time* 26 October 1962: 90). As Jack Ryan, a former missile engineer who went on to head Mattel's research and development department, exclaimed, "We're right out on the frontier of technology" (*Time* 26 October 1962: 90).

Third, the popularity of a doll such as Chatty Cathy that had the physical imperfections of real children proved to the toy industry that dolls need not be the idealized perfection of the human form in order to sell. Over the years, the curvaceous Barbie has been criticized, particularly by women, because, as Stern and Schoenhaus note, she "promotes an unattainable physical ideal that will leave little girls feeling inadequate when they grow up and cannot look like Barbie" (63). The Chatty series dolls paved the way for more flawed, less attractive dolls—perhaps best exemplified by Coleco Toys' Cabbage Patch Kids, which became the best selling toy of 1983. These dolls, by not setting up unrealistic models of perfection, may help children to feel better about themselves and their own appearances.

Fourth, and most important, Chatty Cathy affirmed for Mattel and the entire industry the power of television advertising to sell toys to baby-boom children. In a 1962 article titled "All's Swell at Mattel," *Time* magazine attributed Mattel's economic success to "saturation selling on TV" and noted that Mattel's strategy encouraged other toy companies to advertise not only at Christmastime but all year round on television and to concentrate not on individual items but on accenting the brand name (26 October 1962: 90). Mattel, with a 1962 advertising budget of $5,700,000, led the pack (26 October 1962: 90).

When advertising on television, Mattel never lost sight of its key formula, which Elliot Handler coined "the razor and the razor blade technique." In his words, "You get hooked on one and you have to buy the other" (*Time* 26 October 1962: 90). In one television commercial for Chatty Cathy, for example, an announcer emphasizes the doll's "wardrobe of pretty clothes" while visuals show Chatty Cathy in several outfits, among them a playsuit, swim wear, a winter coat with a fur collar, and pajamas. The advertisement concludes with a little girl clutching two Chatty Cathy dolls, one with dark hair and one with light hair, each wearing a different outfit, while the announcer booms, "You'll find Chatty Cathy and her costume sets wherever toys are sold." Another television commercial for Chatty Cathy centers on her versatile stroller, which can be assembled in five different ways—as a front facing stroller, a back facing stroller, a carriage bed, a carry-all, and a car seat. Accompanying the visuals is a voice-over that says, "Wherever you go, now you can take Chatty Cathy with you in Mattel's new Chatty Cathy stroller." The commercial ends with a little girl being picked up in a convertible by her mother and placing Chatty Cathy in a car seat version of the stroller for the ride home. Chatty Cathy coos "I love you," followed by a voice-over affirming, "Chatty Cathy will love her new stroller, and you will too." Television commercials such as these suggest to children that having a particular doll is not enough; that initial purchase must be supplemented by wardrobe items, additional dolls, and accessories.

The use of television advertising aimed at children has only become more sophisticated in recent years. Teddy Ruxpin, the best selling toy of the Christmas 1985 season, was a talking toy with little play value—one that children watched passively rather than played with—but one who appeared irresistible on television. And the many toy series aimed at children over the years—lines such as the Barbie doll, Strawberry Shortcake, Care Bears, My Little Pony, Smurfs, Hot Wheels, and Teenage Mutant Ninja Turtles—all use the television sell to persuade children that the purchase of the first item is just a gateway to acquiring an entire set. Finally, the effectiveness of television to reach the child audience has led to the popularity of toy-based programs, set off by "He-Man and Masters of the Universe" in 1983, which are essentially one-half hour advertisements. Mattel's successful use of television to promote its Chatty series dolls to baby-boom children contributed to these trends and, in so doing, helped to establish marketing strategies and an image of the child consumer audience that still characterize the toy industry today.

Bibliography

"All's Swell at Mattel." *Time* 26 Oct. 1962: 90. A discussion of Mattel's successful use of television to advertise toys such as Chatty Cathy and Barbie.

"Annual Toy Fair Opens Showings." *New York Times* 8 Mar. 1960: 53. A brief description of toys showcased at the ten-day New York toy fair, noting many variations of the previous year's toys but few new concepts.

Bagala, Rita. "Still Chattin' After All These Years." *Dolls* Nov. 1990: 103-106. A chronicle of Chatty Cathy on the occasion of her 30th birthday; notes other dolls in Mattel's Chatty series spawned by Chatty Cathy's popularity.

Comstock, George, with Haejung Paik. *Television and the American Child.* San Diego, CA: Academic, 1991. A comprehensive, scholarly overview of the research conducted on the relationship between children and television in America.

Jones, Landon Y. *Great Expectations: America and the Baby Boom Generation.* New York: Ballantine, 1980. A readable, fascinating study of the baby-boom generation and its continuing impact on American culture.

Lewis, Kathy. "Chatty Cathy: Popular as Ever." *International Doll World* Dec. 1990: 42-45. An article discussing the collectibles market for Chatty Cathy and other Mattel Chatty series dolls.

Mandeville, A. Glenn. "The Chatty Cathy Story." *Doll Reader* November 1988: 162-67. An article addressing the appeal of Chatty Cathy and other Mattel Chatty series dolls to children of the 1960s.

Newson, John, and Elizabeth Newson. *Toys and Playthings.* New York: Pantheon, 1979. An analysis of children's playthings, citing psychological reasons for their popularity.

Schneider, Cy. *Children's Television: How It Works and Its Influence on Children.* Lincolnwood, IL: NTC Business Books, 1989. An insider's account of children's television's history and effects written by an advertising executive who was an influential buyer of children's programs; offers insight into the business decisions characterizing children's television.

Stern, Sydney Ladensohn, and Ted Schoenhaus. *Toyland: The High-Stakes Game of the Toy Industry.* Chicago: Contemporary, 1990. A readable, insightful history of the toy industry: its products, manufacturers, marketers, and consumers.

Thomas, Bob. *Walt Disney: An American Original.* New York: Pocket, 1976. A well-written biography of Walt Disney; provides insight into his personality, business decisions, and influence worldwide.

Little Women in the 21st Century

Christy Rishoi Minadeo

Reading *Little Women* used to be easy. Before feminism changed the way American girls looked at the future, Louisa May Alcott's book was simply a manual showing girls how to be ideal women. From Alcott's book girls learned to serve others and forget themselves, to put ambition aside for marriage and family, and to hide their negative feelings. Reading *Little Women* these days is much more confusing because feminism has helped girls understand the future isn't limited by gender—that biology is *not* destiny. It is difficult to read *Little Women* anymore without resisting its overt messages about the nature of femininity. The March sisters' journey to little womanhood seems to involve a degree of self-renunciation that is no longer realistic, emotionally healthy, or even fashionable. Contemporary readers feel let down by Jo March's eventual capitulation to marriage and motherhood after her long-standing insistence on "paddling her own canoe." Yet if we remember the novel is a product of its time and place, post-Civil War New England, and that the outcomes of the plot are dependent on those factors, we're left with a novel of female development that reflects not only the cultural norms of its time, but also specifically female conflicts that are not significantly reduced despite the passage of more than 100 years. Even so, *Little Women* has a strong undercurrent of resistance to cultural restrictions placed on girls; the March girls' gentle rebellion against the cultural imperative that makes domestic work their domain suggests the possibility that there are (or should be) choices.

Still, modern girls are no more exempt from expectations they be agreeable, nurturing, and giving than the March sisters were. If they are to achieve success in school and in the workplace, girls are expected to do so without unseemly displays of ambition, aggression, or competitiveness. In the end, as Marmee March tells her daughters, many modern females are still taught that "to be loved and chosen by a good man is the best and sweetest thing which can happen to a woman" (118). As regressive as Marmee's philosophy sounds, an updated version would likely sound like a description for

199

Superwoman (modern women *should* have successful careers, happy marriages, well-behaved children, home-cooked meals, and spotless homes), a role as restrictive in its way as that of "little woman." *Little Women* does depict limited roles for women, and the plot of the novel does serve to rein in the one character who doesn't fit the mold, but modern expectations differ only in specifics—girls must now be high achievers in academics, athletics, and the arts as well as cultivate many old-fashioned girlish virtues, such as selflessness, docility, and patience. The trajectory of girls' lives remains carefully defined, and that is why *Little Women* remains relevant to contemporary readers.

That modern readers still identify with Jo, the rebellious March sister, suggests they too feel at odds with social and cultural expectations. The central problem for Jo in becoming a woman is deciding how she will reconcile her unwomanly ambitions and tendencies with the immutable fact of her gender. What does it mean to be a woman? What can a woman have in life and still be acceptable to society? What must she give up? This is the basis for Jo's conflict; her resolution of these questions and the reconciliation of seemingly irreconcilable desires is at the core of *Little Women*. It is this theme that elevates what many have seen as a sentimental girls' book into an important work in the American canon. The struggle to find a definition of womanhood one can live with is a critical, perhaps universal rite of passage for girls.

And yet there's much in *Little Women* to make any self-respecting feminist cringe. The entire novel seems bent on maintaining the health of the patriarchy by stamping out any tendencies toward feminine self-reliance and self-esteem. The March sisters learn to renounce themselves and serve others, to repress anger and other negative feelings, but most of all that nothing is more important than to be "loved and chosen by a good man."

Marmee March is the model of little womanhood for her girls. Never angry, always ready to serve others, and in possession of a good (though thoroughly useless) husband,[1] Marmee guides her girls toward fulfillment of their destinies. Expressing her dreams and hopes for her girls, she says:

I want my girls to be beautiful, accomplished, and good; to be admired, loved and respected; to have a happy youth, to be well and wisely married, and to lead useful, pleasant lives with as little care and sorrow to try them as God sees fit to send. (118)

The only challenges and ambitions Marmee foresees for her daughters are domestic; there seems to be no room for worldly success and achievement. The March sisters must suppress any ambitions beyond the domestic sphere; that they are successful in doing so is perhaps the most difficult plot outcome for modern readers to accept. Yet this discomfort is useful to girls reading *Little Women* today, allowing them an intimate view of how girls' lives used to be, and enabling them to favorably contrast their own options with those of the March sisters.

In contrast to Marmee's hopes for her girls are their own dreams for the future; each girl reveals her fondest hopes in a chapter titled "Castles in the Air." Their innocent wishes contrast in varying degrees with the path their mother envisions for them; the extent to which each girl's dream reflects the ideal of little womanhood reveals just how difficult each one's fulfillment of it will be.

Beth's "castle in the air" is to "stay at home safe with Father and Mother and help take care of the family" (173). She is "perfectly satisfied" with that and her piano. A perfect specimen of little woman, Beth has successfully collapsed almost all interest in self into a desire to serve others. She is associated with domestic accoutrements—"a little mop" and an "old brush," and is so diligent in serving others without thought of her own safety that she contracts scarlet fever. There are no struggles for Beth in becoming a little woman, because wherever there might be a conflict, she gives in. Tired from her domestic labors, Beth forces herself to visit the destitute (and ailing) Hummel family their mother has adopted. Not able to give in to her own selfish desire to skip the visit, Beth dutifully carries a basket of food to the Hummels, and returns with the scarlet fever that causes her death.

According to feminist scholar Judith Fetterley, the implication is that "to be a little woman is to be dead" (380). The character and history of Beth March do not provide a good rebuttal to Fetterley's view. Beth is saintly, and although readers often weep at her death, they do not usually identify with her. Beth's selflessness is so extreme it leeches the life out of her as effectively as the scarlet fever does. Despite her apparent perfection in meeting the ideals of little womanhood, Beth has a terrible self-image; everyone loves her, but she thinks of herself as "stupid little Beth." She even provides justification for her own death, telling Jo that she is "of no use anywhere but [at home]" (452). There is no need to indoctrinate Beth into the role of little woman; she has embraced the definition wholeheartedly, obliterating herself literally and symbolically in the process.

Meg, the eldest sister, is also destined to fulfill the ideal with a minimum of difficulty, but her outcome is much less extreme than Beth's. Meg's "castle in the air" is a nearly perfect reflection of her mother's hopes for her:

I should like a lovely house, full of all sorts of luxurious things—nice food, pretty clothes, handsome furniture, pleasant people, and heaps of money. I am to be mistress of it, and manage it as I like, with plenty of servants, so I should never need to work a bit.... I wouldn't be idle, but do good, and make everyone love me dearly. (172)

The deviations from the ideal are relatively minor, and are disposed of in due course. Meg struggles with a longing for luxury from the beginning, but when she vacations with wealthy friends she gives in to pressure to dress in the latest fashions and preen before stylish lads. But having been raised well, she is ashamed of her foolish vanity when she finds herself face to face with Laurie, the boy next door, who clearly prefers the unaffected Meg. When Meg returns home after her visit, she confesses her foolishness to Marmee, who is well pleased that the lesson was not lost on Meg. While Marmee wishes good and wise marriages for her girls, she tells Meg and Jo that it is "better [to] be happy old maids than unhappy wives or unmaidenly girls running about to find husbands" (119). It is obviously not acceptable for a little woman to choose and pursue a good husband; she must be chosen and pursued by *him*.

Humility is not taught in one simple lesson, however, and Meg must fall a few more notable times before she finally accepts her place. Falling in love with John Brooke, while sweet for Meg, poses a bit of a conflict for her. He is not wealthy, and will probably never be able to build her the castle in the air she dreamt of. Still, she accepts this, because she has internalized her mother's teaching about wise marriages, and because she loves John. After her marriage, when Meg rebels against the limitations of his modest income, the consequences for her are understated but pointedly clear. Meg gives in to the urge to buy a $50 silk dress in order to keep up with a wealthy friend. John is kind and understanding, but he cancels his own order for an overcoat, telling Meg it is too expensive. Consumed with guilt, Meg prevails upon her wealthy friend to buy the dress so John can have his coat. The selfish desire to satisfy herself falls out in two ways for Meg: first, she realizes that John earns money for his work, so he is entitled to whatever he wants to get: he has earned it. On the other hand, Meg's work carries no economic value so she feels she isn't entitled to buy things for herself. Second, Meg learns that domestic harmony is ensured only when she puts herself and her needs after her husband and his needs.

In Marmee, Meg finds the role model for the kind of wife she was raised to be: always sweet, happy, and smiling, with dinner ready at the end of the day. Meg desires to be a good wife, and so tells John that he should feel free to bring home dinner guests any time he pleases; he needn't so much as warn her, because she will always be prepared to welcome guests with open arms. Predictably, John takes her at her word, but chooses a day when Meg has tried all day (without success) to make currant jelly. The house is closed up, uninviting, no dinner is ready, and Meg is hot and tired; most unforgivably, she is angry with John for not warning her he was bringing a guest. John quietly but effectively punishes her by going away with his friend. When he returns, she is still angry, but while they peck at each other, Meg recalls her mother's advice:

Be careful, very careful, not to wake John's anger against yourself, for peace and happiness depend on keeping his respect. Watch yourself, be the first to ask pardon if you both err.... (338)

A husband's anger and lack of respect are to be feared and avoided at all costs. A wife must repress her perhaps justifiable anger, because domestic peace rests on her willingness to ensure it by avoiding the expression of negative feelings. So Meg internalizes the suggestion that the whole problem is hers, the necessary repairs to the relationship her responsibility alone. She apologizes, and bliss is thus restored. Meg successfully submerges herself in John's superiority.

Later when Meg is frazzled with caring for newborn twins, she neglects her appearance, her housework, and her husband. Once again John's reaction and her mother's advice serve to remind Meg of the consequences of not placing John first. He is driven to look for companionship elsewhere, which he finds in the parlor of another young couple whose wife is not worn down by the demanding chores of young motherhood. Marmee does not hesitate long in letting Meg know she is to blame for John's desire to avoid home.

You have only made the mistake that most young wives make—forgotten your duty to your husband in your love for your children.... Make it so pleasant he won't want to go away. (472)

The sermon is not wasted on Meg, who desires to be a good little woman, and who runs herself ragged to give the appearance that the management of house and children doesn't impede her ability and desire to please her husband. Meg must bear the responsibility for keeping the marriage happy, and if her husband doesn't want to be at home, she must be at fault. There's no mandate for the husband to participate in needed changes; it's the wife's duty to be forever pleasant, attractive, and available to her husband.

The major differences between Meg's girlish "castle in the air" and her married reality is that she is *not* to manage her home as she likes, but rather how her husband prefers it. And she learns the necessity of work, because without some work to do, she is left to feel useless, as if she doesn't deserve anything of value if she doesn't create some work by which to earn her keep. With husband and mother guiding her to the correct path, Meg is finally indoctrinated into the ways of little womanhood, with hardly a whimper of protest. Her reward is, by the time she has finally reached little womanhood, everyone loves her as dearly as she had wished in her girlhood fantasy. Clearly, to be loved and chosen by a good man is indeed the sweetest thing that could happen to Meg, and she recognizes the necessity of keeping herself in his good graces.

The kind of oppression Meg endures in her marriage is not extinct today, a fact not likely to be lost on modern adult readers, but perhaps not fully understood by the book's usual audience of 10-13-year-olds. Still, a modern girl will be certainly be dismayed by Meg's subservience, thus increasing the value of *Little Women* to postfeminist generations. Rather than being an exemplary model of young womanhood, Meg's gradual capitulation to the restrictions imposed on her can help emphasize the degree to which things have changed for the better. Young women of the postfeminist generation often claim they're not feminists, but faced with a portrait of prefeminist attitudes about women, they find they are more feminist than they thought.

Meg's inability to buy a dress for herself because she believes she doesn't do anything to earn it is echoed in the modern need women have to delineate the value (both economic and cultural) of traditional women's work: housework, child-rearing, and family management. Though attitudes have changed a good deal since *Little Women* was written, housewives still aren't valued much. Meg's story serves as an excellent cautionary tale. As a result, many girls will respond to Meg's subservience with repugnance, rather than admiration, and may even feel renewed dedication to achieving equality for women.

The youngest March daughter, Amy, is perhaps the most unsympathetic character in the novel, but she is also useful in shaping the images of themselves that contemporary readers hold. Being of an artistic bent, Amy's "castle in the air" involves going to Rome, painting fine pictures and becoming "the best artist in the whole world" (172). Notably absent from Amy's castle is any mention of traditional womanly fulfillment, but even so, it is not too difficult to tame her aspirations. Amy, like Meg, delights in the finer things in life, and because she possesses a disposition that pleases, she gains opportunities her less socially adept sisters miss. In spite of her pronounced vanity, Amy works hard at her art, and is often depicted working on her projects with single-minded zeal. But faced with the genius of Michelangelo on her European tour, she gives up on her art, realizing that talent isn't genius. Claiming "I want to be great or nothing" (489), Amy opts for nothingness, which opens her up to the new possibility of fulfillment through marriage to Laurie. Through him she becomes a patron of the arts, thus fulfilling the womanly dictum that she serve others, not herself.

Amy does not even require a motherly sermon to accept the tenets of little womanhood. The model of genius Amy finds in Michelangelo is enough to suggest to her that she cannot be a great artist and be a woman. As a woman, Amy can never be more than a dabbler, if she is also to fulfill her womanly roles. It does not occur to her to create a new, uniquely female model of artistic achievement; she gracefully capitulates to socially acceptable pursuits, like philanthropy, which always appealed to her anyway. Again, the pattern is reinforced; in the world of *Little Women,* the only acceptable pursuits are in service to others and fulfillment lies in being loved and chosen by a good man.

Like Amy, Jo's ambitions have nothing to do with fulfillment in the domestic sphere. Meg characterizes Jo's "castle in the air" as full of "nothing but horses, inkstands, and novels"; Jo wants to do "something heroic or wonderful that won't be forgotten after I'm dead. I don't know what, but I'm on the watch for it and mean to astonish you all someday" (172). Jo's conflicts are the most difficult because of all the girls, she is the farthest from the ideal. Her journey to little womanhood is fraught with disappointments, bitter lessons and bewilderment, leaving Jo and her readers with the unmistakable impression that becoming a woman is a series of compromises of one's individuality. The novel resolves neatly because even ornery Jo finally accepts the role society defines for her by the end, although she does put her own imprint on it.

Jo refers to herself as "the man of the house" while her father serves in the Civil War, introduces herself to Laurie as a "businessman—girl, I mean," and generally bemoans the great injustice in her fate of being born female. She seems to suffer from rather serious gender confusion, enjoying playing all the swashbuckling, romantic male roles in the sisters' homemade melodramas, and fancying the role of breadwinner for her genteel (but poor) family. The action of the novel serves to help Jo discover and relish her place among women. In a society with distinctly drawn roles for men and women, it is critical for Jo to recognize and accept her womanly attributes.

The first and most difficult fault Jo is asked to overcome is her wild temper. Alcott writes that "[P]oor Jo tried desperately to be good, but her bosom enemy was always ready to flare up and defeat her, and it took years of patient effort to subdue it" (90). Jo's lessons in repressing her anger come, as many do, at her mother's knee. Having been angry for days at Amy for burning a treasured manuscript, Jo fails to warn Amy about thin ice when they are skating. Amy falls through and nearly drowns, but is rescued in time by Laurie. Jo is tearfully repentant for not forgiving Amy sooner, thus connecting her anger to guilt for Amy's accident. She calls her temper "savage," and fears she will do great harm with it someday. Jo is astonished to learn that Marmee used to have an even worse temper than Jo.

I've been trying to cure it for forty years and have only succeeded in controlling it. I am angry nearly every day of my life, but I have learned not to show it, and I still hope to learn not to feel it.... I've learned to check the hasty words that rise to my lips, and when I feel that they mean to break out against my will, I just go away a minute and give myself a little shake for being so weak and wicked. (97)

The consequences for Jo "having her feelings" is that her sister nearly dies. As Judith Fetterley points out, "in the world of 'little women,' female anger is so unacceptable that there are no degrees to it;" all anger has terrible consequences. Marmee reinforces this view by her firm repression of all angry feelings. This is a turning point for Jo; she is deeply penitent, and vows to repress her anger in the same purportedly admirable way her mother has demonstrated (Fetterley 380).

The reasons for Marmee's anger are never articulated; indeed it seems possible she has repressed her feelings so well that she might be unable to articulate them herself. But the overt message of this episode teaches that women should *not* be angry, regardless of whether there might be just cause for it. The barely disguised message is that a woman is "weak and wicked" if she gives vent to her anger. Still, the idea of anyone trying so sincerely to eliminate all hints of anger, even to herself, is so preposterous it seems reasonable to wonder if Alcott wasn't perhaps being ironic. It does seem like an absurd notion to contemporary readers; encouraged everywhere to express our feelings, good or bad, Marmee ends up looking like the hopelessly repressed Victorian she was. By presenting an extreme characterization, Alcott imbedded a message of protest in her homily. Jo is never completely successful in repressing her feelings (and readers applaud because her individuality is her most appealing characteristic), but with the simple passage of time and the indoctrination she receives, she finds more acceptable outlets for her sometimes unmanageable feelings. While Jo is still somewhat "wild" at novel's end, the fact that girls sometimes feel disappointed by the path she chooses points to one of Alcott's most important covert messages. There is value in this disappointment readers feel as it helps girls see that they needn't give up whole parts of themselves to fit a mold. It was a cultural and social necessity for Jo, but needn't be for her readers.

Jo and Amy have ambitious dreams in common, but unlike Amy, Jo has a true vocation for writing; Jo doesn't much care if her work fits standard notions of what literature is. She simply *must* write. The action of the plot, then, pushes Jo to place her writing in its proper place—in a secondary position at best. The desire to be a genius doesn't drive Jo so much as her enjoyment of the power she has in earning a living for herself and her family. Skilled at writing "sensation fiction," Jo makes good money selling her stories. She is, however, ashamed of her subject matter, publishing her work without attribution while hoping her family will not recognize her style. Jo

thought she was prospering finely, but unconsciously she was beginning to desecrate some of the womanliest attributes of a woman's character. Wrongdoing always brings its own punishment, and when Jo most needed hers, she got it. (*Little Women* 422-23)

Jo's real crime was not writing lurid fiction, but rather in straying from the confines of subject matter deemed appropriate for women. Appropriately enough, it is a man, in the form of her future husband, who chastens her. Discreetly, Professor Bhaer tells Jo that sensation stories are "bad trash" and making a living from selling them is dishonest—like putting "poison in a sugar plum" and letting others eat it.

Thoroughly ashamed, Jo burns all her manuscripts, and resolves to hold herself to higher standards in her future writings. Her next tale is moral and didactic, but no one will buy it. The public, it seems, wants only their women to be morally correct, not their fiction. Soon after this episode, Jo returns to her family home to take up the more acceptable vocation of caring for her dying sister, putting aside her writing for the time being.

Jo doesn't takes her writing seriously, calling it "scribbling," but when she writes, it consumes her. After a period of intense writing, Jo returns to the real world, cross and hungry. Her art is not romanticized; it is literary "labors," and eventually Jo feels it is not enough to sustain her. With Meg happily tucked in her nest, and Amy crooning blissfully with Laurie, Jo is finally bothered by her solitude. "An old maid, that's what I'm to be. A literary spinster with a pen for a spouse, a family of stories for children, and twenty years hence a morsel of fame, perhaps" (530). This is clearly an unhappy vision, for despite Marmee's sermon to the contrary, it is apparently not all right to be an old maid under any circumstances. Jo's discomfort at the prospect of old-maidhood reinforces the notion that a little woman is happily and wisely married. It isn't possible to be an old maid and a little woman; old maids do not meet the criteria.

After Beth's death, Jo plunges into a deep depression. With Beth's shining example no longer before her, Jo finds it difficult to keep her promise of self-abnegation. She despairs at the thought of spending the rest of her days tied to her parents' house, endless duty, and few pleasures. She is guided out of her grief by her parents, who try to teach her to "accept life without despondency or distrust, and to use its beautiful opportunities with gratitude and power" (522). But she is also converted to domesticity at this stage; she begins to see the beauty in "brooms and dishcloths [that] could never be as distasteful as they had once been" because they were Beth's magic implements (522). And, as if sprinkled with fairy dust, Jo begins to take pride in making home cozy and clean. She notices and appreciates Meg's domestic wizardry for the first time, noting "Marriage is an excellent thing after all. I wonder if I should blossom out half as well as you have if I tried it" (523). Jo has nearly made it. Now she is ready to be accept Professor Bhaer's courtship with gratitude and pleasure, but not necessarily because he's perfect for her. Looking about her, seeing everyone neatly paired off, and wondering what morsels will be left for her, Jo essentially jumps at her last chance to become a little woman.

And here the notion of a woman being "little" must be discussed. Jo cannot marry Laurie when he proposes, because not only are they too much alike, they're also too equal in age, intellect, and personality. Laurie is more properly married to Amy who is immature enough and young enough to be his clear inferior—not unlike a parent/child relationship (Fetterley 381). Meg, as we have seen, has also learned her place as the lesser half of her marriage to John. These two couples, interestingly, do interact on a fairly equal level until they marry, when their roles revert to socially accept-able form. Professor Bhaer is significantly older than Jo, but more important, his educational and moral superiority to Jo are immediately evident. Temperamentally, intellectually, morally, and chronologically, Bhaer is depicted as superior to Jo, making him the ideal mate for her to play little woman to. The end of *Little Women* shows Jo and the professor happily ensconced at Plumfield, a home and school for orphan boys (she always did feel more akin to boys) where Professor Bhaer does all the teaching and Jo presides over the meals, contenting herself with mothering her own two boys and all the other needy lads. She doesn't seem to be writing at all (she will, however, return to her vocation in the sequels), although she claims that marriage and motherhood will make her a better writer. A radical thought for its time, and while it sounds like rationalization, there is no hint of irony in Jo's philosophy. Alcott validates female life experiences by having Jo believe they will enrich her art. But for all Jo's spunkiness and creativity, she ends up taking the only socially acceptable path in life available to her.

Having enumerated the ways in which the ideology of *Little Women* is antifeminist, it seems reasonable to wonder if the novel has any value today, and if it might not actually give future feminists some very regressive ideas. Feminists are no more monolithic than any other group, so their responses to the novel do vary. Judith Fetterley writes that it is difficult to see Jo's capitulation to the doctrines of little womanhood with "unqualified rejoicing" (382), and indeed, many readers seem disappointed with Jo's marriage, or at least by her rejection of Laurie. She has married a man who is a father figure and mentor, rather than the soul mate she might have had in Laurie. Her marriage to an authority figure serves to dampen her considerable vitality—symbolized by her renunciation of writing—and to severely curtail her image of herself as a person of value. During the first months of their friendship, Jo darns Professor

Bhaer's socks in return for German lessons, clearly signaling that the only thing of value she has to barter with is her domestic skills. In marrying Bhaer, Fetterley asserts, Jo's rebellion is neutralized and she proves once and for all that she is a good little woman who wishes for nothing more than the chance to realize herself in the service of some superior male (382). It is difficult to argue against this vision; Jo is indeed tamed, and brought into her proper sphere. By the end of the novel, Mr. and Mrs. March are pleased with the fruit borne by their teaching, and note that all their "little women" have realized their parents' brightest hopes for them. It is the reader who cannot forget that Jo's own dreams have been severely restricted as she internalized the cultural norm of self-abnegation in women.

Yet Elaine Showalter sees in *Little Women* "Alcott's belief that the fullest art came from women who had fulfilled both their sexual and intellectual needs, and her effort to imagine such a fulfillment for Jo" (61). Seen in this light, Jo's story is one of discovery of her whole self, not simply buying into the acceptable role for women, or completely rejecting it in favor of an alternative lifestyle either. Jo's marriage to Bhaer can then be seen as a positive step for her, given Jo's unconventional style, for Bhaer is no conventional man. Nurturing, loving and expressive, Bhaer does eventually give Jo a room of her own to pursue her vocation as a writer, which does not diminish after her marriage. This marriage provides Jo with the framework that eventually allows her to see her writing for the gift it is, rather than denigrating it as merely "scribbling." Showalter points out that although modern readers might wish Jo had gone off and lived independently, such a wish is really not true to Jo's time, place, or personality. Jo is rather a foremother to those women who came after her, who had fewer limitations than Jo had to contend with (64).

Women readers of many generations have identified with Jo, in spite of her limited options. My octogenarian aunt read *Little Women* as a young girl, admiring Jo for being the "doer." Though she wouldn't describe herself as a feminist, this aunt supported herself and her family, put herself through college and graduate school, and married late by choice. My mother, growing up in the conformist early 1950s, thought Jo a "brick." A college sophomore likes Jo because she was the "hard worker who intended to do something outside the house." Apparently girls still feel that they are housebound, and admire Jo because she didn't want to be burdened with domestic duties either. Few girls can truly put themselves in Beth's saintly shoes, for how many girls are as good at erasing themselves as Beth was? Amy also fails as a role model, primarily because, through

Jo's eyes, we see her as selfish and vain. Meg may be admired by a scattered few readers, but she fails to sustain interest because she is brought into line with such ease.

If my attempt to find out what young girls think of *Little Women* is any indication, this book is not much in fashion any more.[2] It is easy to see why—at nearly 600 pages, it takes fairly sustained concentration to complete, something that may be difficult for a generation weaned on Sesame Street, the Berenstein Bears, and MTV. Unlike those contemporary shapers of adolescent self-image, the messages in the novel are subtle and require active intellectual engagement. *Little Women* asks its readers to compare themselves to each of the characters to find where they stand. Among women who have read *Little Women,* it is a time-honored tradition to compare which March sister was the favorite. And the answer to that question always seemed to reveal a great deal about the character of the reader. The differences in the characters seem to invite self-examination, asking each girl, who are you most like? Are you vain like Amy? Or sweet and loving like Beth? Or spunky like Jo? Is that what you want to be like? The act of sizing herself up helps the young reader define herself, perhaps for the first time, even if it is by negative comparison (I know I'm not like *that!*). Yet those I found who had read it share with previous generations of readers an appreciation of Jo's strength and empathy with her struggles to fit in. They seem to understand that, for her time, Jo did what was right for her.

And while the plot of *Little Women* inarguably reinforces androcentric stereotypes of womanhood, it also makes some covert suggestions that run contrary to those stereotypes. For all its reinforcement of the superiority of men, or "the lords or creation," the world of the novel is that of self-reliant, self-sustaining women. Father March is physically absent in the first half of the book, tucked away in his study for most of the second half, and while he is the nominal head of the household, it is his wife and daughters who hold it together, physically, financially, and emotionally. But it is through Jo that Alcott makes her veiled suggestions resisting social norms for women. Jo steadfastly clings to a platonic relationship with Laurie despite social pressure to view male/female relationships as possible only within marriage. While readers are invariably disappointed that Jo rejects Laurie's proposal of marriage, they still admire her for going her own way.

Jo is also the only member of her family, including her father, who is able to earn a living, and although she later puts it aside, this fact serves to emphasize her strength and self-reliance, attributes she never entirely puts aside. Although Jo does put aside her writing to take care of domestic duties, her mother recognizes its importance to Jo's sense of self, and suggests that Jo write to work through her grief over Beth's death. Writing is then seen as an acceptable outlet through which Jo can express her feelings. The result of this therapeutic writing is that she finds, as her father proudly notes, her "true style." It is clear that through her life experiences, *as a woman,* Jo has finally come into her own as an artist, creating her best work thus far. In making an unconventional marriage, Jo completes her own unique definition of womanhood, blending her own needs with the expectations of society, and thus creating a new female model of artistic and marital success.

I suggest readers tend to identify with Jo because so many girls have experienced Jo's conflicts. The desire for independence, rebellion against the drudgery of domestic burdens, and straining against the limits placed on girls' horizons are far more universal in women's literature and lives than often recognized. Reading *Little Women* at age ten, Simone de Beauvoir focused on the choices Jo made, identifying with Jo and learning that

marriage was not necessary for me…. I saw that all the March girls hated housework because it kept them from what really interested them, the writing and drawing and music and so on. And I think somehow, even when very young, I must have perceived that Jo was always making choices and sometimes they were neither well reasoned nor good. The idea of choice must have frightened me a little, but it was exhilarating as well. (qtd. in Showalter 64)

Little Women is, as many others have asserted, *the* American female myth, having profoundly influenced generations of women, and not simply to be good little wives and mothers who never lose their tempers. In 1989, there were only three women governors in America; two of them named *Little Women* as their favorite childhood book (Showalter 42). While the novel explicitly extols the place of women in the home, implicitly it suggests the availability of options. With each succeeding generation of readers interpreting the message through the lens of their times, *Little Women* continues to be a vital role model of the passage from girlhood to womanhood.

Acknowledgments

My thinking about literature in general and *Little Women* in particular has been greatly influenced by the work of Judith Fetterley. Her article on *Little Women*, cited in this essay, is a clear, direct influence. But Fetterley's concept of the "resisting reader," detailed in her book of the same name, was the catalyst to a profound change in the way I understood my life-long experiences as a female reader. I am deeply indebted to her insights and arguments.

I'd also like to thank Helen Rishoi for introducing me to *Little Women* and feminist ideas; Larry Juchartz, for much-valued feedback; Harry Eiss, for his encouragement and advice; and Alan Minadeo, for a giant leap of faith.

Notes

[1]Although a warm and loving man, Mr. March contributes little to the financial and emotional health of his family. Having lost the modest family fortune, Mr. March is away serving with the Union forces for the first half of the novel. Although he comes home for the second half, he is mostly in his study, above and beyond the machinery of daily living. Incapable of managing day-to-day affairs, or even earning a living, Mr. March leaves it all in the capable hands of his wife and daughters.

[2]I handed out over 100 reader surveys to female middle schoolers in Ann Arbor, Michigan, seeking answers to the following questions:

1. How old were you when you first read *Little Women*?
2. Which of the four sisters did you identify with most closely? Why?
3. Did you identify with the March sisters' struggle to become "little women"? Why or why not?
4. Do you feel pressured by your family, teachers, or friends to behave a certain way because you're female? What is it like? How do you feel about that pressure?

Having no means by which to require the return of my surveys, I received a disappointing five completed surveys. While I have no way of knowing, I do suspect the wording of the questions encouraged girls who had not read the book to simply toss out the questionnaire.

I also asked another dozen women, ranging in age from 20-82, what their memories were of reading *Little Women*. Without exception, these women felt that reading *Little Women* was a special and important part of their growing up years. Each found something to admire in at least one of the March sisters (usually Jo) and each recognized the specifically female growing pains experienced by their fictional counterparts.

Works Cited

Primary Sources
Alcott, Louisa May. *Little Women*. 1869. New York: Dell-Yearling, 1869.

Secondary Sources
Alcott, Louisa May. *Alternative Alcott*. Ed. Elaine Showalter. New Brunswick: Rutgers UP, 1988. A collection of Alcott's sensation and feminist stories, some originally published pseudonymously. Showalter's introduction provides an excellent overview of Alcott's career and thematic concerns.

Baym, Nina. *Woman's Fiction*. Ithaca, NY: Cornell UP, 1979. A comprehensive study of the evolution of women's fiction.

Fetterley, Judith. "*Little Women*: Alcott's Civil War." *Feminist Studies* 5.2 (1979): 369-83. Alcott did not particularly like writing girls' books, but they brought her financial security. Her feminist stories were much more to her own liking, but did not enjoy great popular success. In this article, Fetterley maintains the use of the American Civil War as a backdrop to *Little Women* provides a particularly apt metaphor for Alcott's internal struggle over her true style.

Showalter, Elaine. *Sister's Choice: Tradition and Change in American Women's Writing*. Oxford: Clarendon, 1991. An analysis of the writing of American women in a specifically historical, national context. Examines Alcott, Chopin, and Wharton in depth.

Bad Boys/Black Misfits:
Ruth McEnery Stuart's Humor
and "The Negro Question"

Judy E. Sneller

> The childhood of southerners, white and colored, has been lived on trembling earth: let us accept this, and the hurt that comes from a realization of what it means to the human spirit, and meant to me.
>
> —Lillian Smith, *Killers of the Dream*

Although generally unknown today, at the turn of the century Ruth McEnery Stuart was so popular a writer that an article in *The Bookman* proclaimed that "now there is no woman whose work is more widely known and loved, and whose personality has a further reaching influence" (Tutwiler 633).[1] From 1888 until the time of her death in 1917, Stuart won national acclaim for her fiction about life in Louisiana and Arkansas. Furthermore, and rare for women of her day raised as "Southern Ladies," Stuart was well known as a *humorist*, who, according to some critics, was "the foremost of southern humorists" ("Sharps and Flats").[2] Today Stuart's humorous fiction remains a valuable window into the people, customs, values, and social organization of the post-war South, that "trembling earth" which Stuart had experienced first-hand.

Generally speaking, humor is a useful way of investigating a particular culture, because it is usually a shared activity whose subjects, forms, and limits are determined by that culture. However, Stuart's work illustrates that humor is not simply a benign tool whose main purpose is always to entertain or amuse. She shows how humor is a powerful two-edged sword that can be employed both to *challenge* existing ideologies and hierarchies and to *reinforce* them; it can be used by the oppressed as a method of coping and empowerment and by the oppressors as a method of aggression and social control.[3] Indeed, Stuart's comic, but ultimately demeaning, images of black boys indicate that sometimes humor is neither innocent nor harmless.

Stuart's particular brand of humor cannot be properly understood without reference to her particular time and region—the

215

post-war South, especially Louisiana. In fact, southern women writers like Stuart often identified not only with a specific locale of the South but with the *idea* of the South, what Anne Goodwyn Jones has described as "the South as a region of mind" (47). For Stuart, this "region of the mind" included an unwavering support of the defeated Confederacy and a fervent loyalty to the "southern way of life," which, of course, had long included blacks in subservient roles to whites. Because the social, political, and economic plantation system of the South had in large part been built on traditional concepts of paternalism which idealized the supposedly harmonious relationship between strong, protective white "parent" owners and their dependent, black "children" servants, the presence of millions of free blacks following the Civil War was a particularly acute problem. One way Stuart and other southerners could cope with the changed circumstances brought by the Civil War, Emancipation, and Reconstruction was to recreate the paternalistic ideology of race relations. According to Guion Griffis Johnson, by the turn of the 20th century, the old concepts of paternalistic treatment of southern blacks had, in fact, been adapted to fit the new circumstances. As Johnson states, "The paternalistic concepts of slavery had become neatly placed within the framework of emancipation" (483).

In Stuart's post-war Louisiana, for example, the political power which registered black voters had initially gained following Emancipation soon dissolved, and by 1898 a series of educational and property qualifications had disfranchised blacks and reinstated whites to political power (Dethloff and Jones 310-16). Jim Crow legislation of the 1890s legalized the segregation of the races, thereby officially marking blacks as the inferior "Other" to be set apart. Jim Crowism also fostered a new surge of violence against blacks and, as George Fredrickson sadly notes, "the vicious custom of taking accused Negro offenders out of the hands of authorities and hanging, shooting, or burning them alive reached a high point in the 1890s..." (271-72). Thus, in the last decades of the century—the years during which Stuart was most actively writing—the "Negro Problem" in her beloved southern homeland was being handled in a variety of ways, most of which ultimately sought to (re)enslave blacks socially, economically, and politically, and to (re)define black identity and roles to the advantage of whites.

Stuart's humorous fiction indicates she did not escape the racism of her historical or cultural milieu. In fact, in Stuart's hands humor was far more than the passive amusement many consider it, and an active participant in the ongoing social construction of race, class, and gender codes.[4] Stuart's humor not only *reflects* the deteriorating social, economic, and political relationship between southern blacks and white bourgeois society after the end of Reconstruction in 1877 and into the new century, but it also provides images and stereotypes which *contribute to* the increasing pressure to exclude blacks from the "good life" of the reconstructed South. While stereotypes are not in themselves inherently negative or positive, their continued use in humor by whites can help to perpetuate negative concepts of blacks and to foster discrimination. Stereotyping blacks as lazy, dishonest, sexually immoral, and ugly helps whites to maintain their social distance, to rationalize black subservience, and to justify black exclusion from equal participation in American society (Starke 45-55). Unfortunately, Stuart's humorous fiction seems to confirm John Burma's conclusion that "a not inconsequential amount of humor...has as its primary purpose the continuation of race conflict" (714).

As will be illustrated with examples from a cross-section of her stories, Stuart's consistent stereotyping of black boys as "Grotesque Misfits" and "Bad Boy Pranksters" ultimately perpetuates a racist ideology supporting two main types of renewed paternalism in the post-war South. First, Stuart's comic images of black boys as Grotesque Misfits support a "benevolent" or "new" paternalism which argues that blacks are a weak and backward race dependent upon the superior white race for economic, political, and moral instruction. Blacks could "fit in" southern society or at least improve their day-to-day lives if they relied upon whites for guidance and availed themselves of education which was "appropriate" (i.e., the industrial education provided for blacks by benevolent whites). This "new" paternalism sought the continued dependence of blacks but without the close personal ties which once bound the races (Johnson 489-94; Fredrickson 198-227).

Second, Stuart's images of Bad Black Boys align with late 19th-century views, which defined blacks as a degenerating race with an "innate" tendency for crime and immorality or as savage "black beasts" to be tolerated by patient whites as long as they were "good Negroes" who "knew their place" and worked cheaply. This type of paternalism, fostered especially by scientific theories such as Darwin's *Origin of the Species* (1859), was a cornerstone of increasing segregation, arguing that since blacks were permanently inferior and had no real future, they should be kept strictly within their own race (Johnson 498; Fredrickson 228-55, 275-82).

Stuart incorporates both the Grotesque Misfit and the Bad Boy Prankster stereotypes in her second published story, "Lamentations of Jeremiah Johnson" (first published in *Harper's* in 1888). In this story about a 12-year-old black boy, Stuart joins a long list of southern writers and humorists—including the earlier school of Old Southwest humorists and contemporaries like Mark Twain—who use the grotesque as a technique of humor. Although the concept of the grotesque is actually a complex one with psychological, social, and symbolic relevance, on a simple physical level the word "grotesque" often refers to the "bizarre, incongruous, ugly, unnatural, fantastic, abnormal" (Holman 206-07).[5] It is this definition to which J. Stanley Lemons refers when he notes that during the 1880s, when this story was published, various forms of popular culture, such as advertisements and illustrations, increasingly portrayed blacks as grotesque caricatures. Lemons attributes this increasing use of the grotesque to theories which argued that blacks were less than human, as well as to a willingness on the part of whites to wash their hands of the whole race question that had plagued them since the war (104-05, 113).

In Stuart's story, the black boy's appearance and actions, as well as his name—"Lamentations of Jeremiah Johnson"—mark him as a ludicrous grotesque, a black figure to be laughed at by white readers. When the Johnsons were pondering over a name for their first son, their preacher had suggested the names of the gospels. However, the new father laughingly refused them all, noting, for example, that neither Mark nor Luke would do because "'...a black mark never stan's for no good'" and because just last Sunday the sermon was "'ag'in Lukewarm Christians'" (53). The dilemma is solved the next Sunday when the scripture about Jeremiah is from the book of "Lamentations," a name all feel is dignified enough for the boy.

While the boy's strange name initially hints he is a comic grotesque, his bizarre physical appearance and ludicrous actions confirm it. Not only is he ugly—"tall, black, unkempt" and "not a thing of beauty"—but he is also arrayed in ill-fitting *frocks* (57). As the only survivor in a family of ten daughters, Lamentations is forced by his mother to wear hand-me-downs from his departed sisters in order to save money. As he sits on a fence watching his mother's wash dry in the sun, he wears a yellow calico dress "caught by a rusty pin" and which "boasted a long skirt which...fell in foliated curves, from which the slender black legs dangled as dark stamens project from the yellow calyx of the marsh-lily" (46). The boy "laments" his position as pre-pubescent cross-dresser but realizes that the only way out of his dilemma was through it, "and so, if he prayed at all, he prayed to *grow*" (47).

One day Lamentations tries to break out of this state of mother-imposed emasculation by trying on some of the Judge's clothes drying in the field. As he struts around admiring his shadow, his reverie is broken by his mother's screams that he has let the hogs into the clean clothes. Although the terror-stricken boy scrambles to get out of the Judge's clothes before his mother sees him, he ends up before her "a pitiful nude statute of terror" (59). He then makes a desperate leap for the yellow dress behind him, gets his feet and legs entwined in the pant legs, and flails around trying to escape both the Judge's pants and his mother's blows, thus completing Stuart's portrayal of this black boy as a grotesque, emasculated buffoon.

Supposedly Lamentations' grotesque appearance also points to his potential for low morals and even "evil," for "If suspicion of any sort fell upon him, his appearance went far toward its confirmation, not only on account of his ugliness of person, but his peculiar dress gave him a sort of nondescript character, and seemed to brand him as an evil spirit" (57). Because Lamentations is outside the prevailing (white) standards of beauty and gender dressing, he is deemed not just odd and ugly, but dangerous, someone who should be cast to the fringes of proper (white) society. Then, too, Lamentations has a bad moral example in his mother, a "typical negro—improvident,...dishonest, idle...the tips of her fingers led her easily into sin by fastening themselves to her neighbor's goods..." (56). It is no surprise, therefore, when this "innately" immoral black boy does embark on a life of petty crime stealing (true to the stereotype) chickens and watermelons.

When Lamentations is brought into a courtroom to face charges for stealing two of the Judge's turkeys, he is again described in comic, exaggerated terms:

A murmur of suppressed mirth ran through the court as the tall, gaunt wearer of a white swiss dress stalked gawkily upon the stand.... [T]he fluted ruffles came just to the knees, which, with his legs and feet, were bare. His sunburned hair, usually fluffing out like a mop, was now braided, and stood up in stiff spikes all over his head. (62)

However, when Lamentations confesses his wrongdoing, the white Judge takes pity on the ludicrous criminal and insists that Lamentations leave his mother's cabin and work in the Judge's home. "This was the turning point in Lamentations' life," for at 13, Lamentations is given his first pair of trousers by the Judge (63). Despite "many faults of character, such as idleness and mischief,"

Lamentations goes on to establish himself as a trusted servant in the Judge's home and as a beloved preacher in his black community (63). Thus, with white help, Lamentations is able to complete his journey to "manhood" and begin life as an obedient and "good Negro." Lamentations' story thus symbolizes the social, political, and economic regression of southern blacks occurring in the late 19th century, for he, too, has been made economically and legally subordinate to a white benefactor. Any competition the free black Lamentations might have posed to whites is removed by carefully confining him within the boundaries of lawfully imposed servitude. The "new" paternalism is in place.

However, in this story law is not the only institution working to keep Lamentations in "his place." By aligning Lamentations with religion, Stuart also eliminates him as an intellectual or sexual threat to whites. According to Burma, the "nigger preacher" was, in fact, a favorite type of humor used by whites to lampoon blacks' supposed ignorance and emotionalism (712). Although Lamentations has been to the negro free school, he is not a black man destined to become "uppity" as many whites feared. Instead he turns back to the Good Book of old, proudly exclaiming, "I tell yer, my bredren, some o' dese heah preachers is gradgerated f'om dishere college...but *I's gradgerated f'om on high!*" (66). Aligning Lamentations with religion also relates to the white paranoia over black sexuality and issues such as miscegenation. Once Lamentations leaves boyhood, he was (supposedly) likely to become a sexual black beast ready to besmirch the purity of white women. While his mother had symbolically emasculated the boy Lamentations by forcing him to wear dresses, a second emasculation is enacted upon the adult Lamentations by confining him within religion, a realm associated in the public imagination of this time with passive, domestic, and submissive women. Although by the end of the story Lamentations is a black *man*, Stuart continues to surround him with comic images of a meek, non-sexual, subservient *boy*, perhaps as a way to diffuse white fear about black sexuality. Thus, while his age, social role, and even gender identity may change over time, Lamentations remains a black boy who can be, and must be, controlled by white men through the institutions of law and religion. His blackness remains a constant source of oppression.

"Lamentations of Jeremiah Johnson" is not the only story in which the comic image of the Grotesque Misfit prevails over that of the "Bad Black Boy" or in which Stuart maintains a demeaning image of a black *boy*, regardless of actual age. For example, in "Picayune: A

Child Story" (1899), Stuart relates the childhood experiences of a severely bow-legged black boy, who, although now actually aged "anywhere from twenty to thirty-five," will never leave the "prolonged childhood" of a nine-year-old boy (192, 197). Stuart's portrayal of this black boy as a physical grotesque begins with his comic name, "Picayune Steve," and continues with a painstaking description of the boy who stands only four feet one, has "bushy" hair on his "wooly head," is covered with "nature's chocolate-colored enameling," and was a "last-born ugly duckling" (192-93, 194). Luckily, he has the good fortune to be living with his mother's white mistress, "Miss Annie," who lovingly continues to care for the poor boy. Little Steve occupies his days helping Miss Annie and doing circus tricks for other children. That Steve's disabilities are never treated with dignity or compassion, but as a focal point of humor, is seen when he tells Miss Annie about his dream about having straight legs, and she responds:

But think how much fun you'd lose, Steve...You couldn't play circus for the boys. Remember, you are the only fellow they have who can scratch his ears with his toes, or put the soles of his feet together and rock like a cradle. And then, too, if you had straight, strong legs, maybe you would run away and leave me, and I would be so lonely. I wouldn't have a nice little servant-boy... (200-01)

Miss Annie's remarks define the boy either by his ability to entertain and amuse or by his ability to serve her, duties which both reinstate a paternalistic relationship between blacks and whites. Then, too, as was the case with Lamentations, Picayune Steve's grotesque physical nature also points to his supposedly innate propensity for immorality. Miss Annie fears "lest he should prove normally susceptible to vice," and that he will "go to the bad" without her guidance (203).

Years pass, and when the "Golden Star Museum of America's Greatest Collection of Living Wonders" wants Picayune Steve for their "freak show," a now-elderly Miss Annie agrees. The remainder of the boy's story is again a study in the subordination of blacks to whites. Steve's mother, Violet, who had abandoned him as a baby because he was so ugly and simple-minded, returns to partake of his newfound success (194, 207). She, like the mother of Lamentations, is characterized as a comic black figure who is "naturally depraved." Violet is so huge a black woman—having six chins!—that she is signed for the show, too. The reunion of mother and son is short-lived, however, for Violet soon abandons her son for a second time—to run off and marry the chinless man from New Munster (210).

The story ends when Picayune Steve is sent to board with the "Living Mermaid." Of course, this lovingly maternal white woman is not a "real" freak like the black characters, but only occasionally dons her mermaid appendage. Not unexpectedly, this kindly white woman does not smoke or drink, and she begins reading chapters from the Bible to Steve, who becomes so devoted to her that he considers her a "goddess" or an "angel" and sits for hours at a time rubbing her feet (213). With the story's ending, the cycle has come full circle for Picayune Steve the Grotesque Misfit, who has no place in mainstream (white) society except to serve whites, either as a focal point for their laughter or as their humble servant. Like Lamentations, Picayune Steve is a "Good Negro" who knows his place and keeps it.

In other stories Stuart switches the emphasis from the Grotesque Misfit to the Bad Boy Prankster or black degenerate, although she never created a fully developed "black beast" character. For example, an 1896 story, "Solomon Crow's Christmas Pockets," features a black boy whose immoral traits turn him from prankster to thief and whose attempts to subvert white authority are quickly thwarted. The boy is subdued with enforced instruction in Christianity and must undergo a symbolic castration before he is "fit" to reenter proper (white) society.

The ten-year-old black boy in this story shares many of the traits of humorous grotesque like Lamentations and Picayune Steve, for he, too, has a ludicrous name—"Solomon Crow"—and an unusual appearance. In fact, "he was so very black and polished and thin, and had so peaked and bright a face, that no one who had any sense of humor could hear him called Crow without smiling" (3-4). However, Solomon Crow's chief resemblance to Lamentations lies in his "natural" tendency toward dishonesty. Solomon Crow, in fact, is an enterprising little con man. "It is a pity to have to write it, but his weak point was exactly that he was not quite honest...[H]e had long ago begun doing 'tricky' things" (8). This black boy's disposition for tricks and thievery had also been nurtured by his "lazy and broad" black mother, Tempest, who "had never been very honest" and who steals enough to feed "herself and Crow and a pig and the chickens" (4). Stuart feels compelled to speak directly to her (white) readers, noting that they should "be patient with him [Solomon]. If we could not trace our honesty back to our mothers, how many of us would love the truth?" (4). Thus, early in the story, the humorous images of both boy and mother have set up the dichotomy between comic, immoral (unworthy) blacks and patient, moral (worthy) whites which the rest of the story will develop.

When a kind and generous white family, the Carys, hire him to pick figs, Solomon continues the "family tradition" of thievery and soon gets caught stealing eggs (11). The boy's disgraceful act is first handled by old Mrs. Cary who, with a kind voice, delivers a long lesson in God's love and mercy to all his children. She then delivers the boy to stern old Mr. Cary, who declares that he is not at all sure the "dirty little thief" deserves another chance (13). With a voice which was "really quite terrible," the old white patriarch tells Solomon to turn his pockets out so he can rip them off (14). However, the boy himself gets a scissors from Mrs. Cary, cuts the pockets off, and gives them to Mrs. Cary, who promises to restore them when he proves he is once again an honest boy. In this scene Mr. Cary symbolically castrates the little black boy, but the fact that the black boy does the severing himself relieves the white man of any guilt he might have felt over the task. The act completes Solomon's subordination to white authority which was begun, in fact, with Mrs. Cary's lesson of the love and justice of God the (white) Father. The only way the little black boy, Solomon Crow, is going to get along in the Carys' white world is to associate himself willingly with allegedly "feminine" traits (lack of authority, passivity, weakness), and thereby pose no threat to white male power. In other words, like Lamentations and Picayune, Solomon Crow must become a "Good Negro."

In the next weeks, Solomon works to prove to his white benefactors that he has "turned over a new leaf." When Mrs. Cary asks him what he would like for Christmas, he replied "Needle—an' thrade—an'—an'—you knows, lady. Pockets" (18). To his utter delight, the old woman presents him with a brand new set of clothes containing *eleven* pockets in all. The story ends with the "ragged urchin" donning the new clothes so quickly that "it seemed scarcely a minute before a 'tailor-made boy' strutted out..." (19). The new clothes symbolize the white couple's transformation ("tailor-making") of Solomon Crow from a potential "black beast" to a docile "black pet." Thus, in this supposedly harmless and amusing story the happy-go-lucky little black prankster/thief learns what every white supremacist would have all blacks learn, namely, obedience and submission to white authority.

Stuart also features black Bad Boys as pranksters in stories such as "Duke's Christmas" and "Tobe Taylor's April Foolishness." In "Duke's Christmas," Little Duke is a nine-year-old boy, "black as a raven...agile and shrewd as a little fox," who often helps his old grandfather with his "poultry fishing." The two live in a ramshackle cabin set on stilts along the levee, and Duke's grandfather keeps a fishing line baited and set out the back and front doors to help supplement their meagre food supply. He doesn't, however, always catch *fish*, for occasionally his neighbors' chickens wander into the area, swallow innocent-looking grain, and are suddenly whisked into the floor above (167). Duke accelerates this "accidental" occurrence by dropping a trail of grain from their cabin to where the chickens are kept, and then driving them backwards along the trail toward the waiting line (169). Duke's grandfather explains this thievery by declaring that "when strange chickens come a-foolin' roun' bitin' on my fish lines, I des twisses dey necks ter put 'em out'n dey misery" (167). In "Tobe Taylor's April Foolishness," Tobe Taylor is a black boy who cannot resist playing practical jokes of all kinds. Indeed, "Tobe was no respecter of persons, times, or places, and a setting hen or the bishop of the diocese invited him about equally as possible victims of a practical joke" (69-70). On one memorable occasion he puts sorghum syrup into the baptismal font and "had ten mothers struggling to keep the flies off their eleven babies during the rest of the ceremony" (70). On the occasion memorialized in this story, he has the mothers of his community in an uproar when he goes around switching babies in cribs while their mothers are attending to other household tasks. Although the events set forth in these two stories are surely more light-hearted than those of Lamentations or Solomon Crow, nevertheless they, too, posit blacks as not-to-be-trusted inferiors who need white guidance to be "Good Negroes."

During Stuart's long writing career, she did occasionally use humor for the more progressive ends of challenging traditional perspectives on gender codes. However, as the foregoing stories have shown, she also frequently used humor to reinforce the reigning white supremacist ideology. While Stuart's repeated depiction of the amusing antics of wayward black boys and kindly whites may on the surface seem innocent, her continued use of these demeaning images of blacks contributed to the reinstatement of a paternalistic relationship between black and white southerners. Her images of Bad Boy Pranksters and Grotesque Misfits participated in the debate over the "Negro Problem" by implying that free blacks are unfit to function as equal social, economic, and political partners with whites in the emerging "New" South. Regrettably, much of Stuart's humor is used to depict the role many southern whites desired for free blacks, namely, their submission to white power and authority, or, blacks who "knew their place."

Although contemporary critics may aptly consider Stuart's humorous fiction flawed by its sometimes overt racism, an analysis of her work can lead not only to a more enlightened understanding of the values motivating people in the late 19th-century South, but also to a new realization that one reason southerners like Stuart lived on such "trembling earth" was because of the oppressive paternalistic racial codes which were being reinstated. For those of us in the late 20th century, this knowledge can, hopefully, be used to address the racial discord which continues to damage the human spirits of black and white Americans.

Notes

[1]For the most comprehensive study of Stuart to date, see Helen Taylor, 84-137.

[2]In the Ruth McEnery Stuart Collection at Tulane University, scrapbooks of newspaper clippings such as "Sharps and Flats" have been preserved which attest to Stuart's fame, both as a woman writer and as a southern humorist.

[3]Although a detailed discussion of the various definitions of or approaches to humor is outside the scope of this essay, Regenia Gagnier provides a good overview of humor theory and its relationship to women's writing, and Paul Lewis provides a good overview of interdisciplinary approaches to literary humor.

[4]My analysis of the relationship between literary humor and the reinstatement of paternalistic racial codes in this essay has been informed by Peter L. Berger and Thomas Luckmann's study of the social construction of reality.

[5]For an excellent historical/linguistic study of the grotesque, see Mikhail Bakhtin.

Annotated Bibliography

Bakhtin, Mikhail. *Rabelais and His World*. Trans. Helene Iswolsky. Bloomington: Indiana UP, 1984. Historical/linguistic study arguing that the humor of folk culture—more particularly, the spirit of carnival with its marketplace language and images of the grotesque—is a regenerating social force.

Berger, Peter L., and Thomas Luckmann. *The Social Construction of Reality*. Garden City, NY: Doubleday-Anchor, 1967. Explores the ongoing dialectic between society as objective reality (social institutions, laws) and society as subjective reality (personal, individual). Argues that the three dialectical moments in the construction of social reality are externalization, objectivation, and internalization.

Burma, John H. "Humor as a Technique in Race Conflict." *American Sociological Review* 11.1 (Feb. 1946): 710-15. Argues that humor is often employed as a conflict device to gain ascendancy or temporal advantage in racial conflict. Gives examples of humor by both blacks and whites targeting such features as sexual relationships, avarice, ignorance, and emotionalism.

Dethloff, Henry C., and Robert R. Jones. "Race Relations in Louisiana, 1877-1898." *Louisiana History* 9 (Fall 1968): 301-23. Reviews C. Vann Woodward's much-debated thesis of the gradual imposition of a permanent and thorough system of segregation in the South and argues that this thesis is sound for Louisiana.

Fredrickson, George M. *The Black Image in the White Mind. The Debate on Afro-American Character and Destiny, 1817-1914.* New York: Harper, 1971. Study of the development of intellectualized racist theory and ideology in the United States. Explores slavery and racism, romantic racialism, racism during Reconstruction, the post-Civil War "new" paternalism, scientific theories of racism, and accommodationist racism.

Gagnier, Regenia. "Between Women: A Cross-class Analysis of Status and Anarchic Humor." *Last Laughs. Perspectives on Women and Comedy.* Ed. Regina Barreca. New York: Gordon and Breach, 1988. 135-48. Argues that British women during Victorian period did not use humor particularly for disparagement or for temporary psychological release, but as an assault upon the codes constricting them as women.

Holman, C. Hugh. *A Handbook to Literature.* 4th ed. Indianapolis: Bobbs-Merrill, 1980. Provides definitions and examples of terms and concepts commonly associated with the study of literature.

Johnson, Guion Griffis. "Southern Paternalism toward Negroes after Emancipation." *The Journal of Southern History* XXIII (Feb.-Nov. 1957): 483-509. Argues that by the turn of the 20th century the paternalistic concepts of slavery had been adapted and readopted to fit the changed social, political, and economic circumstances of the "reconstructed" South.

Jones, Anne Goodwyn. *Tomorrow Is Another Day: The Woman Writer in the South, 1859-1936.* Baton Rouge: Louisiana State UP, 1981. Using the writing of seven southern women, argues that southern women writers used their writing to come to terms with, or to challenge more aggressively, not only the prevailing conservative codes of Southern

Womanhood, but also the intertwining class and race ideologies of their region.

Lemons, J. Stanley. "Black Stereotypes as Reflected in Popular Culture, 1880-1920." *American Quarterly* 29.1 (Spring 1977): 102-16. Explores how a variety of negative stereotypes of blacks were used in the humor of this period in response to the growth of racist ide-ologies.

Lewis, Paul. Comic Effects. *Interdisciplinary Approaches to Humor in Literature.* New York: State U of New York P, 1989. An inter-disciplinary study exploring literary humor in three contexts: political and social competition, processes of maturation, and experiences of fear.

"Sharps and Flats." *Chicago Record* 19 Mar. 1895. Ruth McEnery Stuart Collection No. 139. Special Collections Division. Howard-Tilton Memorial Library, Tulane U, New Orleans. Clipping in the Stuart Collection which favorably reviews Stuart's visit to Chicago and which praises her as a southern humorist and a master in the use of negro dialect.

Smith, Lillian. *Killers of the Dream.* New York: Norton, 1949. A southern woman's account of growing up in the segregated South, her socialization into racist ideology as a child, and her gradual recognition of how destructive racism is to both black and white southerners.

Starke, Catherine Juanita. *Black Portraiture in American Fiction. Stock Characters, Archetypes, and Individuals.* New York: Basic, 1971. Investigates three flexible, overlapping categories of images of blacks presented in literature since 1800. Concludes that the shifts in portraiture significantly paralleled changes in cultural belief and attitudes.

Stuart, Ruth McEnery. "Duke's Christmas." *Solomon Crow's Christmas Pockets and Other Tales.* 1896. Rpt. New York: Books for Libraries, 1969. 165-89. Story relating how the Christmas wish of a poor black boy and his grandfather comes true when they by accident discover the old man's former white owners.

———. "Lamentations of Jeremiah Johnson." *A Golden Wedding, and Other Tales.* 1893. Rpt. New York: Garrett, 1969. 45-66. Story relating how an ugly, thieving black boy is rescued by white benefactors and becomes a loyal servant and a beloved black preacher.

———. "Picayune: A Child Story." *Holly and Pizen and Other Stories.* 1899. Rpt. New York: Books for Libraries, 1969. 192-216. Story relating the trials of a crippled black boy who joins a freak show and once again finds kindness in the home of a white caretaker.

———. "Solomon Crow's Christmas Pockets." *Solomon Crow's Christmas Pockets and Other Tales.* 1896. Rpt. New York: Books for Libraries,

1969, 3-19. Story relating how a thieving black boy is brought back to the straight path by a couple of white benefactors.

———. *Sonny. A Christmas Guest.* New York: Century, 1904. Series of stories by a rustic Arkansas farmer about the birth and early years of his long-awaited son.

———. *Sonny's Father.* New York: Century, 1910. Series of stories continuing to relate a rustic Arkansas father's memories about his son's early years, marriage, and career.

———. "Tobe Taylor's April Foolishness." *The Second Wooing of Salina Sue.* New York: Harper, 1905. 69-100. Story relating the adventures of a black boy whose April Fool's Day pranks are renowned in his community.

Taylor, Helen. *Gender, Race, and Region in the Writings of Grace King, Ruth McEnery Stuart, and Kate Chopin.* Baton Rouge: Louisiana State UP, 1989. Study of three New Orleans women writers and how issues of race, class, region, and historical moment—as well as gender—were integral to their writing.

Tutwiler, Julia R. "The Southern Woman in New York." *The Bookman* 18 (Feb. 1904): 624-34. First of a two-part series describing the lives of southern women who moved to New York to pursue literary careers. Includes such women as Stuart, Elizabeth Bisland, Sarah Barnwell Elliott, and Eulabee Dix.

Creating a Legacy:
Black Women Writing for Children

Kathleen L. Ward

Some years ago black feminist and literary critic Mary Helen Washington asserted the following: "Black women cannot fully comprehend their lives without [black women writers], for they celebrate and rename our experiences in powerful ways" (*Midnight* xxiv). Washington could just as accurately have said, "Black children cannot comprehend their lives without writers who will define and celebrate their experiences for them." For years, black children in America could not find themselves in the books written for children. When they did, their depictions were often shallow and demeaning, reflecting ingrained racist attitudes and saying to them, "[You] do not really matter or count" (*Children's* 107). Fortunately, black women writers have not only placed black women at the center of much of their work, they have also written for children. Some of today's most distinguished literary black women have written children's books— Gwendolyn Brooks, Sonia Sanchez, Alice Childress, Lucille Clifton, Alexis DeVeaux, Nikki Giovanni, June Jordan, Alice Walker. Their writings spring out of deep regard for children and reflect the same themes that characterize their adult works: individual importance, family dynamics, the role of community, and strong cultural pride.

While my awareness of literature especially for black children has come through a study of black women literary figures (children's titles kept popping up until finally I began making a list), research reveals quickly that the literary women I am acquainted with have linked arms with another significant group: black women and men who write and illustrate exclusively for children. Together, they are creating a literary legacy, countering years of absent and distorted images to offer black children, and all children, authentic views of black life and childhood experience.

There is ample proof that both self-esteem and prejudice begin to form at an early age (Katz 125-54). Evidence also supports that children are influenced, both subtly and profoundly, by what they read. I have thought further of Washington's call for fortifying depictions of black womanhood. Would her call have been so necessary, so urgent, had black children (both genders) of two, three, and four generations ago found themselves and their lives richly represented in quality children's literature? And had that literature been accessible to them? That they did not and that it was not are irrefutable. Instead, many have had to battle what children's writer Eloise Greenfield calls "a lifetime of conditioning," with literature a frequent accomplice:

In this society, our conditioning has been, to a great extent, irrational and harmful. This country was built on a foundation of racism, a foundation which is only slightly less firm after centuries of Black struggle. Attitudes toward women, toward men, attitudes regarding age, height, beauty, mental and physical disabilities have been largely of the kind that constrain rather than encourage human development. To perpetuate these attitudes through the use of the written word constitutes a gross and arrogant misuse of talent and skill. ("Writing" 19)

Greenfield is adamant that those who write for children recognize their influence and assume the responsibility—as well as the joy—that comes with their writing. Unlike adult literature where an unlimited range of material can be treated if done artistically, children's literature, believes Greenfield (and hers is a position shared by many), must be evaluated on content, as well as literary merit. Images that damage self-esteem or distort a child's view of her or his group have no place in children's literature, however skillfully and artistically they are conveyed. "No matter how entertaining a book is," insists Jessie M. Birtha, long-time children's literature expert, "one group of children should never be entertained at the expense of another group's feelings" (119). The NAACP's recommended reading list includes no book that to any degree promotes a racist premise or image, which, incidentally, means the exclusion of "a number of poignant and stirring [children's] stories...because they [are] marred by racial slurs" (Alexander 53). According to Greenfield, books warranting children's time and "emotional investment" must meet specific criteria:

The books that reach children should: authentically depict and interpret their lives and their history; build self-respect and encourage the development of positive values; make children aware of their strength and leave them with a sense of hope and direction. ("Writing" 21)

Illustration by Floyd Cooper reprinted by permission of Philomel Books from *Grandpa's Face* by Eloise Greenfield. Illustration copyright © 1988 by Floyd Cooper.

Should, then, life's harsh realities be spared children? No. Nor should they be portrayed as inevitable or all that life has to offer or as the accepted, expected lot of any one group. The challenge of those writing for children is to communicate through the power of language—and art, if illustrations are included—the great range of characters, settings, and experiences (good and bad) that exist within all human groups.

To understand the impetus for black women's turn to children's literature we must recognize the dismal failure of past writers to communicate individual and collective worth to black children. Today's African American children have inherited what I call a literary non-legacy, non-legacy because I choose to attribute to "legacy" its positive connotation—something strengthening, power generating, handed down from the past. Children's written literature of the past has not provided a legacy of pride and identity for black children but rather has perpetuated disparaging images and myths. Nor has it given white children and children from other groups multi-dimensional and humane depictions of black people upon which to build their racial consciousness.

The racist ideology of the 19th century guaranteed the absence of a sustaining literary legacy for black children. Out of the premises of that ideology—the intellectual inferiority of blacks, the inherent suitability of blacks to subordination and servitude, and so on—evolved degrading racial stereotypes, still familiar today with various adaptions: the Contented Slave, the Wretched Freeman, the Ample Mammy, the Haunted Mulatta, the Comic Buffoon. All were reflected in and endorsed by 19th century literature, including works read by and to children. In her essay, "Racism in Children's Books: An Afro-American Perspective," Beryle Banfield examines the work of Edgar Allan Poe, one of 19th century America's most popular writers with both youth and adults (a popularity that continues today). In 1843 Poe received a literary award for "The Gold Bug," a story which relies heavily on racist stereotypes in its characterization of Jupiter, a manumitted slave who chooses to stay with his "Massa Will" and plays the role of the gullible, shuffling comic. Banfield includes in her essay an excerpt from a short story written over a century later by black writer A.F. Watts. Titled, "Integration: Northern Style," the story tells of a modern black student's response to "The Gold Bug":

We are reading Poe's *Gold Bug*...Now this is what kills me. Jupiter is afraid of the dead bug!...Here's Jupiter acting like a jackass. None of the white fellows are afraid. Nobody's scared but Jupiter. He's rolling his eye-balls which are, of course, very white and talking like an ignoramus and murdering the king's English. Then there's this word "nigger" that's going to be read out loud by somebody in just a few minutes. And there's me, the only one of me in the whole class.... (qtd. in Banfield 26)

The narrator cites the pleasure of his white classmates who find the whole matter a joke. Clearly it is no joke to the black student, nor has it been to black Americans, young or old, at any time since Poe wrote it.

Poe is joined by numerous other writers who, having absorbed 19th century racist views, further entrench them through their writing. Well-known children's writers Thomas Nelson Page and Joel Chandler Harris wrote during the Reconstruction and Jim Crow periods, and both promoted the docile, fun-loving-but-inept-and-lazy stereotype of black Americans. Little hint of the degradation of slavery nor of the dignity and variety of black people made it into their works, read by and to generations of black and white children.

Harris's *The Tales of Uncle Remus,* to my knowledge, has never been out of print since its publication in 1881. In spite of its longevity, no child or adult has ever learned of real black culture through Uncle Remus and his stories. Supposedly providing creative renditions of African folktales, with Harris consequently applauded as one who knew the black perspective, Uncle Remus is, in fact, "the epitome of the 'plantation Negro' [stereotype]: in the words of [Harris himself], 'an old Negro who had nothing but pleasant memories of the discipline of slavery'" (Banfield 29). Banfield continues:

Harris' racism blinded him to the true nature of the slave's use of the folk-tale. In the African homeland, the folk-tale was a vehicle of moral instruction and the trickster-hero was often punished. Under slavery, it became an instrument of political retaliation and a technique of survival under an oppressive system. (29)

Inaccurate depictions of black children and their culture continued into the 20th century. The popular Bobbsey Twins series which began in 1904 included the Mammy Dinah, stereotypically devoted to her white family and entertaining all with her watermelon-eating, eye-rolling, "Negro ways." Though the 1950 edition attempted to subdue the over-done dialect and overt racism, the following passage from *The Bobbsey Twins in the Country* illustrates the tenacity of racist images:

"That sure is a ghost," whispered Dinah to Martha in the hall above. "Ghosts always lub music," and her big eyes rolled around in that way coloured people have of expressing themselves. (qtd. in Banfield 30)

Some consider *Little Black Sambo* (1929) a fairly innocuous piece—the story is not about an African child but a child in India— yet it has enraged many and over the years contributed little to a literary legacy. The long-time pejorative, "Sambo," caused Birtha to conclude over 20 years ago: "The usefulness of *Little Black Sambo* is dead.... [A] librarian will never offer this book to a black child if he stops to realize that the name Sambo has been used so often to refer to a Negro in a derogatory sense" (119). Yet copies of *Little Black Sambo* remain in the children's sections of most libraries.

In reality, few books were available for children of any race or group during the first decades of the century. When they did include African American children, they generally failed to get beyond images of "little darkeys" and "mischievous pickininnies." Dharathula H. Millender contends people of that time "wanted books about the Negro, who was really a puzzle to many" (114). She recalls that books showing black children in school surprised whites of the 1930s who didn't realize black children in the South attended school.

Needed at this point were stories of the happiness within the Negro communities, north and south. The Negro always found a way to give hope to his youth and show the brighter side of a very bleak life. This spirit often gave the outside world the wrong impression.... Handed down to us...were many false stereotypes of Negro life. (114)

Black writers were the logical refuters of the stereotypes. Yet where were they? Millander and others assure us they "could and did create" (117). Yet limited publishing opportunities and editorial restrictions kept most black writers out of print. An exception was Arna Bontemps who, as a child searched the public libraries in Los Angeles, "seeking a recognizable reflection of himself and his world" (Sterling 167). Two decades later when he still found nothing better than *The Pickaninny Twins*, he began writing stories for his own children. Though he had problems getting his works accurately illustrated, he persisted and numerous Bontemps works, some in collaboration with Langston Hughes, remain in print today. (If we are to attach a time to the beginning of a literary legacy for black children, the early efforts of Bontemps is a logical choice.)

New stereotypes of black American life surfaced in children's fiction during the 1940s and 1950s: the street hoodlum, Welfare mother, fatherless home. There was a breakthrough, however, in the nonfiction biographies of notable African Americans. We must remember, black children were not only invisible or marginalized in children's books, they and the contributions of their culture were also absent in school history texts. Children's writer and literary critic Dorothy Sterling tells of the exhilaration of discovering for the first time, along with thousands of others, the life of Frederick Douglass in Shirley Graham's 1947 award-winning book, *There Once Was a Slave*. Sterling tells also of listening with a black friend to a radio adaptation of Graham's *Story of Phyllis Wheatley*. The friend, overcome by her first introduction to the poet Wheatley, began to weep and implored, "Why didn't somebody tell me about this?" (167-68).

It is a disturbing question. All children deserve to have their heritage shared with them. They deserve, as well, to find themselves and their day-to-day lives reflected in the books they read and in those read to them. The rigorous turn of African Americans to their culture during the Civil Rights period of the 1960s, and the consequent interest of the publishing world, generated a deliberate effort to place black children and black culture into books for children. The highly important Council on Interracial Books for Children was established in 1966 and began its campaign against racism in children's literature (and sexism and all forms of discrimination, an effort that continues today). Contests and awards, most notably the Coretta Scott King Award, encouraged new black writers and illustrators and advanced the careers of those already writing. Works by non-black writers more frequently included black characters in contemporary settings and with more substantive roles than in the past. It is at this point in the 1970s that numerous black women literary writers and critics became increasingly aware of the negative—or non-literary—legacy of black children. Black feminism was taking form and black women had begun their own efforts to retrieve a literary tradition and to depict (and "celebrate") women's lives and experiences. Many chose to do the same for children.

One of the most prolific contributors to both adult and children's literature is poet Lucille Clifton. Great-great-granddaughter of a slave, Clifton began writing for children in the early 1970s, her works rich in universal appeal but aimed specifically at the world and experiences of black children. One illustration is *Good, Says Jerome* (1973), in which Jerome's sister explains death by saying life "ends when they meet old cousins and brothers and others at the meeting place. They'll wait for us, too. Me and you." The work was lauded by Beryle Banfield and Geraldine L. Wilson as the only children's book of its time to present an African-American view of heaven. Several of Clifton's award-winning *Everett Anderson* books appeared in the 1970s. One, *Everett Anderson's Nine Month Long* (1978), is a poetic depiction of a child awaiting the birth of a new sibling. More significantly, however, it treats the complex issue of being a step-child:

> Mama is Mrs. Perry now, and it's fun
> that Mr. Tom Perry is almost a dad
> and doesn't mind that Everett Anderson
> plans to keep the name he had.

"When I write, especially for children," says Clifton, "I try to get... across, that...whatever your circumstance, you are capable of being the best of people and that best, as a human, does not come from the outside in, it comes from the inside out" (137).

June Jordan, also an established poet, has written for both young and older children and since the 1970s has involved herself in organizations addressing children's issues. Her small, child-sized *Kimako's Story* (1981) depicts numerous urban neighborhood scenes familiar to city children, including a man sleeping in an open pipe and older people playing board games. Jordan also includes Kimako sitting between her mother's knees while her hair is fixed, a bonding activity especially meaningful to black women and children (and one mentioned frequently in the critical and creative works of black women writers).

Other women with established reputations who contributed in the 1970s to black children's growing literary legacy were Maya Angelou and Alice Childress. Angelou's *I Know Why the Caged Bird Sings*, though aimed at an adult audience, also appeals to children and was a Coretta Scott King Honorable Mention book in 1971, and Childress's *A Hero Ain't Nothin' but a Sandwich* received honorable mention in 1974. Numerous women writers creating exclusively for children also began (or advanced) their careers in the pivotal 1970s—Jeannette Caines, Eloise Greenfield, Virginia Hamilton, Sharon Mathis, Mildred Taylor are several who remain prominent today. In various interviews, each speaks of her desire to convey the richness and diversity of black culture to as wide an audience as will hear and see, but particularly to black children. Mildred Taylor, when accepting her Newbery Award for *Roll of Thunder, Hear My Cry* (1977), stated that as early as high school she had "a driving compulsion to paint a true picture of Black people":

I wanted to show the endurance of the Black world, with strong fathers and concerned mothers; I wanted to show happy, loved children about whom other children, both Black and white, could say: "Hey, I really like them! I feel what they feel." I wanted to show a Black family united in love and pride, of which the reader would like to be a part. (405)

Increasingly, the works by black writers were illustrated by accomplished black artists, so that by the decade's end, a wide range of cultural images were available to children, on library shelves, in the bookstores, and in a growing number of homes.

Yet there is a downside to this. During the very time of increased success, several award-winning books were reflecting the same racial affronts and stereotypes black writers were striving to erase. *The Cay* (1969), *Sounder* (1969), *Slave Dancer* (1973) and *Words by Heart* (1980) all received awards and critical attention that kept them (and keep them) among the most read and read-from children's books. Yet each contains characterizations and situations demeaning to black children and black culture. The more racially aware climate of the 1970s ensured swift response to the selections, with *The Interracial Books for Children Bulletin* an especially valuable forum for analyses and debate. Sharon Bell Mathis's "The *Slave Dancer* Is an Insult to Black Children" first appeared in the *Bulletin*. In it Mathis, herself an award-winning writer, charges: "So this year *again* the ALA has chosen as 'a distinguished book' one that insults my children and, yes, all Black people. A book that perpetuates stereotypes about Africa and about Blacks in general—stereotypes that in my writing I do my best to demolish" (146). Similar protest voiced by others within the black literary and educational communities denounced the subordinate position of Timothy, the elderly West Indian in *The Cay*, and the passivity of the nameless sharecropper family in *Sounder*. Yet objections were more a matter of record than influence, reaching an audience minute beside that of the highly promoted winners. Walter Dean Myers, in his impassioned plea for responsible screening of children's books (particularly, I would interject, a responsible screening of those receiving awards), states:

I personally would rather have my children exposed to prurient sex, which librarians do not mind censoring, than racist books. I believe that the human values I give my children will help them deal with filth. It is a far more difficult task to help them deal with the concept of being less worthy because they are black. (225-26)

Eloise Greenfield confronts a second concern clouding the accomplishments of the 1970s. In a 1986 address before the Council on Interracial Books for Children, she asserted: "Children's literature ...is suffering a reversal of many of the gains that were realized during the last few decades. Many of the books that we welcomed just a few years ago are no longer in existence" ("African" 5). She continues by calling the failure to keep a book in print "censorship at its most lethal and effective level—a publisher's decision to discontinue a book is quiet and efficient, and you don't have to waste a match on a book that is never printed" (5).

Greenfield is not alone in her conclusions. A look at publication lists and mail order catalogs of the last five years verifies the disappearance of titles and the scarcity of new works by African American writers and artists. To be sure, fine works still exist and new ones continue to be published. The difficulty of getting and staying in print, however, must not be underestimated nor must the consequences to children.

Currently, and I think of the last decade and now into the 1990s as current, the struggle for publication and recognition long familiar to black writers continues. Fortunately, the literary legacy for black children also continues, reinforced and expanded by the works of both established and new black writers, many of whom are women. Literary figures such as Nikki Giovanni, Alexis DeVeaux, Rosa Guy, and Sonia Sanchez have turned their talents to the young audience, creating images of family cohesion, friendship, and individuality within a variety of skillfully rendered frameworks. DeVeaux's *An Enchanted Hair Tale* (1987) reflects the same free-spirited element typical of her adult work in its accepting portrait of a child who doesn't fit because of his Rasta dreadlocks yet finds friendship among circus acrobats and within his family.

Alice Walker, one of the most widely known black women writing today, has contributed to black children's literary legacy with her childhood account, *To Hell With Dying*. Written in 1965 and published as a children's book in 1986, the story underscores the deep connection between generations. Events focus on a young girl's relationship with a fun-loving, elderly neighbor whom, for years, she and her brother coax and love back from death each time his health falters. Years later, however, no amount of coaxing will postpone death, and she is left with his guitar and a vast store of memories to comfort her.

Ancestral influence is a frequent theme in books for today's black children, just as it is in those written for adults. The great surge of racial pride fostered by the Civil Rights movement has been sustained within black culture through literary returns to the past. Those for children are among the most crucial. Patricia McKissack's *Flossie and the Fox* (1986), a story set in the past and resembling a folktale, shows the young Flossie cleverly outsmarting the fox. McKissack captures both the child's wit and intelligence and the rich black vernacular which effectively bridges past and present for many of today's black children. In the preface to *Flossie*, McKissack credits the older generations of her family, particularly her grandfather, with nurturing the oral tradition and love of past that shape her writing: "[My grandfather] was a master storyteller who charmed his audience with humorous stories told in the rich and colorful dialect of the rural South. I never wanted to forget them. So, it is through me that my family's storytelling legacy lives on."

Also through her, and others like her, the literary legacy for black children persists. Works featuring various African cultures and traditions reinforce black children's link to Africa, at the same time advancing the role of family and community. Children cheer Emeke, the young African boy who wants to fly, in Mildred Pitts Walter's *Brother to the Wind* (1985). Armed with guidance from the animals and his grandmother's unwavering belief in him, he builds a kite, listens for whisperings from the wind, and flies. McKissack's *Mirandy and Brother Wind* (1988) also draws on the African legends of wind and flying, but more pointedly on the early African American cakewalk tradition (a dance first introduced by the slaves). Young Mirandy, like Emeke, needs the wind to help her win the upcoming cakewalk competition. She also needs the help of numerous neighbors and family members, all of whom applaud her and her dancing partner at the community's big Saturday night social: "When Grandmother Beasley had seen Mirandy and Ezel turning and spinning, moving like shadows in the flickering candlelight, she'd thrown back her head, laughed, and said, 'Them chullin' is dancing with the wind!'" Children reading Emeke's and Mirandy's stories feel attuned to the past and see themselves as important, part of a broad community that values them.

Not only is the past a frequent setting for stories by black women writers (and men, as well, though my focus here is on women), but their stories with contemporary settings often include past events, traditions, and individuals, creating as they do, a significant racial memory for children. *Aunt Flossie's Hats (and Crab Cakes Later)* (1991) by Elizabeth Fitzgerald Howard weaves past and present as two young girls try on Great-great-aunt Flossie's old hats and hear her recall the occasions when they were worn. In this way they learn of a parade that honored America's black soldiers returning from World War I and about the huge Baltimore fire of 1904. The girls also relive more recent events, ones they are part of, securing as they do family memories that in time they will share with a younger generation.

Teaching modern black children about their slave past is another contribution of today's literary legacy, one approached with a clarity and strength accumulated by writers over the past two decades. Author and critic Sherely Anne Williams acknowledged in 1972 the "estrangement which Black people feel toward that part of themselves which is bound up in slavery and segregation" (*Give Birth* 216). The same unease is caught in Gayl Jones's question from her novel *Corregidora*: "How could she bear witness to what she'd never lived?" (qtd. in McDowell 44). Since those expressions, writers have confronted their slave past and found, as did Williams, that "slavery eliminated neither heroism nor love; it provided occasions for their expressions" (*Dessa Rose* x). Out of such a recognition many have "borne witness" to what, though not personally experienced, is vital to personal and collective identities. Gradually, children have been included in their audience.

Virginia Hamilton's *The People Could Fly: American Black Folktales* (1985) and *Many Thousand Gone: African Americans from Slavery to Freedom* (1993) capture the dignity and variety of those who lived and resisted the slave experience. A collection by McKissack entitled *The Dark Thirty: Southern Tales of the Supernatural* (1992) includes important, straightforward references to lynchings and discriminations but makes clear racism was not all that comprised life for past black Americans. Humor, good times, courage, faith, just going about life, all are part of the portraits offered by Hamilton and McKissack.

Mildred Taylor also reaches back to speak to children of the present. Her works, frequently autobiographical, appeal to various ages, each reflecting both private and group struggles and the ever-present possibility of triumph. Her own strong upbringing is apparent in all Taylor writes. In *The Gold Cadillac* (1987) she tells of the fancy car her father bought against her mother's wishes. Before long, the car is returned, causing speculation that they had been unable to afford it. She narrates: "We and the family knew the truth. 'As fine as the Cadillac had been,' [her father] said, 'it had pulled us apart for awhile.' Now, as ragged and noisy as that old Ford was, we all rode in it together and we were a family again. So I held my head high."

But the gold Cadillac symbolizes more than family unity. Taylor and her family drive South to visit relatives and for the first time she sees "Whites Only" signs. She watches her father demeaned by a policeman and eats and sleeps in the car because restaurants and motels will not serve black people. The following words conclude her book:

We had the Cadillac only a little more than a month, but I wouldn't soon forget its splendor or how I'd felt riding around inside it. I wouldn't soon forget, either, the ride we had taken South in it. I wouldn't soon forget the signs, the policemen, or my fear. I would remember that ride and the gold Cadillac all my life.

Taylor writes of her childhood and places her story several decades into the past. Few black readers, however, young or old, will divorce themselves entirely from the incident. In some respects and in many places, it is today's reality as well. For that reason, it, and other stories like it, have a strategic place in black children's literary legacy.

As important as the past is to black cultural identity, it is not more important than the present, and this truth is evident to black women writing for children. The here and now and development of the individual child are frequently central to the books they write. Those writing for young adults (Candy Dawson, Rosa Guy, Virginia Hamilton, Eleanora Tate, Joyce Carol Thomas, to name several) address the many social issues facing young people today. Those who write for younger children include issues that pertain to children's well-being. Lucille Clifton writes of a father's abandonment of his family and also traces a child's journey through grief when his father dies. Mildred Pitts Walters depicts the anxiety of replacement when a new baby joins the family. In recent poetry, Eloise Greenfield addresses father-son relations, local drug dealing, and a child's fear of nighttime noises. Perhaps the most challenging of all issues, child sexual abuse, is faced in Jeannette Caines' *Chilly Stomach* (1986) in which the hugs and kisses of an uncle do not feel right to a young girl and she is encouraged by a friend to share her secret with her parents.

I hasten to point out there are books contributing to black children's literary legacy written primarily to delight, and in that delighting, to build the child. Caines has another book entitled *Just Us Women* (1982) in which a young girl and her aunt take a trip in the aunt's new car, "No boys and no men,/just us women." There are no incidents, no tensions, just the two preparing for and enjoying a carefree time together. Similar is Greenfield's *First Pink Light* (1991), a young boy's effort to stay awake late to welcome his father home. Even Walters's *My Mama Needs Me* (1983), while portraying the arrival of a new sibling, is primarily about the love of a boy for his mother and the reassurance she gives him before he runs out to play.

Whether today's works turn on serious issues, draw upon the past, or exist simply to please and entertain children, they share in common the power and purpose to fortify their audience. Eloise Greenfield says it is her intent in all she writes "to give [children] words of love, to grow on" (jacket, *Grandpa's Face* [1988]). Jeannette Caines "looks upon herself as a role model for black kids," visiting schools to share both her books and herself (Raymond 25). One of the newest black women writers in the children's field, Angela Medearis, declares: "I like to make people laugh. I...like to make kids laugh. It's one of the happiest sounds in the world" (Olendorf 177).

Clearly, writers of enormous commitment and talent are creating an identifiable literary legacy for black children. Their skillful use of language, joined with the illustrations of gifted artists, yields genuine images of black culture for black children, contributing at a most fundamental level to their positive self-concepts. Even as we celebrate these accomplishments, however, we must recognize that many more African American writers and artists are needed. Children's literature by black writers falls far below the ten percent that African Americans make up of the total population (Greenfield, "African" 5). Those writers with established reputations should not, nor would they wish to, become "racial representatives," as it seems may be happening.

Racism did not begin with children's literature, nor will it end there. Yet we know literature and art are reflectors and shapers of humane societies. All groups within a society, if they are to be valued and advanced, must be included in that society's aesthetic renderings. Thus the contributions of today's black women writing for children are essential to black culture and to the broader American culture. As they convey strong individual, family, and community images, they reinforce the identities of black children and provide for all children full, authentic views of African American people and their culture.

Works Cited

Alexander, Rae. "What Is a Racist Book?" MacCann and Woodard 52-56. Alexander establishes the characteristics of a racist book, citing specific works rejected by the NAACP. She also discusses works that foster positive images for black children.

Banfield, Beryle. "Racism in Children's Books: An Afro-American Perspective." MacCann and Woodard 23-38. This historical overview of children's literature underscores Banfield's premise that racist myths and stereotypes thrived not only in past publications but continue in contemporary works.

Birtha, Jessie M. "Portrayal of the Black in Children's Literature" (excerpt). MacCann and Woodard 57-65. Birtha offers guidelines to librarians (and others) responsible for selecting children's books that accurately depict African American life.

Children's Literature Review Board. "Starting out Right: Choosing Books about Black People for Young Children. *Cultural Conformity in Books for Children.* Ed. Donnarae MacCann and Gloria Woodard. Metuchen, NJ: Scarecrow, 1977. 107-33. The board establishes guides for evaluating and choosing books that reflect black culture.

Clifton, Lucille. "A Simple Language." *Black Women Writers: 1950-1980.* Ed. Mari Evans. Garden City, NY: Doubleday-Anchor, 1984. 137-38. Clifton talks of her life as writer and her interest in "trying to render big ideas in a simple way."

Greenfield, Eloise. "African American Literature: A New Challenge." *Interracial Books for Children Bulletin* 17.2 (1986): 4-5. In an anniversary address to the Council on Interracial Books for Children, Greenfield applauds the accomplishments of the Council but emphasizes remaining challenges, particularly in the area of publishing.

____. "Writing for Children—A Joy and a Responsibility." MacCann and Woodard 19-22. Greenfield stresses the responsibility of writers and publishers to provide full, accurate portraits of black American life for all children.

Katz, Phyllis A. "The Acquisition of Racial Attitudes in Children." *Towards the Elimination of Racism.* Ed. Phyllis A. Katz. New York: Pergamon, 1976. 125-54. Studies reveal development of racial awareness and attitudes in children begins at pre-school age.

MacCann, Donnarae, and Gloria Woodard, eds. *The Black American in Books for Children: Readings in Racism.* 2nd ed. Metuchen, NJ: Scarecrow, 1985.

Mathis, Sharon Bell. "*The Slave Dancer* Is an Insult to Black Children." *Cultural Conformity in Books for Children: Further Readings in*

Racism. Ed. Donnarae MacCann and Gloria Woodard. Metuchen, NJ: Scarecrow, 1977. 146-48. Mathis objects to the Newbery being awarded to a work offensive and demeaning to black people.

McDowell, Deborah E. "Negotiating between Tenses: Witnessing Slavery after Freedom—*Dessa Rose.*" *Slavery and the Literary Tradition.* Ed. Deborah McDowell and Arnold Rampersad. Baltimore: Johns Hopkins UP, 1989. 144-63. McDowell analyzes strategies used by Sherley Anne Williams to connect past and present African American life through her novel *Dessa Rose.*

Millender, Dharathula H. "Through a Glass, Darkly" (excerpt). MacCann and Woodard 110-18. Traditionally, children's books have mirrored society's racist views, entrenching stereotypes rather than reflecting authentic black culture and daily life.

Myers, William Dean. "The Black Experience in Children's Books: One Step Forward, Two Steps Back." MacCann and Woodard 222-26. Myers tells why it is *not* time to stop "harping on the issue of racism in children's books."

Olendorf, Donna, ed. *Something about the Author.* Vol. 72. Detroit: Gale Research, 1993. Angela Shelf Medearis talks about herself and her writing.

Raymond, Allen. "Jeannette Caines: A Proud Author, With Good Reason." *Early Years* Mar. 1983: 24-25. Raymond interviews Jeannette Caines about her experiences and goals as a writer of children's books.

Sterling, Dorothy. "The Soul of Learning." *English Journal* 29 (Feb. 1968): 166-80. In the 1967 speech given at the NDEA Institute in English at the University of Wisconsin—Milwaukee, Sterling acknowledges numerous works of quality for black children but stresses the need for far more African American writers and for knowledgeable teaching of their books.

Taylor, Mildred D. "Newbery Award Acceptance." *The Horn Book* Aug. 1977: 401-09. Taylor accepts her Newbery award for *Roll of Thunder, Hear My Cry* and talks of her background and goals as a writer.

Washington, Mary Helen. *Midnight Birds: Stories of Contemporary Black Women Writers.* New York: Doubleday-Anchor, 1980.

Williams, Sherley Anne. *Dessa Rose.* New York: Berkeley, 1986. In the fictional recreation of the slave community, Williams depicts black family life and gender relations and the collaboration of a black and a white woman.

_____. *Give Birth to Brightness: A Thematic Study in Neo-Black Literature.* New York: Dial, 1972. Literature written in the wake of the Civil Rights Movement focuses on black experience and culture "as a means of edifying Blacks first and whoever else can understand...second."

A Special Female Voice:
The Heroine in Series Books for Girls

Mary Welek Atwell

Several years ago I began a study focusing on the heroines of series books for girls. The investigation grew out of an interest in the influences on young females that led them to define their aspirations and to develop their expectations. I began with the notion that just as books such as the Horatio Algers had helped to mold a code of behavior for boys in the late 19th and early 20th century, so there must be books that had a comparable impact on girls. Even 20th-century textbooks in U.S. history referred to the Algers as they encouraged adherence to the work ethic, offered a material definition of success, upheld Social Darwinism, and lauded a business culture. Yet these books and their values spoke to only one sex. The values and codes of the Alger books, rather than being American values, were *male* American values and codes. However, one may search for *female* values in popular literature written for an audience of girls. In my view, some of the series books for girls offered not only female role models of various types, but also alternative codes of behavior.[1]

My examination of heroines has included Elsie Dinsmore by Martha Finley; Patty Fairfield by Carolyn Wells; Anne Shirley and Emily Byrd Starr by L.M. Montgomery; Betsy Ray by Maud Hart Lovelace; Maida Westabrook by Inez Haynes Irwin; Judy Bolton by Margaret Sutton; and Anastasia Krupnik by Lois Lowry. Of the older series, only the L.M. Montgomery books remain popular and readily available today. Several of the Betsy books have been reissued, and a considerable body of Lovelace fans is agitating to see the entire series back in print. The Anastasia series, published in the last decade, can easily be found in libraries and bookstores. The other books are more obscure, likely to be found in attics, in the occasional second hand book shop, or in special collections. Several series were chosen for this study because of my own fond memories of them; others were recommended by women colleagues who had read them with pleasure. Still others were suggested by my daughter. Thus the sample of books is subjective and non-scientific. Nonetheless, there are some features common to all the series and questions to be asked of each heroine.

Each series is the work of a single female author, rather than a syndicate, and all can reveal codes of behavior directed to young readers. American women were well represented in the reading and writing of children's literature. Since at least the early 19th century, women have been charged with the education of children—inside the home and in the schools.[2] Their socially defined gender role as educators, as well as the belief that women had an intuitive affinity for and knowledge of children, may have led to a fortuitous match between the female writer and the youthful reader.

Among the types of young people's literature, series books have long been a staple. The series books form part of a culture women writers have helped to create for girls. The series books provide additional pieces of the puzzle of women's past. While it is difficult to measure their precise influence, surely those who seek to appreciate the texture of women's experience can enhance their understanding by examining the heroines offered to young girls in series fiction.

Each series heroine in this study offers a formula for success and happiness, each is empowered, at least temporarily, by subscribing to a code and mastering it. In each case the code suggests an alternative to the dominant masculine value system.

The late 19th-century Elsie (1868-1905) embodied the stereotyped female virtues—chastity, filial obedience, a world encompassed by her extended family, and an intense preoccupation with evangelical Christianity.[3] Elsie seemed at first glance to be submissive in the extreme. Actually, she exerted great power over her family and friends through her virtuous example and preaching. In the patriarchal setting of the stories, Elsie, a female Christ figure, was the instrument of salvation for dozens of characters. The message that women could exert a profound influence for good in the domestic sphere, and through their converts, in the wider world, is not far below the surface of the Elsie books.

The substance of the series is included in the first seven of the 28 books. By the time Martha Finley concluded the series, Elsie was a widow, a grandmother, and in fact, a matriarch. The quality of the novels deteriorated, becoming purely didactic, virtually without plot or characterization. Rather, the author, in Elsie's voice, inflicted upon her readers incessant lectures on the Bible and an extremely jingoistic version of American history.

In a series published between 1901 and 1919, Patty Fairfield was at first glance a much more modern heroine.[4] Patty went to school and competed with her peers, while Elsie studied at home with her father. Patty is active and energetic, while Elsie was sedentary. Patty goes to dances and parties—activities that would shock the Dinsmores. And most significantly, the whole matter of religion, so central to the lives of Elsie et al., is absent from the concerns of Patty, her family, and friends. But despite such contrasts between the series, conventional notions about women's place persist. Patty's mission in life during her late adolescence is to choose the best husband material from among her numerous suitors. Her goal is to be married. If she approaches that goal without unseemly haste, she nonetheless pursues it with avid dedication.

Patty's code is based on a sense of proportion, an attempt to create a tasteful, harmonious, comfortable environment. She cultivates her beauty, her good temper, and a firm devotion to the rules of etiquette. Driven by a sense of noblesse oblige, Patty's social conscience moves beyond saving souls to individual acts of private charity, but lacks any sense of a need for political action or reform. Patty is successful, on her terms. She marries a rich man and lives happily ensconced with husband and baby, doing battle against gaucheries in Westchester County.

Anne Shirley, in the books which begin with *Anne of Green Gables*, written and set at the same time as the Patty series, shows both similarities and differences to the other heroines.[5] Like Elsie Dinsmore, Anne began in her author's mind as a character in a Sunday School serial; and like Elsie and Patty, Anne grew up in the series from a little girl into a mature married woman. On the other hand, the Anne books have enjoyed much greater longevity than the others, both in her native Canada and in the United States.

To understand fully Anne's evolution, one must go beyond the series heroines and look at the character who may be the prototype of the series heroine. In many ways, Anne's development from irrepressible to conventional most resembles Jo March in *Little Women*. Both are full of spunk and imagination, both want to be writers, both are unconventional and independent in mind and spirit. Both young women were intelligent, both left home for careers and economic independence, both returned and married. Before their marriages, both Anne and Jo lived in a largely female environment, where they formed strong bonds of support and encouragement with other girls and women. In the feminine world of their youth, the heroines had dreams and kindred spirits to share them.[6]

But marriage to her childhood friend and academic rival, Gilbert Blythe, seemed to diminish Anne. She moved into Gilbert's world—

cozy and loving—but one in which she became Mrs. Dr. Blythe, one in which she became less empowered, less and less a person with her own goals and talents.

Like Anne, Emily Byrd Starr is a creation of L.M. Montgomery.[7] The author uses the metaphors of the climb and the quest to place Emily in the heroic tradition. But because Emily was female, her quest was carried on within a set of boundaries imposed by her family and her conditioning. Emily's goal, indeed her very essence, was to write and to have her writing add to the world's happiness and beauty. Hers was the universal female struggle to find and speak in her own voice, a struggle that was often played out between Emily's personal ambitions and the family claim. Emily's writing was at times her salvation, at times a gift, at other times a disappointment or a burden, but always integral to her self. But traditions, conventions, ambitions, relations, romances—all threatened to thwart Emily in the expression of her voice. Circumstances in her personal life seemed to conspire to interfere with or tarnish her success.

The resolution of Emily's struggle is ambiguous at best. She must write to be true to herself, to express her voice, and yet when men are involved romantically, she cannot or does not write, her voice is muted. As Emily marries at the end of the trilogy, the reader never knows whether she has, in the end, made a choice between love and work.

The Betsy books (or the Betsy-Tacy books as they are often called) are also set in the first decades of the 20th century. They differ from the other series in several ways.[8] Most noticeably, while all the books in the other series are written in a style suitable for a single age group, Lovelace has designed the stories of little Betsy for an elementary audience, whereas the later books are longer and more sophisticated in style, vocabulary, and content for young adult readers. Set in the early 20th century, the first five books deal with Betsy up to the age of 12, her family and friends. They are simply written and simply illustrated. The remaining six books cover Betsy's years in high school, college (very briefly), her trip abroad, and her early married life.

Betsy is part of a traditional nuclear family—a slim, fun-loving red-haired mother, a solid sensible father whose wife and three daughters took top priority in his life—and a network of friends who are an integral part of the series. The atmosphere in Deep Valley, Minnesota, is stable, loving, and supportive. The biggest challenges Betsy faces involve reconciling her private dreams and aspirations with her social needs. In essence, Betsy's story is a tale of a real girl growing up, of learning lessons about religion, friendship, work, and relationships with men, that help her clarify her values and become the kind of person she hoped to be. Betsy learns the rules of becoming a successful, mature person, not through severe moral trials, but through the ordinary dilemmas of life.[9] She develops her code of behavior not by being instructed in principles, but by deriving lessons from pragmatic self-evaluation and from positive reinforcement. As Carol Gilligan and other feminist writers have shown, women are more likely to develop their moral values through relationships than through the application of abstract principles.[10] Betsy seems to embody this pattern.

As the series ends, Betsy remains an unfinished heroine. Like Anne and Emily, she wants to be a wife and mother as well as a writer. The time is 1917, her husband is in the army, Betsy has taken a job writing for a publicity bureau. Despite the uncertainty of the war, Betsy has her family, her friends, her writing, and her partnership with a husband who thinks she is important—"as a human being, not just as a girl."[11] If Betsy's future is not resolved, at least it is promising.

Maida Westabrook, in books written between 1909 and 1953, provides a much more autonomous and androgynous female model.[12] Unlike the other heroines, Maida does not grow up beyond the age of about 12. Her father, a Wall Street tycoon, could afford to provide a full range of experiences, including an entire house, trips, a school, a farm, and a camp, for Maida and her friends. His wealth supports a world of children, with little or no control by adults. The author, feminist Inez Haynes Irwin, provides a code of behavior directed equally toward boys and girls. The characters in the series strive for honesty, love of learning, tolerance, responsibility for the less fortunate, and good sportsmanship. Maida finds her reward in good health, friends, and plans to major in economics and pursue her own career on Wall Street after college. Although the children live in a definitely paternalistic world, the Maida books provide at least one positive adult female character—a happily married teacher and writer, who was also an accomplished storyteller and a fine athlete.

Detective heroine Judy Bolton (1932-67) is courageous and caring, with a strong sense of social responsibility.[13] Margaret Sutton develops Judy's story from high school to young married woman. Judy enjoyed a sense of accomplishment from setting things right and seeing justice done; emotional satisfaction from a loving husband, family and friends; and the extended youth that comes from an inquisitive spirit. Judy comes from a realistic middle-class family and home. Unlike most of her predecessors, (and her contemporary Nancy Drew), Judy has a mother, as well as a father who is not a superpatriarch. She lives in a house with a reasonable number of rooms and without a staff of servants. The heroine never identifies with the elite or the powerful. Indeed, the social values of the books reflect a sort of populist New Deal liberalism. Judy hated and set out to rectify the exploitation of the poor by the privileged. Judy is more than a successful and clever detective—she is connected with other people, she works on her relationships, she makes the people she helps a part of her life. She has made the choice to be both autonomous and committed.

Marriage does not end life as a detective or as an individual for Judy. More than half of the series takes place after Judy marries Peter Dobbs, who as an FBI agent shares her interest in detecting. Unlike many series heroines, she has both a husband and a career, suggesting that life as an adult can continue to offer growth and adventure, as well as contentment.

A heroine for the current generation, Anastasia Krupnik is a precocious ten-year-old at the beginning of Lois Lowry's eight-volume series (so far), and a precocious 13 in the most recent book.[14] Carol Gilligan's work indicates that these years of early adolescence are critical in the development of young girls' identities. It is often during those years that girls move from self-confident, assertive and independent-minded persons to conform themselves into an apparently more socially acceptable role that limits their self-esteem and security. Not so Anastasia. This eminently believable heroine experiences failure and challenges, yet through her interaction with her environment she is developing into a strong, thoughtful young woman with a positive code of behavior, a sense of humor, and an ongoing skepticism about superficial values.

Through her family and friends, Anastasia has the opportunity to encounter and respond to contemporary issues, such as divorce, sexuality, racism, and sexism. Anastasia's relationships with African-American peers and adults are mutually respectful—recognizing differences in a positive way. Relationships among men and women and marriage are frequent topics, always without an aura of make-believe romance, and never as the goal of a woman's life. Unlike work, which is necessary for everyone, marriage is an option.

Lowry's presentation of the complexity of female options is a definite strength of the series. Of all the books in this study, these are extraordinary for their strong adult female characters. Unlike many earlier series which had no mothers in them, with the implicit suggestion that mothers are boring, a hindrance to individual development, or both, Mrs. Krupnik offers a model of what Anastasia could grow up to be—a talented, creative, intelligent woman, with a family, a career, and a congenial, supportive husband. Here perhaps is one of the significant feminist messages in the Anastasia books— that one can become a successful adult through relationships of connection and continuity, not through separation and competition.

All of the series, with the exception of the Elsies, feature lively young heroines, but the problem of sustaining strong series characters into adulthood affects even well developed and appealing heroines. The larger question arises—why are there so few positive adult female characters in children's literature, and why do such characters who start well fade as they go along?

It may be that authors who are successful in portraying children and young people do not enjoy the same skill in drawing adult characters (and vice versa). In other words, someone *becomes* a juvenile author because of a talent for characterizing children. The imagination that draws a wonderful 11-year-old Anne Shirley, for example, may fail when it comes to the same character at 40.

Possibly juvenile authors conclude that young people aren't very interested in grownups, so they move them out of the way. It is, however, difficult to know whether children are interested in adults or not, as they have so few chances to decide.

Some authors may have felt that strong adult female models were invalid, that the opportunities for an autonomous life for adult women were limited, that conformity was the penalty for growing up. A truly feminist author such as Inez Haynes Irwin may have solved the problem for Maida by keeping her a child, thus avoiding any real conflict between personal growth and family responsibilities.

But perhaps what the young readers remember from the series heroines is not their limitations and their truncated adult careers, but their sense of possibility. As Perri Klass describes the literary characters she loves, "Emily and Jo and Anne and Rebecca and Betsy...are permanent residents of my mind, and I suspect they go on colonizing new young minds year after year. They brought me information, details about life as a writer, vicarious triumphs and agonies. But above all they brought me reinforcement in my determination that I would grow up to write books."[15]

Women series writers have helped to create a culture for girls—a culture in which people like themselves, other female children, are agents of change. This is surely an empowering experience for young girls. Perhaps one lesson this historical examination of girls' books has shown is that, if Anastasia is in any way typical, the barriers to the development of contemporary heroines are different from those in the past. The obstacles are not, as with earlier heroines, only their own bows to convention or the restraints imposed by family, but the structural inequities of society. The young reader may look to find more than individual inspiration from her heroines. She will need to make common cause with other potential real-life heroines to bring down these barriers.

Notes

[1] See Mary Welek Atwell, "'Little' Maida: The Heroine Progresses," *Children's Literature Association Quarterly* (Summer 1987).

[2] See for example, Kathryn Kish Sklar, *Catharine Beecher: A Study in American Domesticity* (New Haven: Yale UP, 1973), and the essays on teaching in Anne Firor Scott, *Making the Invisible Woman Visible* (Urbana: U of Illinois P, 1984).

[3] See Martha Finley, *Elsie Dinsmore* series (New York: Dodd, Mead, 1868-1905).

[4] See Carolyn Wells, *Patty Fairfield* series (New York: Grosset, 1901-19).

[5] See L.M. Montgomery, *Anne* series (New York: Stokes; Boston: Page, 1908-39).

[6] See Ann B. Murphy, "The Borders of Ethical, Erotic, and Artistic Possibilities in *Little Women*," *Signs* XV (Spring 1990): 562-85.

[7] See L.M. Montgomery, *Emily* trilogy (New York: Stokes, 1923-27).

[8] See Maud Hart Lovelace *Betsy* series (New York: Crowell, 1940-55).

[9] Many of the issues in the Betsy high school books involve courtship patterns and adolescent male-female relations. Beth Bailey's *From Front Porch to Back Seat* (Baltimore: Johns Hopkins Press, 1988), offers some provocative ideas for understanding the popularity of the Betsy books. For example, the books were set in the "front porch" period, when young women and their families had the initiative in courtship as hosts for the young men who came to call. Later in the 20th century, when the books were written, the relationship had changed. In dating, young men held the power and the initiative, as they paid for the date. Some of the appeal of the Betsys may relate to nostalgia for a time when women exercised more control in courtships.

[10] Carol Gilligan, *In a Different Voice* (Cambridge, MA: Harvard UP, 1982).

[11]Maud Hart Lovelace, *Betsy's Wedding* (New York: Crowell, 1955): 204.

[12]See Inez Haynes Irwin, *Maida* series (New York: Grosset, 1909-53).

[13]See Margaret Sutton, *Judy Bolton* series (New York: Grosset, 1932-67).

[14]See Lois Lowry, *Anastasia* series (New York: Dell-Yearling; Boston: Houghton Mifflin, 1980-91).

[15]Perri Klass, "Stories for Girls About Girls Who Write Stories," *New York Times Books Review* 17 May 1992: 39.

The Reproduction of Gendering: Imaging Kids in Ads for Adults

Barbara Gottfried

The notion that gender is a social construction has become a truism of much feminist, and more recently, men's studies, as evidenced in a recent volume of essays on *Men, Masculinity, and the Media*. In the introduction, editor Steve Craig points out as a working assumption of the various essays that if we grant that "gender is a concept that is culturally constructed...[m]asculinity and femininity can then be examined as sets of social expectations, created and maintained in a patriarchal society."[1] In one of the volume's essays, Stan Denski and David Sholle further elaborate upon gender as a construct, rather than an essential biological "fact," using Judith Butler's Foucauldian reading of gender and sexuality in *Gender Trouble: Feminism and the Subversion of Identity* to call attention to the performativity of gender:

sexuality is not a fixed, natural fact, but is better understood as the "set of effects produced in bodies, behaviors, and social relations by a certain deployment deriving from a complex political technology" [Foucault, 1980, 127]. This complex cultural apparatus of sexuality results in the production of the binaries of gender and sexual difference as seemingly normal or natural categories. Thus what we read as gender is constructed through a performance that is repeated. Since the reality of gender is created through sustained social performances, the suggestion is that the idea of a true or essential masculinity or femininity is an illusion.[2]

No matter how you cut it, social construction theory calls into question the essentializing of gender. Nevertheless, as Jean Bethke Elshtain puts it elsewhere, "ours is a culture [that gives] gender a strong reading, highlighting its many markers, constraining and inciting men and women to characteristic modes of action and reaction,"[3] perhaps, one might speculate, as an expression of our anxiety about the very illusoriness of gender; but more to the point, because ours is a culture that is heavily invested in gender as (binary) difference. As Teresa De Lauretis explains what is at stake:

If at any one time there are several competing, even contradictory, discourses on sexuality—rather than a single, all-encompassing or monolithic, ideology—then what makes one take up a position in a certain discourse rather than another is an "investment"...something between an emotional commitment, and a vested interest, in the relative power (satisfaction, reward, payoff) which that position promises (but does not necessarily fulfill).[4]

Thus there is "a vested interest," a politics, to sexual orientation and the construction of gender identity as a set of complementary opposites, that uncovers the "payoff" which is our pleasure in difference, and which enlists every aspect of our culture in its production, or, more precisely, its reproduction.

Exploring the media's role in the cultural reproduction of gender in "Gender Ideology in Television Commercials," Denise Kervin points out that "[t]he process of conveying lessons about gender— what it means to be or takes to be properly masculine and feminine—is undertaken by the major institutions in our lives, such as the family, schools, church and peer groups,"[5] almost from the moment of birth. She then goes on to argue that given the pre-dominance of the visual media in late 20th-century America, especially movies and television, those media, too, should be counted as significant contributors to the social construction of gender.

Extending Kervin's point, I would argue that glossy magazines, a significant portion of whose contents are full-page color ads, also figure in the reproduction of gender ideology. Indeed, polls suggest that people respond more favorably to magazine advertising than to advertising on TV.[6] What distinguishes print ads' representations of men and women from those in films or television, especially as they embody current notions about masculinity and femininity, is their immediacy and compression, one might almost call it their overdetermination. Ads are created to respond to an immediate need to successfully market a particular product to a particular audience in a very short space of time: the time it takes to air an ad on TV (15-60 seconds) or the time it takes to turn the page of a magazine (1-5 seconds). The creation of effective ads for magazines is particularly challenging because those ads rely on static, silent images with which advertisers must nevertheless create the same kinds of dramatic stories as they do in television ads.

At the same time, advertisements' quality of immediacy and compression, their overdetermination, is reminiscent of Freud's dreamwork, which figures forth potent fantasies in compressed, over-determined images that have to be decoded, unpacked, and interpreted to be apprehended. As in advertising, the touchstone of dreamwork as Freud has it, is its quality of wish-fulfillment, and in this sense, as John Berger paradoxically suggests, by drawing on nostalgic images of a rarefied past, advertising wishfulfillingly promises a rarefied future, contingent upon the purchase of whatever is for sale. What we see in ads is not ourselves or our world *per se*, but ourselves and our world as they ought to be, and could be, purged of ugliness, poverty, problems, should we be persuaded to purchase the latest talismanic product.[7] Thus ads, in their endless self-recreation, contribute to the ideological work of culture by helping both to create and expose our world as we see it, "continually working over beliefs and counter-beliefs about women and men"[8] and, I would add, about what constitutes masculinity or femininity, even in very young children, at a particular cultural moment.

In keeping with advertising's nostalgic, yet wishful, imaging, advertisements which picture children nostalgically reproduce a world in which girls are girls and boys are boys, and gender works as a simple binary opposition, reproducing our cultural fantasy that gender is an unproblematic category of perceptual organization. Only a very small spectrum of gender possibilities is imaged (or imagined): variations of any sort from a strict gendering of boys and girls are rarely represented in advertising; and the exceptions are rarely more than slight aberrations of appearance, which often unintentionally reconfirm gender stereotypes despite superficial efforts to undercut them. As Jo Spence explains the significance of the oversimpli-fications of advertising, "An important concern in decoding images should be that of understanding the ways in which dominant forms of visual representation reduce complex issues and relationships to a few 'recognisable' aspects which appear to constitute an acceptable reality."[9] Thus advertising that pictures children often schematizes the representation of gender, and in so doing, points to our culture's nostalgia for gender certainties, when boys were boys, and girls were "sugar and spice and all things nice," inadvertently revealing our cultural anxiety about the very notion that gender is a construct.

In terms of the on-going process of the social construction of gender identity, this paper will ask how representations of children in advertisements reflect, corroborate, and/or expose current gender ideology as those representations reveal both innovations and anxieties with regard to the propagation and performance of gender roles and identities. Much has been written about how children as audience are exploited by the insidious ways products are marketed to them on TV. But children appear frequently in magazine ads for products they can hardly be interested in; and, even more commonly, in ads for products that are for children, but which appear in magazines that children can hardly be supposed to read. Indeed, these ads are not addressed to children, but to the women who are usually the primary caretakers and instructors of young children, and who are therefore important mediators in the process of identity construction for those young children. These ads contribute to the reproduction of gendering by imaging for parents representations of desirable traits for their children, which work, though often unintentionally, to underscore distinctions of gender. In so doing, "film, TV, and other media help to constitute gender difference, rather than simply reflect or represent that difference,"[10] as the evidence of the ads discussed below will confirm.

To obtain a representative sample of advertising addressed to parents which pictures kids, I looked through a wide variety of magazines that target parents, especially mothers, including: *Parents, Baby Talk* [a free Diaper Service magazine], *American Baby, Mothering, Good Housekeeping, Woman's Day, Family Circle, People, Time,* the *Sesame Street Parents Guide, Parenting,* and *Child. Good Housekeeping, Parents, Parenting,* and the *Sesame Street Parents Guide* contained many ads which pictured children either alone, with other children, or with adults. *Woman's Day* and *Family Circle* contained surprisingly few ads which included children, suggesting that these particular women's magazines target women whose children have reached the age of adolescence or older, and who are therefore no longer interested in ads for toys, disposable diapers, baby food, etc. *Time* and *People* also did not contain many ads that pictured children, perhaps because they target both men and women of various age groups and demographics, significant numbers of whom are either not parents, or do not have young children, so that companies that wish to optimally target the market of parents with young children might better spend their advertising budgets elsewhere.

Decoding these advertisements raises questions about the ways in which ads addressed to adults instruct them about what constitutes gender identity in children, or, put another way, how masculinity and femininity are coded for reproduction and consumption in the ways children are represented in advertisements. I will consider the spectrum of portrayals of children in magazine ads addressed to adults, examining the ways in which masculinity and femininity are coded to cue the adult reader of the ad to dress boy children and girl children in particular ways, treat them in gender specific ways, allow or foster gender specific behaviors and activities, etc. Finally, I will turn to the sexualization of children, especially young girls, in ads as a way of looking at how adults' attitudes contribute to girls' beginning to internalize notions of themselves as sexualized objects of the male gaze, even at a very young age. Magazine ads are ideal for such an investigation because in crystallizing a particular cultural moment, they become sophisticated, if evanescent, cultural icons which mingle insight with cliché, easy explanations with the cutting edge's trace of anxiety and ambivalence about the potential breakdown of the (gendered) status quo.

Children learn their gender roles from a variety of sources in a variety of ways. The major institutions of our culture are an important source of social knowledge, but even before children have been to school they have begun to develop a sense of what is expected of boys or girls which they learn from TV, peers, parents, and other family members. Inevitably in our culture, the first question asked about a newborn after inquiring into its health, is whether it is a boy or a girl. Indeed, the evidence, both anecdotal and that garnered from formal research, indicates that gender role imprinting begins virtually at birth: that parents and other adults treat even the youngest boy babies and girl babies differently. To understand why this is so, we must look at how parents understand and reproduce gender in their children. The evidence from the advertising in glossy magazines addressed to the parents, especially the mothers, of young children suggests that what gets communicated to parents about their kids encourages them to reproduce a rather limited range of gender-stereotyped appearances and reinforce a rather limited range of gender-bound behaviors. The crystallized moments of magazine advertising make clear that a lot of ideological work goes into reproducing gender differentiation in kids even at a very young age.

Many children display gender-stereotyped toy preferences and behaviors by 18 to 24 months of age both at home, and in group settings;[11] and the evidence suggests that parents encourage the gender-differentiated play preferences of even very young children.[12] By the time they are three, "children are well aware of the socially prescribed nature of the kind of toys with which they play and not only request gender-stereotyped toys, but appear to avoid objects labeled as appropriate for the other sex."[13] In addition, children "police" each other's choice of toys, and while girls can usually get away with playing with boys' toys, both boys and girls will rarely allow a boy to get away with playing with anything that is obviously associated with girls,[14] clearly because there is a stigma attached to femininity that makes a transgressive manifestation in relation to it much more taboo than the other way around.

In keeping with the notion of the strict gendering of children from a very young age, a now classic study was made of the furnishings and toys of 48 boys and 48 girls under the age of six of relatively well-to-do, university-affiliated, highly educated parents, on the assumption that children that young don't choose their own things, so that what was there would indicate the parents' ideological perspective on gender socialization.[15] The investigators found no differences in the number of books, musical objects or stuffed toys in children's rooms, but did find significant differences in several categories of toys. The number of vehicles for boys was 375 versus 17 for girls. No girl's room contained a wagon, boat, kiddie car, motorcycle, snowmobile, or military toys, the toys boys most typically play with, while only 8 of the boys' rooms contained a female doll, compared to 41 of the girls' rooms. Only girls were provided with toys that encourage nurturance, or toys that emphasize domestic concerns such as cooking or housekeeping, or a concern with fashion. The investigators also discovered that boys had more toys, and more different toys than girls, which, in addition to vehicles, included sports equipment, toy animals, machines, and live animals, while girls' toys were almost exclusively focused on domestic concerns.

Boys' toys were found to promote rough-house and fantasy play, motor activity, competition, constructiveness, handling, and aggressiveness, thus stressing achievement and autonomy, whereas girls' toys were found to foster cooperation and nurturance, and perhaps not surprisingly, activities directed toward the home, especially housekeeping and childcare. Thus girls' toys were found to promote creativity, but also lady-like behavior, staying clean and neat, and a concern with mirrors and physical attractiveness; while boys' toys promoted self-reliance, independence, and, crucially, activities directed away from the home, all of which parents encourage much more in boys than in girls.[16] According to Hilary Lips, "Even the different toys and play activities parents encourage for boys and girls influence not only children's conceptions of what activities are appropriate for females and males, but also what thinking, problem-solving, and social skills these children develop."[17]

Thus, according to Lips, "Parental gender-role socialization has a more global impact than does the communication of a particular set of 'gender-appropriate' behaviors. Parents give male infants more stimulation and varied responses, and allow boys to explore more than they do girls. Furthermore, girls and boys are taught by their parents to take different approaches to problem-solving, to challenge, and to life in general." Thus, as Jeanne Block argues, boys are socialized to "develop a premise system that presumes or anticipates mastery, efficacy and instrumental competence, [while] the socialization practices directed at girls tend toward fostering proximity, discouraging independent problem solving by premature or excessive intervention, restricting exploration, and discouraging active play." The net result has repercussions that reverberate throughout their lives: boys develop "wings—which permit leaving the nest, exploring far reaches, and flying alone, while girls develop roots—that anchor, stabilize, and support growth, but allow fewer chances to master the environment."[18]

The findings of the sociologists, psychologists, and anthropologists detailed above with regard to the virtually unrelenting reproduction of gendering in young children by parents and other invested adults, are borne out in the advertisements that depict children in a broad range of magazines. As glossy ads make clear to even the most casual observer, the color-coding of little boys and girls begins pretty much at birth, "help[ing] to mark a human being as a gendered subject,"[19] and persists with few exceptions in advertisements for everything from "his" and "her" Huggies to Mickey and Minnie Mouse inflatable rocking chairs. Though a number of contemporary ads gesture toward breaking color, and therefore, implicitly, gender taboos, their efforts rarely move beyond the superficial or obvious. For instance, in an ad for the inflatable rockers [© 1991], though the little girl is dressed in light blue and yellow rather than pink, she is sitting on a pink Minnie rocker, as if it were impossible, or somehow transgressive, for a boy to sit on a Minnie rocker, or a girl to sit on a Mickey rocker.

For somewhat older children, Huggies gender-specific training pants come in blue and pink packages, ostensibly to alert the purchaser to differences necessitated by biological gender distinctions, since the two kinds of training pants are designed to correspond to the anatomical differences between boys and girls. But this pragmatic distinction in the packaging does not explain why it seemed necessary to the designers of Huggies to make the decorations on the boys' pants pictures of cars and trucks in bold, primary colors, while the pictures on the girls' pants are of animals in pastel colors. Though kids themselves can tell the difference between vehicles and animals, it is unlikely that at that age they necessarily make gender distinctions based on the illustrations. It seems more likely that the decorative character of the training pants confirms gender distinctions for those who see and notice them, that is to say, caretakers, whether parents, day-care operators, babysitters, relatives, or the other adults who come into contact with the children, and to whom it is (apparently) important to "mark human being[s] as gendered subject[s]."[20]

Fruit of the Loom [© 1992] also emphasizes gender distinctions in an ad with three separate images for their children's underwear line. According to the ad's three captions, each of which corresponds to a picture depicted on a different example of the underwear itself, the boy's underwear "gives him a chance to stomp around with Dinosaurs," whereas the girl's underwear "let[s] her sing along with the Little Mermaid," more lady-like and feminine than the boy's activity; or, already emphasizing the importance of appearance for girls, "Help[s] your Beauty save the Beast." Looking at these three images, I can't help wondering if it is entirely a coincidence that not only are two of the three pictures in the underwear ad of girls, whereas the majority of the children pictured in toy ads are boys; but also, if is entirely coincidental that in those two images the girls are pictured in full frontal poses, while in the third image the boy is pictured with his back to the magazine audience, as if already to suggest that the girls, like their older counterparts in fashion magazines, are pictured in the ads as objects for the viewers' visual consumption, whereas the boy is modestly allowed to deflect attention from the part of his body which is sexually vulnerable, and which, culturally, marks him as a sexual subject, rather than a sexual object.

The research which suggests that boys are encouraged to be active and do things, while girls, like their mothers, are pictured in the house, engaged in passive or at-home activities, is borne out by a number of ads like the one for a Fisher-Price wagon and scooter in *American Baby* magazine [© 1990]. In it, a child who is clearly a little boy is pictured pulling a wagon in one shot, and pushing himself on a scooter in another. While there are no gendered pronouns in the ad (the gender-free words "child" and "toddlers" are used), the caption, which begins, "Remember how wonderful it felt to get your first set of wheels?," seems to address the fathers of sons, playing on the stereotype of the American male's obsession with owning and driving a car, and reinforcing the notion, traditionally associated with masculinity, that being in control of your own movements is a form of asserting independence and autonomy. Similarly, a Fisher-Price ad for a Pic Up 'N Go Dump Truck [© 1990] not only pictures a boy in the ad and refers to him as "he," the front of the toy itself includes a picture of the dump truck driver, who is clearly a male, reinforcing the notion that it is boys who play with and drive vehicles and toys that create motion, not girls. Even ads for a walker and a rocking horse "for your little buckaroo" [© 1990] picture boys, as if it is boys who have a premium on "getting around" while little girls are content to remain sedentary.

When girls are allowed to have a car, it isn't a Safari jeep, "perfect for little campers," with a "pretend engine...to tinker with," or a replica of a Suzuki dirt bike for your "little rider" [© 1992], but a hot pink Barbie-Corvette, which includes a "play cellular phone—essential for Barbie business calls and hours of chit chat" [© 1988]. However, the little girl in the picture does not look like she is making business calls, but rather, like she is engaged in "chit chat," and the caption makes no reference to her being able to "tinker with" the car. Perhaps, however, someone pointed out this discrepancy to Power Wheels, because in a more recent ad [© 1990], though the little girl is still pictured in a pink "sweetheart" car, the caption does mention "tinker[ing]."

Some advertisers and product manufacturers do seem to be aware both of the power of advertising to perpetuate gender stereotypes and of the desire of at least a certain segment of their [parental] audience to break down the rigid strictures of gender stereotyping, especially in toys for children.[21] For instance, a series of ads for Playskool toys seems relatively gender neutral. Both boys and girls are pictured in the ads, and when girls are pictured, they are wearing pragmatic, utilitarian, dark-colored, boy-like clothing, rather than the pink or white, frilly, feminine clothes stereotypically associated with little girls. But closer attention to the images reveals a gendering of the children's activities that nevertheless works to reinforce cultural stereotypes. Both a little girl and a little boy are pictured in facing page Playskool ads riding on rocker ponies and dressed in gender neutral colors [© 1992]. But an ad for a "Busy Poppin' Farm" [© 1991], includes no female figures—a boy is pictured playing with it, and the farm itself includes a (male) farmer and a boy who pops up if you push the barn roof. And while it is a girl pictured "talk[ing] and listen[ing]" on a a Big Bird Talking Phone [© 1991], it is a boy who gets to use "SoundsAround" to learn his letters; and even more tellingly, it is a boy pictured in the ad for Alphie II, My First Computer [© 1990]. In addition, in keeping with the notion that it is boys who are better at constructiveness and building or making things, Fisher-Price pictures a boy in its ads for its Action Tools [© 1991], as does Playskool's ad for its Tinkertoys [© 1992], even though the ads never use the male pronoun. Interestingly, when Fisher-Price advertises a kitchen, the ad deliberately pictures both a boy and a girl, rather than just girls, and the long narrative virtually surrounding the image seems to go out of its way to avoid gendered names or pronouns, referring to the children as "little chefs" and "kids" to suggest that both boys and girls can have fun or belong in the kitchen. But, for some reason which undercuts the gender-inclusive impact of the ad, the girl is talking on the phone rather than cooking or eating the food in front of her, or engaging with the boy with whom she is, ostensibly, playing, while the boy is about to eat an egg he may or may not have prepared (though, male-like, he has not put his food on a plate but is about to eat it directly from the frying pan), so that it is not clear who has done the cooking. The ad does seem to suggest, however, that girls would rather talk on the phone than perform culinary or "wifely" duties, and that, like grown men and women, male and female children have little to say to each other.

In a series of ads on successive pages, Disney/Mattel [© The Walt Disney Company, no date] lets a boy talk on the phone, an activity more usually assigned to girls, but the next ad, more traditionally shows a boy using a tape player, and in the following image shows a boy playing with a train that includes a "*rugged* collection of accessories" (emphasis mine). The only one of the four ads to picture a girl is for a Baby Minnie doll "specially designed so that little ones can learn to care." Though like many of the ads for toys addressed to middle- and upper-middle class parents, this ad would appear to carefully avoid using a gendered pronoun to refer to the child in the ad, she is quite clearly a girl, and the advertiser does manage to get gender into the description by referring to the doll twice as "she." Thus the Disney/Mattel ads, like the Fisher-Price and Playskool ads described above, contribute to the reproduction of gendering in ads addressed to adults by making it clear that even though their ads are carefully constructed to avoid gendered pronouns, dolls are intended for girls, and trains for boys; and, even more insidiously, toys that can go either way are also for boys.

Again, even ads that seem to go out of their way to be gender-neutral often undercut their own best intentions. For instance, an ad for Mattel's Farmer Says Doll [© 1991], a male doll which says the name of its body parts when squeezed in the appropriate places, and which is clearly not a baby doll, pictures the doll standing alone as if to suggest that the doll could be given either to a boy or a girl. In addition, the ad copy uses the gender-free words "your child" to refer to the doll's potential audience. Nevertheless, a smaller image in the ad shows the Farmer Says Doll being held not by a little boy, but by a little girl.

In addition to simply indicating which toys are most appropriate for which gender child, many toy ads provide adult caretakers of children with further cues to gender appropriate behavior for kids. In an advertisement for Mattel toys at Kmart's Toyland Express [© The Walt Disney Company, no date] two little girls are playing with a Barbie and a Mickey doll. Pictured in front of them are Barbie accessories all in pink. Interestingly, in addition to the stereotypical color associations, and the girls' traditionally feminine activities, they are shown looking at each other, stressing their engagement with each other and their mutual involvement in their play, interpersonal qualities more often associated with girls than with boys. In a two-page ad for a Little Tikes Beauty Salon [© 1992] two girls are again engaged in stereotypically female activities, playing dress-up and hair-dresser with each other (even though virtually every hairdresser I've ever had has been male). And this time they are overtly shown in an activity that both stresses appearance and mimics what adult women do to be attractive. In addition, although they are pictured outdoors, they are playing on the terrace of a house which is clearly separated off from the overgrown garden beyond it by a balustrade to enclose and protect the girls.

Another ad with cues to gender specific activities is an ad for Ovaltine [© 1992] which pictures a boy on a scooter, and creates an image very different from the images of girls at play described above. Not only is the boy engaged in an activity outside the house, and defined by its mobility, but his house is nowhere to be seen, suggesting autonomy, independence and freedom of movement— he is apparently whistling in self-possession and unconcern, although alone in a wooded area. It is no coincidence that it is a boy pictured alone, away from home, rather than a girl: girls are almost always pictured in or near the home, or near an adult, as in the Beauty Salon ad described above; and parents, both mothers and fathers, are not comfortable with the notion of their young daughters out and about alone. In addition, the boy's solitariness and self-sufficiency suggest a childhood version of the Marlboro man, that cultural icon of the modern cowboy, who, in owing nothing to anyone, bodies forth the collective fantasy of macho integrity that haunts the American male psyche. Indeed, I suspect we would be hard pressed to find an ad like this one which pictured a girl rather than a boy.

Beyond appropriate activities and behaviors, other gender stereotypes associated with males and females are continually reproduced in the ways kids are pictured in ads addressed to adults. For instance, an ad for Carnation Good Start Infant Formula, which pictures a mother with her baby in a close-up, uses both color-coding and particular adjectives that connote femininity and gentleness to sell its product. The large caption, "Made To Be Gentle," that runs across the top of the page in pink letters, and the rose tone of the ad as a whole, underscore the literal sense of the caption, and the words of the ad below reinforce gentleness by invoking stereotypes associated with girl children, though boy babies are, of course, just as "soft and tender, and so special." Another ad, this time for Dreft detergent for baby clothes [© 1990], also connotes gentleness by bathing the image in the ad in rose tones and showing soft, frilly, pink baby clothes strewn all around a baby one then assumes is a girl. Boys, on the other hand, are used to connote the opposite of gentleness, as in a PopQwiz microwave popcorn ad in which a boy is pictured eating some (by throwing it up into the air and catching it in his mouth) because the popcorn has "passe[d] the *tough*est test." Yet, in an ad that makes explicit use of the gender qualities associated with girls, Fisher-Price, seemingly unintentionally markets its ungendered "Puffalump Kids" [© 1991] for girls only, billing them as "the sweetest dolls your little doll will ever cuddle." In doing so, the company both encourages parents to think of their little girls as doll-like, cute, cuddly, and passive, and seemingly excludes boys from wanting one, even though the company originally seems to have gone to the trouble of calling the dolls the ungendered "kids" to make them appropriate for both girls and boys.

Ads that include adults in the picture with children fall into two categories: those ads which depict parental figures in ads for products for children, as in the Carnation Good Start Infant Formula described above; and those in which children are used to connote some quality associated with children in a product for adults. Thus children, like women, are sometimes used to sell products that have nothing to do with the children themselves. For instance, in an ad for a Norelco Ladyshave electric razor, a girl baby is used to connote legs that are "baby soft and silky smooth," just as children are often used to suggest that by using a particular hair color, a woman, assumedly the mother of the child, can achieve the same child-like shiny, bright hair color.

In the last few years, more and more advertisers seem to be cashing in on images of the "New [non-macho] Man," to sell products. In a number of those ads, a man is pictured, not as the "head of the household," with his whole family, but alone with a child, as if to suggest not just his traditional sense of responsibility, but his caring and involvement with the child as well. In an ad for a Simmons Beautyrest [© 1993] which has appeared in a number of magazines, a man, who is naked to the waist, but whose chest has absolutely no hair on it, is pictured cradling a baby of indeterminate gender, with whom he is making deeply engaged eye contact. The caption reads "Only one thing has ever cradled you as perfectly as a Beautyrest can," likening the mattress and box spring to the strong, yet gentle embrace of a loving father. What is not clear, however, is why the man needs to be unclothed to the waist. Because I first saw the ad in *Good Housekeeping*, I thought it was, perhaps, because the ad figured forth a female fantasy of the perfect husband/father, engaged with his young infant, yet still desirable (which is, perhaps, an inversion of the male fantasy of a wife and mother who is still a desirable woman). But I have since seen the ad in magazines whose target audiences include both men and women. An ad for a La-Z-boy recliner also pictures a father and a baby together, but this time, the child is quite clearly a boy, even though he is only wearing a diaper, so that it is not his clothes that signal to the reader the baby's gender. Rather, it is the manner in which the father is engaged with the child, showing "him" a soccer ball, as if to interest him, even as a baby, in sports, an appropriately masculine activity. Furthermore, the room's furnishings connote masculinity: the recliner is upholstered in neutrally colored leather, the carpet and bookcase are in dark colors, and the books suggest the (male) domain of knowledge, which is further suggested by the mention of college in the ad's narrative, as if it were a foregone conclusion that a male child will attend college.[22]

Perhaps most insidious of all is an ad for Quaker Oat Life cereal [© 1992]. A boy and a girl are fighting over a box of the cereal. The boy has apparently finished his cereal, whereas the girl has not yet eaten hers. The caption over the boy's head reads, "'I really want more Life Cereal'" and the caption over the girl's head reads "'Don't even think about it.'" To me the ad suggests all the negative stereotypes of the mother/wife's prohibitory and inhibitory roles in relation to the male, since it is not clear why he can't or shouldn't have more. In addition, the girl is looking at the boy, as if she is fully engaged with him, while he looks directly out at the viewer of the ad as if to make eye contact, and thus to enlist the viewer on his side in this "power struggle." As Carol Moog suggests in *Are They Selling Her Lips*, it is the ads in which children are made to mimic adults ("Don't even think about it"), rather than just being kids, which least successfully make use of the images of children to market their products.[23]

I did, however, find at least one ad which seemed to be playing with viewers by deliberately undercutting their gender expectations. In an all black-and-white ad for Gerber baby foods [© 1992], which appeared in several different magazines, an adult, who is clearly a man though only his arms and legs can be seen, is holding a barefoot toddler dressed in jeans, an undershirt, and a little boater hat in a dark color. The clothes, the dark color of the hat, and the fact that it is a man helping the child all connote maleness, according to traditional gender coding in ads, yet the sex of the child is not clearly determinate, and the very end of the narrative in the ad refers to the child as "she." However, two earlier Gerber ads [© 1991] and [© 1988] are not as successfully ambiguous, suggesting that it took Gerber several years to perfect their notion of gender ambiguity in an ad. The 1991 ad shows a woman feeding a baby what the narrative informs us is applesauce. As in the 1992 ad, the child is not dressed in any way that gives away its gender, though the ad's narrative refers to the child as "she," and the fact that the baby is pictured with its mother this time further connotes its femaleness. The 1988 ad for Gerber Meats: Body builders for babies, shows a baby in an undershirt and diaper touching barbells, suggesting that the child is male, though the caption does not say "he" anywhere. Thus an ad for "sweet," nutritious applesauce pictures a girl baby with her mother, upholding the stereotype of a delicate girl, who is, and can live on, sugar and spice; while an ad for body building meat pictures a baby whose gender is ambiguous in such a way that it reveals our gender assumptions about maleness, reinforcing the stereotype that it is a hearty, thriving boy who needs to eat meat to grow big and strong.

A Nike ad shows child athletes, and in what appears to be an attempt to be gender-inclusive, pictures a girl as one of the three children in the ad; but the boys are shown in uniforms, dressed for a team sport, while the girl is dressed for tennis, a sport which has been acceptable for girls to play for quite some time. And, an ad for Benadryl allergy medicine which picture kids as doctors, and features one of the few children of color in these ads, suggests that anyone, girl or boy, can grow up to be a doctor. However, the absence of nurses is conspicuous, unless the girl in the back row is meant to be a nurse (since we can't see her doctor's name tag), and if that is so, then the boy doctors would outnumber the girl doctors three to one instead of three to two.

Finally, I would like to turn to the eroticizing of girls in advertising for adults. The most famous image of a coy, eroticized young girl is probably the one in the Coppertone ads, now no longer for suntan lotion, but for sunblock, in which a rather stylized dog is pulling at the panties of a little girl, who is looking over her shoulder with her mouth open and her hand pressed charmingly against her cheek, a look Erving Goffman in *Gender Advertisements* reads (though not with reference to this particular ad) as connoting a sexual come-on.[24] Though the ad's narrative nowhere mentions the gender of the children for whom the sunblock is appropriate, in all the years Coppertone has been running this ad, or some variation of it, the company has never once run the ad picturing a boy invitingly revealed, rather than a girl. Jordache Kids' ads are also guilty of making girls into miniature sexy women. For instance, in an ad for their clothes at Macy's [© 1990], two girls are pictured, very neatly dressed in denim outfits complete with matching jackets and pants, and, in one case, belted with a bandanna, in imitation of a certain grown-up chic. The girls' hair is very curly, as if permed, and in both cases, is decorated with a bow; their hairdos make them look very feminine, even though they aren't wearing dresses. The girls are having a tea party at a simple white table decorated with flowers; one of the girls is sitting very properly with her teacup and saucer daintily in hand, looking at the other, who is standing with her back toward the magazine-viewing audience. The ankles of this girl's pants are decorated with denim hearts, as if to suggest she is a "sweetheart"; and even more tellingly, her right knee is coyly crooked so that her hips and rear end are presented to the viewer in a subtly sexualized pose. Thus the girls are constrained, like Victorian children, to be proper little adults: they are not allowed the freedom to be "little outlaws" like the boys in an ad for Billy the Kid clothes.

Children learn their gender roles from a variety of sources in a variety of ways. The major institutions of our culture are an important source of social knowledge, but even before children have been to school they begin to develop a sense of what is expected of boys or girls which they learn from parents, peers, TV, children's books, etc. The findings of sociologists, psychologists, and anthropologists with regard to the virtually unrelenting reproduction of gendering in young children by parents and other invested adults, are borne out in the advertisements that depict children in a broad range of magazines.

The evidence from the advertising in glossy magazines addressed to the parents, especially the mothers, of young children suggests that what gets communicated to parents about their kids encourages them to reproduce a rather limited range of gender-stereotyped appearances and reinforce a rather limited range of gender-bound behaviors and activities. These ads contribute to the reproduction of gendering by imaging for parents crystallized representations of desirable traits for their children, which work, though often unintentionally, to emphasize distinctions of gender. In so doing, magazine advertisements and other visual media help to constitute gender difference, rather than simply reflecting or representing that difference. Thus the cultural work of making kids into gendered subjects reproduces our current cultural notions of gender-appropriate appearances, behaviors, and activities, as they work toward the reproduction of the (gendered) status quo.

My paper raises the question *why* ours is a culture that "gives gender a strong reading;" or, more to the point, what is at stake in our heavy investment in gender as (binary) difference? Extending Teresa de Lauretis's argument that we have a "vested interest" in gender identity as a set of complementary opposites, I have suggested above that the payoff of the reproduction of gender as binary opposition is our pleasure in difference: the problem is that that difference has thus far been constructed not out of a broad spectrum of different possibilities, but out of fundamental inequalities between the sexes, which are reproduced in our children almost from the moment of birth.

We have yet to imagine a sex-gender system in which agency is equally distributed, where there is no (gendered) division between sexual subjects and sexual objects; indeed where all are subjects, none are objects. This is not to argue for a *genderless* world, but for a world in which differences of gender do not mean differences of power or possibility. When we can imagine such a world, we will have achieved what is not yet pictured in advertisements: images which actualize the full range of possibilities for both boys and girls, and men and women, in our society.

Notes

[1]Newbury Park, CA: Sage Publications, 1992: 2.

[2]"Metal Men and Glamour Boys: Gender Performance in Heavy Metal," in Craig, 47. I have taken the liberty of slightly reorganizing their ideas. They further quote Butler (1990, 137-38)—"In imitating gender drag implicitly reveals the imitative nature of gender itself—as well as its contingency. Indeed, part of the pleasure, the giddiness of the performance is in the recognition of a radical contingency in the relation between sex and gender in the face of cultural configurations of causal unities that are regularly assumed to be natural and necessary" (51-52).

[3]"Cultural Conundrums and Gender: America's Present Past," *Cultural Politics in Contemporary America*, eds. Ian Angus and Sut Jhally (New York: Routledge, 1989) 123.

[4]*Technologies of Gender: Essays on Theory, Film, and Fiction* (Bloomington: Indiana UP, 1987) 16. The ellipsis omits the information that "investment" "translates the German *Besetzung*, a word used by Freud and rendered in English as *cathexis*."

[5]"Gender Ideology in Television Commercials," *Television Criticism: Approaches and Applications*, eds. Leah R. Vande Berg and Lawrence A. Wenner (New York: Longman, 1991) 238.

[6]Christenson and Redmond, 1990, quoted in Diane Barthel, "When Men Put on Appearances: Advertising and the Social Construction of Masculinity," *Cultural Politics in Contemporary America*, eds. Ian Angus and Sut Jhally (New York: Routledge, 1989) 137-38.

[7]John Berger, *Ways of Seeing* (New York: Penguin, 1977) chapter seven.

[8]Kervin, 239.

[9]Kath Davies, Julienne Dickey, and Teresa Stratford, eds. *Out of Focus: Writings on Women and the Media* (London: The Women's Press, 1987) 53.

[10]Diane Saco, "Masculinity as Signs: Post-Structuralist Feminist Approaches to the Study of Gender," *Men, Masculinity, and the Media*, ed. Steve Craig (Newbury Park, CA: Sage, 1992) 25.

[11]O'Brien and Huston, 1985a; Perry, White, & Perry, 1984, cited in Rhoda Unger and Mary Crawford, *Women and Gender: A Feminist Psychology* (New York: McGraw-Hill, 1992) 238.

[12]Caldera, Huston, & O'Brien, 1989, cited in Unger and Crawford (1992) 238.

[13]In keeping with the more rigid demands for gender-role conformity from boys than from girls, three-fourths of all the three- to five-year-old boys

studied requested gender stereotyped toys for Christmas (Robinson & Morris, 1986), while it took till age five for such a high percentage of girls to request stereotypically feminine toys. Unger and Crawford (1992) 239, 243.

[14]Barrie Thorne, "Girls and Boys Together...But Mostly Apart: Gender Arrangements in Elementary Schools," *Feminist Frontiers II: Rethinking Sex, Gender, and Society,* eds. Laurel Richardson and Vera Taylor (New York: McGraw, 1989, 1986) 76.

[15]The study, by Rheingold and Cook, 1975 is cited in Unger and Crawford (1992) 238; and in Ungar (1979) 172-73.

[16]Unger and Crawford, 244.

[17]"Gender-Role Socialization: Lessons in Femininity,"*Women: A Feminist Perspective,* ed. Jo Freeman, 4th ed. (Mountain View, CA: Mayfield, 1989) 199.

[18]The entire paragraph is reconstructed from Lips, 198. The first direct quote is from Lips herself; the other two quotes are Lips quoting Jean Block.

[19]Saco, 25.

[20]*ibid.*

[21]Steven Kline notes that children's toys, cartoons, stories, etc. are highly gendered since boys and girls respond to different things. "Action is necessary for boys and caring and social relations for girls. Boys like to engage in conflict and solve problems in play; girls like to touch, cuddle, stroke, dress, and care for their toys." "The same exclusion by imagination is at the root of a growing divide between boys and girls at play. Since the marketing targets and features different emotional and narrative elements (action/conflict vs. emotional attachment and maintenance) boys and girls also experience difficulty in playing together with these toys. The advertisements, which most precisely represent marketing's conception of how children play with toys, reveal single sex groupings in 95 percent of ads." In "Limits to the Imagination: Marketing and Children's Culture," *Cultural Politics in Contemporary America,* Ian Angus and Sut Jhally, eds. (New York: Routledge, 1989) 314, 315.

[22]Fathers are particularly potent constructors of gender; and fathers more than mothers see children as conforming to gender stereotypes (McGuire 1988), cited in Ungar and Crawford, 234. The gender coding of this ad was first pointed out by a student of mine, Tammy Jipson, in her final term paper for my "Rhetoric and Research" class on advertising and gender, May, 1992.

[23]New York: Morrow, 1990, 167-88.

[24]Cambridge: Harvard UP, 1979.

Creating Gender Expectations through Children's Advertising

Nancie Kahan
and
Nanette Norris

When the issue of advertising aimed at children came to the forefront in the 1970s, the focus of concern and study was primarily the effect of television violence on the behavior and thinking of young viewers. Less attention was paid to the socializing influences of gender orientation in the ads, a focus which remains largely uncharted today. The purpose of this study is to examine gender orientation in the advertising that children are most likely to watch—advertising which appears on Saturday morning at the same time as the children's cartoons—for the messages present-day ads are sending to young viewers. The ads are aimed at specific age groups—young children, preteens, and teenagers (Thornburn 167). The study was limited to ads designed to reach young children.

We approached the ads with three questions in mind, questions which intrinsically assume a standard of equality of opportunity for both sexes.

1. Would the ads show boys and girls playing together?
2. Would equal time on-air be devoted to the two sexes?
3. Are there differences in the imaging of gender orientation?

Reading the Ads

Separation of the sexes is the norm for 1990s' advertising. Only one ad in ten showed boys and girls playing together. (This was an ad for craft and drawing products.) Boys and girls were presented separately in the majority of the ads, with the ads sequenced girl/boy/girl.

The advertisers seem equally interested in reaching girls as reaching boys, since as many ads were directed at girls as at boys. Girl ads, however, had very few girls (three girls maximum). The girl ads featured close-up shots and personal views of the girls. Boy ads had more boys (gangs of boys) which meant that no particular boy was focused on.

Boys and girls were definitely presented in gender-specific roles. More than this, the underlying psychological premise of the ads, the manipulative attempt to create the desire for the products presented in the ads, is most disturbing. The ads are designed to do far more than image the product for young viewers. Present-day ads are involved in the creation of gender differences in susceptible young viewers, in a manner which C.G. Jung would have considered pathologically unbalanced.

The Business of Advertising

The advertisers clearly have one basic purpose: to sell the product. Advertising is a multi-billion dollar industry. In 1990, over $96 billion was allocated for all forms of advertising in the U.S., and $9 billion in Canada (Gillam 16). The billions of dollars poured into advertising production are having an effect on the sophisticated production of these ads. They are slick, compelling, and carefully designed. The messages which the ads encode are carefully constructed, "a series of subtle codes...are conveyed and are dependent on the type of program and the target audience" (Thornburn 167). The advertisers try to ensure results for their investment of money; therefore, they draw upon the findings of research into effective advertising for children in order to develop the ads (see Geis). Research has shown, for instance, that children identify with same-sex characters. This would explain why ads aimed at girls show only girls (see Signorielli).

Identification with same-sex characters doesn't account for the clear stereotyping of Barbie as a girls'-only doll. (Ads for Barbie dolls show only girls.) Role stereotyping is alive and well in the 1990s, with no solution in sight. Many of us who grew up in the 1960s and 1970s were determined to bring up children in gender-neutral roles, and were quite surprised to find our little boys and girls preferred different toys, different games, in spite of our best efforts. Is it nature or nurture? To what degree are gender differences naturally present, and to what degree are they socialized? As Myriam Miedzian points out in *Boys Will Be Boys*, recent brain research suggests that "there may well be differences in the brain which will ensure some emotional, cognitive, and behavioural variance between males and females as a group, under any conditions" (293). No matter what we do, boys and girls will be different. There is no danger of a boy becoming a 'wimp' if he plays with dolls.

However, Miedzian's study does not negate the role of socialization in the process of gender orientation. There is a danger that young children will identify with the stereotyped roles presented as the norm by the ads. Thornburn describes commercial television as a "cultural experience" (167) which contributes to the socializing of the young viewers who are active participants in the decoding and transformation of the television message (see Wright).

A second advertising aim which goes unmentioned more often than not is market creation. Advertisers are concerned not only with creating a market for a particular product, but also with feeding one market into another. The child who is interested in Barbie clothes may become the teenager who is interested in Alfred Sung creations. Molding the viewer thus becomes important for future markets.

Is such molding possible? The kind of continuity we glimpsed between the categories of advertising, divided as they were by age group, suggests that the advertisers consider molding a possibility.

Analysis of Two Ads

"Nerf Bow and Arrow" by Parker Brothers is an ad which is designed with boys in mind. (See Lyrics in Appendix 1.) Research has shown that boys are visually attentive, more so than girls (see Rolandelli). The visual excitement of this ad is therefore designed to attract young boys' attention to the television screen. The ad has strong colors—bright green, red, yellow—much action, and the images change quickly. The ad also has a primordial appeal to basic male aggression. The soundtrack is the beat of war drums. The action is reminiscent of the Arnold Schwarzenegger film *Predator*, which was very popular with a certain young set for a time. In addition, the ad evokes the world the boys are familiar with, showing little boys at play.

At the same time, it appeals to the boys' natural desire to grow up and become men: the narrator's voice is a deep, husky, man's voice. The characters transform from little boys playing a game to full-grown adult commandos. The auditory message supports this transition from childhood to adulthood by focussing on the word 'business.' "Nerf Bow and Arrow is coming your way, and it means business!" The use of the word business is idiomatic, as in 'Don't mess with me!' However, the 'business reality' with which most children are familiar is the mundane world of work—the business world which commands so much of their parents' time and attention. The word 'business' reverberates beyond its obvious idiomatic use into the 'real' world of work.

In "Nerf Bow and Arrow," the boys are encouraged to identify aggressive play with adulthood—in this case the game becomes 'real,' real war. The images of reality are seductive. The children become adults, the war play becomes real war. The sub-text encourages the boys to see the 'real' adult world as dangerous, competitive, and filled with enemies to be combatted. Playing on the natural insecurities and fear of the children, the sense of powerlessness in the face of authority that children often have, the ad promises to empower the boys: "The power is pumping!" They are ironically reinforced in their sense of youth = powerless and are encouraged to think that they will need to be violent and combative if they are to succeed when they grow up and "Get Real!"

"Starbright Sparkles" by Mattel is less visually exciting than the ad aimed at boys. It features pastel colors and very little action. One stereotypical blonde girl—the human equivalent of the doll being marketed—alternately hugs and shows off the doll. One dark-haired friend joins her for a brief moment. The setting is a small bedroom, and we see only the back wall, which appears to be sloping. It is a very small, enclosed space, as opposed to the outdoor setting of the boy ad. From the top of the doll's head a beam of light projects a pastel-colored flower motif onto the sloping wall.

Research has shown that girls process auditory-verbal content better than boys (see Rolandelli). They listen better and pay attention to the words. They don't have to be watching the screen. The visual images and the auditory track of "Starbright Sparkles" are artfully combined to complement each other; however, because the girls are especially atuned to auditory-verbal processes, the soundtrack is of particular importance.

Susan McClary points out that "music teaches us how to experience our own emotions, our own desires, and even (especially in dance) our own bodies. For better or for worse, it socializes us" (53). The music in "Starbright Sparkles" is reminiscent of a simple nursery rhyme—'Ring Around the Rosies,' for instance. Like the nursery rhyme, this song also has a serious purpose beyond the world of play in preparing the child for the world she will join as a grown-up. The contours of this world are presented in the images: a world of narrow confines, enclosed and cell-like. The child's horizons are limited, her role passive. The images are of passive sexuality. The focus of the girl-child's adulation is a circle penetrated by a beam of light. Womb imagery? She ends up in a bed where, at night, she is "filled" with love: "When I go to sleep tonight, no other love will shine so bright!" The lyrics tell her, in fact, that she needs to be "filled" with love.

In this ad the music, the visuals, and the lyrics combine to socialize the girls. The ad implies an emptiness in the child's life at present. Her world is narrow; she lacks friends (what a contrast to the group fun promised the boys), and she is desperately in need of love. The implication is that, in order to fulfill herself as a female, she must be a passive spectator. The focus is on beauty and her own identification with beauty. She is being socialized for a future role as passive mother.

The Creation of Gender Expectations

The advertisers intend far more than a simple depiction of boys as active and girls as passive; they draw on sources beyond established research in advertising. More is going on here than meets the eye or ear. The advertisers are not simply creating 'visual' ads to appeal to boys and 'auditory-verbal' ads to reach girls. They are also drawing on Jungian archetypes of the male and female.

Jung formulated his theory of the archetype decades ago. He hypothesized that in each of us is a "collective unconscious" (Jung 3), a way of knowing that is sub-verbal and which we possess as a species. It differs from instinct by the nature of its potential for interchange with our conscious thoughts and actions (4). The collective unconscious is expressed and made tangible through archetypal images (4), which are essentially 'things' or tangible objects to which the contents of the collective unconscious become attached and with which they become associated.

Fundamental concepts of the collective unconscious include the 'masculine' and the 'feminine' (which are particularly ill-named as every human possesses these aspects as the building-blocks of personality). At its most primitive, our knowledge of the world is initially differentiated into masculine and feminine, with feminine predominant through our infant dependence upon the mother, the 'mother-goddess' (see Neumann). The feminine aspect of the collective unconscious is associated with security and fulfillment very early on in a child's psychic development. As a child's sense of self becomes associated with 'things' (an on-going process throughout childhood), the feminine becomes associated with circles, with flowers, with images of enclosure and security (Jung 15). On the other hand, the masculine becomes associated with symbols of dominance and power, images of the phallus, of action, of war (see Neumann).

The intent of the ads was to draw upon established symbols of masculinity and femininity. The advertisers are commingling with the creation of the collective unconscious in the children's formative period, possibly causing the contents of the children's collective unconscious to become attached to gender-differentiated objects and ideas. The concepts of masculinity and femininity are inherent in the collective unconscious; the objects to which these concepts become attached are not. Socialization and the "cultural experience" (Thornburn 167) of the ads dictate the direction of the archetypal association. Whether or not we accept the validity of these theories, the advertisers are using them for the purpose of marketing their products.

Implication for Teaching Media Literacy

If we can speculate on the use or abuse of Jungian psychology, we can also speculate on his concept of consciousness and resistance in teaching children how to read the ads. In spite of the great power of the images of the unconscious, and the symbolic force of the things with which they become associated for us, Jung felt that we could nonetheless resist being manipulated. Knowledge is the key. If we are conscious of the archetype, we can resist it because we are empowered and the archetype is transformed into 'something' manageable.

To demonstrate the effectiveness of conscious resistance, we asked two girls, four and eight, to respond to the two ads in question. The four-year-old was unaware of the issue of male/female stereotyping. Her response was entirely undiscriminating: she wanted each toy and reveled in each image. The eight-year-old was aware of the issue, having had open discussions with her parents. Her response to the "Starbright Sparkles" ad was to point out that the girl didn't do anything, that she was in a small, indoor space, and that she was alone—in vivid contrast to the "Nerf Bow and Arrow" ad. She was aware of the difference of portrayal, and the potential implications, and was resistant to the ad. Consequently, the ad failed in its effectiveness both as a tool for sales and as a tool for subliminal gender-role stereotyping.

The ad failed in its effectiveness at this point in time with this resistant viewer perhaps because, at the age of eight, she was psychologically ready to be resistant, to assert her independence and individuality. The question remains as to whether she would be resistant later in her development when, as a young teen, other socialization processes have kicked in and her instinct is to conform rather than to criticize. Much study is needed in this area to determine the best method of maintaining critical awareness in view of increasing social pressure for girls (and boys) to be subsumed by a cultural reality which, as Robyn Gillam points out, is created by a mass culture which is largely manipulated by the agenda of a few.

Collaborative learning may prove to be the most effective mode of media literacy training in the classroom setting. As Kenneth Bruffee points out, it is in the nature of collaborative learning to challenge the "traditional authority of knowledge" (649). The font of knowledge moves from the teacher to the students themselves, and the repositioning of authority of knowledge readily supports other intellectual challenges, such as the repositioning of role-model acceptance when viewing ads. Students could be asked to watch television for homework, to look for ads which depict boys and girls, and to be prepared to describe what they see. The messy issue of copyright and using the VCR in the classroom is thus effectively sidestepped. The groups themselves could challenge the premise of the ads, challenge the role models being offered, and could become more aware of the archetypes and their potential manipulation. The teacher's role would be that of facilitator, offering the concepts of role modeling, of manipulation, of gender roles and equality for perusal. As in the tradition of Kathleen Weiler, where she calls for a critical interrogation of the text, collaborative writing would support an active 'reading the texts' of the ads, and thus empower the children to resist them.

Bibliography

Best, Raphaela. *We've All Got Scars*. Bloomington: Indiana UP, 1983. Best argues that the present elementary school system is actively creating gender role expectations—and limitations—in young students.

Bruffee, Kenneth A. "Collaborative Learning and the 'Conversation of Mankind.'" *College English*. 46.7 (1984): 635-52. Bruffee argues that 'collaborative learning' helps students to bridge gaps between knowledge communities.

Geis, Michael L. *The Language of Television Advertising*. New York: Academic, 1982. Geis discusses specific approaches and images to be found in television advertising.

Gillam, Robyn. "The Fiction of Media Education: Truth or Dare?" *Paragraph*. 14.1 (1992): 14-17. Gillam discusses the problematic role of media education in North American schools and questions its efficacy in our present teacher-centered structure.

Jung, C.G. *Four Archetypes: Mother, Rebirth, Spirit, Trickster. From The Collected Works of C.G. Jung*. Vol. 9. Part 1. Bollingen Series XX.

Trans. R.F.C. Hull. Princeton, NJ: Princeton UP, (1959) 1973. A detailed discussion of four archetypes which Jung considered key to every person's psychological constitution.

McClary, Susan. *Feminine Endings: Music, Gender and Sexuality.* Minnesota: U of Minnesota P, 1991. McClary argues that musicology has been inherently patriarchal.

Miedzian, Myriam. *Boys Will Be Boys: Breaking the Link Between Masculinity and Violence.* New York: Doubleday, 1991. While arguing that there seem to be inherently masculine behaviors, Miedzian addresses the link our society has created between perceptions of masculinity and violence.

Mitchell, Claudia A. "Michelangelo Takes On Barbie: Pleasure, Politics, Pedagogy and Popular Culture: Dimension of gendered culture in the elementary school classroom." The Popular Culture Association, Louisville, KY, 18-21 May 1992. Mitchell argues that learning in the classroom takes place in the context of popular culture.

Neumann, Erich. *The Mother Goddess: An Analysis of the Archetype.* Bollingen Series XLVII. Trans. Ralph Macheim. Princeton, NJ: Princeton UP, 1955. Neumann expands upon Jung's concept of 'the feminine' in psychology.

Rolandelli, David R., et al. "Children's Auditory and Visual Processing of Narrated and Non-narrated Television Programming." *Journal of Experimental Child Psychology* 51 (1991): 90-122. A thoroughly documented research study of the ways in which children process auditory and visual television programming, the results of which strongly suggest gender differences.

Signorielli, Nancy. "Television and Conceptions About Sex Roles: Maintaining Conventionality and the Status Quo." *Sex Roles* 21.5, 21.6 (1989): 341-59. Signorielli discusses the role of television in developing and maintaining our expectations concerning gender and sex roles.

Thornburn, David. "Television as an Aesthetic Medium." *Critical Studies in Mass Communication* 4 (1987): 161-73. Television ads, although carefully constructed and encoded, nonetheless become a cultural experience for viewers.

Wright, John C., et al. Working Paper for *American Psychological Association,* 1978. Cited in Rother, Irving. "An Analysis of Children's Television." *The ATEQ* 11.3 (1992): 9-16. Research of Wright et al. shows that children are active participants in the decoding and transformation of the television message. This study is cited by Rother in his exploration of children's semiotic understanding of the television message.

Appendix 1
Lyrics

Nerf Bow and Arrow

Man's voice:	Nerf Bow and Arrow is coming your way, and it means business!
Male singer:	The power is pumping, an arrow's in your hand Now your heart is pumping, fire as quick as you can!
Male chorus:	Nerf Bow and Arrow!
Male singer:	The enemy's coming Now they're in your sights
Male chorus:	Nerf Bow and Arrow!
Male singer:	You're the front of the line, in the thick of the fight
Male chorus:	Nerf Bow and Arrow!
Male voice:	The mightiest Nerf adventure yet!
Script on screen:	GET REAL......GET NERF

Starbright Sparkles

Female chorus: What girls do:

Starbright Sparkles
Shiny, how you love me
Sparkle when I hug you
Light my world above

                                                                 Girl in ad: "Ooooh!"

Starbright Sparkles
When I turn your crown   (girls giggle)

See the colored stars go round
You fill my world with love!

Girl: "Wow!"
Friend: "Aah!"

Through your magic star
Your love sparkles near and far

Girl: "Beautiful!"

When I go to sleep tonight
No other love
Will shine so bright

Girl: "Wow!"

Girl: "Sweet dreams!"
(kisses doll)

Starbright Sparkles!

Breathless Female Voice: "Batteries not included."

Appendix 2
Transcript of Interviews with Amy
(four years old) and Sarah (eight years old)

AMY
(soundtrack of ad for "Starbright Sparkles"
begins to play in background)

A: I want that toy, Mom. Mom, did you know I wanted that toy?
N: Well, I'm beginning to have an idea, Amy.
A: Can you get it for me? For my birthday? (soundtrack ends)
N: Well, let's talk about it first, okay? What did you like about that ad?
A: (begins to sing) "Star..." Uh, the stars...and, um, the sparkles.
N: The stars and the sparkles. And, um, what didn't you like about the ad?
A: I liked everything!
N: You liked everything! What colour did you see the most of?
A: Pink.
N: Uh-hum...
A: No, actually, not pink but...um...white.
N: White? Uh-hum...
A: And sparkles.
N: And sparkles. And what were the people doing?
A: Singing to...to the...to the toy.

N: Singing, okay. And what were the people saying?

A: (sings) "Starbright Sparkles."

N: Okay. And do you wish you were like someone in this ad?

A: (pause) Starbright Sparkles!

N: You'd like to be the dolly?

A: Yeah!

N: Yeah.

A: But I would like to get it!

SARAH
(soundtrack of "Nerf Bow and Arrow" plays)

N: What did you like about this ad?

S: What did I like about this ad? Music. I like the music.

N: You like the music?

S: Yeah.

N: Okay, anything else?

S: No.

N: What about the music? Did you find it..uh...

S: My kind...my style!

N: Your style?

S: Yeah.

N: What didn't you like?

S: That all they had was boys playing with those things, not girls, and girls can play with those things, too.

N: What colour did you see the most of?

S: Uh, yellow and blue...

N: Okay...

S: And red.

N: What were the people doing?

S: Shooting Nerf Bow and Arrows.

N: That's all? Were they indoors?

S: No, they were outdoors. And they were pretending that they were going "Pow! Pow!" at...um...enemies.

N: Enemies? Who were the enemies?

S: Enemies. Uh...ninjas.

N: Ah! Okay. Um, what were the people saying?

S: Uhhh...they were talking about Nerf Bow and Arrow, and, uh...

N: Who's talking?

S: A man.

N: Uh-huh. Do you wish you were like someone in the ad?

S: I'm a girl. I wouldn't rather be a boy.

N: What makes it, "I'm a girl..." Explain.

S: Explain? Well...because..the people in the ad...you asked me, would I like to be like somebody in the ad? Does that include changing the person? Or...

N: I don't know.

S: Because if...if I could change the person to a girl, then, I might like to be like the person in the ad...but if I'm not allowed to change anybody, no.

N: Okay, so the way it's set up right now you feel as though, um...

S: No...

N: ...only a boy is going to be there.

S: Yeah, I don't, I've...

N: And you don't...

S: And I've got no..no place in it.

N: Is this ad for a toy anyone might like?

S: I might like it.

N: So it's a toy that's, uh...

S: Mostly boys would get.

N: Why?

S: Because the...some people are really, really sexist, some parents, and they get their girls the dollies, (tone of voice changes and is sneering) little cupcakes, and (voice returns to normal) they get their boys these toy guns and such.

N: So the parents would make these choices?

S: Yeah. Or the children would...boys would want the cupcake dolls...they would take the bow and arrows...

N: But you wouldn't mind having the Bow and Arrow?

S: No. I wouldn't mind. No, no, not me! I get the best...I get the best of both worlds.

N: (laughs) Okay...

S: ...My parents aren't as sexist. My mom tries to avoid the sexist world.

N: Okay. Let me show you another ad.

(soundtrack of "Starbright Sparkles" plays)

N: Okay. What do you like about this ad?

S: (pause) Nice colors. (pause)

N: Anything else?

S: Not really...nice colors when you're looking through the magic star.

N: What didn't you like?

S: That the girls were playing with it. Like, cause...(pause) why, why wouldn't a boy like that?

N: Well, you've already told me.

S: I know. (pause) I have?

N: Yeah. You've told me for the other ad, "Well, boys wouldn't want the little cupcakes."

S: I know, but...

N: Don't think a boy would like that?

S: And...the...they put it so sweet and comfortable and sort of cuddly and such like that for the girls...and the Nerf Bow and Arrow one...they're outside, they had red flashing, they were shooting enemies. I don't know why they had to do that.

N: What colour did you see the most of?

S: Pink.

N: Okay. What were the people doing?

S: People? Looking up at the ceiling, watching the bright colors, and seeing the colors of this, uh, little dolly and such like that, going "Oooh, aah, eee."

N: (laughs) Uh, what were the people saying?

S: (sings) "Starbright Sparkles, shining room above..."

N: Who was saying that?

S: A woman. A choir of people.

N: A choir, yeah. So it's not the person in the ad.

S: No. The woman. A choir of women. And the other one is a choir of men.

N: Do you wish you were like someone in this ad?

S: (pause) So-so.

N: Can you see yourself in this ad?

S: (pause) No.

N: No?

S: No.

N: Why?

S: Cause I'm not that kind of kid!

N: Oh, okay. So tell me about that.

S: (sighs) Aaaah...

N: What kind of kid is this?

S: This is a little girl who sticks to little girls' things and doesn't go beyond that. She always plays with dollies and she probably—how will I put this?...um...probably doesn't have a boy thing that I have. (laughs) What boy thing do I have? A kitten! Tch.

N: Okay. Is this ad for a toy anybody might like?

S: No.

N: Why not?

S: Because the boys don't necessarily play with dolls. Unless they're boys that get the best of both worlds.

The Eva and Topsy Dichotomy in Advertising

Robert M. MacGregor

In October 1991, a Benetton advertisement appeared in numerous fashion magazines throughout North America and Europe. The ad under the banner slogan "United Colors of Benetton" showed a smiling, blond-haired white child juxtaposed to a very serious looking black child that appeared to have her hair styled in the form of two horns. The image of a "horned" black child immediately created a strong negative reaction within the black communities, especially. This image of opprobrium evoked a message of the black devil that was seen to send out a barrage of subliminal, negative, and pejorative stereotypical messages.[1]

This essay will try to place the 1991 advertisement into a historical perspective using initially a structuralist approach to the analysis. Later, a functionalist focus will discuss some reasons why the images that evolved were used. The characters in the central position of the analysis will be Topsy and Eva, two of the children that appeared in Harriet Beecher Stowe's novel *Uncle Tom's Cabin*. Given the protestations over the Benetton ad, was there a possible historical perspective, a previous precedent(s) to view, to read, to cognitively accept the rationale that was used against the acceptance of the Benetton ad? Have there been Eva and Topsy ads that heretofore portrayed the angelic white child in oppositional terms to the devilish black child?

The Multi-Media Success of Uncle Tom's Cabin

The first edition of Harriet Beecher Stowe's novel was published in March 1852; 3,000 copies were sold the first day, 10,000 the first week, and over 300,000 copies sold in America within the year. These figures pale in comparison, however, when viewed alongside the sales of the book in Britain. Published there in May 1852, one year later over one million copies had been purchased. By 1878, The British Museum had copies of the book in 20 different languages including Russian and Siamese.

The first stage version called *The Southern Uncle Tom*, was performed at the Baltimore Museum on January 1852, two months before the book was published. The book was serialized in *The National Era* before it was issued in book form. Throughout most of 1852, the play did not play all that well and its acceptance was rather slow. By 1854, the play version of the novel was playing throughout the United States in large and small locales. Stock companies performed the play in San Francisco, Chicago, St. Louis, Cincinnati, Detroit, New York, Washington, Philadelphia, Salt Lake City, Cleveland, and Baltimore. No play, before and since, had captured the imagination of so many Americans. By 1925, one researcher was known to have said "...no play in the world, probably, has ever had half so many productions."[2] Berlin first saw the play called *Negersleben in Nord-Amerika* in December 1853, Paris saw *La Case do l'Oncle Tom* in January 1853, and by 1901 it was stated that all capitals of Europe had seen some play or other alleged to be *Uncle Tom's Cabin*.

In Britain, by the fall of 1852, six productions were running in London and for the season 1852-53, Manchester, Glasgow, and Edinburgh each had their own companies of "Tommers." For the rest of the century, the play was a standard fixture on the London stage as it was throughout the United States.

Twentieth-century "Tomming" continued into the late 1950s and in 1955 a college in Ohio performed the play then called *Eliza on the Ohio*. Birdoff (1955) suggested the era of 1852-1900 was called "The Uncle Tomic Age." The excitement and enthusiasm was so great that a new word was coined, "tomitudes."

Throughout this time, consumers in the Western world believed and embraced their world that they saw was being "Uncle Tomized." Products such as dolls, toys, games, wall and household furnishings, dinnerware, knick-knacks, clothes, foods, store names and related decor were being changed to reflect the immense popularity of the book, the play, and the songs that all were so widely diffused throughout the Western world.

The first film of the book was made in 1903 by Edwin S. Porter. The second production was in 1907, two appeared in 1910, three films in 1913, and one each in 1914 and 1918. In 1927, United Artists screened the Duncan sisters in *Topsy and Eva*. In 1936, Twentieth-Century Fox shaped the early career of Shirley Temple as Dimples which featured a Topsy and Eva scene. Judy Garland played a Topsy character in the 1938 production of *Everybody Sings*. Betty Grable and June Haver played double Topsies in the 1945 film *The Dolly Sisters*. Abbott and Costello played Simon Legree and Eva in the 1945 film by Universal Productions called *Naughty Nineties*.

Two animated cartoons made in 1927 also played their part in the diffusion of the Eva and Topsy images to the very young. Felix the Cat outwitted Simon Legree in *Topsy Turvy* (Paramount Pictures); and *Uncle Tom Crabbin* was produced by the Educational Company.[3] Jorgenson (1952) thought that the book *Uncle Tom's Cabin* overshadowed all other books in the reading world.[4]

The following section will now explore numerous aspects of the imagery that came to surround Topsy and Eva throughout a period of at least 90 years, or more, when you include the Benetton ad.

Portrayals of Eva and Topsy

At this juncture of the presentation, the following discussion will be placed and conducted within a structuralist paradigm. A bipolar/oppositional schema will focus on the white child as the angel figure and the black child as the satanic persona. This dichotomy of two of the central characters of the novel will compare the written representations that Mrs. Stowe used in her portrayal of Eva and Topsy.

The major idea behind the concept of the polarization of the Western mind was that all things good are white and that all things bad are black. How this concept and the resultant ideology came to be, have to be explained.

In the production and representation of the "Other," images, beliefs, values, and attitudes which categorize people in terms of the "Other" have to be constructed. These constructed categories allow the "Self" to compare and to be compared with the "Other." Therefore, there is always a dialectic process taking place between the "Self" and the "Other" in which the attributed characteristics of the "Other" refract contrasting characteristics of the "Self" and vice versa, through time and space. Historically, at least from the 15th century, the "Other" was represented in thought through a structural process in terms of binary opposites with the foundation being that of skin colour.

With the expansion of capitalism, colonialism, and Christianity around the world, there appeared to be a correlation between these ideologies and the growth and spread of early racism. For example, Western Christianity associated certain colours with a range of meanings with the result that it embodied a colour symbolism mirroring that of the preceding classical world. The perceived biological differences gave rise to a biological hierarchializing of different people based mainly on the colour of their skin. Eventually skin colour expressed a hierarchial religious evaluation which attained a widespread secular content within Western cultures. Where distinctions between people were based on this colour symbolism it had powerful evaluative implications. Monstrousness, sinfulness, and blackness, therefore, constituted a rather different form of Trinity in the Western cultures of that time.[5]

This superior/inferior dichotomy was a powerful foundational basis that appeared in ethnic and race relations. There were many complex variables that arose in this binary/oppositional relationship process and some of these significant labelling variables between blacks and whites included the following:

Superior Label	Inferior Label
white	black
Christ	Satan
Heaven	Hell
salvation	damnation
good	evil
spiritual	carnal
pure	diabolical
clean	dirty

These bipolar/oppositional labels clearly separated the two races as they did Eva and Topsy in the book *Uncle Tom's Cabin*.

The first time that we meet Eva was on the river boat that was taking Tom down the river to be sold. The description of Eva was one of a truly positive nature. This is in stark contrast to the pictures and the images that we read later on concerning Topsy.

The appearance of Eva read as:

Her form was the perfection of childish beauty without its usual chubbiness and squareness of outline. There was about it an undulating and aerial grace, such as one might dream of for some mythic, and allegorical being. Her face was remarkable less for its perfect beauty of feature than for a singular and dreamy earnestness of expression, which made the ideal start when they looked at her, and by which the dullest and most literal were impressed, without exactly knowing why. The shape of her head and the turn of her neck and the bust was particularly noble, and the long golden-brown hair that floated like a cloud around it, the deep spiritual gravity of her violet-blue eyes, shaded by the heavy fringes of golden brown—all marked her out from other children and made everyone turn and look at her.... (171)[6]

In striking opposition to this, "perfection of childish beauty," the child, Eva, Topsy's description personifies blackness and impishness. Topsy was described as:

She was one of the blackest of her race; and her round shining eyes, glittering as glassbeads, moved with quick and restless glances over everything in the room. Her mouth, half open with astonishment at the wonders of the new Mas'r's parlor, displayed a white and brilliant set of teeth. Her woolly hair was braided in sundry little tails, which stuck out in every direction. The expression of her face was an odd mixture of shrewdness and cunning, over which was oddly drawn, like a kind of veil, an expression of the most doleful gravity and solemnity. She was dressed in a single filthy, ragged garment, made of bagging; and stood with her hands demurely folded in front of her. Altogether, there was something odd and goblin-like about her appearance—something, as Miss Ophelia afterwards said, "so heathenish...." (278)[7]

Topsy was described as a "thing," and, as St. Clare, her new master, was introducing the new slave-girl to his cousin, Miss Ophelia, he whistled to Topsy, like one would a dog, to perform her maniacal tricks and contortions. Early on in the discourse between various characters the reader discovered that Topsy believed she had not been born of a mother, Topsy just happened. Some of the descriptive metaphors that Mrs. Stowe used to describe Topsy included: Topsy was a "black spider," "the thing," "a heathen," "a freshly caught speciman," "the sooty gnome from the land of Diablerie." These labels clearly linked Topsy to past historical invectives that were frequently used to describe the "Other" and to dehumanize and to marginalize the black. In this Eva/Topsy dichotomy, Topsy herself equates her being as a child of the devil, an insect, something to be trapped to be put on display and to be used to perform, to entertain her white owners.

The bipolar perception of the races was clearly illustrated when the two children are described as they appear side-by-side in a later scene in the novel. Their looks read as:

There stood the two children, representatives of the two extremes of society. The fair, high-bred child, with her golden head, her deep eyes, her spiritual, noble brow, and prince-like movements; and her black, keen, subtle, cringing, yet acute neighbor. They stood the representatives of their races. The Saxon, born of ages of civilization, command, education, physical and moral eminence; the Afric, born of ages of oppression, submission, ignorance, toil, and vice! (287)[8]

As has been previously discussed, the play and the novel were immensely popular. The acceptance of the works were later reflected in the marketplace with the widespread commercialization of "Tomist" images and products. Continuing within this process of commercialization, was the bipolar/oppositional labels and images of the two children perpetuated by advertising? The next section of the essay will try to answer this question.

Topsy and Eva in Advertising

Given the mass acceptance of the novel and the play, it must have seemed reasonable for others, other than those in the artistic communities, to exploit the images of the two children, Eva and Topsy. This did happen in a number of ways that I believe continued to exploit and to perpetuate the oppositional labels that were congruent with the values and the outlooks that many whites had of blacks throughout the 19th and 20th centuries.

An early promotional throwaway card to advertise the annual arrival of the play, *Uncle Tom's Cabin*, clearly highlighted and reinforced the dialectic between Eva and Topsy. This card read as shown:

T   is for Topsy, impish and wild;
           Only sweet Eva can tame this poor child.
O's for Ophelia, a spinster unblest;
           An angel to Eva, to Topsy, a pest.
P   is for Platform, where Tom was on sale,
           And also where Eva saved Topsy from jail.
S   is for Shelby, a gallant young blade,
           Whom Topsy and Eva helped win a fair maid.
Y   is for Yore, the old cabin days,
           In Topsy and Eva, the brightest of plays.
E   is for Eva, who pined to get back
           Topsy her playmate so ragged and black.
V   is for Vivian, whose "Eva's" the pal,
           For Rosetta's "Topsy", the wickedest gal."
A's for Amusement, which mounts to a shriek
           In Topsy and Eva arriving next week. (Birdoff 392)[9]

In the material, Topsy is the wild imp whom Eva rescues from jail, a perpetuation of the image of Eva, the Saviour.

In an early tradecard (circa 1870-90), we saw a frequently recurring theme that was used in advertising for well over one hundred years—the theme of the durability of the colour black and black persons used to reinforce this fact, this product benefit. The colour black of the human had been inextricably linked to the colour of the product—the subject and the object both became objectified and the person was dehumanized. In the J. and P. Coats black thread tradecard, Eva admonishes Topsy by saying, "Come in Topsey out of the rain You'll get Wet." Topsy replied, "Oh! it won't hurt me Missy I'm like COATS BLACK THREAD De Color won't come off by wettin." In this early promotional material, Topsy was telling the reader of the durability of the dye and was reflecting this benefit when she compared that fact by durability of her own skin colour, black (figure 1).

In what could be termed an early advertising jingle, the following four-line song was used to raise money for the Abolitionist Movement in Boston, 1852:

> Come and list to little Topsy,
> Hear a little slave-girl's tale,
> Sure I am, her simple story
> Oft will make my cheek turn pale.

This song was used as an invitation to donate $10 to the $1,000 fund for the F. Douglass anti-slavery newspaper.[10] Songs were also very important in reinforcing stereotypes of the two children. These songs were mainly in the various renditions of the play, based on the book. The purity of Eva was sung about in the song "Uncle Tom's Lament For Eva," the wish of Tom was to be with Eva in Heaven and to join with her and be "There," "mid seraphic beings"; in "Uncle Tom's Glimpse of Glory," Tom wanted to have a glimpse of Heaven when they opened the door so wide to welcome little Eva home to be with God. The song that Topsy sang opened a vast, and potent subject for the exploitation of the black by establishing the figure of the mischievous black child. The song, "Oh! I'se So Wicked," was the unquestioned model for songwriters who subsequently produced thousands of songs of the type and thereby created the figure into an enduring stereotype.[11] Some of the verses clearly outline the invectives that added to the pejorative epithets of the day, and future:

> Oh, white-folks I was never born,
> Aunt Sue, raise me on de corn,

Fig. 1.

Send me errands night and morn,
Ching a ring a ring a ricked.
She used to knock me on de floor,
Den bang my head agin de door,
And tare my hair out by de core,
Oh! cause I was so wicked.[12]

When Topsy sang, this song, and the wild antics that she used in its presentation, caused an uproar. Topsy's torch-singing set the audiences on their ears; with her raucous voice, like that of a cricket with laryngitis, the wild waif of Mrs. Stowe's imagination became the living embodiment of the "wickedest nigger on earth" (Birdoff 219).

In a British advertisement (circa 1900s), Topsy's Testimonial—"It am good fo' de cumplekshun," was another example of how the black female character was treated by advertisers of the day. The product, James' "Dome" Black Lead Stove Polish followed a popular genre of themes in advertising. A major dimension of invective in this submission was the vulgarization of the English language. As a sort of usage testimonial, Topsy was telling the reader that the product was good for her complexion. The objectification of the "Other" was illustrated in this ad by the extremely poor usage of the language and the fact that the head, the face area, was completely blackened out so that there were no humanly recognizable features. This was a technique that was used to marginalize the black, the "Other."

In the novel, *Uncle Tom's Cabin*, Topsy was the "blackest of her race," as she appeared to be in the ad for James' Dome Stove Polish (figure 2).

In the Beecham's Pills and toothpaste advertisement (figure 3), the image is of a black female domestic. She appeared to be rummaging through the personal belongings of the mistress of the house. In the act of looking at items in the room, it seemed as though the maid tried, or would try later, some of the products that were available in the bureau of the "Missus." The line spoken by the Topsy (adult figure) read as: "What am good for de Missus am good for me." In the novel, Topsy, early on in the St. Clare household, starts to steal things. This stereotypical action reflecting that whites perceived blacks to be inveterate thieves appeared to be reinforced in the Beecham ad. The vulgarized language also was used to marginalize the black domestic from the mainstream of white society.

Several more recent advertisements (circa 1940s) showed Eva, the angelic white child. The J. Walter Thompson Company ad was

Fig. 2.

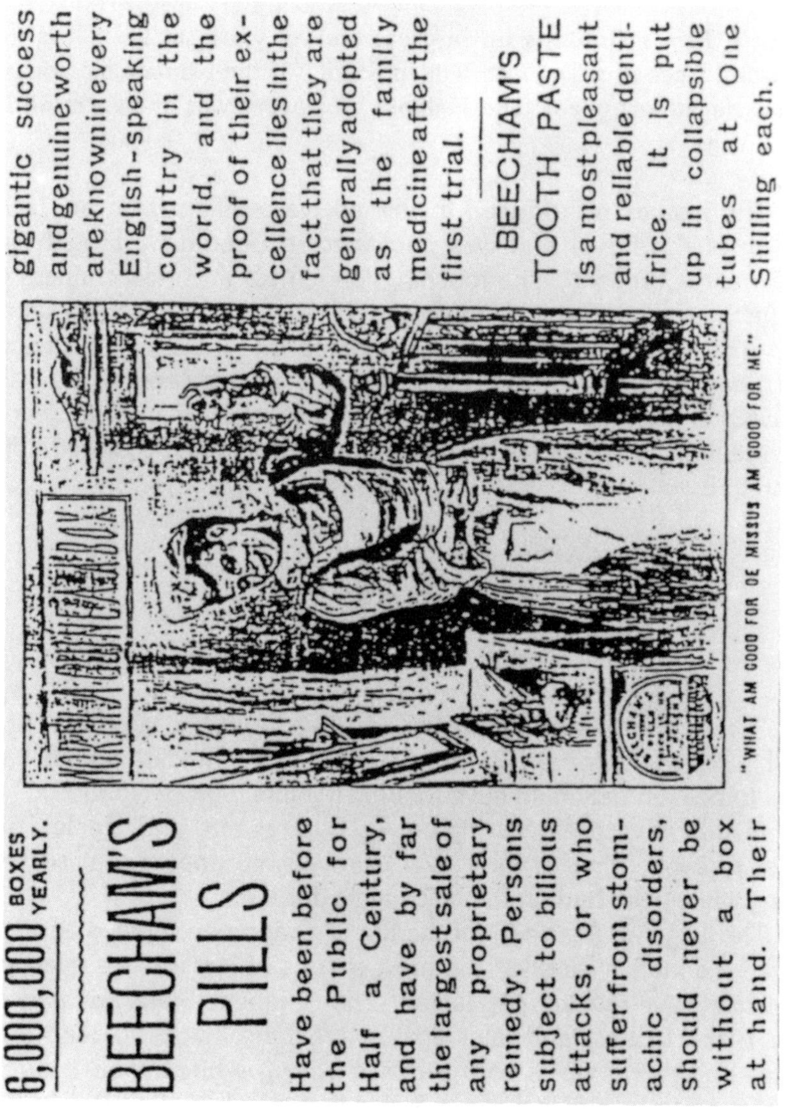
6,000,000 BOXES YEARLY.
BEECHAM'S PILLS
Have been before the Public for Half a Century, and have by far the largest sale of any proprietary remedy. Persons subject to bilious attacks, or who suffer from stomachic disorders, should never be without a box at hand. Their gigantic success and genuine worth are known in every English-speaking country in the world, and the proof of their excellence lies in the fact that they are generally adopted as the family medicine after the first trial.
BEECHAM'S TOOTH PASTE
is a most pleasant and reliable dentifrice. It is put up in collapsible tubes at One Shilling each.
WORTH A GUINEA A BOX
"WHAT AM GOOD FOR DE MISSUS AM GOOD FOR ME."

Fig. 3.

used to sell the services of one of the world's largest ad agencies. The opening paragraph of the body read as:

If *Uncle Tom's Cabin* is not a great literary work, at least it is the shrewdest piece of selling ever written. Here was the ultimate blossoming of the Negative Appeal. The Halitosis of slavery was shown in all its dreadfulness.

The images reproduced in this ad were taken from an 1897 edition of the novel that was published in Boston by Houghton, Mifflin and Company. The touching tenderness and peacefulness of the first image of Eva leaning on the knee of Uncle Tom was taken from a section of the book that reinforced the angelical qualities of Eva. Leading the reader into this image was the circularity of the lash, the whip of the master that was so frequently used against the slaves. The scene in the book was when Tom was singing an old Methodist hymn to Eva:

> I see a band of spirits bright,
> Than taste the glories there;
> They all are robed in spotless white,
> And conquering palms they bear.

"Uncle Tom, I've seen them," said Eva. Tom had no doubt of it at all; it did not surprise him in the least. If Eva told him she had been to heaven he would have thought it entirely probable (303).[13]

In this advertisement (figure 4), Eva, as she and Uncle Tom relate to each other in the novel, showed the impact that such a young white child had on the black male domestic.

The 1946 ad (figure 5) for the Ink-O-Graph pen showed another powerful dynamic that had the most serious of implications even for the white slave-owning population. The Southern States, as part of their Black Codes, had laws against teaching blacks to read and write. In several parts of the novel young whites took it upon themselves to teach Uncle Tom the rudiments of the two R's. In the ad we see Eva instructing the adult black male. The ad was significant because in the United States women were very much a part of the Abolitionist movement and it was imagically appropriate that Mrs. Stowe chose a young girl to complete the educational task that young Martin had started at the beginning of the novel before the adventures of Uncle Tom started. Did the ad also have a more subtle hidden message? The ad appeared in 1946, a few years ahead

Fig. 4.

of the Brown v. Board of Education of Topeka which sought to eradicate the segregation of schools in America. This ad, then, had a degree of poignancy that could not be missed in that here we have an early (then reproduced) integrated educational scene albeit a child and an adult.

In the five ads that I have presented to this point, three of the pieces showed elements that were analyzed to show how Topsy was marginalized as the "Other": the vulgarized language usage; the featureless face, the objectification of the human image to show the

Fig. 5.

blackening features of the products in question; and the Beecham ad that shows the black domestic basically stealing some of the mistress's items. These ads were part of numerous themes that were and continued to be used when the black child and the black female were portrayed (as were black males). Since the focus of the paper is on the two characters of the novel *Uncle Tom's Cabin* I have kept the analysis to Topsy and Eva. Eva, on the other hand, was shown protected and in the position of teacher, the opposite types of images that included really nothing negative. This type of imagic representation was clearly distinctively different from that of the black child/adult, Topsy.

If we now fast forward to 1991, we witness the Benetton ad, one that caused so many people to protest the juxtaposing of the white and black children in the elements of the ads that were found to be unacceptable.

Since 1985, Luciano Benetton had used integrated advertisements to promote his soft-fashion goods throughout the world. Part of the advertising strategy was to use models that represented the races of the world. These images also had a direct tie-in to the universally used slogan of the firm "United Colors of Benetton."

Benetton believed that with this type of campaign, the company was making its contribution to the war against racism. In the ads all races were shown kissing, holding hands, frolicking, and in many other forms of behavioural interplay. The emphasis appeared to be that togetherness fosters greater human understanding regardless of race. The models that were used reflect the market niche, the customers of Benetton, children and young adults. However, in the 1991 campaign, some segments of society found the image of the "horned" black child unacceptable (figure 6). The image of the child they believed evoked images of the past that were negative, stereotypically laden caricatures of blacks that were created by whites.

It appeared that the "hair as horns" was too powerful, too painful a sign, and signified evil and the devil. It drew protestations from the black community, in particular. They believed, and I have tried to show, that the "horned" child was a 1991 version of the "sooty gnome," "the thing"; the child of the devil, Topsy, as she appeared and was portrayed negatively in the 1852 novel *Uncle Tom's Cabin*. The image, this characterization, was eventually used by a number of advertisers in the later part of the 19th century and into the present time.

Early after the widespread success and popularity of the book and the play, and the many songs that came from versions of the stage presentations, both in America and Western Europe, images of some of the characters appeared in the marketplaces of many countries of the world. This widespread commercialization could be seen as an earlier version of the mass acceptance of, say, the Disney

Fig. 6.

characters, the Ninja turtles that are presently so commercially exploited. Eva and Topsy had, and have, been shown in numerous bipolar/oppositional situations. Eva, the high status child with all that image entailed, and Topsy the lowly child with all the imagic signifiers that status entailed. The Benetton ad did not have the names, Eva and Topsy, shown. However, eventually some community members took strong exception to the message that they believed the ad was sending to the viewing public in the United States and in Canada.

Discussion

The analysis of this essay has focused on the structural, hierarchializing of the races that was based on the binary/ oppositional uses of colour as a major signifier. A functionalist discussion also indicated that the images of Eva and Topsy were used by many different types of commercial ventures in their efforts to sell and to promote products in a wide variety of categories. The following portion of the essay will now discuss additional dimensions of these two approaches within the concept of "symbolic slavery."

Dubin (1987) focused on the use of everyday material objects and how they represented blacks in a series of gross/negative caricatures. He believed that these objects conveyed a powerful symbolic message. These widely distributed everyday objects—salt and pepper shakers, clothes, dolls, dishes, cleaning utensils, wall calendars, packages, labels on goods, golf tees, candies, placemats, and many other items were a form of visual apartheid in that they frequently showed blacks in the lowest status positions within society. His analysis showed that for centuries these types of images were indicative of the slave system in America and the occupational segregation that was an integral part of America's history. These material artifacts of our culture connoted a form of psychological violence based on power relationships that were institutionalized on the basis of skin colour. He believed that these systemic, institutionalized values were transmitted by these material artifacts that soon were reflected in the actions, the values, the attitudes of numerous segments of the American society.[14]

In one of her recent works, Morrison (1992) discussed how the Africanist presence in American fiction was carefully invented, constructed, and crafted, and how the colour of the participants in the fictional works was used to demonize blacks and to valorize whites. These basic points have been previously discussed in this essay. The approach that I took was to show the reader how Western Christian and capitalist ideologies, beginning about the mid 15th century, also constructed a biological and class hierarchy based on skin colour. Morrison believed that numerous, and some of the most popular, American authors used the binary oppositional schema in their literary works. These authors, such as Melville and Hemingway, for example, contextualized power, control, and degradation in relations between blacks and whites by exploiting and fabricating the evil and the power of blackness.

Morrison argued that the slave system in America was unlike many other slave systems in that it was based mainly on the visible variable of skin colour. Americans absorbed Western European ideologies that stated that colour meant something—a system of racial hierarchializing and human degradation.

She went on to state that black fictional characters were constructed to be shown as alien, as "Other" to the normative white characters in the white literary discourses. One area of her analysis was the continued use of vulgarized language. The speech patterns, the spelling, the expressions that were all shown to be used by black fictional characters created tension between the "Self" and the "Other."[15] This form of mongrelized language use was another major factor that helped to marginalize the black from the mainstream of American society. This form of marginalizing the black helped to create a cognitive world split between blacks and whites. I have shown that the ads of Topsy clearly used this type of language and probably helped to reinforce class and race distinctions of "Otherness" as well as to assert class privileges, power, and high status to the white elites, in particular.

Dubin also argued that the widespread negative stereotypes of blacks that were so pervasive throughout society also helped the white underclasses realize that their position was not completely rock bottom. They could always see blacks and images of blacks that indicated to the poor whites that blacks were much worse off within a segregated society.

Cultural identities are formed by the informed in a nation's literature. Uncle Tom's Cabin was one of America's most widely read books of the last century. The novel and the numerous versions of the play also made major impacts in Europe. What I have tried to argue is that with the widespread diffusion and acceptance of these works the images that emanated from them eventually added to the vast repertoire of pejorative images of blacks that some have argued are forms of symbolic slavery, visual and psychological violence. I have presented the idea of visual apartheid, in that in the ads discussed, there is treatment of the subjects but that the significations of the black and white persons of the images are treated in many different ways.

In Mrs. Stowe's novel, Eva and Topsy were clearly created to show a binary/oppositional set of relationships. It has been well documented that Mrs. Stowe as an ardent and lifelong Abolitionist wanted her book to expose the dreadfulness of the evils of American slavery. In so doing by way of the plot she used she was also showing the structural social hierarchy that existed within the South and the world of the slave-owners. With the immense success of the work, in various forms, commercial interests, which did not have the same intent as that of Mrs. Stowe, used the Eva and Topsy imagery for their own functional reasons. In many cases the function was to advertise and to sell products. However, in so doing, what I believe was in fact taking place was that these images of Eva and Topsy were in fact reinforcing the binary/oppositional relationships based on skin colour that had existed for almost five hundred years in the Western world.

Eventually, in October 1991, some concerned societal members took strong exception to the Benetton advertisement, which I have tried to present as a modernized version of the Eva and Topsy dichotomy. The protestions even went so far as to demand a public apology from the company, the quick withdrawal of all billboards that carried the ad, and a threatened boycott of the Benetton products; all demands were ignored.

Because significant features of the "Other" can change over time, one has to analyze the stereotype(s) so that they are placed within, and according to, their cultural contexts.

With respect to the images of Eva and Topsy, some variations have occurred. Some of these changes have been illustrated and discussed. However, even though the Benetton advertising campaign was believed to be based on racial tolerance and understanding, significant numbers of people viewed the "horned" black child and the angelic white child as evocative signifiers of an image that was thought to be long forgotten—a satanically portrayed black child "thick" with negative significations that represented a bygone era that was a part of *Uncle Tom's Cabin*.

Notes

The six tradecards and advertisements that were discussed in the essay range in time from approximately the early 1870s (the J. & P. Coats tradecard) to the widely circulated "United Colors of Benetton" ad that appeared in 1991. The span of time would be about 120 years of the type of binary/oppositional material that are included in the essay.

[1]Robert M. MacGregor, "The Coloring of the Race Issue." A paper presented at the Northeast Popular Culture Association's Conference, Boston, Oct. 1992.

[2]Chester E. Jorgenson, *Uncle Tom's Cabin As Book and Legend. A Guide to an Exhibition* (Detroit, MI: sponsored by the Friends of the Detroit Public Library, 1952) 10.

[3]J. Frank Davis, "Tom Shows," *Scribner's* Magazine 77 (Jan.-June 1925): 350-60.

J. Winston Coleman, Jr., "Mrs. Stowe, Kentucky, and Uncle Tom's Cabin," *Lincoln Herald* June 1946: 2-9.

F. Lauriston Bullard, "Uncle Tom on the Stage," *Lincoln Herald* June 1946: 19-22.

Ralph G. Newman, "Uncle Tom's Cabin," *Lincoln Herald* June 1946: 23-25.

Richard Moody, "Uncle Tom, The Theater, and Mrs. Stowe," *American Heritage* 6.6 (Oct. 1955): 29-33, 102.

[4]Ibid., 36.

[5]Robert Miles, *Racism* (London: Routledge, 1989).

Jan Nederveen Pieterse, *White on Black* (New Haven: Yale UP, 1992).

[6]Harriet Beecher Stowe, *Uncle Tom's Cabin* (Boston: Houghton, 1897).

[7]Ibid.

[8]Ibid.

[9]Harry Birdoff, *The World's Greatest Hit: Uncle Tom's Cabin— Illustrated with Old-Time Playbills, Daguerrotype, Vignettes, Music-Sheets Poems, and Cartoons* (New York: S.P. Vanni, 1947).

[10]Ibid.

[11]Sam Dennison, *Scandalize My Name* (New York: Garland, 1982) 176.

[12]Ibid.

[13]Ibid.

[14]Steven C. Dubin, "Symbolic Slavery: Black Representations in Popular Culture," *Social Problems* 34.2 (Apr. 1987): 122-40.

[15]Toni Morrison, *Playing in the Dark* (Cambridge, MA: Harvard UP, 1992).

"What are you going to make out of this boy?": The Role of Poetry in the "Management" of Boys, 1875-1900

Stanley S. Blair

In industrialized late 19th-century America, before the general affordability of life insurance policies and old age homes and the creation of viable pension plans and the Social Security system, in an age of extended families in which aged parents who outlived their economic usefulness had to rely on their children's support, many middle-class parents thought it crucial that they direct their daughters to be desirable brides and their sons to be dutiful breadwinners. Wanting a better life for their children, economic insurance against their own old age, and better social standing for their family, these parents saw their children as a resource, a raw material they could fashion and develop to their advantage through what they called "child-culture," "child-training," or, more frequently, "child management."[1]

While there have been many fine studies of the children's literature of the period, the corresponding popular nonfiction child-management literature is, as scholars such as historians John and Virginia Demos and psychohistorian Lloyd deMause observe, a largely unexplored phenomenon.[2] This lack of scholarship is all the more surprising in light of cultural anthropologist James Spradley's observation that "The richest settings for discovering the rules of a society are those where novices of one sort or another are being instructed in appropriate behavior" (21). Child-management literature attempts not only to instruct children in appropriate behavior but also to instruct their parents in appropriate behavior toward their children; in effect, it tries to make a continuity out of the potential discontinuity between generations, to be, in R. Gordon Kelly's words, "productive both of individual identity as well as of the continued existence of the group" (36-37). Partly because of how late 19th-century child-management books influenced middle-class adults and partly because of how they reflect what was at the time parents' commonsense approaches to raising boys, these books shed light on how in the process of socializing their sons—the adult males of the early 20th century—fathers and mothers disagreed on what sort of men to make out of their boys, reflecting even larger tensions in the cultural logic of late 19th-century America.

As Bernard Wishy notes, the late 19th-century men who wrote about child management were, for the most part, not scientists or child psychologists but simply fathers who sought to share with other fathers their own successful practical experiences in dealing with their sons (ix). The Demoses observe that some of these writers "were struck by a kind of aimlessness and indecision that seemed increasingly common among American young people" (634). These writers see an entire generation of weak, listless, and lazy boys. For example, John Harvey Kellogg's popular *Plain Facts for Old and Young* (which went through 13 printings between 1877 and 1895) discusses the forces that are "undermining the health of the race and sapping the constitutions of our American men." "The boys of today," Kellogg notes, "would be no match in physical strength for the sturdy youths of a century ago who are now their grandparents," which explains why "we hear very little of remarkable feats of labor accomplished by our modern boys" (436-37). In his popular book *Education*, Herbert Spencer also sees an increasing debilitation of manhood; the middle-class men of his generation appeared to him to be weaker than their grandfathers, and the current generation of boys is even "less robust" and "on the average, neither so well grown nor so strong as their seniors." Most children, he says, "do not reach the stature of their parents; and, in massiveness, making due allowance for difference of age, there seems a like inferiority. In health, the contrast appears still greater."[3] Like many at the close of the 19th century, these men see nothing less than a crisis in masculinity, and accordingly they encourage fathers to become more involved in the raising of their sons.[4]

These men see their own progress to adulthood and their status as adult males as paradigms for how boys become men. Since, like many of their peers, they are the primary—and often only—economic providers for their families, they associate their biological sex with their economic function, so much so that they blur the line between being a man and being a breadwinner. In effect, they define the masculine gender economically. In managing boys, therefore, their goal is at once economic and social: to prepare boys to become recognizable as men to other men. They do this chiefly by depicting being a man in terms of being an economic provider, the prerequisite for which is duty: the more dutiful a boy was, the better a breadwinner and man he would become. For example, in William Augustus Mowry's *Talks With My Boys*, which was first published in 1885 and reached a fourth revised and enlarged edition seven years later, schoolmaster Mowry writes that a sense of duty would prepare boys for being men: "You all need to learn to be *industrious*. You should all have some duties to do at home, every day. These duties should always be performed with care and fidelity," says Mowry, "you *can* and you *ought* to have a high and laudable ambition to prepare yourself for *manhood*, and for the duties which manhood shall bring to you."[5] A boy lacking such a sense of duty would not grow up to be a man capable of meeting his future duty as economic provider; in fact, some of these writers believe that such a boy would not grow up to be a true man at all, but only a biologically male entity unprepared for manhood. In his *Lectures to Young Men*, which remained in print for over 30 years, Henry Ward Beecher explains to boys that in order to secure a livelihood they must above all cultivate the quality of industriousness, not because it will necessarily make them rich men, but because it will make them real men: "The poor man with Industry, is happier than the rich man in Idleness; for labor makes the one more manly, and riches unmans the other" (13). Those males who lack the mental quality of Industry lack the external sign by which it is known, labor; such unindustrious and unmanly males are, in effect, economic castrati. To avoid such a fate, Beecher says, boys should develop Industry through having "the intention of usefulness" (7), "usefulness" that he celebrates as "the manly joy" (12).

In the management of boys, these male writers' female counterparts have priorities that somewhat differ. These women also are interested in usefulness and efficiency, but less for their sons than for themselves as mothers, and less for economic reasons than for social and cultural ones: late 19th-century mothers were trying to reduce the amount of time they spent on maintaining the house so they could both spend more time with their children and develop themselves intellectually. This is the project of Mary Blake's *Twenty-Six Hours a Day*, which (as the title suggests) shows overworked, harried housewives ways to save two hours each day on their housework, two hours that they can then spend on reading and the arts so as better to cultivate themselves and their children. Another such project is that of Charlotte Perkins Gilman in *Concerning Children*. Showing that in nine-tenths of American homes women have to perform both mothering and housekeeping duties, and that in the other one-tenth both duties are performed by socially inferior domestic servants (233), Gilman contends that women must spend more time raising their children and becoming socially active; for her, being a good mother and being a social activist are one and the same:

Sunk in the constant contemplation of their own families, our female citizens let the days and the years pass by, utterly ignoring their civic duties. While women are supported by men, they have more time to spare for such broad interests than men have; and one would naturally think that even the lowest sense of honor would lead them to some form of public usefulness in return for this immunity.... The care of children is certainly the duty of women. The best care of children means the best education. The woman who has not done her best to improve the educational advantages of her city, State and country,—of the world—has not done her duty as a citizen or as a woman.[6]

Women can free enough time to become more socially active and better mothers, Gilman explains, if they realize that child care is a task best performed not by one mother individually but by several collectively. To this end she suggests that groups of six women get together and each day take turns caring for each other's children; in this way, by caring for all the children one day a week and for her own children in the evenings, each mother will have five working days each week to devote to housework, rest, self-cultivation, and social activism.[7]

These women's attitudes toward self-cultivation and social activism carry over into how they raised their sons. While these women acknowledge that boys should grow up to be economic providers, they view that economic role as achieved through and subordinate to a higher, more noble duty, that of being a moral person. Sarepta Henry, the author of *Studies in Home and Child Life*, says that "'What are you going to make out of this boy?' is a common question, and it is often answered just as though he were a stick of timber, a block of stone, or a lump of potter's clay, to be shaped according to the will of his teachers.—'I shall make a doctor,' 'a lawyer,' 'a business man,' 'a preacher, out of this boy'" (151). But unlike her male peers, Henry sees the management of boys in these materially practical directions to be in fact "misdirected" and impractical: viewing the values of the male-dominated material world with contempt, she contends that "The 'hard sound sense' of the world, the 'business shrewdness' which is counted as so necessary to 'success,' can not be built into the foundation of a Christian home without so modifying and nullifying the Christian part of it as to make it worse than useless" (175). Since what is ultimately "useful" is not material things but spiritual qualities, children should achieve true usefulness through developing not materialist abilities but spiritual values. In this way she is able to confute the arguments of her male peers by asserting that "the end to be attained in child culture is the making of men and women who shall be strong" not because they know how the material world works but "because they are pure" (128). "The one thing to be kept in mind," she says, "is that he is to be *developed* for an eternal existence; that he is to be taught how to use his abilities in the best possible manner for the sake of those around him; that work is simply one of the means to this end, and, like any other tool, should be kept in its own place, and made to serve its legitimate purpose" (125). The linkage of God and boy through the middlewoman of the mother is expressed eloquently by Mrs. Frank Malleson in her popular *Notes on the Early Training of Children*, which had reached a third edition by 1887 and a fourth by 1897: "...we must train so that our boy will grow up to take a useful and honorable place in the world...but we desire this for him because *we aim at the greater which includes it*. We will, with God's help, try our best to train the boy for manhood, fitting him for work and usefulness in the century in which he lives, but otherwise possessing character and aspirations which belong to human excellence at any time, and in any position."[8] Similarly, mothers should "not be content if the 'right,' to him, as he grows onward to man's estate, means the current morality of his generation, in views of trade, politics, social ethics. In accordance with our training, we shall demand higher conceptions of his duty" (113). One can see why Henry's and Malleson's male peers might object to their practical spirituality: while the men think that it is essential for those boys growing "onward to man's estate" to immerse themselves in the "current morality" of "trade, politics, and social ethics," Henry and Malleson contend that for boys such worldly concerns are relatively unimportant, for boys can succeed in the material world through spiritual excellence.

According to these women, boys can gain access to the moral, the true, and the beautiful (and consequently material success) through reading literature, especially poetry. Among the several women who discuss the importance of literature as a whole in the raising of sons,[9] Henry makes the general point that the reading of literature has two functions, one of which is worldly, the other spiritual. The worldly function of literature enables the middle-class citizen to pass for upper-class, as if one had the economic resources to have much leisure time; but this worldly and dissembling function of literature is one to which she objects: "Literature represents to the student about all there is in culture. To be uncultured, according to the law of this world, is worse than to be sinful; and every aspiring, intelligent child must sooner or later feel the force of this influence, and overcome it, or be overcome by it" (196). That is, in "this world" the worst sin is failing to have some passing knowledge of great literature. The other, non-worldly, spiritual function of literature—the one Henry prefers—contributes to a child's moral well-being and in turn to society's well-being. "The object of the printed page," she says, "is to turn thought into desired channels, to capture brain and heart, and train them to certain habits of opinion and belief, and so produce a given course of action, which shall be to the advantage of the power behind the scenes" (192). Because of its role in the formation of boys' spiritual values, literature is somewhat subversive; who exactly this "power behind the scenes" actually is—God or women—is not as important as who it is not: the economic power currently on the scenes, masculine breadwinning men. Why Henry thinks it important for boys to read literature, then, has to do not only with making them better men, but also with engineering a better society.

These women mention frequently and describe in detail the merits of particular types and particular collections of poetry. Although some of these women encourage the reading of verse written specifically for children, they tend to prefer the same poetry adults read. Discussing the importance of "the learning of poetry from the lips of the mother," Malleson objects to "the repeating of mere rhyme," "inferior literature," or "doggerel," preferring instead that mothers read to their children "a number of our finest poems which appeal to the world of children as thoroughly as to older readers. There are others scattered amidst the treasures of English literature, and it is these which should be taught to children."[10] Similarly, Mary Blake suggests to mothers: "If you make wise selections, the children will surely listen. They are naturally fond of melody and rhyme; if they never hear anything better, they will be satisfied with mere jingle. But try spirited ballads and little poems by our best authors and see how quickly they will learn to appreciate them." This poetry pervaded settings in which women interacted frequently with children. "Almost every household possesses some of our standard poets, or selections from their works," Blake notes, and there are also a number of poetry anthologies, "little compilations."[11]

In fact, the creator of the Shaw Childhood in Poetry Collection at Florida State University, John Mackay Shaw, recalls that "this kind of clear, rhythmical, musical poetry...confronted us 19th-century children wherever we turned—in the home, in the school, in church, and in the periodicals that were our delight. We read it, we memorized it, we declaimed it, not always willingly, sometimes resentfully, but so constantly and in such profusion that it burned into our souls."[12]

In short, these little poems by the best authors not only occupied the leisure time of middle-class housewives but also educated the souls of both their daughters and their sons into spiritual maturity, into, as Shaw calls it, wisdom. In fact, Shaw suggests that in the 20th century the decreasing importance of poetry in rearing children is responsible for many of the world's current problems. Noting that poetry became "the neglected art" because high modernist poetry "could not very well be read to children," Shaw calls for his readers to restore poetry to "its proper place as the mother of the arts," a matter that he says is "of vital importance to the future" of the human race: "poetry in the preceding ten centuries has been the channel through which each generation has transmitted its wisdom to the one that follows it. And of what value is all our knowledge if it does not walk hand in hand with wisdom? May not mankind's increasing understanding of the ways of nature be actually destructive if there be not wise minds to direct its use?"[13] Like Malleson and Henry, Shaw reasons that poetry, "the mother of the arts," is the medium of eternal wisdom, and in turn that wisdom is of true "value"—more valuable than anything in the material world of "knowledge" and "use." The material world is potentially self-destructive without wisdom; but with wisdom there are no limits to what the human race may achieve. As his call to action indicates, Shaw has a tremendous passion for and commitment to improving the human condition through poetry—testimony to the constructive impact of his own childhood reading of poetry. In this way the spiritual and social imperatives of having children read poetry transcend sexual division. Both girls and boys, and the world in which they lived, could benefit from the wise truths imparted by poetry.

Many of the men writing about managing boys disagree. Rather than viewing poetry as the means for improving boys' moral virtues, they see much fiction and poetry as amusements that distract boys from the business at hand, which is learning to be effective breadwinners. These men attempt to direct boys' reading towards what are for them useful subjects, and in so doing direct them not only away from many sorts of fiction—historical and Algeresque fiction being the exceptions—but also away from most poetry. In his *Hints on Child-Training* (first published in 1891 and reprinted in 1893, 1896, 1898, and well into the 20th century), Henry Clay Trumbull explains that first among the factors to "be borne in mind in the choice and presentation of the book or books for a child's reading" is sex, for books, like other amusements, "ought to be... such as will aid in developing a child's manliness or womanliness." Accordingly he tells parents that in boys' reading "fiction ought not to be the chief factor" because it "would not tend to the development of his highest mental faculties, or to the fostering of his truest manhood."[14] To foster this manhood, Trumbull recommends that parents should lead boys to read "books that are likely to be helpful," "books of history, of biography, of travel, of popular science, and of other useful knowledge, that they will find in these books a higher and more satisfying pleasure than is found by their companions in the exciting or delusive narrations of fiction and fancy."[15] Such parental manipulation of a boy's reading, Trumbull says, "is work that is remunerative beyond its extremest cost" (82): what a boy reads will influence his future ability to have and support a family. Similarly, Spencer claims that parents make a wise economic investment when they acquaint their sons with the sciences: "Whoever is immediately or remotely implicated in any form of industry (and few are not) has a direct interest in understanding something of the mathematical, physical, and chemical properties of things; perhaps, also, has a direct interest in biology; and certainly has in sociology. Whether he does or does not succeed well in that indirect self-preservation which we call getting a good livelihood, depends on his knowledge of one or more of these sciences..." (52). Since reading in scientific subjects is the best preparation for achieving a good livelihood, Spencer contends, literature "should be wholly subordinate," for it constitutes "the efflorescence of civilization": as the arts "occupy the leisure part of life, so should they occupy the leisure part of education."[16]

Some of these men choose to direct boys' reading not positively but negatively, by recommending not what they should read but what they should avoid; they direct boys away from certain types of literature both directly and indirectly. In characterizing certain types of literature as being read primarily by boys or by girls, some of these men indirectly portray poetry as effeminate. For example, in *The Aim of Life*, first published in 1894 and reaching a third edition by 1900, Philip Moxom expresses concern for what girls and boys read. Both girls and boys are reading too many sensational novels; girls are reading too much poetry and boys too much pulp fiction. Since what children read will determine their character as adults, Moxom believes, reading such things will have severe consequences for them later in life: "If I find a young woman absorbed in the works of Mrs. Southworth or the author [Tennyson] of 'Airy, fairy Lilian,' I am at once of the opinion that she will never startle her friends with the profundity or originality of her thoughts. If I find a young man devoted to Emile Zola or the Police Gazette, I am not surprised by-and-by to learn that his name has appeared in the records of the criminal court." In effect what Moxom has done is to gender certain types of literature: poetry is girlish, pulp fiction boyish. In light of his assertion that "An analysis of the books which a man habitually reads will reveal at once the quality of his mind and the tendency of his character," one can infer that Moxom's reaction upon finding his young man absorbed in "Airy, fairy Lilian" would have been unfavorable.[17]

But some of these men are much more direct in depicting much of then-contemporary poetry as effeminate.[18] One of the most virulent attacks is Beecher's. Through a mildly circuitous logic he contrasts the qualities of true Industry, which he renders as manly, and feigned Genius, which he depicts as effeminate. According to Beecher, "Industry has a firmer muscle" than Genius and "can do anything which Genius can do; and very many things which it cannot." In fact, if a boy would like to be like most men, Industry is indispensable: "the vast bulk of men," he says, "have less need of Genius than of intellectual Industry and patient Enterprise." While a man with true Genius has "one or more faculties" that are "in the highest state of development," he observes, most people have a mistaken notion of Genius as being a "rare facility of mind" that can do "anything without labor" and that "loathes the sweat of toils, the vexations of life, and the dull burden of care." While he acknowledges that such geniuses "may exist," they must be even less common than true geniuses. Thus, Beecher concludes, there are many young men who pretend to possess the quality of genius but who in fact lack it. He depicts these false geniuses as effeminate males interested in poetry:

So far as my observations have ascertained the species, they abound in academies, colleges, and Thespian societies; in village debating clubs; in coteries of young artists, and among young professional aspirants. They are to be known by a reserved air, excessive sensitiveness, and utter indolence;

by very long hair, and very open shirt collars; by the reading of much wretched poetry, and the writing of much, yet more wretched; by being very conceited, very affected, very disagreeable, and very useless:—beings whom no man wants for friend, pupil, or companion.

According to Beecher, the reading and writing of poetry renders males into "beings" that lack the "firmer muscle" of Industry and are therefore unlike "the vast bulk of men" who shun them (16-17). Reinforcing such beings' association with art and poetry, Beecher later writes that their dissoluteness threatens to contaminate other males, tempting them "with the lying lyric of 'classic drama,' and 'human life,' 'morality,' 'poetry,' and 'divine comedy.' Disguise it as you will, these men of pleasure are the world over, CORRUPTERS OF YOUTH."[19]

Late 19th-century child-management books suggest that their male and female authors see, respectively, masculinity in terms of economic power and femininity in terms of spiritual influence.[20] Defining masculinity economically, the men concern themselves primarily with how to manage boys so that those boys can fulfill their future duties (toward their wives, children, and parents) as economic providers. Like the men, the women acknowledge that men should be adequate breadwinners, but they subordinate that economic function to the more important need for boys, like girls, both to learn about and to embody positive moral values. For these women, boys would succeed economically less through knowing specific skills than through developing their moral character through reading literature in general and poetry in particular. On the other hand, the men authors advise parents to direct sons' reading toward those subjects that will enhance their economic competitiveness and away from less economically profitable subjects such as fiction and poetry, viewing those boys interested in reading and writing poetry as economically irresponsible, as being non-masculine and, by default, effeminate. If these works on child management accurately reflect the concerns and the common sense about raising boys in late 19th-century middle-class America, many mothers and fathers agreed on the ends but not the means of raising their sons, in effect drawing boys between the economic duty of breadwinning and the need to transcend that duty in favor of spiritual excellence.

Notes

For their criticisms and suggestions I wish to thank Lawrence Berkove, Louis Budd, Celeste Fraser Delgado, and Frank Lentricchia.

[1]See C. Gilman 161-64. On the use of the term "management," see *Nineteenth Century Readers Guide to Periodical Literature, 1890-1899*, 2 vols., ed. Helen Grant Cushing and Adah V. Morris (New York: H. W. Wilson, 1944), I: 492, II: 198; the *Subject Headings used in the Dictionary Catalogs of the Library of Congress* [from 1897 through 1928], 3rd ed., ed. Mary Wilson MacNair (Washington: U.S. G.P.O., 1928), which cross-lists "Child Management" and "Moral Education" (237); and the *List of Subject Headings for Small Libraries*, 5th ed., ed. Minnie Earl Sears (1st ed. 1923; New York: H.W. Wilson, 1944), which notes that the heading of "Child management" should be "used for books on child training and discipline. These books may include psychological matter such as is entered under the heading Child study, but their content and purpose is more practical. Books on management of children in school are entered under School discipline" (88).

[2]On children's literature see *American Writers for Children before 1900*, ed. Glenn E. Estes (Detroit: Gale Research, 1985) and Suzanne Rahn, *Children's Literature: An Annotated Bibliography of the History and Criticism* (New York: Garland, 1981). On the lack of studies of child management literature, see deMause 2, Demos 632-33, and Wishy ix-x, as well as Edward N. Saveth, "The Problem of American Family History," *American Quarterly* 21 (1969): 311-29. The sheer number of late 19th-century child-management books—not to mention periodicals—is considerable: see the Appendix.

[3]Spencer 258-59. Spencer's book passed through at least 30 American printings in the 40 years between its first publication in 1860 and the close of the century; it was perhaps the single most popular and most often quoted statement of child management principles. See also Beecher 25: "Manhood seems debilitated." Similarly, Trumbull decries boys' "reluctance" to apply themselves "in the line of wise expediency" as "a failing which, if not trained out of that boy, will stand as a barrier to his truest manhood, and will make him a second-rate man when he might be a first-rate one; a one-sided man instead of a well-proportioned man" (32): that is, without the guidance of fathers boys will grow up to be false, second-rate, and one-sided men, and that assisting those boys to become true, first-rate, and well-proportioned men is the father's duty.

[4]This was a trend that had begun in American culture relatively recently, only in the 19th century (see deMause 52); it was reflected in the

"Mothers Congress" changing its name to the "Parents Congress" near the end of the century (see C. Gilman 76). Middle- and upper-class men's perception of a crisis in masculinity and their determination to have their sons avoid effeminacy is also reflected in the popularity of "strenuosity": see Theodore Roosevelt, *The Strenuous Life* (New York: Century, 1902); John Tunis, *The American Way in Sport* (New York: Duell, Sloan, and Pearce, 1958), 21-32; Edwin Cady, "'The Strenuous Life' as a Theme in American Cultural History," 59-66 in *New Voices in American Studies*, eds. Ray Browne, Donald Winkelman, and Allen Hayman (West Lafayette, IN: Purdue University Studies, 1966); John Higham, *Writing American History* (Bloomington: Indiana University Press, 1970), 77-88; and T.J. Jackson Lears, *No Place of Grace* (New York: Pantheon, 1981), 102, 107-09.

[5]Mowry 211, 33 (emphases in original). Similarly, Kellogg warns boys that those males who are unfit "for the important duties and responsibilities of life" (419) will be unable to fulfill "The Two Objects of Human Existence," which are "the maintenance of an individual life" and "the production of similar individuals which shall also have the power of maintaining individual lives" (423); in effect Kellogg fuses economic and sexual virility and dooms those without such virility to extinction. See also Beecher 14.

[6]C. Gilman 154-55; see 283-91.

[7]C. Gilman 201-202; see 200-211. See also her *Women and Economics* (Boston: Small, Maynard, and Co., 1898).

[8]Malleson 68-69 (my emphases). See also Henry 24, 79.

[9]For example, see S. Gilman 62-76; Blake 38-83, 128-39, and 141-45; Malleson 56-58.

[10]Malleson 57-58; she continues, "...I have found children between four and six years of age, love, and repeat, with touching emphasis and beauty, a large variety of English poems, the Percy Ballads as a matter of course, and Macaulay's fine modern ballads; some of Browning's lyrics, many of Tennyson's, and scattered simple gems of Shakespeare, Coleridge, Wordsworth, Keats, and many others." For an account of showing the fallaciousness of distinguishing children's or adult's verse in terms of authorial intention, see Donald Hall's introduction to his edition of *The Oxford Book of Children's Verse in America* (New York: Oxford University Press, 1985), xxiii-xxxviii, especially xxiii-xxiv, xxxiv.

[11]Blake 142-43 (see her chapter on "The Cultivation of Literary Taste in Children," 128-39); among the anthologies she names are "Lucy Larcom's 'Hillside and Roadside Poems,' Mrs. Giles's 'Hymns and Rhymes for Home and School,' 'Hymns for Mothers and Children,' Elliot's 'Poetry for Children,' to say nothing of the school readers, which contain many excellent selections. Of larger and more expensive works, there are Dana's

'Household Book of Poetry,' Mackay's 'Thousand and One Gems,' or, best of all for children, Whittier's 'Child Life' in prose and poetry." Other poetry anthologies deemed appropriate by Mrs. George Elgin include Coventry Patmore's *Children's Garland* and Francis Turner Palgrave's popular *Children's Treasury of English Song* (Elgin cited in S. Gilman 70; see 62-76, especially 69-70).

[12]Shaw 135; see his *Childhood in Poetry: The Forty-Year History of a Collection, 1929-1969* (Tallahassee: Friends of the Library, Florida State University, 1970) and his annotated catalogue of his collection, *Childhood in Poetry*, 5 vols. (with 2 suppl.) (Detroit: Gale Research Co., 1967-68).

[13]Shaw 134, 140, 142, 134.

[14]Trumbull 183, 160, 178-79; see 155-56, 176, 182. Trumbull's book has recently been reprinted by a Christian press in a trade paperback edition, the back cover blurb of which notes that "this book is filled with practical guidelines for parenting that possess timeless value."

[15]Trumbull 183, 180.

[16]Spencer 74-75; see 73 and Trumbull 177-78. See also Mowry 240: "What study, then, can be more vital in interest, more attractive in material, or more fruitful in utility than the study of the annals of mankind?"

[17]Moxom 254-55. He is disparaging the first line of Tennyson's "Lilian." Curiously enough, he himself then cites Tennyson twice in epigraphs to the beginning of his next chapter; see 278-79. See also Kellogg 462-63, 465-66, 485-86.

[18]For an extended study of effeminacy in genteel poetry, see F. Brett Cox's "The Genteel Tradition in American Poetry and Criticism" (Diss. Duke University, 1992). See also Frank Lentricchia's *Ariel and the Police* (Madison: University of Wisconsin Press, 1987).

[19]Beecher 149 (emphasis in original). The linking of poetry and homosexuality in late 19th-century American culture is explored at length in Robert K. Martin's *The Homosexual Tradition in American Poetry* (Austin: University of Texas Press, 1979), 3-114.

[20]For an extended study of this phenomenon, see Ann Douglas's *The Feminization of American Culture* (1977; New York: Anchor Press, 1988).

Works Cited

Beecher, Henry Ward. *Lectures to Young Men.* 1860. Rev. and expanded ed. New York: John B. Alden, 1889.

Blake, Mary. *Twenty-Six Hours a Day.* Boston: Lothrop, 1883.

deMause, Lloyd, ed. *The History of Childhood.* New York: Psychohistory P, 1974.

Demos, John, and Virginia Demos. "Adolescence in Historical Perspective." *Journal of Marriage and the Family* 31 (1969): 632-38.

Gilman, Charlotte Perkins [Stetson]. *Concerning Children.* Boston: Small, Maynard & Co., 1900.

Gilman, Stella Scott. *Mothers in Council.* New York: Harper, 1884.

Henry, Sarepta Myrenda Irish. *Studies in Home and Child Life.* New York and Chicago: Fleming H. Revell Co., 1897.

Kellogg, John Harvey. *Plain Facts for Old and Young.* Rev. 3rd ed. 1877; Burlington, IA: I.F. Segner, 1884.

Kelly, R. Gordon. "Social Factors Shaping Some Late Nineteenth-Century Children's Periodical Fiction." *Society and Children's Literature.* Ed. James H. Fraser. Boston: David R. Godine, 1978. 35-44, 51-52.

Malleson, W. I. (Mrs. Frank). *Notes on the Early Training of Children.* 3rd ed. Boston: Heath, 1887.

Mowry, William Augustus. *Talks With My Boys.* Rev. 2nd ed. Boston: Roberts, 1886.

Moxom, Philip Stafford. *The Aim of Life: Plain Talks to Young Men and Women.* Boston: Roberts, 1894.

National Congress of Mothers. *The Work and Words of the National Congress of Mothers (First Annual Session).* 2nd ed. New York: Appleton, 1897.

Shaw, John Mackay. "Poetry for Children of Two Centuries." *Research About Nineteenth-Century Children and Books: Portrait Studies.* Ed. Selma K. Richardson. Urbana-Champaign: U of Illinois Graduate School of Library Science, 1980. 133-42.

Spencer, Herbert. *Education: Intellectual, Moral, and Physical.* 1860; New York: Appleton, 1885.

Spradley, James, ed. *Culture and Cognition.* San Francisco: Chandler, 1972.

Trumbull, Henry Clay. *Hints on Child-Training.* Philadelphia: Wattles, 1891; Brentwood, TN: Wolgemuth & Hyatt, 1990.

Wishy, Bernard. *The Child and the Republic: The Dawn of Modern American Child Nurture.* Philadelphia: U of Pennsylvania P, 1968.

Appendix

Appended to the proceedings of the first National Congress of Mothers (1897) is a list of "Books practical and helpful to parents, pertaining specially to child culture" (275-77):

A Great Mother. Willard.

A Handbook for Mothers. Mary Louisa Butler.

Apperception. Lange.

As a Matter of Course. Call.

A Study of Child Nature. Harrison.

Beckonings from Little Hands. Du Bois.

Bits of Talk about Home Matters. H. H.

Child Life in Art. Hurll.

Childhood in Literature and Art. Scudder.

Children's Rights. Wiggin.

Children, their Models and Critics. Aldrich.

Children's Ways. Sully.

Comenius's School of Infancy. W.S. Monroe.

Early Training of Children. Malleson.

Education. Spencer.

Education of Man. Froebel.

Essays on Books and Culture. Mabie.

Facts and Fiction. Gardener.

Froebel and Education through Self-Activity. Bowen.

Froebel's Mother Play, Mottoes, and Commentaries. Blow.

Gentle Measures in the Management of the Young. Abbott.

Hints on Child Training. Trumbull.

Home Occupations. Beebe.

Infant Mind. Preyer.

Kindergarten and Child Culture Papers. Barnard.

Law of Childhood. Hailman.

Lectures to Kindergartners. Peabody.

Leonard and Gertrude. Pestalozzi.

Mental Affections of Childhood and Youth. J. Langdon Smith.

Methods of Mind Training. Aiken.

Myths and Mother Plays. Wiltse.

Moral Instruction of Children. Adler.

Nursery Ethics. Florence Hull Winterburn.

Picture Work for Mothers and Teachers. Hervey.

Power through Repose. Call.

Prisoners of Poverty. Campbell.

Reminiscences of Froebel. Bulow.
Republic of Childhood. Wiggin-Smith.
    Vol. I. *Froebel Gifts.*
    Vol. II. *Froebel Occupations.*
    Vol. III. *Kindergarten Principles and Practice.*
Senses and Will. Preyer.
Songs and Music of Froebel's Mother Play. Blow.
Studies of Childhood. Sully.
Studies in Education. Dr. Earl Barnes.
Symbolic Education. Blow.
The Children of the Poor. Riis.
The Child, Its Spiritual Nature. Lewis.
The First Three Years of Childhood. Perez.
The Intellectual and Moral Development of the Child. Compayre.
The Life and Educational Works of John Amos Comenius. Laurie.
The New Womanhood. J.C. Fernald.
The Psychology of Childhood. Tracy.
Your Little Brother James. [sic]

Children on Board:
Images from Candy Lands

Sally Sugarman

Board games are cultural texts. Their traditional forms of race or contest suggest universal themes existing within play, while their content show the interests and concerns of particular times and places. An examination of board games may provide insights into the values of a culture. Huizinga, does, after all, claim that culture arises from play.

Changing images of children and childhood can be traced through board games. However, board games not only show us the dress, the roles and the activities of childhood but, in their depiction of adult occupations, show children society's goals for them. Board games give children an opportunity to practice possible future roles. However, board games are still vehicles of play. Amusement, pleasure and challenge are aspects of their appeal. Parody and irony are elements in successful games which, through exaggeration, often provide a mocking commentary on some of the values they extol.

Board games, dating from 3000 B.C., were found in the royal tombs of Mesopotamia and Egypt (Bell, *Board and Table*; Murray). Adults are pictured playing board games in Egyptian wall paintings, in medieval tapestries, Renaissance landscapes and 17th- and 18th-century genre paintings.

With the onset of a concept of childhood as a specific and unique phase of life, the leisure activities of adults in one generation translated into the activities of children in the next (Aries). In the 18th and 19th centuries, board games, unlike the spontaneous social games of children, were instruments of education and socialization. Along with a separate literature for children, board games were adapted as tools for children's moral and intellectual instruction. A geographical game like Carrington Bowles' Journey Through Europe or the Play of Geography (1759) not only demonstrated mercantile England's fascination with distant places, but represented the types of games which were given middle- and upper-class children. With improved printing technology, board games were produced in greater numbers in the 19th century. Since leisure activities were still

323

considered with some suspicion by religious America, teetotums or spinners were used instead of dice. Games like The Mansion of Happiness (1843) and The Checkered Game of Life (1860) reinforced the lessons adults wished children to learn. "WHOEVER gets into a PASSION must be taken to the water and have a ducking to cool him..." (Kayyem and Sternberger).

The American game industry expanded in the 20th century. Board games were targeted at children, families and adults as separate markets. Before radio and television, board games were an inexpensive leisure activity. Television resulted in increased sales for advertised games; its programs provided subject matter for board games. Eventually, television competed with board games as did computerized games. The golden age of board games may be past, but children of various ages still do play old favorites and their newer variations.

Board games teach children how to take turns, how to follow rules and how to win and lose in the vocabulary of their times. The heroes may be the soldiers of World Wars I and II, frontiersmen, space men or crime fighters or business men. Board games are more content specific, more rule governed and more predictable than sociodramatic and athletic play. Existing as they do in rigidly defined playing spaces that are either square, rectangular or circular, board games restrict options in much the same way that rides in amusement parks do. Children may find security in the predictability of these pastimes.

Games can be organized into age groups; games aimed at preschoolers of four and five; children in the six-to-nine category and ten through early adolescence. Specific images of children are more likely to be found in games for the youngest children although this varies depending upon the decade in which the game is published. The values of the games, however, seem to be reflective more of a specific time than of the age group. For example, games for all ages of children in the 1890s moralize while games from the 1960s emphasize adventure.

Although themes of power, commerce and morality are addressed through the games, gender is perhaps the clearest issue that emerges from a study of board games. The changing views of boys and girls can be traced through different editions of the same games as well as through the subject matter of the games themselves at different times.

America's preoccupation with business, for example, predates the publication of that most popular of games, Monopoly (1935).

The child as worker is depicted in The Game of the District Messenger Boy (1886) where a sturdy adolescent lad maneuvers through the squares of dishonesty and dullness in order to become "a respected banker and a good citizen." In the game of The Errand Boy (1891), a smoking youth is shown in contrast to another who is rushing to deliver his packages, visually demonstrating that initiative will lead to advancement and sloth to failure. In Geschaft or The Game of Business (1897), two young, middle-class boys are shown in a department store with their mother as the advertisement claims this is a game of the Survival of The Fittest. In The Game of Playing Department Store (1898) children are shown playing at department store. Of the nine children pictured on the cover, eight of them are females, dressed in the clothes of the period, clearly younger and less competent than the males depicted on other board games of the same time and same subject.

In the 1959 Leave it to Beaver Money Maker, Beaver's mother is worried about his ambition for money. The cover depicts a photograph of Beaver and a drawing of him shoveling a pile of money into a wheelbarrow. Despite the popularity of business games, not many have had images of children on them. Billionaire (1973), King Oil (1974) and Trump The Game (1989) have drawings or photographs of men in stereotypical poses of power. Some of the cards and consequences in these games, however, do challenge the seriousness of these enterprises. Do Not Pass Go has become a part of our national vocabulary.

Dealing with images of power can be satisfying for children who are less powerful than these adults. Humor is a way of deflating the powerful, while taking on their images. The balance of chance and skill in games also compensates children for their status. The journeys or races that are a part of the structure of many board games provide children with a metaphor for their own journey from childhood to adulthood. Sometimes these are literal as in The Game of Life (1960), whose three-dimensional board and plastic pink and blue children reflect the ideals of the preceding decade clearly. Commerce takes precedence over morality in this version. "If you own stock, sell" is far from The Mansion of Happiness admonition, "WHOEVER possesses AUDACITY, CRUELTY, IMMODESTY, or INGRATI- TUDE, must return to his former situation till his turn comes to spin again, and not even think of HAPPINESS, much less partake of it" (Kayyem and Sternberger).

A game that has religious roots and which also reflects some of the changing attitudes towards gender is Snakes and Ladders. This game is known in the United States as Chutes and Ladders. It is based on Mohska-Patamu, an Indian religious instruction game which was designed to show the way to Nirvana. According to R.C. Bell, the vices and virtues, represented by the snakes and ladders stood for "pap" (good) and "punya" (bad) which existed side by side. In the Indian game one descended from the mouth of the snake to the tail. This indicated that one would be reincarnated in a lesser animal form. Each square in which a ladder or a snake originated represented a particular virtue or vice, with more vices than virtues, a characteristic maintained in subsequent secular versions.

An 1895 English version of the game shows the transformation of the child into the adult. Even as an adult, the player can fall. In the square depicting a man, the player slips because of self-esteem; in another square a woman is dispatched downward because of vanity or in biblical terms, pride goeth before a fall. Of the 20 snakes and ladders, only four squares include females. One such square is bravery, represented by Grace Darling, a popular heroine of the time who as a lighthouse keeper's daughter helped in the rescue of shipwrecked passengers. In the final square is a scroll with the names of men and women whom the players can emulate. There are ten men and two women: Grace Darling and Florence Nightingale. The children must avoid Unpunctuality, Degeneracy, Cruelty, Robbery, Destructiveness and Dishonesty and demonstrate Perseverance, Pentinence, Veneration, Respect, Obedience and Suffering. The drawings of the children are dramatic; a boy is entering a Bank in a square designated as Punctuality whose ladder leads to Opulence.

In another English version of the game, the snakes are reversed and the misfortunes start with the harmless tail and end with the dangerous mouth. Focusing on the hazards of train travel, rather than travel through the world to heaven, as in the Indian original, or from childhood to adulthood in the previous variation, this board shows a boy and a girl encountering difficulties together. They are younger, about ten, as contrasted with the adolescent image in the 1895 game. Generally, they are competent travelers. Some of their misfortunes, such as a train wreck, are not the result of their actions. The sex role stereotyping , typical of later American versions, is more subtle on this board. The boy mischievously opens the train door, almost falling out and he also pulls the stop-the-train cord, which leads to his scolding by the conductor and the girl's weeping into her handkerchief as she does again when they get the wrong train. Throughout the game, the boy is the more active partner. Even so, having a boy and a girl in each square suggests cooperation and comradeship as well as a shared independence. Adults in various roles also exist in this little world of squares.

American versions do not depict a single journey, such as train travel. Chutes and Ladders, however, clearly demonstrates appropriate behaviors and well-defined sex-roles in the good and bad actions of the children. In a 1956 edition of the game, the only negative action the girl takes is to help the boy steal cookies from the cookie jar. In the 1895 English game, the girl did it by herself, it was clearly labeled as dishonesty and she ended up sick in bed. In the American games, the girl's other chute is the result of her dropping a load of dishes which she is carrying. Otherwise, this little girl's life is a series of ladders in which she plants flowers, dries dishes (probably those she later dropped), visits the sick and bandages the boy's knee.

The boy, on the other hand, shoots rubber bands in school, skates on thin ice, breaks a window, pulls a cat's tail, paints on the wall, eats too many green apples, fishes on private property and pulls a girl's pigtails. The boy also reads a book, mows the lawn, returns a lady's pocketbook and is rewarded with an ice cream soda, eats bread and becomes strong, takes the little girl to the circus and gives her a present.

For the last ladder, square 80, both the boy and the girl are shown painting. This square will lead a child, either male or female, to the winning square 100. But woe to the boy who does not land on that square because the last row holds many dangers for him. In squares 93, 96 and 98, his actions lead to chutes. What does this mean? Do boys need to be more prepared for vicissitudes and disappointment than girls? Obviously, both boys and girls landed on chutes and ladders which depicted a child of the opposite sex and advanced or retreated according to the square and not sex identity. However, whoever won the game, certain views about male and female behavior were reinforced with each playing.

The 1979 Chutes and Ladders showed different views of American children, even though the goal on the box remained the same: "...in going up the ladders and down the chutes, a child will learn by the pictures the rewards of good deeds and the consequences of bad ones." Some of these behaviors have remained constant, some have changed. There are black as well as white children now playing on the chutes and ladders, but where there were ten squares which previously showed children together, there is now only one. So much for integration. Where there were four squares indicating an adult presence, albeit a punitive one, there is now only the one square where the boy returns a lady's pocketbook.

Girls now seem more aggressive and boys more nurturing. Square 93 has a black girl drawing on the wall. Squares 94 and 98 still have mischievous boys, but there is a boy rescuing a cat and square 80 has a boy and girl embracing animals as their entry to the winning square. Girls are still generally depicted as more domestic, but they do wear jeans and get into trouble by themselves in two squares. As in the social world, girls' roles seem to be changing more than the boys', at least among younger children. In each succeeding version, the graphics depict younger children.

This declining age is evident in changing editions of other games. A 1962 Candy Land for example provides a race to a cheerful Gingerbread House for a boy and a girl of about seven and eight. Although the other pictures on the board are not as realistic as those in Chutes and Ladders, there are decreasing mileage markers stationed along the winding path through the pleasant images of Lollipop Woods and Gum Drop Mountains. This Candy Land also includes puns like "the cherry pitfall." A 1978 Candy Land game board is similar except that the energetic drawing of the boy and girl has been replaced by a photograph of two children on the go. The girl in pink with pink bows in her hair, a pink dress, white socks and patent leather shoes has a cupcake in one hand and an ice cream cone in the other. The boy in a green striped shirt with a white collar, green slacks and brown leather moccasins holds a large lollipop and points towards the game with pleasure. They are perfect suburban American children, slightly older than the preschoolers for whom this game is designed. Their presence appears to legitimate the game.

The 1984 board for Candy Land rejects the idea that children wish to grow up and shows less realistic and much younger children. Sex-role stereotyping is absent, however, since both children are wide-eyed, unisex caricatures with gender indicated only by the girl's ponytail. The impact of MacDonald's and television is evident in the cartoon characters that now inhabit the once semi-metaphorical terrain. The mileage markers have been replaced by name markers and humor is reduced to alliterative names like King Kandy and Lord Licorice. Home Sweet Home is remodeled into a candy castle inhabited by an infantile king and queen who like the other adult figures on the board seem benign, unrelated refugees from the lands of Smurf and Rainbow Brite.

Gender definition is an increasingly significant element in board games as they develop from their 19th-century origins. Although there are early games specifically designated for boys such as The Game of Battles or Fun for Boys (1889), American Boys State

Camp (1919) or The Boy Scouts Progress Game (1926), games for younger children were not aimed as pointedly at one sex as were the games for older children. From Innocence Abroad (1888) with a boy in knickers pointing out a castle to a girl in knee socks and dress with sash to Disneyland (1965) where a smiling boy and girl wave from a rocket ship ride, there have been games which have been aimed at a mixed audience. In Tip the Bell Boy (1929), it is the girl who is active while the boy watches her. An advertisement for Waterloo (1895), a game about that battle, shows a family sitting around the table playing the game. Mother and daughter, in their long, 19th-century dresses, are as engrossed as are father and son. A photograph on the box cover of a new edition of The Game of Life (1985) displays a similar ideal American family in sweaters with a boy, a girl and two parents—a family who has obviously achieved the goal of the game.

Many games, however, have focused on either boys or girls as the major players. The box cover of Battleship (1967), for example shows a bemused father and a victorious son playing the game, while in the background an aproned mother is doing the dishes as the daughter dries them. The cover of Go to the Head of the Class is equally interesting in its evolution. In a 1967 version, a younger boy hides his face in shame while mother pats his head and older sister points her finger teasingly at her brother. Father sits in the same position as the father on Battleship, arm bent as one hand is behind his head and the other hand holds, in one case, the quiz book and, in the other, a battleship. Both fathers wear sleeveless sweaters and the same astonished expression. Only the colors of the clothes are different. In the 1986 edition of Go to the Head of the Class, a triumphant boy is at the front of the class, his seat tipped back, his hand held high, knowledge shining from his grinning face. No taunting females on this cover. Nor are there any on the board as on the 1967 one, although to be fair, the boy on the earlier board is the figure at the coveted 100 number. He holds a diploma and wears a mortar board and a victorious grin.

The targeting of specific gender audiences occurs as games become a larger and more profitable business and as television is the medium through which they are advertised. A young boy is shown on the cover of Cowboy Roundup (1952) and The Merry Milkman (1954) is a milkman with a young boy's face, recalling the 1890s image of the child as worker. During the 1950s and 1960s, however, television personalities join soldiers, spies and detectives as major board game characters along with cartoon figures like Batman

(1966), The Phantom (1966) and Captain America (1966) or cowboys like The Virginian (1962), Branded (1966) and Lancer (1968) moving the child off the board game. Games with males, adult or child, outnumber those with females. The Nancy Drew Mystery Game (1957), like the books, was an exception; its plucky heroine is shown in red rain slicker, out on a stormy night, her flashlight illuminating a mysterious house.

Barbie, Queen of the Prom is introduced in 1960. She is still around in 1991, looking quite the worse for wear. Slender 1960's Barbie with a crown perched on her ponytailed head looks demure compared to 1990s bouffant Barbie. The 1960 blue box is tasteful next to the electric pink of the 1991 box. Feminists need not despair, however. In another 1991 pink box, there is a We Girls Can Do Anything Game which promises that you can Travel the Path that Leads to the Career of Your Dreams. That mainstay of board game existence, the journey to achievement, lives on. Barbie, and the player, can be a Fashion Designer, a Musician, Pilot, Actress, Doctor or Ballerina. From her costume, Barbie seems to fly for the In-The-Pink Airlines. There is some difficulty, however, inferring what instrument Barbie plays in her short, gauzy tutu and large diamond shaped earrings. Perhaps she is a singer in some camp 1950s cocktail lounge. Every career requires that Barbie be gowned in pink. Even her white doctor's coat covers a pink dress. Although her stethoscope is blue, the patient's chart is pink. A glimpse of her medical office in pink and blue suggests that Barbie's approach to medicine is unique. But the box does say that the game is for ages five and up.

Ages eight and up can enjoy the relative reality of The Baby Sitter's Game and The Sweet Valley High Game. Since these games are based on two popular series books, they have a context which seems almost substantial. Unlike Tammy (1963), Gidget (1965) and Gidget, Fortune Teller Game (1966), these games focus on a group of girls rather than one silly teenager. The telephone also has other uses than as the defining prop on the box cover. In Sweet Valley High, the girls need to find dates, not only for the Junior Prom, but for a Week-end Bike Tour, a Surfing Beach Party and a Sweet Sixteen Party. Their game board is a high school in which serious subjects like economics are taught if not learned. The girls reflect contemporary views of attractive females, regular features, healthy skin, and direct gazes. The box cover shows a white, red tile-roofed high school with palm trees, adolescents on bicycles, a young man in a convertible with a surf board in the back seat. Boys and girls in slacks and shorts converse in friendly clusters.

The Baby Sitter's Game reflects a more diverse group, including African-American and Asian-American girls. Hair-styles are more varied and one girl wears glasses. The cover also shows a dazed blond girl in T-shirt and jeans flopped exhausted on a chair while two young boys are playing cowboys and Indians, a toddler is pulling apart an over-turned potted-plant. The game itself is more complex than the usual game, requiring creative answers and stunts which are judged by the other players. Although the baby-sitters are involved with traditional nurturing tasks, they also are young business women who have moved from baby-sitting as an obligation to it as an occupation. Dates with boys are not their object as they are with Barbie and the Sweet Valley High females. Images for females, although focusing on traditional female roles, are slowly changing.

There are not equivalent preadolescent board games for boys. In the Pizza Power Game (1990), ages six and up, 16 out of 84 squares instruct the player to fight, bringing the violence of the television cartoon to the board. Directions refer to the players as he or she suggesting an expectation that this Ninja Turtle game is a family game. The art work, however, has four pictures of the turtles and their enemies, while April, their newswoman friend, is in only one of them, filming their exploits. This game is the equivalent of the game for the young female child who is playing with her Barbie dolls and her Barbie game.

For the preadolescent group, adult males are usually pictured on the games which preadolescent boys play. Girls are shown as adolescents in games which, like the books on which they are based, are primarily for the preadolescent child. In the world of the board game, boys seem to skip this phase of practicing for adolescence and enter adulthood directly. In the past some of the sport games may have provided this transition. In The Boy's Own Football Game (1901), adolescents are shown scrimmaging on a field. By 1962, the All Star Baseball Game has adult players in action.

As children move into the teen years, games are not specifically aimed at them. They may continue to play familiar adult board games such as Clue (1948), Monopoly (1935), Trivial Pursuit (1985), Scrabble (1953) and Dungeons and Dragons (1970). These games generally tend not to have specific character images. Earlier, adult games like Nellie Bly (1898) or The Game of Golf (1898) depicted adults in action as games for younger children showed children.

Recent games like The Little Mermaid (1990) and Beauty and the Beast (1993), designed for children five years and up may be an indication of the future. These games, developed from the media, show adult versions of the fairy tale characters. The child may be disappearing from the game board as childhood is disappearing as a concept. Postman (1982) has claimed that, when adults and children have access to the same knowledge, childhood as a specific stage of life no longer exists. The isolation of the child from direct knowledge of adult life, characteristic of the print cultures of the 18th and 19th centuries has been eliminated by television. Board games for boys, with their strong adult role models, seem to reflect this shift. Young children may romp on the boards of traditional games, such as Chutes and Ladders and Candy Land, but when five-year-olds are identifying with Barbie and her problems in dating and careers, childhood has changed if not vanished. Several other indicators support this idea. Board games have become collectibles in the last ten years, often a sign of pending rarity. Ironically, children's discards are now being treasured by adults, a turnabout of significance. Game boards, themselves, are becoming more abstract and less picturesque. Fewer board games are being produced. Those that continue will probably not emphasize the ideal two-parent family with time to play games together.

In the first half of the 20th century children could see themselves on board games, winning and losing through adventurous journeys and contests. Young boys and girls played some games together, but the messages they received were different. As they matured, the images they encountered were generally gender specific, giving stronger and more powerful roles to male images. Although a few games challenged these ideas, more provided the old messages in new packages. Children, however, do not always receive ideas in the same form in which they are given. Children play the game according to their own rules. Whatever children may have learned, the cultural pictures of their childhood are left in the legacy of board games.

Bibliography

Aries, P. *Centuries of Childhood.* London: Jonathan Cape, 1962. The classic study of the development of the concept of childhood.

Bell, R.C. *Board and Table Games From Many Civilizations.* New York: Dover, 1979. An historical and cross-cultural examination of board games with useful drawings.

_____. *The Board Game Book.* New York: Exeter Books, 1983. Beautifully illustrated with large full-color reproductions of games.

Goodfellow, C. *A Collector's Guide to Games and Puzzles.* Secaucus, NJ: Chartwell, 1991. The text is brief, but informative. The clear, color illustrations include card games and puzzles. The material is well organized.

Hewett, K., and L. Roomet. *Educational Toys in America: 1800 to the Present.* Burlington, VT: The Robert Hull Fleming Museum, 1979. A thoughtful and informative text. The illustrations are black and white, but still convey the quality of the toys with single pictures to a page.

Huizinga, J. *Homo Ludens.* Boston: Beacon, 1955. One of the first and most significant discussions about the nature of play which all serious students of play should read.

Kayyem, M., and P. Sternberger. *Victorian Pleasures: American Board and Table Games of the Nineteenth Century from the Liman Collection.* New York: Columbia U, 1991. The catalog from an excellent exhibit. The text is informative. The black and white pictures are not as clear as desirable, but the text makes this a valuable historical review.

Murray, H.J.R. *A History of Board Games Other Than Chess.* Oxford: Clarendon, 1952. This is a useful discussion of the development of games.

Polizzi, R. and F. Schaefer. *Spin Again: Board Games from The Fifties and Sixties.* San Francisco: Chronicle, 1991. Very well illustrated in color. The text is minimal, but helpful.

Postman, N. *The Disappearance of Childhood.* New York: Delacorte, 1982. The author contends that television has broken down the boundaries of childhood because knowledge is accessible to children through television. As literacy created childhood, television destroyed it. An interesting companion to the Aries.

Sommer, R.L. *"I Had One of Those": Toys of Our Generation.* New York: Crescent, 1991. A celebration of Yuppie childhood, designed to evoke nostalgia as well as inform. Covers fads, families and the toy industry.

Whitehill, B. *Games: American Boxed Games and Their Makers 1882-1992.* Radnor, PA.: Wallace-Homestead, 1992. Essentially a guide for collectors, this has a lot of history about the toy industry and the changes in games.

The Child in American Advertising, 1890-1960: Reflections of a Changing Society

Eileen Margerum

The picture of American children presented in 20th-century advertising differs considerably from that described in American social or economic history.[1]

Because advertisements are intended to sell a product, both picture and text must work toward that goal. In the late 19th and early 20th century, as the American advertising industry took the form that it still retains, advertising agencies discovered that the buying public wanted "a Zerrspiegel, a distorting mirror that [presented] life as it ought to be," not life as it was (Marchand xvii).

Children were included in the pictures that accompanied ads because their presence implied "family." The image of "family" became a persuasive selling technique as America changed from an agricultural to an industrial society in which workers had little control over their public and economic destiny. In compensation, they turned to their private, family lives for a sense of control and social consequence (Berger 74-76).

When children appeared in advertisements in magazines written for adults, they represented to adult readers a set of social assumptions: adults protected and provided for children; children, in turn, obeyed and emulated adults (Schlereth 275-77). Vulnerable and dependent children intensified in adults both emotions that advertisers sought to reach: the joy of an adult's anticipated success and the bitterness of his dreaded failure. In a society where social mobility was one of the most basic tenets, advertisers could heighten the readers' hopes or exaggerate their fears by showing the fate of children.

Until television became the dominant cultural medium in the mid-1950s, magazines played an important role in American social life. Popular magazines for adults could include three different types of "reality": presumably factual articles about current events, people, and places; acknowledged romantic reality in short stories and serialized fiction; and an idealized reality in advertising. In advertising's reality, marginalized groups such as the poor or racial and

335

ethnic minorities are invisible and no problem is addressed unless the advertised product can solve it.[2]

Over time, the presence of children in American print advertising has changed in both quantity and quality; in part, this reflects the growth and change in the consumer economy. In magazine ads at the end of the 19th century, when mass retail advertising was in its infancy, children were merely anonymous decorations. Some were so depersonalized that the figure might be a child or a tiny winged cherub. In an 1890 ad for Franco-American Soups, for example, naked cherubs sat where children should be: by the fireside as mother prepares a meal. Other naked figures, curly-haired asexual children, appeared in ads for Allcock's Porous Plasters (1888), Cuticura Remedies and Triton playing cards (both 1892). In other ads, children were dressed like miniature adults and stood in the background while adults were the center of action. In an era when children were little seen and never heard, these silent cherubs were an apt representation.[3]

As the consumer economy began to raise the general standard of living in the first two decades of the 20th century, the function of the child in ads changed from anonymous "anychild" to anonymous "child-in-the-family." They became markers of their parents' success. Well-dressed children (never exceeding two, always a boy and a girl) appeared in the background of ads for products that presented themselves as for "the family."

Generic children had only one featured role: "the child in peril." This advertising trope continued in variant forms through the 1950s. Playing on the well-founded fear of children's death,[4] the earliest versions showed a seriously ill child (often a baby or infant) whose cure could be effected only by using the advertised product. As infant mortality rates declined, the trope changed. In ads from the 1930s, the child was generally near or at school age and the "peril" diminished from impending death to an unspecified "grave danger." By the 1950s, it had been redefined as a momentary inconvenience: the school-age child's inability to satisfy some immediate need, such as starring in the school play or keeping a skating date.

Throughout these changes, the child remained passive; it was mother who worried and then acted, using the advertised product to remove the child from danger. From the 1930s onward, the happy ending was always part of the advertisement. In a multi-panel format based on comic strip design (often, however, using photographs or line drawings), the last panel in 1930s ads showed the mother expressing her relief; by the 1950s, it showed the child taking advantage of the almost-missed opportunity.

The only other ads from early in the century that featured children and continued over the decades were those using the Campbell Kids. Created in 1904 by artist Grace Grebbie Drayton, this pair of curly-haired, rosy-cheeked moppets appeared consistently in ads for Campbell Soups until the early 1920s before fading from the scene. They reappeared in the 1950s as school-age children and came back again, transformed into incipient teenagers, in the late 1980s.

In their first incarnation, the Campbell Kids, a boy and a girl, were really nothing more than an answer to "the child in peril." Because they were created to convince mothers that canned soup was a healthy alternative to homemade soup, their appearance exaggerated the popularly accepted signs of health: they were too rosy-cheeked and too fat (with dimples in arms and knees). They were also too cute; in fact, they never grew beyond physiological babyhood. Their heads were always equal in size to their bodies, and their arms and legs remained quite small, even when they were shown performing feats, such as ice skating, that would daunt most young children.

Like all children in ads until the 1920s, the Campbell Kids were silent and their actions related only indirectly to the product. Their cute adventures, described in an accompanying short poem, were totally separate from the advertising pitch.

One significant difference between ads featuring the Campbell Kids and the "the child in peril" is their level of realism. The Kids were idealizations of childhood, happy innocents who were implicitly protected by unseen adults. "Child in peril" ads reminded adults of the real danger of epidemic and childhood illnesses from which even the most conscientious adult could not protect vulnerable children. This difference was underscored by the graphic styles: the Kids were drawn as cartoon-like figures while "child in peril" ads used photographs or line drawings to simulate reality. So long as the potential peril was serious, the ads simulated reality; by the 1950s, when the "peril" had devolved from life-and-death to momentary inconvenience, the situation appeared in ads that ran in the comics section of the Sunday papers.

Only one child in early advertising had a name and defined personality: Buster Brown. When Buster Brown migrated from the comic pages to advertising, he continued to behave as he had since 1902 when R.F. Outcault created the comic strip (Beiswinger 38).

"A masterpiece!"—Campbell's Vegetable Soup. *The Literary Digest,*
December 3, 1921. From The D'Arcy Collection of the Communications
Library, The University of Illinois, Urbana-Champaign.

This spoiled, undisciplined rich little boy was really an upscale version of The Yellow Kid, Outcault's earlier creation. Unlike the passive anonymous middle-class children in advertising, Buster's consciously disruptive behavior involved tricking adults including his parents. He differed from The Yellow Kid, the Katzenjammer Kids and other low-class child-tricksters who populated early newspaper comics pages in two ways: his obvious wealth and the absolute certainty that each cartoon adventure would end with his being spanked. Outcault successfully licensed scores of Buster Brown products from bread to shirt collars; in 1904 he started a long-term relationship with the Brown Shoe Company of St. Louis which ultimately transformed the comic strip into its own commercial (Marschall 32-39). Like the ads using the Campbell Kids, however, the Brown Shoe Company selling message was always separate from Buster's cartoon adventure.

Buster Brown's popularity suggests that middle-class adults were willing to accept a comic strip about a child's bad behavior if the situations didn't challenge their own ideals of child-parent relationship. Although Buster's rich parents bore the brunt of his actions, he always paid in the end. In the last panel, his parents literally got the upper hand; either a parent was shown spanking him or he stood, holding his spanked bottom, next to a list of resolutions to improve.

After World War I, realistically drawn school-age boys and girls began to appear in ads. Even when adults were not seen in the ads, their presence was implied because the children used toys or tools provided by adults. These ads, showing children engaged in outdoor activities, fixed two advertising formulae. First, they reinforced sex-role stereotypes. Boys were presented as active and needing special food to support their activity. Girls were always passive or subsidiary in ads where boys were present; when shown by themselves, girls emulated their mothers' behavior. While boys rode Dayton bicycles, girls washed their doll clothes with Ivory Soap. In one of series of 1919 ads for Brown Beauty Beans, girls and babies watched boys put on a show; in another, a boy carried a frightened girl, piggy-back, across a stream. Perhaps even more telling was a November 1919 ad in *The Ladies Home Journal.* Urging parents to "Buy American-Made Toys," it presented a parade of preschool children, each holding a toy. Every boy carried a different toy: a rocking horse, a toy rifle, a toy automobile, a drum, a scooter, a wagon, a tricycle, and a hoop. The girls' toys mark the narrow limits of play allowed to them: two carried dolls, one held a doll house, another pushed a doll carriage; only one girl's toy, a skipping rope, suggested activity.

Toy Hours
Build Patriotism
THAT is, if the kiddies have American-Made Toys to play with. The splendid teachings, the 100 per cent "Americanism" that boys and girls absorb in school and at home, can be furthered and enriched if the play hour—the toy hour is surrounded by real American things.
Buy
American-Made Toys
Give your children the original conceptions—the careful craftsmanship of American men and women, not the thoughts of foreign countries.
Toy stores—the far-seeing patriotic ones everywhere, are displaying the sign of American-Made Toys. Look for it—look for the circle of Uncle Sam with the happy children on his knee. It represents a national benefit—a great big help—a real toy joy, to the coming generation.
"Made in U. S. A." is the guarantee of American-Made Toys—the best that are procurable.
This space is contributed to the cause of American Industries by the Toy Manufacturers of the U. S. A., Flatiron Building, New York City.
American-Made TOYS

"Toy Hours Build Patriotism." *The Ladies' Home Journal*, November 1919. From The D'Arcy Collection of the Communications Library, The University of Illinois, Urbana-Champaign.

The other trend was the deliberate choice of nonurban locations. As if responding to the reformers of the Progressive Era who urged more play spaces for urban children (Cavallo, Mergen), advertisers moved all children to the country. As late as the 1950s, every discernible locale in ads featuring children is a country or suburban setting. Despite the increasing urbanization of the American populace, a cultural anthropologist using ads to develop a history of the child would have to conclude that no American child ever lived in a city.

In ads throughout the 1920s, boys continued to congregate outdoors, play strenuous sports, and need special nourishment. (At least two advertising campaigns, for Heinz Oven Baked Beans and Butter-Krust Bread, combined boys' special food needs with an answer to the "child in peril" by featuring little boys named "Fatty" whose mothers fed them very well on the advertised product.) Girls, most often preschool age, were cute and passive with no special needs.

Throughout the 1920s, one child often appeared in the background of ads featuring adults. In the economy of advertising signs, a single child could stand for "family"; a well-dressed, apparently healthy child signaled that the family was prosperous and well managed. Two children in an ad meant family togetherness (Marchand 272). They sat next to mother, perfectly behaved and intent on her every word, to show women the best way to use the time gained by using the newest labor-saving devices or they hovered in the living room near mother and father to show how the family enjoyed their new radio. Again, they were silent props in the adults' world.

There was no reason for advertisers to see children as other than silent and passive. Until radio changed their minds, advertisers believed that children had little influence over family expenditures because they had virtually no earning power. Ironically, as American discretionary income declined during the Depression, advertisers found that children had a strong influence on how it was spent. Radio was a democratic medium; even children too young to read could be persuaded by it. When a voice sang to them or told them stories, and then offered them a way to be part of the adventure, they responded. For just a box top or a product insert, they could get a free prize. In a 1932 trade publication, The Kellogg Company told merchandisers that "nearly 100,000 [box] tops a week" were coming in with requests for the Singing Lady's song book. Over 418,000 bought Ovaltine to get a picture of Little Orphan Annie. "And a child shall lead them—to your product," another trade paper headlined (Barnouw 120).

Print advertising quickly responded, but within its own parameters. In magazines for the adult audience, the message had to be repackaged. Famous adults interacted with children (principally boys) and identified their needs; parents were offered a chance to send for a prize or premium for their children and were promised continued health for them. Boys got sports tips from Jack Dempsey and Babe Ruth, along with prize offers from Wheaties cereal; a boy and girl were pictured riding with Tom Mix in a Ralston cereal ad. In the Wheaties ads, the happy ending was made explicit as the boys' parents commented proudly on how "husky" they were getting from eating Wheaties.

The presentation of children in ads during the 1930s was quite contradictory. Even as some children were shown happily fulfilling both their childhood dreams and their parents' ambitions, others became passive victims. As financial conditions deteriorated during the 1930s, ads fostered a special father-son relationship that placed an explicit burden on men: if the father failed now, he doomed his son to future failure. As early as 1930, a Listerine ad showed two boys fighting because one had scrawled "Jimmy's Dad has Halitosis" on a fence. The headline "Not one out of ten escapes this social fault" was just ambiguous enough to describe both the adult's poor hygiene and his needing to be defended by his child.

Life insurance companies tried to capitalize on fathers' fear. The entire copy of a 1930 Prudential Life Insurance ad read: "Children of the Lapse. Many a lapsed policy has deprived a child of its full-time schooling." The text was superimposed on a stark photograph of five boys and a girl, barely in their teens, sitting dejectedly in straight chairs outside a door reading "Working Papers Issued Here" (Goodrum 153). In 1932, Union Central Life Insurance companies began an ambitious campaign that played on adults' fears of dying and leaving their children destitute (Marchand 152).

At the same time, mothers were presented as responsible for their daughters. Little girls (often of preschool age) became surrogates for all ill children; they got the potentially deadly colds, had failed appetites, or suffered sore and chapped hands from playing outdoors. Their return to health was always a personal triumph for mother.

One explicit example of the mother-daughter connection is a 1930 ad headlined "Wait a minute, mother!" which included a line drawing of a little girl in a bathing suit riding in the bowl of a spoon.

This curious graphic ties in with the advertising message: only by choosing Parke-Davis Cod-liver Oil could mother ensure her child's health. Since the mid-1920s, public health officials had urged parents to start babies on a routine of sun baths and daily doses of cod-liver oil to prevent rickets, then prevalent among young children. Although all reports especially noted that dark-skinned children were most susceptible to rickets, the little girl in the Parke-Davis ad is the typical fair-haired and fair-skinned advertising ideal (Bremner 1074-76).

One 1935 comic-style ad neatly incorporated both the positive and negative aspects of ads using children, with fantasies fulfilled and fear overcome. "Billy" was about to lose his "job on our baseball team" to the new kid down the street due to his poor appetite and lack of energy. To reinforce the father-son link, Dad said he was worried how Billy would pitch in the ball game. Once Mother got Quaker Puffed Rice and Wheat, however, Billy won the game and was told by his team captain, "You're on our team for life." His career had been saved and his appetite captivated (see Marchand 228-32 for "The Parable of the Captivated Child").

In the brief time between the perceived lifting of the Depression and the start of World War II (roughly 1937 to early 1942), children (usually at least eight years old) were presented in ads without the pain and stresses of the earlier Depression years. Boys got spending money by doing errands and had sufficient energy to go hiking. In several ads, children became miniature doubles of their parents. Boys mimicked their fathers' actions and ideas. Girls were smaller duplicates of their mothers, cleaning the house and doing the wash.

With the start of World War II, children became signs of problems that no advertiser's product could solve. Babies often meant overcrowding as war brides moved back home or stayed with in-laws while their soldier-husbands were away. Family tensions might be blamed on someone, often the mother-in-law, but only the end of the war and the start of a housing boom would solve them. During the war, older children—too young to work but needing extra food for their growing bodies—were a drain on limited rations. The best way for advertisers to deal with children was to ignore them.[5]

Children reemerged only when the War seemed close to being won. An ad for Norge in early 1944 featured two pictures: "Working for Today" showed a woman in military uniform handing a package to a young man; "Planning for Tomorrow" showed her in frilly apron placing a package in her full-stocked refrigerator as her smiling son sits at the table eating. At the same time, daughters, in this case twins,

Wait a minute, mother!

Are you giving her all the extra "sunshine" that spoon will hold?

It's not cod-liver oil you are giving her, you know—not really. It's straight, strong bones, and sound even teeth, and rosy cheeks, and added protection from the winter ills you dread so much.

This is the magic that the vitamins work. So, of course, when you give her cod-liver oil for the vitamins it contains, you want cod-liver oil that is *rich* in vitamins.

Perhaps you don't realize that there is a world of difference in cod-liver oils. To make sure that every spoonful of Parke-Davis Standardized Cod-liver Oil contains *definitely measured* amounts of both Vitamin A and Vitamin D, we subject it to a series of carefully controlled tests which take thirty-five days to complete.

As a result of these tests made in our own laboratories, we can say to you, "*Every teaspoonful* of Parke-Davis Standardized Cod-liver Oil contains as much of the disease-resisting Vitamin A as 11 pints of whole milk, or 9 eggs, or one pound of butter; and as much of the rickets-preventing 'sunshine' Vitamin D as 7½ eggs or 2 pounds of butter."

This pure, golden oil comes in 4-ounce and 16-ounce bottles, or in convenient, easy-to-take capsules. At drug stores everywhere.

PARKE, DAVIS & CO.
The world's largest makers of pharmaceutical and biological products
DETROIT, MICH.   WALKERVILLE, ONT.

(Parke, Davis & Company supply a number of other cod-liver oil products also, including Cod-liver Oil with Viosterol.)

Parke-Davis
STANDARDIZED
Cod-liver Oil

In 4-ounce and 16-ounce bottles—also in easy-to-take capsules

"Wait a minute, mother!" *The Saturday Evening Post*, November 15, 1930. From The D'Arcy Collection of the Communications Library, The University of Illinois, Urbana-Champaign.

could still be used for household work, cleaning clothes and dishes with "Twin Advantage" Rinso.

Children were part of what had been deferred during the War. So, it is no surprise to see them blossom in ads from 1947 onward. First babies, then infants, then young children appeared, matching the advertisers' perception of the growth of the newly started families. But a new relationship between child and adult had developed, which altered dramatically the presentation of children after World War II.

The post-War world had altered most of the appeals advertisers had used on adults. The perception of boundless prosperity negated the appeal to fear of personal or financial failure and, conversely, blunted the appeal to hope of success; success now seemed a guarantee that didn't require using any specific advertised product. At the same time, new immunizations defeated many childhood illnesses. So, the traditional role of the child as burden and reward to the adult disappeared.

Also at this time, children had taken on a new significance in popular thinking. The burgeoning field of child psychology, codified and pre-digested for popular use in the 500 pages of Benjamin Spock's *The Common Sense Book of Baby and Child Care*, which was first published in 1945, presented the child as a complex social and emotional being whose personal development could be hampered at any stage by the wrong parental action. In this new order, children became the center of attention; their needs were paramount; they were to be listened to. Unless guided by child psychology, parents would inevitably ruin their children's lives.[6] When this view of children gained popular ascendency, it destroyed the basic assumption upon which advertisers had based all previous presentations of children; namely, that parents were the best guardians and guides of their children.

Advertisers responded to these new ideas by presenting children in new roles. If children were to be listened to, advertisers would give them something to say. So children became spokespersons and advice givers. Babies and young children, often photographed looking directly out at the adult ad reader, told adults how to act and react. In 1947, the Bell Telephone System used a picture of a baby under the headline, "A girl needs more than Glamour!" to sell customers on the improving quality of telephone service. In 1951, an infant looked plaintively out from an ad, pleading "Before you scold me, Mom...maybe you'd better light up a Marlboro."

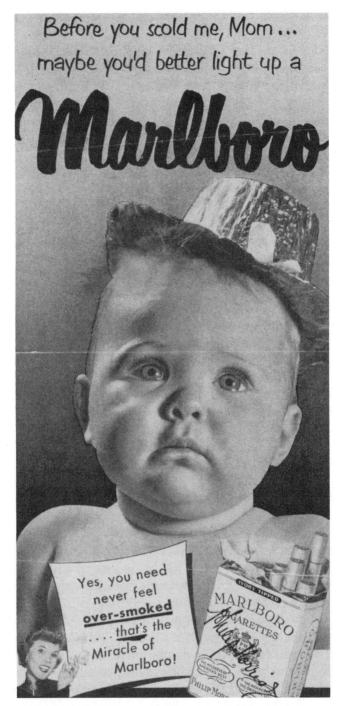

"Before you scold me, Mom..." *The New Yorker Magazine*, June 16, 1951. Private acquisition.

Since parents no longer knew how to raise their children without help, advertisers used children to illustrate the adults' total helplessness in other areas. Mothers became the target of much of the new advertising. In the 1950s, during which Procter & Gamble and General Foods made half their sales on virtually indistinguishable products created since World War II while advertisers lamented the lack of creativity in their field (Fox 178-80), one easy way to convince Mom to try yet another version of a product was to show her gaining a measure of control over her unruly children.

In a decade when middle-class women had fewer economic problems and more labor-saving help than ever before, advertisers created the overworked mom. As presented in ads, the cause of her problem was her children. Dad was absent. Children were chaotic and underfoot (often shown in cowboy suits or Indian headdress). But, advertisers implied, solutions could be bought. All she had to do was use the advertisers' product: Kraft Instant Dinners and Aunt Jemima Pancake Mix to feed them; Duz and Super Suds to clean their messy play clothes and to handle the multitude of spills they made.

As Betty Friedan noted in her ground-breaking study of women in the 20th century, social pressures had broken the intergenerational bond between women and, by the 1950s, the housewife had few sources of advice other than the experts. In the field of commercial products, the advertiser became that expert.[7]

To foster the idea of adult helplessness, some advertisers heightened the activity of children and added a level of mischief. Dennis the Menace and Junior, little boys whose curiosity mirrored the psychologists' idea of preschool behavior[8] and led to inevitable but unplanned disasters, were used to sell cereals. As in the comic-strip versions of these children's adventures, adults stood by in frozen silence as the children created their inevitable chaos. Since these little boys, and the other children who ran through advertisements in the 1950s, intended no harm and were simply expressing their curiosity or venting the energy, there is no consequence to them.[9] No advertiser in the 1950s would ascribe to disruptive children the deliberate trickery of Buster Brown. In fact, the only part of the comic-strip ad pattern that remains from the Buster Brown era is the separation of the child's adventures from the selling message.

Since adults weren't suitable to advise children, children took on the role of advising—both adults and children. Neddy Nestle, a bright alert boy of about ten, starred in a series of cartoon-strip ads in Sunday papers; in each he solved a problem by using Nestle Quik

"Yipe!!" *Ladies Home Journal*, October
1954. From the D'Arcy Collection of the
Communications Library, The University of
Illinois, Urbana-Champaign.

and thus gained the admiration of both his classmates (especially the girls) and his parents.

No longer wise counselors, fathers could be presented as "pals" who played with their children, primarily their sons, outside of the home. In a reversal of the pattern of the early 1940s, fathers now acted like their children, playing their games and getting as dirty as they did—becoming, in effect, another child. Mothers recapitulated their familiar roles as housewives and caregivers; however, since mothers could no longer serve as models or advisors to their daughters, girls virtually disappeared.

When television gained ascendancy in the mid-1950s, the picture of children presented by American print advertising was more varied, but not much more accurate, than it had been at the start of the century. Children in ads were still more likely to be male than female, especially if they were active. Unlike children in prior decades, they were usually healthy and often mischievous. They still lived in a never-land of America that excluded cities and they were always middle class. And, like all the children who had preceded them in American ads, they were inevitably white. The picture of children presented in magazine ads in the 1950s, like that in every previous decade, was based on what would sell.

Advertisers tapped into the dominant attitudes of adults and manipulated them. At those times when children could be used to strike an appropriate chord, they appeared in American ads. When children were inconvenient, they disappeared. Throughout the decades, the picture of children shown in American advertising was an index of how adults felt about children, rather than an accurate presentation of children during the first half of the "American century."

Notes

[1]This essay is based on studying advertisements in publications aimed toward the adult mass market, from the late 1880s through the 1950s. Magazines include *The American Magazine, The Delineator, Everybody's Magazine, Good Housekeeping, Harper's Weekly, Harper's Magazine, The Ladies' Home Journal, Life, The Literary Digest, National Geographic, The New Yorker, The Saturday Evening Post, Sunset* (the Pacific monthly), *Woman's Home Companion*. Newspaper ads come from the *Philadelphia Evening Bulletin, St. Louis Globe-Democrat* and *St. Louis Post*.

These advertisements were found primarily in The D'Arcy Advertising Collection of the University of Illinois at Urbana-Champaign; a small percentage were in the N.W. Ayer Collection at the National Museum of American History, part of the Smithsonian Institution in Washington, D.C.; some were private acquisitions.

This study does not include children used in trademarks such as the Uneeda Biscuit boy, the Morton Salt girl, the "Dutch Boy," or the Silver Dust or Gold Dust Twins.

[2]The most succinct summary of the history and theory of American advertising from the 1880s through the 1950s is "The Institution of Abundance: Advertising," chapter 8 in David M. Potter's seminal work, *People of Plenty: Economic Abundance and the American Character* (Chicago: U of Chicago P, 1954).

[3]In *The Child and The Republic: The Dawn of Modern Child Nurture* (Philadelphia: U of Pennsylvania P, 1968), Bernard Wishy describes the growth of forces that worked against the assumptions that children were merely passive recipients of adult moral training (see especially "The 'New Education' and the Old Ideals," 136-58).

[4]New York City, which had the first consistent public health statistics, reported that 288 infants died per 1,000 live births in 1880; 162 in 1902; 120 in 1911 (Bremner 812).

[5]For a complete discussion of the problem of child care during World War II, see William H. Chafe, *The American Woman: Her Changing Social, Economic, and Political Roles, 1920-1970* (New York: Oxford UP, 1972).

[6]The emphasis shifted to reducing the child's level of frustration by attending to the child's emotional needs. Irene Josselyn, in *Psychosocial Development of Children* (New York: Family Service Association of America, 1948), told teachers and social workers what the child needed for a comfortable adjustment to school: "If he has had an opportunity for satisfying social contacts, if the demands made upon him at school are within his intellectual capacity, if the restrictions on his behavior are reasonably geared to his capacity to tolerate frustration and to renounce his impulses, and if the environment balances demands and frustrations with reasonable gratifications and recognition...(75). In 1954, Florence G. Blake advised hospital nurses that "Children need adults who can empathize or feel with them." (*The Child, His Parents and the Nurse* [Philadelphia: Lippincott, 1954] 245).

[7]In *"Just A Housewife": The Rise and Fall of Domesticity in America* (New York: Oxford UP, 1987), Glenna Matthews argues that "The public discourse of the early twentieth century made nothing available to women that would have given them the leverage to resist the persuasion of

advertisements—especially when the advertisements were echoed by the advice of experts" (259). By the 1950s, the advertising message had become conflated with the expert advice so that there was no need for an "expert" other than the advertiser himself.

[8]Blake's description of the typical three-to-six-year-old is the picture of Dennis's behavior: "...the child needs to discover and to accept his sexuality and his place within his family and to come to find satisfaction in play and in his relationships with children outside his family. He needs to find answers to the many questions that perplex him and to develop wholesome attitudes toward all things concerning his personal development. He also needs to acquire self-dependence which will prepare him to make a good adjustment to experiences outside his home...(*The Child, His Parents* 212).

[9]By the mid-1950s, child care experts were rethinking and redefining the new permissiveness. In an aptly titled pamphlet, *The Controversial Problem of Discipline* (New York: The Child Study Association of America, 1953), Katherine Wolf, R.N., argued for a redefinition of "discipline" that distinguished between the needs and wishes of the child and returned to parents the responsibility of knowing and caring for their children. It was reprinted at least ten times over the next decade.

In 1962, Dr. Spock himself entitled one section of his book *Problems of Parents* (Boston: Houghton Mifflin) "Overpermissiveness, An American Phenomenon." As if describing the antics of "Dennis the Menace" and his ilk, he wrote: "...parents [who] were so properly brought up that they never dared act, speak or even think aggressively...unconsciously enjoy letting [their child] express the impoliteness, selfishness and aggressiveness which they had to suppress so completely.... This blinds them to the fact that the behavior is offensive to others and disturbing to the child. In fact, they manage to express pride in their own progressiveness and its good results" (287). Of his contribution to the revolution in child management, he says mildly, "I think I helped to intimidate...parents by stressing too heavily the risks of severe [toilet] training, in the earlier edition of *Baby and Child Care*" (288).

Bibliography

Barnouw, Erik. *The Sponsor: Notes on a Modern Potentate.* New York: Oxford UP, 1978. A study of modern mass media with the premise that advertising shaped its form and content.

Beiswinger, George L. "The Early Licensing of Comic Characters." *Editor & Publisher* 121 (26 Mar. 1988): 38-39. A short informative article on early commercial uses of characters in comic strips.

Berger, Peter L. "Marriage and the Construction of Reality: An Exercise in the Microsociology of Knowledge." *Social Reality*. Ed. Harvey A. Farberman and Erich Goode. Englewood Cliffs, NJ: Prentice, 1973. A useful essay on familial relationships.

Blackbeard, Bill, and Martin Williams, eds. *The Smithsonian Collection of Newspaper Comics*. Smithsonian Institution Press and Harry N. Abrams, Inc., 1977. A comprehensive history of newspaper comics from the Yellow Kid to publication time with over 700 strips reprinted, many in color.

Blake, Florence G. *The Child, His Parents and the Nurse*. Philadelphia: Lippincott, 1954. Written for nurses, this is a useful look at child development theory in the early 1950s.

Bremner, Robert, et al., eds. *Children and Youth in America: A Documentary History*. Vol. 2. 1866-1932. Parts 7 and 8. Cambridge, MA: Harvard UP, 1971. An excellent source of primary documents from public and private records.

Cavallo, Dominick. "Social Reform and the Movement to Organize Children's Play During the Progressive Era." *History of Childhood Quarterly* 3.4 (Spring 1976): 509-22. Good account of a problem of social and economic justice.

Chafe, William H. *The American Woman: Her Changing Social, Economic, and Political Roles, 1920-1970*. New York: Oxford UP, 1972. One of this author's many excellent works on women in the 20th century.

Fox, Stephen. *The Mirror Makers: A History of American Advertising and Its Creators*. New York: Random, 1984. Perhaps the most readable general history of American advertising.

Friedan, Betty. *The Feminine Mystique*. New York: Dell, 1963. The first volley in the second women's movement. Now an interesting historical and sociological document.

Goodrum, Charles, and Helen Dalrymple. *Advertising in America: The First 200 Years*. New York: Abrams, 1990. Excellent illustrations for a text that is less comprehensive than the title promises.

Josselyn, Irene. *Psychosocial Development of Children*. New York: Family Service Association of America, 1948. This descriptive look at child development was meant as a parents' guide.

Marchand, Roland. *Advertising the American Dream: Making Way for Modernity, 1920-1940*. Berkeley, CA: U of California P, 1985. A well-researched and highly informative scholarly study of advertising's interaction with society during two important decades.

Marschall, Richard. *America's Great Comic-strip Artists*. New York: Abbeville, 1989. Good background on 16 major comic artists from

Outcault to Schulz, with profuse examples of their work, in color and black-and-white.

Matthews, Glenna. *"Just A Housewife": The Rise and Fall of Domesticity in America.* New York: Oxford UP, 1987. Well-reasoned examination of society's attitude toward the role and value of housewives from colonial times to the 1960s.

Mergen, Bernard. "The Discovery of Children's Play." *Atlantic Quarterly* 27.4 (Oct. 1975): 399-408. Historical study of the "discovery" of childhood in the late 1800s and early 1900s.

Potter, David M. *People of Plenty: Economic Abundance and the American Character.* Chicago: U of Chicago P, 1954. Landmark study of how abundance shaped Americans' view of themselves and their world.

Schlereth, Thomas J. *Victorian America: Transformations in Everyday Life, 1876-1915.* New York: Harper Collins, 1991. General introduction to the various aspects of American life in the last quarter of the 19th and first quarter of the 20th century.

Spock, Benjamin, M.D. *The Common Sense Book of Baby and Child Care.* New York: Duell, Sloan and Pearce, 1945; rpt. 1946. Now-classic work on child care.

____. *Problems of Parents.* Boston: Houghton Mifflin, 1962. A rethinking of some of the premises of his 1945 work, with some consideration of child-raising practices in other countries.

Wishy, Bernard. *The Child and The Republic: The Dawn of Modern Child Nurture.* Philadelphia: U of Pennsylvania P, 1968. A well-documented study of attitudes toward child care and education, principally in the 19th century.

Wolf, Katherine, R.N. *The Controversial Problem of Discipline.* New York: The Child Study Association of America, 1953. A brief pamphlet that analyzes the problems faced by parents who took "permissiveness" too literally.

Contributors

Mary Welek Atwell holds a Ph.D. in History from Saint Louis University. Formerly Associate Dean of the College of Arts and Sciences, she is currently an Associate Professor of Criminal Justice at Radford University, Radford, Virginia. Atwell has concentrated most of her scholarship on gender issues. Her daughter, Molly, 15, has encouraged her study of heroines in girls' fiction.

Stanley S. Blair received his doctorate from Duke University and is Assistant Professor of English at James Madison University, Harrisonburg, Virginia. He is currently completing a book manuscript on William Carlos Williams.

Allyson Booth is an Assistant Professor of English at the U.S. Naval Academy in Annapolis. She is currently at work on a book manuscript about the interrelations between modernism and World War I.

Millie R. Creighton, an Assistant Professor at the University of British Columbia, is an anthropologist and a Japan area specialist who has lived in Japan for several years, conducting research on various consumer-oriented industries. She is married and has two small children, Eirin and Sayuri, who helped further the participatory aspects of her research on Japanese children's marketing.

Barbara Gottfried received her Ph.D. in Literature from the University of California, Santa Cruz, in 1985 and has held assistant professorships at the University of Hawaii at Manoa and Bentley College in Waltham, Massachusetts. She is co-author with Murray Baumgarten of *Understanding Philip Roth* and author of articles on Roth, Dickens, and Chaucer. Her current projects include a book-length manuscript on the Brontë sisters, further work on the semiotics of advertising, and pursuit of a new full-time teaching position.

Michael A. Grimm received his B.A. in English and Library Science from Western Michigan University, and his M.A. in English, concentrating in Children's Literature, from Eastern Michigan University. He has participated in presentations dealing with children's literature at several academic conferences. He lives with his wife and son in Fowlerville, Michigan, where he is employed as the Middle School Librarian, facing a variety of challenges as a long-haired rock music fan, as a conservative Christian in a predominantly liberal field (albeit one who does not condone censorship), and as a male in a female-dominated profession.

Alethea K. Helbig, Professor of English Language and Literature at Eastern Michigan University, is a past-president of The Children's Literature Association (ChLA), and Chair of the ChLA Phoenix Award Committee since its inception. She has published more than 100 articles and is co-author with Agnes Perkins of *Dictionary of American Children's Fiction, 1985-1989*, one of a series on award-winning children's books.

Gary Hoppenstand has published numerous books and articles on topics ranging from 19th-century American literature to popular culture studies. His book entitled *Clive Barker's Short Stories: Imagination as Metaphor* will be published by McFarland in 1994. He is an Associate Professor teaching in the Department of American Thought and Language at Michigan State University.

Monica Hughes was born in Liverpool, England, and lived in Egypt as well as England and Scotland. After a stint in the WRNS and two years in Zimbabwe she emigrated to Canada. She finally settled in Edmonton with her husband and four children and began to write for young people. Since 1974 she has had 24 novels published, science fiction and contemporary, as well as two picture books and some short stories.

Kathy Merlock Jackson is an Associate Professor of Communications at Virginia Wesleyan College, where she specializes in mass media and children's culture. She is the author of two books, *Images of Children in American Film* (1986) and *Walt Disney: A Bio-Bibliography* (1993).

Larry Juchartz has been a fan of rock and roll music since the night his parents let him stay up late to watch the Beatles appear on the *Ed Sullivan Show*. As the rhythm guitarist in a high-school garage band, he was once issued a police citation for disturbing the peace. Now a law-abiding instructor of English at Eastern Michigan University, he tries to keep up with the rapid changes in the contemporary music scene so he can have some sense of what his students are writing about.

Nancie Kahan has taught English and writing in both private and public institutions in Montreal. She currently teaches at The Centre for the Study and Teaching of Writing, at McGill University, where she is completing an M.Ed.

Joyce A. Litton holds a Ph.D. in political science from the University of Missouri-Columbia. She is a Library Associate in the Government Documents Department of the Ohio University Library. She has written articles for *Focus* and *The ALAN Review*. She is currently working on a study of teen romances from the 1940s to the 1990s.

Robert M. MacGregor, Professor of Marketing, Bishop's University, Lennoxville, Quebec, is a cultural analyst. One focus of his research interest is racial and ethnic stereotypes in advertising. A recent publication of his, "The Golliwog: Innocent Doll to Symbol of Racism," appeared in *Advertising and Popular Culture*, Sammy R. Dana, ed., Bowling Green State University Popular Press, Bowling Green, Ohio, 1992.

Eileen Margerum is an Assistant Professor at Salem State College in Salem, Massachusetts. She teaches courses in advertising history, theory, and practice in the Communications program, part of the English Department. Her interest is in American advertising history, about which she has written and presented research papers.

Christy Rishoi Minadeo read *Little Women* as a child but became a feminist anyway. She is now a doctoral student in American Studies at Michigan State University, concentrating on the literature of American women.

Nanette Norris teaches English at Marianopolis College in Montreal. She is currently co-writing a software program for grammar studies.

Jennifer Scanlon is Assistant Professor of Women's Studies at the State University of New York College at Plattsburgh. Her research interests include women's magazines, consumer and popular culture, feminist pedagogy, and international feminism. She has published articles in *Women's Studies International Forum*, *Feminist Teacher*, *Transformations*, and *NWSA Journal*.

Judy E. Sneller is Assistant Professor of English at South Dakota School of Mines & Technology. She received her Ph.D. in American Studies at Emory University in 1992. During the last four years, she has presented seven papers on American women's humor at academic conferences and recently published an essay on women's humor in *Gender, Race, and Identity*, Craig Barrow et al., eds., Southern Humanities Press, Chattanooga, 1993.

Joseph Stanton, whose speciality is the study of relations between poetry and visual arts in 19th- and 20th-century America, is the Director of the Center for Arts & Humanities at the University of Hawaii at Manoa. He has recent or forthcoming essays in *Art Criticism, Yearbook of Interdisciplinary Studies in the Fine Arts, The Lion and the Unicorn, Journal of American Culture*, and several other journals. His major critical project at the moment is a book on Winslow Homer for James J. Kery's "Masters of American Art" series. His poems have appeared in *Poetry, Poetry East, Exquisite Corpse, Yankee, New York Quarterly, Harvard Review, Aethlon*, and numerous other magazines.

Sally Sugarman teaches Childhood Studies at Bennington College where she is also the Director of the Bennington College Early Childhood Center. She is Chair of the Vermont State Board of Education. She has a B.A. in Literature and History from NYU, an M.S. in Early Childhood Education from Bank Street College of Education, and a C.A.S. in Educational Research from SUNY, Albany.

Kathleen L. Ward teaches English at Brigham Young University-Hawaii and is Director of the Honors Program there. Her interests in children's literature and in African-American culture led her to a study of children's books written by black women writers.